African Birds of Prey

African Birds
of Prey

Leslie Brown

Collins,
St James's Place, London

To G.

For long-continued interest, help, and good company in this my obsession.

2nd Edition 1972
ISBN 00 0 211044 X
© Leslie Brown 1970
Printed in Great Britain
Collins Clear-Type Press
London and Glasgow

Contents

Part I Introduction

1	What are Birds of Prey?	page 11
2	Behaviour and Physical Adaptations for Predation	16
3	The Variety of African Birds of Prey	35

Part II The African Birds of Prey

4	Cuckoo Falcons, Honey Buzzards and Kites	47
5	Vultures	56
6	Snake Eagles and Fish Eagles	65
7	Harriers	76
8	Sparrowhawks, Goshawks and their Kin	83
9	Buzzards and Small Eagles	92
10	Large and Spectacular Eagles	105
11	Falcons	118
12	Oddities	133
13	Little Owls, Scops Owls and Owlets	143
14	A Variety of Middle-sized Owls	150
15	Eagle Owls and Fishing Owls	159

Part III The Life of African Raptors

16	Some Ecological and Distribution Problems	171
17	Migrant African Birds of Prey	180
18	Migration within Continental Africa	191
19	The Numbers of African Birds of Prey	205
20	The Effects of Predation	216
21	Territory and the Regulation of Raptor Numbers	231
22	Breeding Seasons and Food Supply	245
23	The Breeding Cycle	254

Contents

24 Birds of Prey and Man
    (i) Fable, Fiction and Prejudice   266
    (ii) The Facts   273

Tables   284

Index   315

List of Figures

1	Binocular Vision of Bird of Prey	17
2	Emargination of Primaries	27
3	Ear Openings of an Owl	31
4	Feet of Birds of Prey	33
5	Range of Chanting Goshawks	89
6	Buzzards	95
7	Owlets	176
8	Range of Eagle Owls	177
9	Black Kites—Distribution in Northern Summer	194
10	Black Kites—Distribution in Southern Summer	195
11	Movements of Kites in Africa	197
12	Movements and Breeding Seasons	200
13	Food Requirements of African Raptors	217
14	Food Consumption and Bodyweight of Diurnal Raptors	219
15	Ecological Separation—African Eagles	228
16	Embu District, Census Area 1949-52	232
17	Home Ranges of Seven Pairs of Fish Eagles	237
18	Beneficial or other Effects of Diurnal Raptors in East African Grasslands	283

Illustrations

1	Bat Hawk (*John Pearson*)	facing page 80
	Kites (*Eric Hosking*)	80
2	Cape Vulture (*Peter Steyn*)	81
	Vultures at carcase (*Leslie Brown*)	81
3	Black-breasted Snake Eagle (*Peter Steyn*)	96
	Secretary Bird (*John Karmali*)	96
4	African Fish Eagle (*Peter Steyn*)	97
5	Dark Chanting Goshawk (*Peter Hay*)	112
6	Black Sparrowhawk (*Peter Steyn*)	113
	Augur Buzzard (*Peter Steyn*)	113
7	Ayres Hawk Eagle (*Leslie Brown*)	128
	Wahlberg's Eagle (*Leslie Brown*)	128
8	Tawny Eagles (*V. E. M. Burke*)	129
	African Hawk Eagle (*Peter Johnson*)	129
9	Martial Eagle (*Leslie Brown*)	144
	Verreaux's Eagle (*Peter Steyn*)	144
10	African Hobby (*Peter Steyn*)	145
11	Peregrine Falcon (*Leslie Brown*)	160
	Harrier Hawk (*Peter Steyn*)	160
12	Pearl-spotted Owlet (*Peter Johnson*)	161
	Barn Owl (*Peter Steyn*)	161
	Spotted Eagle Owl (*Peter Steyn*)	161
	Woodford's Owl (*G. J. Broekhuysen*)	161

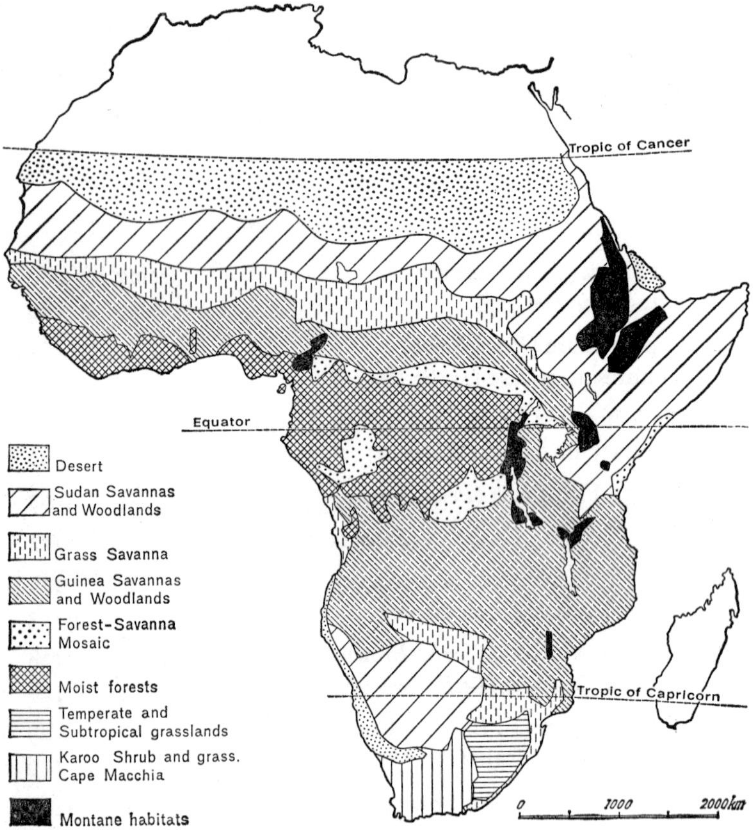

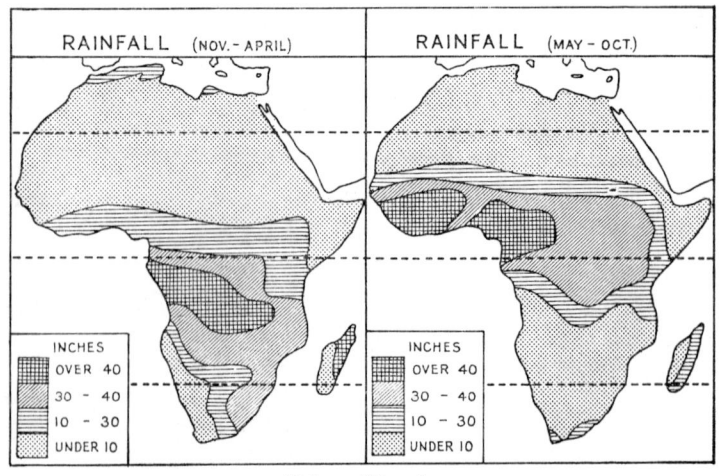

Vegetation of Africa

African Weather

Part 1
Introduction

Chapter 1
What are Birds of Prey?

Theoretically, any species of bird that preys or feeds upon any other living creature is a bird of prey. So broad a definition, however, would include all the insectivorous species, from tiny warblers picking aphids from the underside of forest leaves to big shrikes or starlings feeding on grasshoppers. Indeed, the line of division here is often not very clearly drawn. There is very little obvious difference in behaviour between the tiny Pigmy Falcon and the large White-crowned Bush Shrike. They even live together in the same kind of dry thornbush and can be mistaken for one another when perched on top of a tree. Both feed largely on insects, and it is only when one obtains a close view or handles the birds that the difference become plain.

Likewise Fish Eagles and Fish Owls are birds that feed chiefly on fish and frogs, as do herons, storks, cormorants, pelicans, grebes, gulls, and terns. None of the latter would be called birds of prey, though gulls come nearest to that definition. Many of these species however, especially such large birds as pelicans and cormorants, are far more important predators on fish than are Fish Eagles, while storks are far more important predators on frogs than are, for instance Marsh Harriers. Yet the Marsh Harrier is a bird of prey proper, the Yellow-billed Stork or Wood Ibis is not.

When we consider the species that kill or feed on the larger mammals and birds the true meaning of the definition "birds of prey" becomes clearer. Only the larger eagles can kill monkeys, antelopes and large active birds such as guineafowl or geese; they are the avian equivalent of the lion, leopard and tiger, the largest and most powerful class of avian predators. Vultures are the only important avian scavengers of the larger mammals, feeding on any dead animal from the size of an elephant to that of a gazelle. By night, the larger owls kill such animals as bushbabies and cane-rats, and the chief killers of other birds are the falcons and hawks, though

I have known a Fiscal Shrike kill a Didric Cuckoo almost its own size. Eagles, falcons, hawks, and eagle owls are clearly the most important killers of birds and mammals, and the scavenging vultures are associated with them under the same definition "birds of prey" because of certain basic similarities. Vultures, which seldom or never kill anything which is alive, are not properly birds of prey at all, and in their case some of the usual attributes of birds of prey have atrophied.

This narrow definition of birds of prey includes two groups which have certain physical features in common. They all (except vultures) have powerful grasping feet, equipped with long sharp talons, used both to kill the prey by piercing and gripping it, and to hold it down when feeding. In vultures, which do not need to kill, the long sharp talons are reduced and the foot is more like that of a hen than that of an eagle. But vultures, and other true birds of prey, also have powerful beaks with a hook on the upper mandible, which is used to tear flesh from the body of a dead animal. The true birds of prey are those birds which hunt and feed with the aid of hooked beaks and sharp talons on the feet, whether by day or by night. Pelicans, storks, or gulls, do not possess these attributes, though gulls and cormorants and some shrikes too, do have something of a hook on the beak.

The two groups included in this narrower definition are the eagles, vultures, falcons and hawks, comprising the Order Falconiformes, and the owls, Order Strigiformes. Despite their basic similarities in the possession of talons and hooked beaks they are not very closely related to one another, and they are as a rule sharply differentiated by their habits. The nearest relations of the Falconiformes are, on the one side ducks and gamebirds, and those of the owls are swifts and nightjars on one side and cuckoos on the other. However, such niceties of classification in practice mean little. Both the Falconiformes and the owls have diverged from their near relatives a very long time ago, and have become specialised for their predatory function.

In general the two groups share the hunting time in the twenty-four hours, the Falconiformes hunting or scavenging by day, and the owls by night. There are a few aberrant hawks such as the Bat Hawk which hunt almost in the dark, and some insectivorous species such as the African Hobby commonly hunt in the dusk; in both cases this is because their prey is most abundant at such times. Most of the owls are strictly nocturnal hunters, but some emerge some time before dark and even hunt by daylight. In Africa, Marsh Owls can be seen floating over the plains in search of rats and mice before the last of the diurnal harriers and buzzards have gone to bed.

The basic difference in habits between the two groups accentuate certain physical needs and result in different physical adaptations. A diurnal bird of prey, such as a falcon or eagle, can see well in the strong light of the sun, and hunts mainly or entirely by sight. In such birds the sense of sight is marvellously developed, but the sense of hearing is much less important for the purpose of locating prey, though many diurnal birds of prey make use of such obvious aids as the cries of a bird in distress, or even gunshots to locate their meals. Diurnal raptors such as harriers, which hunt small mice in long grass where they cannot easily see them, probably make use of hearing to a far greater extent than do swift falcons whose main prey is large birds killed in the open or in flight, and always visible. Smell is unimportant, even in the case of vultures, which in Africa hunt entirely by sight. Carrion which has been effectively covered up cannot be found by vultures, no matter how putrid; in this respect African vultures are apparently somewhat different from the American or New World Vultures, which are a different family not even very closely related to the Old World Vultures.

Diurnal birds of prey, then, locate their prey mainly by sight, sometimes assisted by hearing, but apparently never by smell, and kill it by sheer speed or agility in the attack. The different families and genera are adapted in specialised ways to deal with different groups of animals on which they feed, as will be discussed later. But they all must have acute sight, and except for vultures they all must be more or less agile to catch their prey.

Owls, in contrast, hunt mainly by night, or at least in dim light. Consequently the sense of sight becomes less important, and that of hearing more so. This is true for most animals, including human beings. By day we can see a herd of elephants half a mile away and would pay little attention to the noise they make, but by night we could only locate them by ear. Hence, among owls, very acute vision is not necessary, though their eyes are adapted to make the best of poor light; their eyes are designed more to detect movement than to resolve detail. If possible food—such as a dead elephant—does not move, an owl will not feed on it; there are no purely carrion-eating owls and the nocturnal scavengers in Africa are mammals, such as hyenas and jackals, which can detect their prey by scent.

Owls have, however, the most remarkable adaptations to assist them to hear well and to locate their prey by ear. It is generally known that they have soft feathers, but not so generally realised that this is not so much to enable them to approach their prey silently but so that the noise made by their own wings does not distract their attention from minute sounds in the grass. If one is making a noise oneself one cannot hear other things making a noise; one has to stop, look and listen, but a flying owl does not have to do anything of the sort. It can not only move so silently that it is not distracted from any small sounds made by possible prey, but the owls that hunt chiefly or exclusively by night have specially adapted ears that enable them to pinpoint a sound so accurately that they can strike their prey even in almost pitch darkness.

In strong daylight a pigeon attacked by a falcon must be able to hear the loud rushing sounds made by the stoop of its attacker (for no falcon, however fast, is believed to penetrate the sound barrier!), but it may not be able to avoid the speed of the attack, and may be killed before it has properly grasped its danger. In the dim light of evening, or in darkness, the same element of surprise in the attack is best achieved by complete silence. By day, an owl would have very little chance of catching the pigeon, but the falcon would likewise inevitably kill itself if it flew about by night at speed, for it could not see the obstacles against which it might crash.

The essential differences between these two groups of birds of prey are, then, that the diurnal birds of prey, falcons, hawks, eagles, vultures, find their prey by sight, sometimes assisted by hearing, and kill it by speed and agility, while the nocturnal owls locate their prey by hearing, sometimes assisted by sight, and kill it by stealth. At the point of killing, however, the differences disappear and the similarities become obvious. Both kill their prey by grasping it with the talons, which in some species may be so long and powerful that the grip of the predator's foot is capable of driving the long hooked claws into or through the prey. When the prey is dead, both hawks and owls tear it to pieces—if it is too large to swallow whole—with their hooked beaks, holding it down with the taloned foot at the same time. The principle is the same as using a fork to hold down a steak while cutting it with a knife. It is these similarities, the result of parallel evolution among two groups of birds not closely related to one another, that define the meaning of the term "birds of prey".

In the detailed exercise of their various functions there is a degree of overlap between the two groups. But the combination of specialised physical attributes and a degree of overlap means that these two groups of birds are capable of hunting a large variety of animals throughout the twenty-four hours of day or night. It does not help the prey to be exclusively diurnal or nocturnal; if it is not in danger from a buzzard by day, it must look out for an owl by night.

Chapter 2
Behaviour and Physical Adaptations for Predation

For the diurnal birds of prey acute sight and great speed or agility are the most important attributes that enable them to kill their prey. All need acute sight to a varying degree, but some do not require to fly at great speed, or to be extremely agile and quick. Some, that kill large mammals, must be extremely strong (so as to effect the kill quickly without a struggle that might be damaging to themselves) and those that kill fish, or snakes, or bats have special adaptations to enable them to do so more efficiently.

It has long been recognised that the diurnal birds of prey have very remarkable eyesight. The term "eagle-eyed", to denote unusual keenness of vision, is apt, for eagles have exceptionally keen vision. They, and other birds of prey do not see any further than we do, and they probably see very much the same colour, but they see detail very much more clearly than do human beings. Though a buzzard is only about one-fiftieth of a man's weight, its eye is very nearly the same size as that of a man, so that it is very much larger in relation to the size of the bird than is our own eye to ourselves. This very large eye is nearly immovable in its socket. We can move our eyes from side to side, but a buzzard has to keep moving its head round to see in all directions; it may even turn its head upside down to scan places otherwise out of its line of vision.

This proverbial keenness of vision is due to the structure of the retina—the sensitive surface at the back of the eye on which the image of the seen object is cast. The amount of detail perceived by the retina depends on the number of rods and cones (specialised visual cells) per unit area—the more rods and cones the better the detail. The retina of a buzzard's eye is thus able to see detail perhaps three or four times as well as a human eye. Moreover, in the retinas of buzzards and other hawks there are depressions called foveas, in which the number of rods and cones is still greater. The fovea therefore provides an area of still clearer perception. In the retinas of

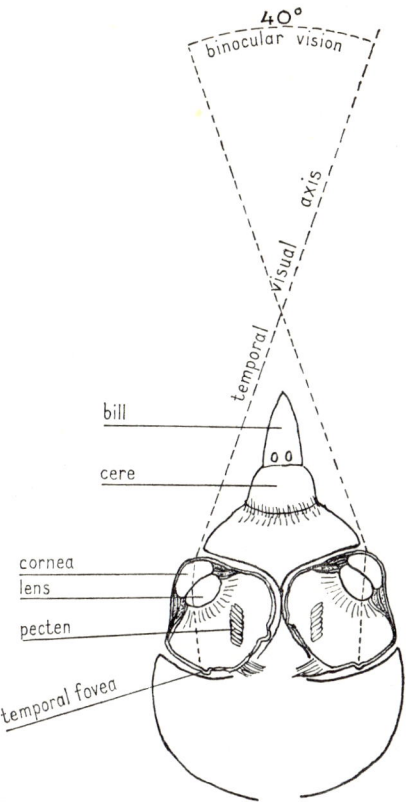

Fig. 1 Diagram of a diurnal bird of prey's binocular vision. Based on *Buteo rufofuscus*. After J. C. Welty, *The Life of Birds*. The area in the centre of the field of vision in front is that in which the bird of prey has binocular vision, extending through about 40° of arc; small adjustments are possible.

hawks there are two foveas in each eye, one directed forward, the other to the side. Binocular vision is obtained in those which look forward, and working in conjunction with the laterally directed foveas they also provide unusually good distance perception, so that the hawk can not only see the detail of its prey clearly but can accurately judge how far away it is. As to detail, according to some authorities on the subject the foveas provide a resolving power at least seven or eight times that of man, though others do not put it quite so high.

What this means in practice is best illustrated from personal experience. I was once sitting at my study window, looking out on an expanse of weeds where there is now a lawn. An Augur Buzzard was perched on a Croton tree which, as I later found, was 110 yards away. It suddenly swept downwards, straight towards me, and alighted not ten feet away, having flown at some prey in the weeds. I then saw that it had killed a small bright green grasshopper about an inch long, and it had clearly seen this little cryptically coloured creature from its perch 110 yards away.

To test my own visual acuity I went out and caught a grasshopper of similar size and placed it in plain view on top of a fence post. I then backed away till I could no longer see the grasshopper at all. From another direction I approached slowly until the grasshopper became visible. I found that I could see the grasshopper with the naked eye at a distance of 33–35 yards, and I could have seen it with X 8 binoculars at about 270 yards. The buzzard had seen it, half hidden as it was in the weeds, from 110 yards and had therefore demonstrated that its vision was at least 3–4 times as acute as mine, and doubtless better, for it probably could only see a portion of the insect when it launched its attack.

Another example, of a different kind, was also provided by an Augur Buzzard. I was watching birds on the edge of the huge Semien escarpment in Ethiopia, a cliff forty miles long and three to five thousand feet high, rich in large birds of prey. An Augur Buzzard was soaring above and behind me, about 1000 feet above the crest of the crag and perhaps half a mile away. Suddenly it started on a deliberate stoop, and I watched it in my binoculars, thinking it was going to kill something. However, it swept right across a great bay in the escarpment, and when it eventually reached the other side I saw that it had flown straight at a Verreaux's Eagle, perched upon a stump, and which I did not see until it took wing to evade the buzzard. The eagle was about three feet long, and about two miles away, so that in this case the buzzard had launched a stoop of about 3500 yards. To it the eagle must have appeared about as big as would a grasshopper at 110 yards, so that the visual acuity displayed by both of these buzzards was about the same. In neither case did I see what they were going for before they reached it.

One would expect big eagles, which at close quarters have a piercingly sharp gaze, to have still better vision than do buzzards, and this may be so, though I know of no evidence on the subject derived from anatomical examination of an eagle's retina. However, again an illustration from personal experience may provide a clue. Verreaux's Eagle is a species that feeds largely or entirely on rock hyrax, animals about a foot or fifteen inches long, weighing two to three pounds. I once watched a Verreaux's Eagle launch a stoop at a Martial Eagle, which was carrying prey. Again, the Verreaux's Eagle flew dead straight at the Martial Eagle and there could be very little doubt that it had seen the prey. At the point of collision the Martial Eagle dropped its prey, and the Verreaux's descended to retrieve it. From knowledge of the ground I was able to estimate the length of this attack as about one and a half miles, or 2600 yards. I also felt fairly certain—since Verreaux's Eagle is not an indiscriminate pirate of other raptors' kills—that it must have recognised the prey as a Hyrax. If this were so, then it displayed a visual acuity about three times as sharp as that of the Augur Buzzard on the Semien escarpment, and it would have been able to see a small green grasshopper an inch long at 300 yards—nearly ten times as far away as I could.

Vultures are reputed to have marvellous eyesight, and doubtless it is good, but actually they probably do not need to have such good sight as does a bird such as a buzzard, which preys very largely on small rodents. Normally vultures cruise in flight at 500–2000 feet above ground. They may appear to be very high up, but travelling in an aeroplane one sees very few at more than 2000 feet above ground level. If from here they display the same visual acuity as the Augur Buzzard in my garden they should be able to see an object three inches long from such a height. Quite obviously, most of the dead animals on which they feed would be much larger than that, usually at least three feet long, rather than three inches. An object three feet long, such as the carcase of a dead gazelle, should thus be visible from a height of 10,000 feet above ground, and vultures are hardly ever seen at such heights.

Likewise a soaring vulture, such as a Griffon, with a wing span approaching eight feet, should be able to see another vulture at a range of four miles or more. The circle of vision of a cruising vulture would then cover about 50 square miles. A hundred vultures, collected at a carcase, could therefore have come from an area of about

5000 square miles. Obviously, in an area of such a size there are likely to be a few dead animals lying around. Their ability to find a large carcase is thus a good deal less miraculous than it seems, especially as they are often led to a dead animal by the movements of other large and conspicuous birds such as kites and ravens.

Speed and/or agility are the other special requirements of the diurnal birds of prey. The large falcons, such as the Peregrine Falcon and the Lanner, can display a combination of speed and precision that seem little short of miraculous. I once saw a Lanner Falcon stoop at a covey of Stone Partridges that were running in single file across a bare slab of rock, 500 feet or so below the soaring predator. The Lanner stooped nearly vertically until, at great speed, it could skim just over the rock surface behind the running file of partridges. Travelling at perhaps a hundred miles an hour, and with a tolerance of a few inches between itself and certain injury or death, it plucked one of the partridges off the rock surface before any of them seemed to be aware of their danger.

Such speed and agility may be used, not only for killing, but in play or in aggressive display. In Nigeria I watched a pair of Lanner Falcons displaying above the nest site of a Crowned Eagle, in a large spreading Silk Cotton tree. Suddenly they took it into their heads to attack the eagle on the nest. Stooping vertically for 400–500 feet, they separated above the tree and flashed through the branches a few inches above the eagle's head in opposite directions, passing each other at a combined velocity of perhaps two hundred miles an hour. A fraction of a second's miscalculation or hesitation would have meant death or injury, yet they missed each other, the eagle (which was most surprised) and the branches of the tree.

Peregrine Falcons are noted for their superlative powers of flight, perhaps superior even to the Lanner. At one easily accessible eyrie in Embu district of Kenya my bull terrier was standing just above me on a grassy ledge while I examined the eyasses—as young Peregrines are called. The falcon was perched on a slab of rock perhaps a hundred feet above us, and suddenly she decided to attack the dog. Plunging down vertically she turned at right angles above the dog's back, put down the hind claw of one foot, and drew it the length of the back through the hair, just grazing the skin in a long scratch. This occurred three feet in front of my face, and as fast as a human being could swipe at a fly. It was only when I examined the dog—who was terrified—that I saw what the falcon had done.

Falling with gravity, she would have achieved a speed of nearly one hundred miles an hour by the time she reached us, and at this speed had shown a combination of agility in a right-angled turn and hairbreadth accuracy of judgment that I have never seen bettered. When one has watched such examples of speed and precision at leisure and at close quarters it is extremely difficult to believe that, if a large falcon attacks quarry with real intention to kill it—as opposed to in play—it can possibly fail, given a fair chance.

A combination of speed and agility is displayed by the little-known Ayres Hawk Eagle, which feeds chiefly on birds and lives in woodland or forest. At a nest I have been lucky enough to watch for nineteen years I have watched the displaying male stooping at speed through the branches of the nest tree where his mate perched on the nest. I have also, once, seen him kill a bird in the treetops by a stoop of breathtaking speed and skill. From a soaring position a hundred feet or so above me he plunged into the treetops 300 feet below, his wings folded to the tail tip so that he presented an almost perfectly heart-shaped silhouette. Thirty-five yards beyond he emerged, clutching a brown bird, perhaps a bulbul, in his talons. I have also seen an Ayres Hawk Eagle swoop into a flock of Superb Starlings in a baobab tree, scattering them in terror, and just failing to catch one despite twirling feats of agility that would have done credit to a small sparrowhawk.

The principal advantage of speed in the attack must be surprise. The killer is on its prey before the latter has the chance to gather its wits and make good its escape. These very fast attacks are often quite noisy—it is often the tearing sound that attracts attention to them in the first place—but it appears that the prey usually does not become aware of or understand the noise till too late. The predator, moving at great speed, has a split second's advantage, and that is enough. A puff of feathers on the wind remains to tell the tale.

The sparrowhawks and goshawks of the genus *Accipiter* and nearly related genera are not capable of very great speed—at least not of the same order as the large falcons and swifter eagles. They achieve surprise by a combination of stealth and agility. They use cover skilfully to approach their prey, and then make a very fast dash over the last few yards to seize the quarry. Sparrowhawks, in Africa as elsewhere in the world, flit silently through the trees, or skim low over flat ground, making use of every bush for concealment, to catch their prey unawares. They may also, on occasion, dart suddenly from cover to seize any bird that is passing. Sir F. J. Jackson records how he saw a Little Sparrowhawk dart up out of low cover and seize a Button-quail in passing.

In open country, such predators may sometimes be able to fly down quarry without having to display either exceptional speed or agility. A Pale Chanting Goshawk once swept over my head in pursuit of a Harlequin Quail I had just flushed from long grass. Pursuing the quail in level flight for about 100 yards it caught it in one outstretched foot without apparent effort. No great speed or agility was needed, for the quail, like most gamebirds, was flying in straight line, and at not more than 30 miles an hour. It was a virtual certainty for the hawk provided that the quail did not drop suddenly into cover. The quail could have avoided the hawk by taking cover but it was evident that it did not realise its danger until too late.

On occasion great strength may be needed by some of the larger eagles to subdue and kill their prey. The most graphic example in my experience was when a Crowned Eagle killed a half grown bushbuck in the forest near my home. I did not see the encounter, but I found the eagle on the remains of the kill, and was able to reconstruct what had happened.

The eagle had dropped upon the luckless bushbuck while it was walking along a track through some bushes, probably launching its attack from a branch about twenty feet above the track. The bushbuck had then jumped to the right, but had been brought down in about four yards. Here there was a big area of flattened vegetation where the flailing legs of the unfortunate antelope had battered the bushes in its struggle. It had been killed, however, presumably by the sheer force of the eagle's clutch, and had been plucked and dismembered at this spot. The dead antelope—far too large for the eagle to handle in one piece—had then been torn in pieces, and the four legs and the head removed to a distance, and cached in trees until needed. The remains of the body had been torn in two at the lumbar joint, and these two pieces had been dragged fifteen yards down a tunnel in the dense bushes to an open space in the shade of the tree from which the eagle had attacked in the first case. Here I found her feeding that evening.

Although the eagle had attacked an animal perhaps twice her own weight, and very strong, she had been able to master its struggles with the loss of a few flecks of down and one small breast feather, whereas the hair of the bushbuck was all over the vegetation. It was impossible to say how long this struggle took, but it seemed evident that the eagle had downed the bushbuck almost at once, and had thereafter held it down until its struggles ceased.

Many diurnal raptors pursue prey which requires neither speed, agility, nor great strength to kill. These would include such diverse birds as the mainly insectivorous falcons, such as Kestrels and the Red-footed Falcon; some Snake Eagles that live partly on frogs; and harriers, buzzards and kites that hunt small or helpless animals in the grass. One or two, such as the Vulturine Fish Eagle, and to a lesser extent the Harrier Hawk, are even largely or partly vegetarian, subsisting on oil palm fruits in tropical forests. When not feeding on oil palm fruit the Vulturine Fish Eagle frequents estuaries and rivers where it can pick up small fish, molluscs or crabs (none of them agile or swift moving) and the Harrier Hawk spends its time flying from tree to tree minutely searching for lizards and insects in crannies and interstices of the bark and among dead leaves, or hanging upside down from the ends of branches taking the young out of weaver birds' nests. For this purpose nature has equipped the Harrier Hawk with a pair of long double-jointed legs, which enable it to strike some truly extraordinary attitudes, and are a peculiar adaptation enabling it to reach prey that is hidden from or inaccessible to other avian predators.

Birds that hunt small animals in the grass, such as kestrels, buzzards, harriers and, for instance, the Black-shouldered Kite, require not so much speed or agility as adaptations that enable them to detect these small animals in thick cover and pounce upon them. Hovering flight is one such adaptation, developed by many birds that hunt in open country. Most buzzards hover—that is, remain stationary in the air, head to wind, retaining a position by gently fanning the wingtips and spreading the tail. So do kestrels, the Black-shouldered Kite, and even some of the larger Snake Eagles, such as the Black-breasted Snake Eagle. Such hovering enables the raptors to remain stationary at a convenient height over terrain where there are no trees or telegraph poles to serve as perches. From a hover they can carefully scan the sector of ground beneath them, and detect a grasshopper or a rat moving in thick cover. When the prey is seen, the raptor usually descends from its hover slowly, as if parachuting down, till within a few feet of the ground, when it raises its wings vertically above the back and plunges the last few feet on to its prey.

It is in such a situation that the supplementary use of hearing may be of most value in detecting prey. Harriers do not hover, but are birds with slim bodies, long tails and long wings, able to fly rather slowly in a characteristic manner for hours at a stretch, beating to and fro over the grassland, checking from time to time, and occasionally dropping on prey. They are constantly moving, even if slowly, and thus have no opportunity to scan minutely any sector of ground as they could from a hover or a perch. In such slow flight it would probably be an advantage if they could first hear the rustle of a moving mouse, so that they could check above it and drop on it. Harriers have developed to some extent the specialised hearing aids brought to perfection in some of the owls. They have a partial facial disc, which gives them an owlish look when facing the observer. They also have rather large ear apertures, sometimes with a decided conch. These structures must assist in funneling sound waves to the ear itself. Although all diurnal birds of prey have good hearing it is only among the harriers (and some South American species of forest falcons) that this sense is strengthened by specialised structures to amplify sounds.

In covering a large area of ground closely it would evidently be an advantage to harriers to fly slowly. One has only to think of the relative difficulty a human being experiences in noting the details of scenery when travelling in a fast moving, as opposed to a slow moving vehicle to appreciate that this must be so. Harriers actually fly at an air speed of 15–25 miles per hour, but against a strongish headwind their ground speed (speed relative to the ground) may be decreased till it is hardly more than a human walking pace. In such a manner the harrier is ideally placed to hear a small sound, check briefly in flight, and drop on possible prey located with the aid of hearing; and field observation will show that this is what they do.

Slow flight is assisted by low wing loading—that is the weight carried per unit of surface area of the wings. Harriers are light-bodied birds with rather large wings, and they all have unusually low wing loading. The wing loading of harriers varies from 0·21–0·30 grams/sq. centimetre, usually less than 0·25 grams/sq. centimetre, whereas in Sparrowhawks of comparable weight it is about 0.4–0.45 grams/sq. centimetre and in a large swift falcon such as the Peregrine it is 0.63 grams/sq. centimetre. Admittedly the Peregrine is a heavier bird, and wing loading automatically increases with increase in bodyweight; but a study of graphs will show that the wing loading of harriers is relatively lower than would be found in other types of raptors of comparable weight.

Low wing loading is associated with buoyant easy flight; in harriers this not only enables them to keep up their flapping and gliding over the grasslands for many hours per day, but it also enables them to migrate more readily over open water. Most birds of prey, especially the larger soaring birds, avoid long water crossings because there are few thermal currents that would aid them to gain height with the minimum of effort. In harriers this is less important, and I have seen them flapping across the open Mediterranean a few feet above the waves, in precisely the same manner as they fly over the open grass plains.

Other birds with unusually buoyant flight include the giant Lammergeier, which also has wing loading lower than vultures of comparable size and weight, and the African Harrier Hawk, which seems so much at the mercy of gusts of wind that it may occasionally be blown far out to sea; one has been found after a storm far out over the ocean near Cape Agulhas, and it must have come from a forested area at least fifty miles away. Harrier Hawks are normally very sedentary forest birds, and they too possess special adaptation which may assist them to fly very slowly, and so assist in the search for small animals and birds in the treetops. Their primaries are rather broad, soft, and flexible, much more so than in most soaring birds of comparable size. Combined with a wing loading which is not known, but is probably low in relation to the weight of the bird, these soft flexible primaries may assist in very slow buoyant flight.

Many large eagles and vultures, and to a lesser extent buzzards and kites, must soar for long periods to detect their prey, or to perform nuptial displays. The Martial Eagle, for instance, hunts largely on the soar, usually at a great height, and the almost equally large Crowned Eagle, a forest species which normally hunts from within the tree canopy, soars to great heights in display. The soaring habits of vultures and buzzards are well known. The function of such soaring is to enable the raptor to gain a position from which it can watch a considerable area of ground without much effort; it is like a man going up in a balloon. To soar without effort for long periods a large heavy vulture requires a great area of wing surface. However, if such birds had long narrow wings, as does, for instance, an Albatross, they would find these very inconvenient when perching on trees or landing on the ground near a carcase. Such large vultures and eagles therefore have wing slots at the end of the wing, formed by the spread ends of the emarginated primary feathers, and so do many other soaring birds such as pelicans and storks.

Such a wing slot is formed by the emargination of the primaries, often on both vanes. The diagrams illustrate how these operate in a spread wing. Emargination of the primaries on both webs produces a square or rectangular wing slot, which is the most efficient type for reducing turbulence at the wing tip. The emarginated primaries apparently have another function as well. Under load, when the bird is flying, and especially under great load, as for instance in taking off and alighting, they bend to a varying degree and when seen from directly in front or behind they lie in different planes. This has the effect of enabling each separate feather to act as an aerofoil, or flying surface, increasing the lift at the tip of the wing by, as it were, having a series of little wings one above another. Thus the spread emarginated primaries of large soaring birds have the dual function of reducing turbulence and increasing lift at the wingtip, while at the same time the wing remains short enough not to hinder the bird unduly when flying among trees or making a landing. It is significant that the Lammergeier, which has unusually long narrow wings, is a bird which lives in open country and feeds largely on bones; Lammergeiers alight with a peculiar pigeon-like fanning of their enormous wings, not with heavy flaps as does a typical large vulture.

The Bateleur is another bird with unusually large narrow wings in relation to its body size; moreover, it has hardly any tail, in adult plumage, and so cannot obtain additional lift by the use of the spread tail. The Bateleur, like the Lammergeier, is an extremely efficient glider. Its mode of foraging is to travel for long distances about 100–300 feet above the ground, at an airspeed of 35–50 miles per hour. It may be on the wing for perhaps 8 hours a day, and may travel up to 300 miles every day of its life. It is in part a snake and bird eater and in part a scavenger, and perhaps this mode of flight enables it to cover a very large area each day and detect small dead

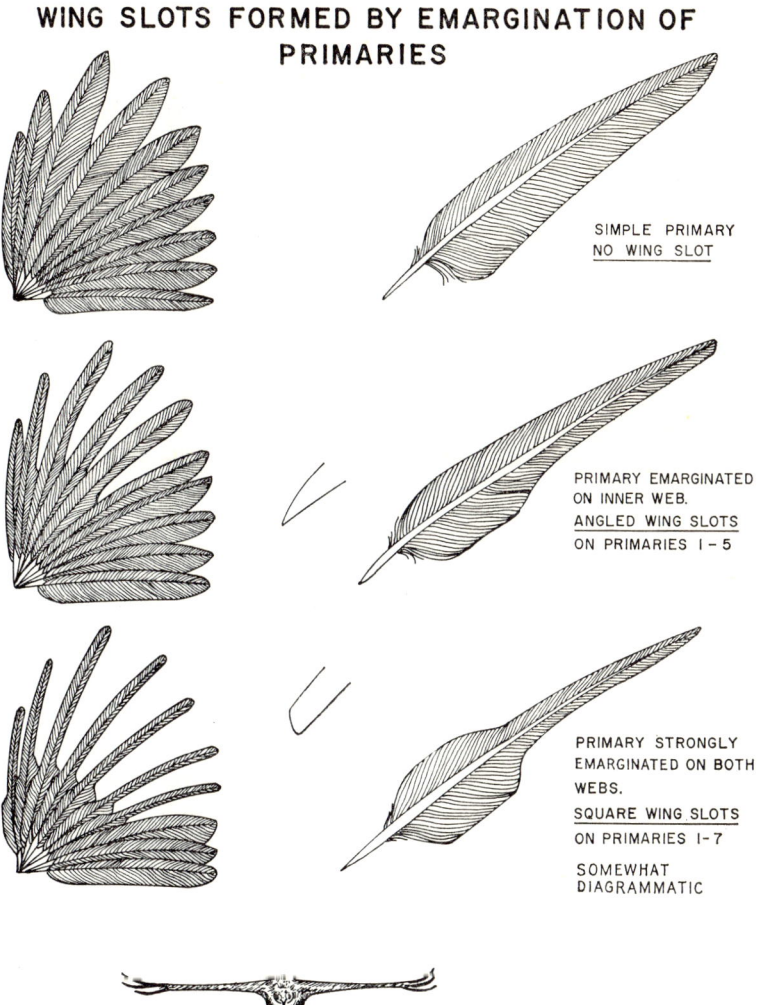

Fig. 2

animals in vast stretches of bush. Bateleurs certainly patrol roads early in the morning, where they may find small dead animals killed during the night by cars. The relatively high aspect-ratio (the ratio of length: breadth) of a Bateleur's wing assists relatively fast, effortless gliding over long distances, and when alighting Bateleurs, like Lammergeiers, have a quick fanning action with the wings.

Before passing on to the specialised adaptations needed by nocturnal raptors, that is, the owls, one may consider two species that habitually hunt in very poor light, the Bat Hawk and the Congo Serpent Eagle. Certain other raptors, such as the African Hobby and the insectivorous Cuckoo Falcon, hunt a good deal in the dusk, but they are also perfectly capable of hunting in bright daylight, and do, whereas Bat Hawks and Congo Serpent Eagles do not.

The Bat Hawk, as its name implies, lives mainly on bats. It seems to catch these mainly or entirely in the evening, when they swarm out of roofs and caves, and must catch its food supply in about half an hour every day. To do this it needs a plentiful supply of bats, so is often found in towns.

The special adaptations of the Bat Hawk include a falcon-like form, unlike that of any of its near relatives, which enables it to fly at very great speed when required. It also has very large eyes which no doubt assist it to see in poor light, and a wide, nightjar-like gape which enables it to swallow bats, swallows, and other such prey without pausing in flight, having first caught its prey in the feet. The Bat Hawk in fact treats a bat in just the same way as a Black Kite or a Hobby treats a flying termite, transferring it from the feet to the beak in flight.

So little is known of the Congo Serpent Eagle that one cannot be dogmatic about the reason for its very large eyes. However, it is a forest representative of a group which generally lives and feeds in open country—and which also have rather unusually large and brilliant eyes, though not to the same extent. The Congo Serpent Eagle apparently lives in the dense shade of the deepest tropical forests, feeding on snakes and chameleons. Its very large eyes probably help it to detect prey in the gloom, which is such that an ordinary photographer's light meter often will not register at all.

Very much less is known about the hunting methods of owls, for the reason that we ourselves cannot see in the dark. We can watch, and appreciate in detail the attack of a Lanner Falcon on a covey of Stone Partridges, but I have never yet met anyone who has watched an eagle owl kill a bushbaby. What we know of such actions must largely be derived from inference or experiment. Some owls have been closely studied under experimental conditions in Europe and America but I know of no such studies for Africa. And when one sets out to try to watch or even to locate owls hunting at night in thick bush one very soon becomes convinced of the futility of the exercise.

However, it can be said at once that owls do not, in general, require the speed or agility displayed by many diurnal birds of prey, though some of the smaller species, such as the Pearl-spotted Owlet, are agile enough. Owls can catch bats on occasion, but anything much less like the swift falcon-like pursuit used by the Bat Hawk in the dusk than the methods used by owls is hard to imagine. No owl is so constructed that it could fly like a falcon or a Bat Hawk, and it is difficult to conjecture exactly how they catch some of the items of their prey.

A certain amount is known about the hunting habits of African owls, and occasionally one can get an insight into the methods used under artificial circumstances. At the celebrated Treetops Hotel near Nyeri and at Kilaguni in the Tsavo National Park artificial light is used to enable the visitors to watch the rhinoceros, elephant, and buffalo that come to the water. In both places I have watched Verreaux's Eagle Owls catching insects and small animals in the light. They perched on trees or on the lamp standards themselves, and from time to time swooped down to catch an insect. At Treetops, earlier in the evening, I had watched a Steppe Buzzard and an Augur Buzzard catching small animals from the same perch used by the owl after dark. The method used by the owl and the buzzards was essentially the same—sighting the prey from the perch and catching it by a quick stoop to the ground, requiring no great speed or agility. It was, however, most entertaining to watch the owl catch an insect within feet of a rhinoceros, fluffing up its feathers in threat display so that the rhino backed uncertainly away from the terrifying apparition.

Again, I was once royally entertained for a whole evening in Nigeria by a Spotted Eagle Owl that came to catch insects in the light of my bush lamp. It was in the early rains and I was camped on a bare swept expanse of hard earth outside a hut, into which I intended to retreat if necessary. Thousands of small round beetles came to the lamp, and crawled about in the bare space. The owl perched on a low limb a few yards away and repeatedly caught the insects within a few feet of me. Sometimes it landed directly on the prey, and sometimes landed on the ground and simply walked up to a chosen insect, grasping it in its foot and transferring it to the beak, where it was audibly crunched. All the time it watched me closely with its great luminous yellow eyes, but as I sat still it became more and more confident. Clearly such helpless prey required no great skill or agility, and from the number of beetle remains found in the castings of such owls one must suppose that they often hunt in a like manner, but without the aid of a lamp. It gave up only after I had gone to bed, by which time it had fairly gorged itself.

These are the only occasions at which I have watched nocturnal owls hunting. One may infer that eagle owls of several species, and some other owls too, regularly hunt in this manner, for one sees them perched on fence posts or rocks, just as one sees buzzards perched by day. The mode of attack used by owls hunting from such perches is likely to be similar to that of a buzzard or a medium-sized eagle. Such specialised habits as hovering are probably not practical in the dark.

However, owls are also known to make use of adaptations not possessed by hawks, just as hawks and falcons behave differently to owls. The Barn Owl, a cosmopolitan and highly successful bird which occurs all over the moister parts of the African continent and is often very common, has been the subject of experiments under controlled conditions in America. These experiments demonstrated conclusively that in pitch darkness the owl could catch prey by the use of its specialised ears. These are asymmetrical, and apparently enable the owl to pinpoint accurately the small sounds made by a mouse among leaves. The owl, in the darkness of a building or under dense tree cover can locate the sound accurately enough to make a successful stoop. But obviously it does not have to fly very fast when doing this, and if the mouse walks about on a soundproof surface the owl cannot locate it. Carrion, which neither moves nor makes a noise, is not eaten by any species of owl, though if one lays a dead mouse out on a stone an owl may sometimes see it and attack it thinking it may be alive.

The owls that hunt by night all have these specialised hearing

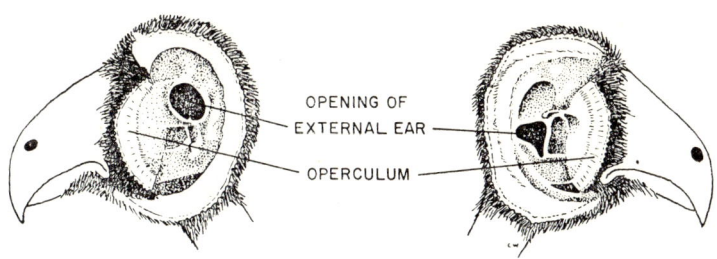

Fig. 3 Left and right external ear openings of an owl (*Asio*), showing their marked asymmetry. After Pycraft. (From J. C. Welty, *The Life of Birds*, Constable.)

adaptations—facial discs and large, sometimes asymmetrical ears—to a lesser or greater degree. The more exclusively they hunt at night the bigger their facial discs and the more specialised their ears. Most owls can use both their eyes and ears, and probably use their eyes at dusk or on moonlight nights and their ears on dark nights or in thick cover to locate their prey. But even with these specialised hearing aids owls seem to be at a disadvantage inside thick tropical forest, and when living in forest country they tend to hunt in the open at the edges, or along river beds and other open spaces within the forest.

Some owls do hunt by day An example is the Marsh Owl, a near relative of the European Short-eared Owl, which also often hunts by day, and has a reduced facial disc. The Marsh Owl emerges from its daytime resting place about an hour or so before dark, and quarters the grassland, flying slowly, rather in the same manner as a harrier. From time to time it drops into the grass and makes a kill after checking in flight just as a harrier does. It takes wing at about the time when hunting harriers can be expected to have stopped hunting and be making for their roosts. It is not known whether the Marsh Owl continues hunting throughout the night, but it probably does, so that the mice and grass rats have no respite from danger during the twenty-four hours.

Occasionally one may even see owls and diurnal birds of prey hunting together. One such occasion was in the Kalahari Desert, when I was watching a Honey Badger (*Mellivora capensis*), an animal so infrequently seen that few people know much about it. The badger spent several hours of the afternoon digging out rat burrows in the soft dune sand, and I followed it for about four miles. It was followed at one stage by both a Chanting Goshawk and a Spotted Eagle Owl, both presumably hoping to be able to catch some rodent that the badger had forced into the open. Such an association of badger, goshawk, and owl would be less likely to occur in a less extreme environment, where each species might find it easier to obtain its normal food.

As noted earlier, it is at the point of killing, done with the feet in all cases, that the similarities between owls and diurnal raptors becomes most marked. Size for size, it appears to me that diurnal raptors have a more powerful grip than owls, and perhaps they kill animals relatively larger than do owls of the same weight. But the feet of a Verreaux's Eagle Owl are strong enough to kill, for instance, bushbabies and giant rats, while one of its favourite foods is the nocturnal hedgehog *Atelerix*, seldom killed by any diurnal African raptor. This largest African owl is not as large and powerful as the largest of African eagles—the Crowned and Martial Eagles, so it is unfair to compare it to these very potent killers. Nevertheless, the feet of Verreaux's and other eagle owls, are more than strong enough to kill the mole rats and grass rats that are their habitual prey.

The feet of both diurnal and nocturnal raptors may be modified in special ways to assist them in killing their prey. Those species that live on fish, frogs, or other slippery animals—the Osprey, and Fish Eagle among diurnal species and the Fishing Owls among owls—have sharp spicules on the soles of their feet to help them grip their quarry. I do not know of any owl that habitually feeds on snakes, though several of the larger owls do kill occasional snakes. But if I found that an owl species had short, thick, very strong toes I should recognise herein a possible evolutionary convergence with the Snake Eagles and the Bateleur. The feet of owls generally exhibit less variation than do those of the diurnal birds of prey, and from this, and what little we know of their hunting habits, we can infer that both their prey and their mode of attack varies less than that of the diurnal raptors. However, the feet of Verreaux's Eagle Owl serve equally well for a hedgehog, a giant rat, a mouse, or a small insect, and the same could be said of some diurnal raptor species.

Among the diurnal raptors the feet and legs are often specially adapted to the type of prey they catch. The legs of sparrowhawks and goshawks are long and thin, equipped with very long thin sharp

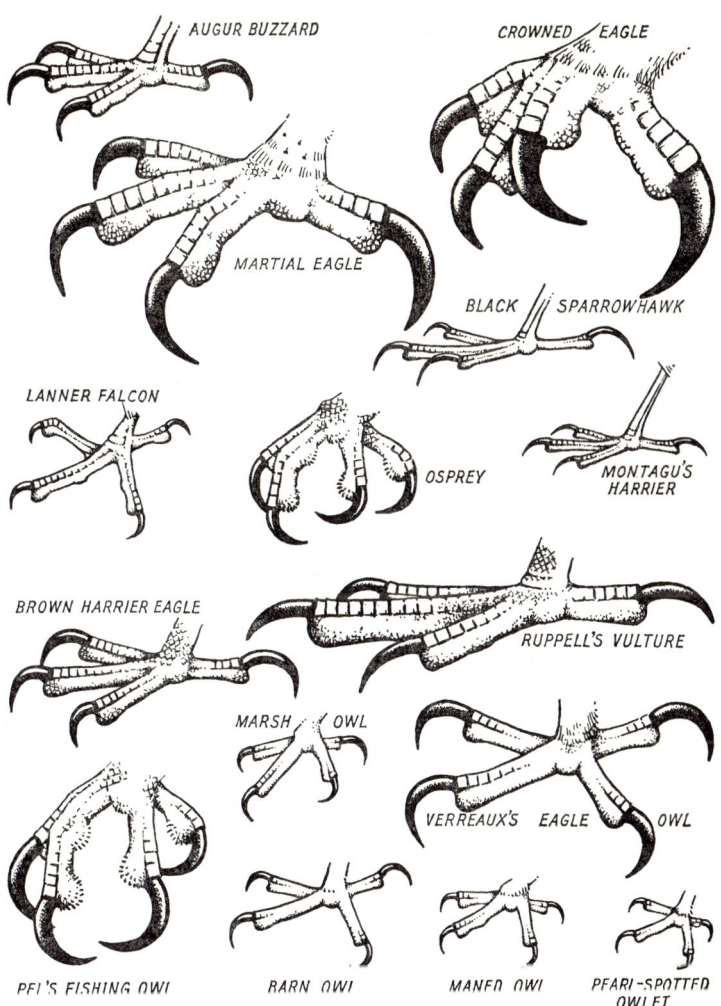

Fig. 4 Feet of birds of prey.

talons, suited to clutching and holding elusive and quick-moving prey, which may have to be snatched off a branch in flight at some difficult angle to the body. Vultures, which essentially do not grasp and kill their food, have accordingly weak feet and blunt claws, though the Egyptian Vulture and Lammergeier, both perhaps more actively predatory than other species, have a more powerful grip and a more serviceable set of talons.

Even in closely related species there may be a difference in the structure of the feet and legs adapted to the type of prey taken. The Crowned Eagle of the forests is primarily a killer of large or fair-sized mammals, and has exceptionally thick, powerful legs and relatively short thick toes, ending in very strong rigid talons. The nearly related Martial Eagle, living mainly in savannas on game birds, has relatively longer legs and thinner toes with a greater spread, perhaps better adapted to catching prey that may be fast moving. Both, however, are strong enough to kill antelope calves.

In the Chanting Goshawks a tendency to hunt insects in the grass has led to the development of long legs, on which they walk about almost in the manner of a miniature Secretary Bird. The Secretary Bird itself has very long legs and short toes, superficially similar to those of a bustard. It kills its prey by stamping, but its feet are not adapted for gripping and carrying prey, which it usually swallows or picks up in the beak.

While it is true to say that a great deal more needs to be learned about the hunting and killing methods of owls in comparison to diurnal raptors it is broadly clear that the diurnal raptors have evolved a much greater variety of methods of attack, and of weapons to assist them to catch and kill their prey, than have owls. Their body structure is so varied as to allow them to hunt in many different ways, whereas it seems that owls usually hunt from perches and at fairly close quarters. To some extent this may be compensated for by the fact that active fast moving creatures may be stationary at night, so that owls do not necessarily need the same physical equipment to catch them. An adult Lanner Falcon has been known to be killed by a Spotted Eagle Owl, and there are other similar records. It is probably still true to say that the various types of prey are exposed to risk of attack, both by day and by night, by one or other sort of owl or diurnal raptor, and that these have evolved all the equipment necessary to enable them to hunt effectively throughout the twenty-four hours.

Chapter 3
The Variety of African Birds of Prey

A great many observers in Africa are discouraged from the study of birds of prey by what they regard as their bewildering variety. It is true that the actual number of species which occur is considerable, and that identification is further complicated by plumages that are different in the immature, subadult, and adult stages, and sometimes between male and female. Of some species several races occur, and may be markedly different from each other—though one may say with confidence that all Black Kites are recognisably Black Kites. Against these difficulties can be set the facts that many birds of prey are large and conspicuous—at least the diurnal species—and are often observed in the open. They do not compare in difficulty with, for instance, some of the skulking forest greenbuls, which can barely be identified at all without shooting them, or the large variety of larks and pipits.

Since this variety appears to confuse and deter many who would otherwise be interested in birds of prey it seems useful to try to break down or analyse the various species according to habitat and habits. In Table 13 (see p. 304) this has been done for both diurnal and nocturnal species.

It is necessary first to give a brief description of the main habitats occurring in most of Africa. In Table 13 the habitats that occur in Africa have been over-simplified. There is, for instance, a very large variety of forest types, from giant St. John's Wort at 11,500 feet in Ethiopia to swampy forests full of Raphia palms in the Niger Delta creeks. However, forest as such has a closed and typically evergreen tree canopy, a rather luxuriant shrub layer, and little or no grass, while the light intensity on the forest floor is often very weak.

There may be a sharp transition from forest to woodland, which in most of Africa includes various types of broad-leaved savanna, deciduous in the dry season, and subject to fires because of the existence of a ground cover of long grass. There is, however, only a steady and gradual transition from woodland and/or broad-leaved savanna to Acacia savanna, which occurs over vast areas in rather lower rainfall, or on different types of soil to broad-leaved savannas. Both types of savanna, however, are characterised by fire-resistant trees which are deciduous in the dry season, a poorly developed shrub layer, and a more or less luxuriant growth of perennial tufted grasses, which dry in the dry season and then carry the fierce fires which reduce the shrub layer and prevent the regeneration of trees. Woodland or savanna protected from fire invariably grows denser, and may eventually form a nearly closed canopy which is, however, still deciduous in the dry season.

Steppe and thornbush have been classified together, though they are very different in character, steppe being open and thornbush dense. However, they are both characterised by a reduction in the perennial grass layer, with consequently less severe fires. There are considerable areas of bare ground, and in thornbush there are often very dense thickets of thorny shrubs, beloved of such animals as Black Rhinoceros, Dikdik, and Lesser Kudu. Not all the species of birds of prey that occur in thorn thickets would be found in the open steppe for preference, but the two habitat types are often intermingled, and one may see a harrier hunting over a small clearing in thornbush or a White-headed Vulture sailing over thickets.

Deserts, aquatic habitats, and towns are more or less self-explanatory, though endless argument rages as to where arid steppe ends and desert begins. Steppes merge imperceptibly into deserts as the rainfall decreases, bare ground increases, and vegetation becomes lower and more specialised. Aquatic habitats may occur in the midst of desert or tropical forest alike, and with them I have included marshlands, which are preferred by some species that do not necessarily obtain much or any of their prey from the water. Towns are a specialised habitat which only a few species of raptors have adopted as their preferred habitat, though those species are sometimes very successful and numerous.

Using this guide, it is possible to narrow the field, to a greater or lesser extent, and to eliminate a proportion of the total possible variety of birds of prey that may be seen. The geographical range of some of the species is a further help. For instance, of two buzzard species inhabiting savanna one occurs in East and South Africa, the other in West and North Central Africa, and there are other examples.

Table 13 is, of course, not infallible, and one may occasionally see certain species out of their preferred or normal habitat, especially if they are migrants. It is intended to be used as a tool to supplement standard identification guides, and the variety is obviously still considerable in some habitats.

In Africa as a whole, excluding Madagascar and other oceanic islands, about 89 species of diurnal and 31 species of nocturnal raptors occur. The exact number is open to argument, and depends on whether one accepts certain forms as good species or merely as races of other species. For instance, one may accept the Mountain Buzzard and the African Marsh Harrier as distinct species or regard them as races of the more widespread Common Buzzard and Marsh Harrier, both of which occur in tropical Africa as migrants. In Table 13(a) concerning the diurnal raptors I have adopted the classification proposed by Dr. Dean Amadon in our joint work, *Hawks, Eagles and Falcons of the World*. Although this disagrees in some respects with other classifications (no two of which agree) we think it an advance on any order yet proposed, though it is of course open to argument.

Of all this large variety, only one family, the Sagittariidae, containing the unmistakable Secretary Bird as its sole representative, is exclusively African. All the other families and most of the genera of birds of prey represented in Africa occur elsewhere, as might be thought reasonable in birds of such powerful flight. There is even some doubt as to whether the Secretary Bird is a true bird of prey—a Falconiform—at all. It eats insects, small mammals, and snakes, which it catches in the grass, and either swallows whole or tears to pieces with its hooked beak. It builds a large stick nest on a thorny tree, much like that of some vultures and performs an undulating display similar to that of many other large soaring species. It looks and behaves like a form of terrestrial eagle. All these similarities, however, may be superficial. Electrical analysis of the egg-white proteins of the Secretary Bird once indicated that it might be more closely allied to bustards than to any known bird of prey. This supports an alternative view, that the Secretary Bird is not actually a Falconiform, but is related to the South American family of Cariamas (Cariamidea). Further samples produced conflicting results indicating that it was a Falconiform. Behaviour studies may help to elucidate this sort of puzzle in due course, and for the moment we say that the Secretary Bird behaves most like a true bird of prey, and probably is one, although highly specialised for a terrestrial existence.

Of the large number of diurnal raptor species twelve breed only in North and North-West Africa, occurring in the rest of the continent only as migrants, if at all. These are properly not raptors of the Ethiopian Region (comprising Africa south of the Sahara and parts of Arabia) but are species of the Palearctic region. A further 11 species are purely migratory, not breeding anywhere in Africa. This with vagrants reduces the number of species that are known to breed in Africa south of the Sahara from 89 to 62, of which a proportion are widespread birds such as the Peregrine Falcon and Black-shouldered Kite. Some of the diurnal raptors that breed in Africa south of the Sahara have a restricted range, for instance the Black Harrier, breeding only in a small part of South Africa. In practice, therefore, between 15 April and 15 September the puzzled observer in Africa south of the Sahara has only to cope with 62 possible species as against 89. And if these are further analysed according to their specific habitats the problem becomes even simpler. Actually one has to try very hard to see more than 25 species of diurnal birds of prey in a day, even in a good area such as the East African Rift Valley, and in the winter, when migrant species are also present.

There are also a few species, five in all, that perform well-marked intra-continental migrations entirely south of the Sahara. The best known of these are the Grasshopper Buzzard, Wahlberg's Eagle, and the beautiful little Swallow-tailed Kite, a delicate, insectivorous species that resembles a tern rather than a bird of prey. When more is known of local movements of some other birds of prey it may appear that others ought to be added to this list. At any rate, the seasonal occurrence of some of these intra-continental migrants can help still further to reduce the identification problem, for they occur in particular areas only at certain times of the year. Their movements are discussed in greater detail later.

The habitat preferences of the diurnal birds of prey, either as migrants or as resident breeders, simplify matters still further. The richest habitats, as one might expect, are woodland and Acacia savannas, each with a possible 63 species. Doubtless this is because both these habitats are relatively open country but with sufficient rainfall to result in a large variety of plants and animals, on which a

The Variety of African Birds of Prey 39

great variety of raptors can prey. However, when these habitats are further analysed on the basis of the numbers of species that prefer to inhabit them, as opposed to living there in small numbers or passing through on migration, we find that the Acacia savanna is poorer, with 20 species as opposed to 32 in woodland. For the field observer what this means is that in Acacia savanna he would be likely to see 20 species regularly, while another 43 would be either rare or of seasonal occurrence. In woodland, he would be likely to see 33 species and less likely to see another 30. Even these reduced numbers would not all be seen in all parts of the continent.

In steppes and thornbush, the next richest habitat, 53 species occur, but only 24 prefer this habitat; a few of these are equally common in Acacia savannas, such as the Chanting Goshawks and, on migration, the Common Kestrel. Here the finer distinction between steppe and thornbush would be helpful, for while one might see numbers of kestrels hunting over semi-arid open steppe they would not be observed in such numbers over extensive thickets of thornbush.

Forests and deserts support nearly the same numbers of species, 29 and 25. However the proportion of species that prefer forest as habitat ($\frac{13}{29}$ or 45%) is very much larger than in deserts, with 3 out of 24 or 12·5%. Doubtless this is because deserts are a very extreme environment which supports little prey. Of the species that occasionally occur in deserts most are large, powerful, wide-ranging species such as large falcons and vultures, or species passing over on migration. In forest, on the other hand, there is a large variety of potential prey living upon the abundant luxuriant vegetation. To make a success of life in such an environment, however, a diurnal raptor may have to be specialised for it. This no doubt accounts for the relatively high proportion of forest species that habitually live only within the dense growth, whereas in deserts a bird of powerful flight may be able to make use of a temporarily favourable situation, as does, for instance, the Lanner Falcon feeding on northward-bound migrant birds in April. Although the numbers are undoubtedly actually much greater in forests, in practice one sees as many or more diurnal raptors in the open desert. It is often possible to spend days in a forest without setting eyes on a hawk or eagle of any sort.

Water and marshlands regularly support ten species, for seven of which they are preferred habitat. However, the edges of lakes are so productive of possible prey, especially carrion or dead fish in one form or another that there may be many adventitious visitors. When large colonies of flamingoes are breeding in the middle of Lake Natron in Tanzania they are preyed upon by Egyptian and White-headed Vultures and Tawny Eagles, all three living in the surrounding steppe and thornbush, but making use of this abundant food supply for the time being without being perennially dependent on it. Equally, I have seen a Fish Eagle perched on a dead tree inside the Mount Kenya forest reserve at 7000 feet, in a place probably 20 miles or more from the nearest supply of fish. Although, therefore, there are certain species of birds of prey that one might expect to see near water or in marshy places, other occasional visitors characteristic of the surrounding country are also likely to be seen.

The diurnal raptors living in towns are either scavengers upon human dejecta and excreta or are specialists in particular types of prey. Among the former, sad to say, must be included the magnificent Lammergeier. Noble though it appears in flight it is actually commoner, in such countries as Ethiopia, round town rubbish dumps than anywhere else. It has, in fact, similar scavenging habits to the even more familiar Egyptian Vulture, which actually feeds, amongst other things, on human excrement. But the scavenger which has exploited this niche to the full is the Black Kite, which is abundant in all eastern and north tropical African cities. In the open bush the Black Kite is a relatively uncommon bird, feeding on any small animal it can catch, or on carrion. In towns it becomes expert at snatching the breakfast from one's plate, and woe betide anyone who tries to keep free-range chickens in his backyard.

Peregrine Falcons breed quite often in towns, and when one comes to think of it it is surprising that they do not breed there more often than they do. Most towns have a large resident population of pigeons, one of the favourite foods of the Peregrine. In Africa, Peregrines used to breed in Nairobi, on the coat of arms on the Law Courts, but when these British insignia were defaced on independence the Peregrines moved away. They tried a concrete statue erected on the wall of the President's Office, but though that would have been appropriate enough, they evidently did not like the hard unyielding substance in which they could not make a satisfactory scrape for the eggs, and they gave it up. Perhaps if town dwellers built suitable nesting sites for Peregrines and Kestrels on tall buildings more would breed, and make use of the potential food supply.

Another unlikely species, which one has a better chance of seeing in towns than almost anywhere else, is the Bat Hawk. The reason is, of course, that bats abound in buildings, and frequently can feed very easily on insects attracted by street lights. I have seen more Bat Hawks in Nairobi and Mombasa than anywhere else, and I have watched them flying over the beaches at Malindi, lit by the electric lights of the tourist hotels. The food chain involved was splendidly exemplified at the Nairobi Agricultural Show in 1966. My wife and I, going to attend a cocktail party after dark, watched a Bat Hawk hunting the bats that were attracted by the insects fluttering around the lights of the arena. The hawk might not have been able to do this everywhere, but in this case it had the open space of the arena in which to catch the bats. The passers-by, watching us gaze steadily into the sky, thought we were hoaxing them in some way.

When it comes to owls, the variety available is very much smaller, only about a third of the number of different sorts of diurnal raptors. Moreover, a good many of these are confined to small areas of habitat, especially those that live in forests. In the case of owls, however, any observations on their distribution patterns must be prefaced by remarking that since they are nocturnal they have been much less observed than have the diurnal raptors. Several species may be commoner and more widespread than we think. One new species of owlet, as yet unnamed, has been discovered in West Africa during the preparation of this book.

Again, woodland is the richest habitat, with 15 species, of which 6 prefer it to other habitats. Two of these, however, are owls which occur only in the north-west, and one is really a mountain moorland species, so that in most of Africa this habitat supports only 12 species, four of them more regular than the others. Two of the more regular species in woodland, the Scops Owl and the Pearl-spotted Owlet, are almost or quite as common in some other habitats.

Acacia savanna, with 12 (one properly a mountain species), and thornbush and steppe have fewer species, but a greater proportion, 5/10, as compared to 3/12, make the thornbush and steppe their preferred habitat. All of these 5, however, in practice prefer thornbush to open steppe, and all but one are small insectivorous species. Anybody who has camped in thornbush knows that the terrain abounds with night-flying insects, especially in the early rains. In fact it is a type of light open woodland, ideal for certain species of owls.

The species that hunt in the open steppe, the Grass Owl and the Short-eared and Marsh Owls, are quite different in their general habits to the small owls that live in the thornbush, for the last two are partly diurnal and may be seen hunting in the evening. And not all of the small species occur in the same area. In practice one would be unlikely to see more than three species of small owls in the same area of thornbush—the Scops, the White-faced Owl, and one of the Owlets.

Five owls are exclusively aquatic or prefer marshlands as habitat. Of these the fishing owls are so little known that no reasonable explanation for their exclusive habits can be advanced at present. The Marsh Owl and the Short-eared Owl, which for practical purposes replace each other geographically, north and south of the Sahara, are likely also to be seen hunting over open grassland or steppe and so are less strictly aquatic than the fishing owls.

In many ways the most remarkable of all habitats, where owls are concerned, is the forests. Of thirteen species occurring in forests eleven occur nowhere else. This proportion would be still further increased, and seem still more remarkable, if the fishing owls were added to the forest species. Although they are classed here as aquatic two species are confined to riversides inside the Equatorial forests, and the third, Pel's Fishing Owl, is in practice not found along rivers devoid of a strip of tall fringing trees or forest.

Of the eleven species occurring in forests exclusively at least nine are, so far as is known, confined to very small areas. One is confined to a few square miles of forest on the Congo border, another to a few square miles of the Arabuko-Sokoke forest on the Kenya Coast, while an Eagle Owl, *Bubo poensis*, has two races, one living in small areas of forest on the West Coast and the other right at the other side of the continent, in the Usambara Mountains. The observer wishing to identify forest owls need not be afraid that he will have to cope with a large variety. He will be lucky if he can locate more than a few individuals of one species alone. Again, however, one must note that few observers ever have tried to locate and watch owls in a tropical forest by night.

Towns attract two species of owls, but only one, the Barn Owl, prefers to live in towns. It can and does also live in open country, breeding, for instance, in abandoned or commandeered nests of the Hammerkop, a habit it shares with the Grey Kestrel. Generally, however, Barn Owls are associates of man, either in agricultural areas or in towns. The little Scops Owls that often call in villages and in well-treed city squares are simply making use of a sort of woodland, but the Barn Owls are benefiting from the presence of man, his garbage, and the relatively dense and vulnerable population of rats and mice found in and around human dwellings.

The Barn Owl, unlike the Black Kite and several vultures, is not directly a scavenger on man's leavings. It is, rather, like the feral domestic cats so common at the present time in the Roman Forum, a killer of mice and rats which are themselves attracted by scraps and refuse. It is not for nothing that the Barn Owl is a cosmopolitan bird, and that the Black Kite is probably the most numerous and successful diurnal raptor of its size anywhere in the world. Both these species have demonstrated that, even for birds of prey, the man-made habitat of towns has its points.

Part II
The African Birds of Prey

Chapter 4
Cuckoo Falcons, Honey Buzzards and Kites

In this and subsequent chapters I shall discuss the different groups, families and species of African raptors, first the diurnal, and then the nocturnal types, more or less in order of classification. If I depart from the order of species as in the list for Chapter 3 it is only for convenience. I have broadly grouped related species together, but in one or two cases I shall deal with species which are not closely related in the same chapter, where it appears to me that they perform the same function in nature.

The first of the natural groups with which we have to deal is actually one of the more diverse in appearance and habits. They may all be broadly called "kites", and include the Honey Buzzard, which is only a migrant to Africa, the Cuckoo Falcon, the Bat Hawk, and the several species of true kites. Some of the latter will later be mentioned or discussed at some length, particularly in relation to migration, so I shall here confine myself to other aspects of their behaviour.

The **Honey Buzzard** is the only one of this group which does not breed in Africa. In itself this fact is something of a mystery, for there appears no reason at all why Honey Buzzards should *not* breed in Africa—at least in the woodlands of North Africa. In the eastern tropics there are resident breeding races, and other species, of Honey Buzzards, so it seems odd that they do not breed in Africa. No other species here fills the specialised ecological niche while they are away from Africa, and their only competitor for their food— the contents of bees' and wasps' nests—would be the Honey Badger or Ratel. Since this is a largely nocturnal animal it is difficult to see how it could directly compete with a diurnal bird of prey, and one would think that there were enough wasps and hornets to suffice both.

Honey Buzzards are, in fact, altogether something of a mystery in Africa. Anyone who has watched the spring or autumn migration at Cape Spartel or Malta knows that they do leave and enter Africa in numbers by these routes, though few of them seem to enter Africa at Suez—the other great entry point for soaring birds. However, once they enter Africa they seem to become very unobtrusive, and are very little noticed. They are even rather scarce in collections. In thirty years' residence I have only seen two, both at my home in Kenya, and I will not believe that I would not have seen more if they often passed through Kenya. Nor have I ever met an ornithologist in Africa who described them as common, except in Rhodesia where there are, nevertheless, very few authentic records of occurrence. Recent information indicates that they are quite common in winter in the forests of Gabon.

As is well known Honey Buzzards live on the grubs in wasps' and bees' nests, which they either dig out of the ground like a terrier or snatch from beneath the eaves of houses or branches of trees. The number of available hornets' nests of one kind and another will be plain to anyone who has spent any time in Africa; they depend from the thatch of almost every native hut, and from the branches of many trees, even in arid areas. Honey Buzzards, which are not shy in their breeding quarters, though they are secretive, ought therefore to be fairly obvious in Africa, but they are not. They should be at least as common and evident as, say, the migrant races of the Tawny Eagle, for their numbers are large; more than 20,000 have been counted at Falsterbo, in Scania, in one autumn migration season, and the total number entering Africa must be very much greater. Yet once they are in their wintering grounds they seem almost to disappear; even in Gabon there is no evidence of the sort of numbers mentioned above.

These wintering grounds are probably in the western part of tropical Africa, perhaps in the Brachystegia woodland belt in the southern tropics, or in the Equatorial forests. In their breeding grounds they are woodland birds so that, except when migrating across more open terrain, one would expect them to settle in woodland or forest. Yet there seem to be only a few records from any African country. Possibly the main wintering ground is in the great Equatorial forest, where ornithologists are scarce, and birds of prey difficult to see. Yet a country such as Nigeria has in the past been well studded with keen observers, and the later Dr. J. P. Chapin covered the former Belgian Congo very thoroughly for many years, but did not see many wintering Honey Buzzards. The only place where I have heard anyone speak of them as common is in Rhodesia, where my friend Richard Brooke tells me they are often seen; but here again the scanty museum records do not support the idea that they are numerous. The main wintering ground of the Honey Buzzard is still something of a mystery.

The **Cuckoo Falcon** is the nearest relative of the Honey Buzzard in Africa. It is a resident, but nowhere very common, and this again is rather a mystery, for it feeds mainly on insects, which abound. It is a thoroughly badly-named bird, for in habits it bears little relation to a falcon of any sort. The original reason for its name appears to have been the fact that, like falcons, it has notches, or teeth, on the upper mandible. In falcons these teeth are used to break the necks of their prey, but as Cuckoo Falcons do not feed on large animals or birds—except a few lizards and perhaps an occasional rat—the purpose of these teeth is obscure. Perhaps they are necessary to chop up large insects, though most insectivorous birds do not possess such teeth and recent work on the Northern Shrike in America does not indicate that such "teeth" are indispensable for breaking up prey.

Whatever the reason for the teeth "falcon" is a thoroughly inappropriate name. Cuckoo Falcons are inhabitants of woodland and forest, and when seen they resemble a sparrowhawk or goshawk when perched, and in flight look rather like a small kite. When perched they often droop their wings in the manner of a cuckoo and this, together with the striking barring of the breast, is doubtless the reason for that part of the name. Their calls resemble those of a buzzard—a musical whistling "pee-ew" with variations. They are altogether odd birds.

Inoffensive and insectivorous, it is possible that their superficial resemblance to a sparrowhawk may be a form of mimicry. When encountered they are often quite tame, and will allow close approach; I have come across one seeking insects in the undergrowth of the forest near my home, peering about among the foliage, almost like a parrot. The large eye, bright yellow, was very conspicuous.

Cuckoo Falcons are most obvious in the early breeding season when they soar and call in nuptial display. All members of this genus (which is mainly oriental) seem to indulge in vigorous aerial displays tumbling about high up, and in the African species displaying the chestnut underwing coverts. No full account of their nesting exists, but from scattered observations it seems likely that they breed in the rains when insects are plentiful, like most other insectivorous birds. They make a slight nest in a tree, usually among thick foliage, but I had never had a chance to observe one until 1967 when a possible explanation of the curious teeth on the mandible occurred to me.

In this case we watched a male Cuckoo Falcon collecting the green branches which his mate worked into a slight nest. He collected branch after branch in full view of us, and in each case his method was the same. He first perched, looking up, down and sideways till he selected a suitable green spray. Then, flying up to the end of the branch so chosen, he hung by his feet from the spray, stretched up, and nipped it off with his beak, with no wrenching or straining, as neatly as one would with a pair of secateurs. It is of course too soon to say whether this single observation on the building habits of the male Cuckoo Falcon is the real explanation of those curious teeth, but it is possible. Unfortunately the eggs in this nest failed to hatch, so the full details of the breeding behaviour remain unknown. However, the female only incubated in this case, and the nest was one which had been built and perhaps used the previous year—when it also failed.

The **Bat Hawk** is a near relative of the Cuckoo Falcon, another "aberrant" kite. But it is as different from the Cuckoo Falcon as chalk from cheese. Although not called a falcon, it strongly resembles one in general build and habits; long winged, swift flying, and highly predatory. It is a scarce species of very wide distribution, occurring in much of Africa, and in Malaysia and Indonesia.

Bat Hawks feed almost exclusively on bats, though they also take a few swallows and swifts, and some insects. They are to a bat what a Peregrine is to a grouse, a danger in flight but not while the bat is perched. To find its prey the Bat Hawk frequents the vicinity of caves wherein bats roost in clusters, or towns where they roost in numbers in the roofs of houses. To catch a bat the hawk needs a clear open space where its great speed can be fully used to advantage; in thick cover it would probably injure itself when in swift pursuit. Such an open space is provided by a still pool on a forest river, a beach, a creek in mangroves, a large open lawn, a football ground, or even a railway station platform. Makindu Railway Station in Kenya used to be a great place for seeing Bat Hawks, and I have watched them around the tourist hotels in Malindi, lit from beneath by the electric lights.

Bats emerge from their daytime roosts at dusk. From the eaves of houses they burst out in little flocks together, and dash off into the gloaming, twisting and turning this way and that. Later they may be found hunting insects over water. It is at these times that they are in danger from the hawk, which pursues them at speed, catches them in mid air in its feet, transfers them to the beak, and swallows them whole, aided by a wide gape, like that of a Nightjar. Bat Hawks must obtain most of their food in about an hour each day, in the late evening and just after dark. Apparently they do not hunt in full night, and evidently do not catch much in the early morning—they only feed their young in the nest in the late evening. This is probably because the bats on which they feed are really vulnerable to attack only when they emerge in numbers together from their daytime roosts. Any insects, swallows, and so on that are also caught are just snapped up in passing, when the real object of the evening hunt is bats.

When breeding Bat Hawks behave much like other birds of prey, making a stick nest in a tree. They can see perfectly well by day, and their display flights are carried out in daylight; and I have seen a male stooping at his mate over the sea near the Likoni ferry, on Mombasa Island. The only nests that have been observed for any length of time have been one in Sumatra and one in the grounds of the Civil Hospital at Dar-es-Salaam. Observations at these nests indicate that the incubation period is about a month, the fledging period about 35-40 days, that the female sits on the eggs and that (in common with kites) she is likely to be very aggressive to an observer who climbs to the nest. Apart from the fact that all feeding of the young takes place late in the evening, and the birds are largely inactive by day, the breeding cycle in this species is not very different from that of many others of about the same size. It is in their specialised feeding habits that Bat Hawks are remarkable.

Of the species called kites in Africa two are what might be called aberrant kites—the Swallow-tailed and Black-shouldered Kites. Neither resembles the true kites—the Red Kite and the Black Kite, large birds with forked tails, graceful soaring flight, living in woodlands or scavenging in towns and villages. Both the Black-shouldered Kite and the Swallow-tailed Kite frequent open savannas, grasslands, and semi-arid steppes, but the Swallow-tailed Kite inhabits more arid country from choice and only migrates into moister savannas outside the breeding season.

Anyone seeing a **Swallow-tailed Kite** in the field for the first time could be forgiven for thinking it not a bird of prey at all, but a tern. Very small, grey and white, with a long forked tail, it hawks over open country with most exquisite grace. It is only at close quarters that the head with short hooked bill proclaims it a bird of prey. A party of them seen hawking over grim desert country, such as that in Turkana west of Lake Rudolf, seems quite out of place; one feels that they ought instead to be over some sheltered backwater.

Swallow-tailed Kites are usually gregarious, hunting and migrating in small groups, nesting and roosting together. They hunt for insects in the grass, turning into the wind to hang poised, with light hovering motions of the wings, then glide down to pick up their prey. They are entirely harmless and completely satisfying to watch. Throughout their range they are rather little known, but some account of their regular migrations in West Africa is given later. They breed in the northern, more arid parts of their range.

Little is known of their breeding, except that they breed in small colonies in Acacias or other thorny trees. In some cases these colonies are associated with the nest of another large bird of prey, such as a Brown Snake Eagle, but whether this is because they deliberately seek the company and possible protection of another larger and more powerful raptor, or whether it is because only certain trees are big enough to attract both is obscure. At breeding colonies they are excitable and noisy, in contrast to their normal silence on migration. In some cases at any rate they seem to feed their young on more solid prey—such as skinks—than the insects they themselves eat when on migration. Anyone having the luck to find a colony should observe it closely.

The **Black-shouldered Kite** is also a grey and white bird with black patches on the wings, and a beautiful coral-red eye. It is a very much more familiar species than the Swallow-tailed Kite, occurring in open country of all sorts almost all over Africa. It even breeds in open patches derived from cultivation and habitation on the edges, and perhaps within the equatorial forest. As it occurs so commonly in places where it can be readily observed it is much better known than the Swallow-tailed Kite. However, it is far from being fully known; and no very complete account of the breeding behaviour exists.

Black-shouldered Kites, in much of Africa, seem to occupy the ecological niche of Kestrels in temperate climates. They hunt over the grassland, hovering at intervals, and dropping on insects or rats. Their method of hovering is essentially rather like that of a Kestrel, with fanning wings and spread tail, but the body is usually more acutely angled upwards, and the wings are held higher. The whole process appears more graceful than in the Kestrel. When prey is sighted the Kite gently parachutes down, controlling the speed of its descent by the angle at which the wings are held, and finally, in the last few feet, it raises them vertically above the back and plunges on its prey. It often takes surprisingly large rats and kills more of such mammals than insects.

The Black-shouldered Kite is one of a very successful group of four species with an almost world-wide distribution in savannas and grasslands in tropical and subtropical latitudes. Some consider that there are properly only two species, our Black-shouldered Kite and the Letter-winged Kite in Australia. However, it is perhaps safer at present to distinguish four, one in America, one in Africa and Asia, and two in Australia. In all the group, the Black-shouldered Kite of Africa included, there is a tendency for the numbers to fluctuate with the numbers of the rodents and insects on which they prey. In East Africa general observations indicate that in favourable years for rodents the kites might breed more often and rear larger broods than usual; this results in a temporary increase in the population which decreases later.

Black-shouldered kites do not resemble the larger kites in appearance, but they share the kite-like habit of gregarious roosting at times. They are nomadic rather than truly migratory, but undoubtedly perform local movements over considerable distances. These movements have not been fully studied, but will probably be found to be connected with fluctuations in food supply. As they can hardly be properly elucidated without making counts in different parts of Africa at different seasons, it is likely they will remain obscure for some time.

To conclude, we come to the true kites of the genus *Milvus*, the **Red** and the **Black Kite**. The former is a breeding species only in North-West Africa, and does not migrate to the tropical parts of the continent. The Black Kite is the commonest, boldest, most ubiquitous, and most adaptable species of large raptor in Africa—and elsewhere in the eastern and Australian tropics. Much will be said later about its movements, so I shall here touch only on other aspects of its behaviour.

Both these large Kites are inhabitants of woodland and also scavenge in towns and villages, preying upon anything they can get. The Red Kite is much the less adaptable of the two, and it only appears to fill the scavenger niche where Black Kites are absent. Thus, it was the species that used to scavenge in the streets of London, and in the Cape Verde Islands, where it is the only resident Kite, it behaves much as the Black Kite does in other inhabited localities. I should like to watch the Red Kites of the Cape Verde Islands for to me it seems, from museum specimens, that there is some doubt that they are Red and not Black Kites. They have shorter tails than other Red Kites, and are browner above.

Red Kites have been studied quite fully in Europe, but not in Africa. There is no reason to suppose that their behaviour in Morocco differs much from that in Spain. They like mature woods of deciduous timber, and are generally shyer than Black Kites. Perhaps this is why they are often ousted by the bolder, smaller, but more aggressive Black Kite in areas where both occur together.

Black Kites were probably originally birds of woodland which have adapted with conspicuous success to domicile alongside man. They are commonest in long-inhabited areas, and do not breed commonly in uninhabited savannas. In a small but ancient Ethiopian town, such as Gondar, many pairs breed close together, but nowhere in Africa do they swarm in towns quite as they do in India. It is likely that as the human population of Africa increases, and towns become larger, the Black Kite will increase in numbers rather than otherwise.

The Black Kite is called by a variety of opprobrious names, derived from its scavenging habits. It picks up offal and scraps, feeds on carrion when available, but not, in my opinion, on human or other excrement. In natural conditions, when breeding away from towns, it feeds upon insects, small mammals, young birds, and the like, and cannot kill anything very large. In towns it is a nuisance to those who leave their poultry unattended, but probably on balance does as much good as harm. While it will take the breakfast off your

Cuckoo Falcons, Honey Buzzards and Kites

camp table if you let it this does not seem to me a reason for condemning it. Its flight is always beautiful to watch, and one should admire and commend its adaptability and success.

The strangest thing about it is that although it is so common and obvious in all parts of the continent it still remains something of a mystery. Its movements have never been fully studied, and so far as I know only one nest in Africa has ever been watched throughout the breeding cycle. It is an admirable object for further detailed study, and it is to be hoped that someone will forgive the fact that it is common, and will observe it as fully as it deserves.

Chapter 5
Vultures

Ten species of vultures occur in Africa. Of these, two—the European Griffon and the Black Vulture—are Palearctic birds which occur only in the North and North-West; the Black Vulture is not proven to breed in Africa and may only be a scarce visitor. Of the remaining eight all but the Egyptian Vulture, which occurs also in Asia, are exclusively African, though they have relatives or ecological counterparts in Asia. There are actually more species of Old World Vultures in Africa than in Eurasia, but they do not all occur together. Even so there are places, such as the Nairobi National Park, where up to six species can be seen together at the same carcase.

All vultures are basically scavengers and carrion eaters, and as a result, they are regarded with disgust by many people. However, with a few doubtful exceptions, they are unquestionably beneficial birds and are rightly protected by most Governments, or are unmolested by African peoples. Of the ten species only four, the Egyptian Vulture, Lammergeier, Lappet-faced Vulture, and White-headed Vulture kill any living prey—and for some of these the evidence is doubtful. One other species, the Cape Vulture, may recently have taken to killing living prey through shortage of its natural food—carrion.

All the vultures are large to very large birds. The European Black Vulture, fractionally larger than the Lappet-faced, is the largest African bird of prey, and the third largest in the world, exceeded only by two American Condors. Next in order of size are the three species of Griffons, the White-headed Vulture, and the White-backed Vulture. The Lammergeier has actually a greater wing-span—about nine feet—than have the Griffons, but weighs less and is much slimmer. The two smallest species are the Hooded Vulture which is the only one of the group that occurs at all commonly in forests, and the Egyptian Vulture, conspicuously black and white in adult plumage, but dark brown in immature dress. No vulture but the

Lammergeier, and perhaps the White-headed Vulture, can be described as beautiful, but they are all impressive in flight, and when on the wing the Lammergeier has a grace and magnificence all its own.

The **Egyptian Vulture**, the smallest, is still the size of a medium-sized eagle. It is commonest in the North African desert country, rare in the south, and does not occur in country with much more than 30 inches of rainfall per annum. It is a partial migrant from Europe and Asia in the winter, but also a regular resident in suitable country as far south as the Equator and rarely further south. In North African towns and villages it is a scavenger feeding *inter alia* on human and other excrement; it is the only species of bird of prey that does this. Unattractive as it may be in this respect, it has other claims to distinction.

The Egyptian Vulture has much more powerful feet than have most vultures which—since they feed entirely on dead animals— do not require a powerful killing talon grasp. Egyptian Vultures do prey upon the young of such colonial breeding birds as flamingos. At Lake Magadi, in 1962, when there was an enormous breeding colony of flamingos, Egyptian Vultures were the most persistent predators, and the downy young flamingos in herds were able to distinguish them as dangerous from the harmless scavenging Black Kites. They preyed more upon eggs than upon the young flamingos themselves, mounting nests in the face of determined opposition from the adult flamingos, and damaging far more eggs than they actually ate. I have also seen them feeding on pelicans' eggs, picking them up in the bill, and throwing them hard against the rocks of the breeding island. But the really unique habit of the Egyptian Vulture concerns ostrich eggs.

I had long known that Egyptian Vultures managed to break ostrich eggs to eat the contents—indeed this was reported by Africans to Victorian naturalists seventy years ago—but did not know how. Now this has been established by the Van Lawicks in Tanzania. The Egyptian Vulture is a tool-user. It picks up a stone, and hurls this with sufficient force against the ostrich egg to crack the shell. It often misses, and evidently some birds are more adept than others, but in the end the shell is cracked and the contents can be eaten. The action is the same as that used to smash a pelican's or a flamingo's egg; but of course it is one thing to pick up an egg and smash it by a quick downward throw, and quite another dimension of action to use a tool—a stone—to do it. The Egyptian Vulture, the despised Pharaoh's Chicken, thus joins the distinguished company of the higher apes, a finch in the Galapagos islands, perhaps a Bower Bird, and man, as a user of tools to obtain food.

The **Lammergeier**—reluctant as we may be to admit it—is probably the Egyptian Vulture's closest relative. Both breed singly in nests that are usually situated in caverns or overhung ledges. Both have long narrow wings and a diamond-shaped tail, unique among vultures. Their eggs are also similar, white, heavily marked with red-brown, sometimes obscuring the ground colour. They display in a similar manner and thorough comparative studies will probably show that their breeding habits are closely akin.

One does not like to think of the Lammergeier, impressive, even draconian, in appearance, magnificent and of matchless grace in flight, as a near relative of Pharaoh's Chicken, or even of other scavenging vultures. One likes to think of Lammergeiers as superb eagle-like birds inhabiting the wildest mountain terrain, with a specialised habit of eating bones and killing some live prey. But where they are common, as in Ethiopia and Tibet, this impression is soon dispelled. For all its magnificent appearance, the Lammergeier then turns out to be a scavenger associated with man, following the plough in Tibet to pick up the grubs in manure, and in Ethiopia frequenting the town garbage heaps for scraps. It is sad, but it is true. Myself, I believe that the Lammergeier can only be common where man, in particular primitive pastoral man, maintains large herds of stock subject to a heavy mortality. Such primitive pastoral communities, lacking good veterinary services, are likely to provide a more reliable supply of bones and scraps than will any wild and uninhabited mountain area—though a few Lammergeiers do occur in such places too.

Nothing detracts, however, from the magnificent flight of the Lammergeier, and to see one—as I have so often seen them—mounting slowly on imperceptible updraughts while following closely the contours of some titanic Ethiopian cliff, is inspiring indeed. Like other vultures they eat carrion. I have seen one waddle into thick bushes and drag out the putrefying remains of a Gelada Monkey. They may also kill some living prey. On Muruanisigar in Turkana, my brother has seen one carrying a monitor lizard, which was probably alive when taken, and they are said to kill hyrax on Mount Kenya. But their most remarkable habit is bone-eating.

The Lammergeier splits bones by dropping them on hard surfaces, rock slabs or scree. It is supposed to be the species which dropped the tortoise on the head of Aeschylus, and in many parts of its range is known as the bone-breaker. Until rather recently I could find only a few good accounts of the habit in the literature, and had only seen it done once myself, in Spain. But in Ethiopia, where the species is common, I have seen it done many times, and the process has been filmed by Jeffery Boswall of the BBC.

The Lammergeier has a favourite slab or two in its range where it drops bones. Such places, from the accumulation of fragments, are known as ossuaries. To split a bone the Lammergeier approaches such a place *downwind*, thereby gaining speed. Approaching the chosen slab it dips or dives in flight, further increasing speed, and releases the bone at a height of 100–200 feet. At that range it can hit a rock 15 feet square, though larger flat slabs are preferred. The bird then turns instantly *into wind* and alights with a quick pigeon-like fanning of those mighty wings. Obviously it must turn upwind to alight, like any flying machine; hence the process is nicely controlled by aerodynamic laws. It is often followed by ravens, which will rob it of the fragments of bone if it is not quick to alight before they do. It will drop the piece of bone three or four times before abandoning it, and often flies some distance to gain height for another approach. It has a specialised tongue, like a marrow scoop, which it can perhaps thrust into the bone cavity for the marrow. What the beard—the stiff tuft of down-pointed bristles on either side of the beak—is for we do not know; but it seems possible that it is a tactile organ, perhaps connected with feeding on bones.

Lammergeiers do not only eat bones, but they must have bones in their diet. Fed only on meat in zoos they do not thrive. Their other special claim to renown is that they are cosmeticians. Recent work on captive birds indicates that the rufous or orange colour of the breast is none other than iron oxide, obtained from dusting or squatting in fine red earth, which also accounts for the powder in the plumage. Systematists have divided the Lammergeier into races partly on the ground that the orange or rufous colour varies. But this is not a true plumage colour, only staining; the deepest rufous birds are in Africa, where the soil is redder than elsewhere in the range of the Lammergeier. Well!

Hooded Vultures form a sort of medium-sized link between Egyptian Vultures and the larger colonial species. They are even placed sometimes in the same genus *Neophron*. To my mind this is absurd, for in no other physical respect but shape of beak do they resemble Egyptian Vultures. They normally inhabit well-wooded or well-watered country, but also occur in deserts. They are the only vultures in Africa that penetrate far into forests; and they only do so in association with man. I know from personal experience that a Hooded Vulture can find a carcase hidden in a tree in woodland, but they cannot find one inside dense forest, and when they occur here it is in villages.

The Hooded Vulture is the only species of African vulture whose breeding habits have been thoroughly described and that only by Dr. Van Someren near Nairobi. From his study we learn that the incubation period and fledging periods are long—46 and 120 days respectively. In larger vultures we can expect the cycle to be still longer, within limits. When bringing food or a green branch to the nest, the bare skin on the face of the Hooded Vulture blushes red in excitement—a feature also seen in some other species such as the Harrier Hawk.

The Hooded is one of the commonest vultures in Africa, in places the commonest. But the large vultures of the plains are actually more numerous, and they are the vultures seen in the greatest numbers at a carcase. The **White-backed Vulture**, and the three species of **Griffons** are all gregarious species that usually feed, roost, and breed in some numbers together. They differ in that the White-backed Vulture breeds in trees, while all the African Griffons breed in rocks and cliffs. There are rare records of Griffons building in trees, or White-backed Vultures on cliffs, but some of these may be questionable.

White-backed Vultures are slightly smaller than the true Griffons, but have a wider range than any of the three. They do not share the range of the European Griffon, but occur alongside both Ruppell's Griffon and the Cape Vulture. The rock-nesting Griffons are mainly birds of arid country, found right out in stark deserts, and seldom breeding in well-watered or wooded areas. White-backed Vultures are generally birds of Acacia savanna and grass plains, breeding for preference in trees along river banks. There is thus some ecological separation between these two types, but both may compete for a carcase. The three species of Griffons, all with similar habits, all very large, divide up the continent between them and do not compete with each other. The European Griffon breeds only in the Atlas, and occurs as a migrant in the north. Ruppell's Griffon is the common big vulture of arid steppes and deserts of the northern tropics, and the Cape Vulture takes over in South Africa. While one may see White-backed Vultures with one or other of the griffons it is most unlikely that one will see two species of griffons at the same carcase.

The remaining species of large vultures, the **European Black**, the **Lappet-faced**, and the **White-headed** are all large, all solitary breeders on trees or rocks and, in at least the last two, certainly kill some live prey. This may only be in the shape of helpless young flamingos or other colonial birds, but the White-headed Vulture is credited by Somalis, who probably know, with ability to kill Dikdik. I have on occasion come on both White-headed and Lappet-faced Vultures in circumstances suggesting they had killed a small animal and eaten it where it was, and there is more recent circumstantial evidence of killing from Tanzania. However, I think that no naturalist has as yet seen the act actually performed—except in the case of young and helpless flamingos, which were certainly killed by both White-headed and Lappet-faced Vultures at Magadi in 1962.

These seven large species—the White-backed, the Griffons, and the three large solitary species—are the birds that clear up the carcases of large dead wild or domestic animals, wherever they are found in the plains. I have already discussed the method by which they find these carcases, which is less remarkable than it might seem. They do not come to every carcase, as anyone who has tried putting out a putrefying dog or goat in the hope of photographing vultures will know. But when they do come to a carcase they finish it off very quickly, leaving only the bones for the hyenas or, in some cases, Lammergeiers. The large solitary species, such as the Lappet-faced and White-headed Vultures, will come to the same carcases as the others, but can also be seen feeding by themselves. A mob of larger vultures is also, sometimes, attended by a few Hooded and Egyptian Vultures; in places on the East African plains one can see these two, the White-backed and Ruppell's Griffon, the Lappet-faced and White-headed at the same carcase.

Really thorough work on the comparative behaviour of large vultures at a carcase has recently been done in the Serengeti. These studies have shown that there is ecological separation in their feeding habits, and a dominance heirarchy between the large and small species. The Lappet-faced—the largest and most powerful, with a huge heavy beak—is the species which can first break into a carcase, and it can sometimes be seen slogging at a dead animal with sideways swipes of the beak while others look on. It is large and powerful enough to enforce dominance over any of the others if it wishes, is very aggressive, and obtains some of its prey by snatching pieces of flesh from other vultures. Both Lappet-faced and White-headed Vultures tear off pieces of rough skin and sinew, while the Griffons and White-backed Vultures feed on flesh and intestines, thrusting their long snaky necks far inside any opening.

Griffons come next to Lappet-faced Vultures in size, then White-headed and White-backed Vultures. But there is often a squabbling mêlée of several species in which all manage to get something; even the smaller Egyptian and Hooded Vultures, whose slender beaks permit them to nibble morsels from places where coarser broader beaks cannot reach, or collect small scraps of flesh torn off and discarded by the squabbling mass of bigger birds. I have also seen Lappet-faced Vultures attending such a mêlée snatching pieces of flesh that have been torn off by Griffons, and pursuing jackals in an attempt to pirate what they may have secured. One jackal can put eighty or more large vultures to flight, and dominate the whole scene.

Ecological separation, in some degree, may also be brought about by aerodynamic laws. The larger vultures are all very heavy birds, and moreover their wing-loading is high, especially after they have fed. Thus in most tropical areas, they cannot get on the wing very early in the morning, since they can only gain height on the larger thermal bubbles, which normally do not rise till the sun is well up. Both the Egyptian Vulture and the Lammergeier have lower wing-loading than Griffons or White-backed Vultures and can thus get on the wing earlier in the morning. So, presumably, can the Hooded Vulture. Thus these smaller species, which might not be able to obtain any food in conditions of intense competition from larger more powerful birds, should at worst have an hour or two at any available carcase before Griffons or White-backed Vultures can reach it at all. I have repeatedly observed that Egyptian Vultures are on the wing almost as soon as it is light, and in Ethiopia Lammergeiers can soar on updraughts far too weak for the heavier Griffons.

One thinks of vultures as soaring birds of the air. But in fact the larger species at least spend more of their time perched, on trees or on rocks at roosts, and near their nests. Griffons and White-backed Vultures, in tropical Africa, are on the wing only for six or seven hours of the twenty-four at best, mounting on thermals between nine and ten in the morning, and back on a roost before five in the evening. The Lappet-faced and White-headed Vultures are similarly limited. In mountainous country winds may enable vultures to soar when in flat country they could not. In the colder parts of Africa (and elsewhere) where rising thermal bubbles are not so regular as in the tropics, large vultures are almost exclusively birds of mountains.

When at a carcase vultures of any species have a dominance hierarchy which appears to be dictated by the hunger of the individual concerned. Naturally, the first-comer has no competition. But it is not long before first one, then half-a-dozen, and finally up to fifty or more potential competitors arrive. A very hungry vulture will rush at others feeding on the carcase, in an attitude of threat display, neck stretched up or outwards, wings partly spread, sometimes, as in Ruppell's Griffon, bounding several feet into the air as it approaches. A less hungry vulture, faced with this apparition, gives way. The hungry bird starts to feed, but is likely to be soon challenged by another, equally famished. It will repel the newcomer, pursuing it for as much as fifty yards, then return. It gets little peace to feed, but in a few minutes its first hunger can be satiated. It is then less aggressive in repelling others.

Eventually, many vultures can get at the same carcase, but usually there are only a few of those present actively feeding. A group of fifty or more vultures round a carcase is divided into a single, or a small group of dominants actually in possession, a bunch of sub-dominants hungry but waiting their turn, and another or several groups of birds which have fed and are merely resting. Size affects dominance. The Lappet-faced Vulture can repel any others if it wishes and a hungry Ruppell's Griffon will be dominant over an equally hungry but smaller White-backed Vulture.

Given a chance, large vultures will gorge themselves to repletion, so that they have difficulty in rising and may be caught on the ground if pursued by a vehicle. They seldom gorge to the point where they cannot fly at all, which would leave them at the mercy of other predators. Despite much that has been written on the subject I know of no accurate data as to how much a large vulture can eat at a sitting. I would expect a bird such as the Lappet-faced Vulture, weighing 15 lb. to have a daily need of about $\frac{3}{4}$–1 lb. but to be able to eat 3–4 lb. when gorging itself. Some of the claims that have been made by quite reputable observers are absurd. Meinertzhagen, for instance, claims to have known a vulture contain 15 lb. of dead donkey—a heavier meal than itself. Rubbish!

A large crop, the ability to eat a heavy meal, and then fly away to a safe perch or roost, would evidently be an advantage for birds that must sometimes have to go for long periods without food. Probably a vulture can live for several weeks once it has gorged. And periods of privation and death for the animals of the plains are periods of abundance for vultures. Conversely, in woodlands and forests, or during the rains when grass is long and mortality among animals is low, vultures not only have difficult in finding prey by sight but, in really wet weather when thermals are lacking, may not even be able to fly in order to seek it. It is not really surprising that large vultures are commonest in semi-arid savannas or deserts, for that is where they can most easily find their prey.

Chapter 6
Snake Eagles and Fish Eagles

The two groups of large birds of prey known as snake or harrier eagles (usually included in a subfamily *Circaetinae*), and fish or sea eagles (sometimes included in a subfamily *Haliaetinae*) are not very closely related to each other and are included in this chapter mainly for convenience. Both are specialised feeders, the first chiefly on snakes and other reptiles, and the second on fish. Apart from this one common feature they are rather unlike one another and are not apparently closely related. The fish eagles are related to kites on the one hand, and possibly to the Old World vultures on the other. Snake eagles seem to be related to Old World vultures on one hand, and to harriers on the other, and in modern classifications are placed between these two groups. To both fish eagles and snake eagles one may attach an aberrant member that does not fit easily elsewhere. In the case of the fish eagles this is that strange bird the Vulturine Fish Eagle or Palm-nut Vulture, which perhaps forms a link between vultures and fish eagles. In the case of the snake eagles it is the Bateleur which seems to be a true snake eagle, if a highly specialised one.

To take the snake eagles first, they are a group of raptors in which Africa is very rich; there are six species in three genera—*Circaetus* (4), *Terathopius* (1) and *Dryotriorchis* (1). With one exception in Madagascar, all other snake eagles occur in India and the east and belong to one genus, *Spilornis*.

Snake eagles are often called harrier eagles because of a fancied resemblance to harriers in flight. Many observers have said that they often fly in this way, a few flaps followed by a short glide. As a matter of fact, the name is very inappropriate, for they very seldom fly in this way, and are normally seen soaring at a considerable height, or perched on a tree intently watching their surroundings. When they do fly close to the ground their flight does consist of a few flaps and a glide, but many other eagles also fly in the same way at low altitudes or on calm days. when soaring is difficult. The name "harrier eagle" should therefore be dropped, and the birds be referred to as snake eagles.

Snake eagles, with one excepion—the aberrant Bateleur—have certain physical features in common. They are medium-sized to large eagles with bare tarsi, which have thick smooth scales. The toes are short, and the undersurface of the foot is rough. These are probably adaptations to help them grasp and quickly kill reptilian and possibly dangerous prey. They also tend to have a cowl or hood of feathers which make them look very big-headed in the field, and makes them easy to recognise at times from other eagles. In all but the Bateleur the eyes are a brilliant yellow, and very large; in the Bateleur they are large and brown. Possibly these large and brilliant eyes indicate exceptionally keen vision, which indeed might be necessary to enable them to catch their unobtrusive prey. At any rate a snake eagle has been seen to launch an attack from a range estimated at 1500 feet, and to detect a snake at all at a range of more than a quarter of a mile indicates unusually keen eyesight, even for a bird of prey.

Only one of the African snake eagles extends outside Africa. It is the Short-toed or **Serpent Eagle** *Circaetus gallicus* which breeds from southern Europe to China. Besides the European race *C. g. gallicus* two other races of this bird occur in Africa; Beaudouin's Snake Eagle *C. g. beaudouini* and the Black-breasted Snake Eagle *C. g. pectoralis*. By some these have all been thought to be different species, but Beaudouin's interbreeds with the Black-breasted where their ranges overlap in western Kenya and Uganda, and cannot therefore be a separate species, while it is also intermediate between the rather distinct Black-breasted race and the European Serpent Eagle. It seems best to regard these as all races of one widespread species, which occupies most of the warmer parts of the Old World.

In flight, general behaviour, and nesting habits so far as is known all three are strikingly similar. They are all very graceful fliers, soaring well at a considerable height and coasting along ridge tops without a wing beat. They hover head to wind with gently fanning wings, like giant kestrels, and they are the largest birds in Africa that regularly hover in this way. All three show bars on the wing quills in both adult and immature plumage, which distinguishes them from other large African snake eagles. Of the three races

Beaudouin's is the least-known but its behaviour seems to be just like the other two.

Throughout its range the Serpent Eagle is for preference an inhabitant of open desert, steppe, or lightly wooded country, though it is found sometimes in quite heavy woodland. It tends to perch less than do other members of the genus, probably because in the type of habitat it frequents good high perches are scarce. Hovering is a fair substitute for perching, and this is the only snake eagle that regularly hovers. It is a handsome bird, especially the Black-breasted race, which is dark grey-brown above and on the breast, and pure shining white on most of the underside; the brilliant yellow eye is very striking at close range.

The other snake eagles of this genus are less distinguished-looking birds, chiefly brown in colour with some barring below and white bars across the tail feathers. All are rather more thickset, heavier-bodied, shorter-tailed, and shorter-winged than the Serpent Eagle, and are consequently less graceful in flight, and less inclined to soar. They tend to spend most of the day perched on a tall dead tree, from which they survey their surroundings very intently. They usually make rather short flights from perch to perch, but they all can soar well on occasion and I have once seen a Brown Snake Eagle hover very briefly.

These three species tend to inhabit thornbush, savanna, or the edges of forest country for preference. The Brown Snake Eagle, which is the largest of the three, and of the genus, inhabits rather dry savannas over most of Africa south of the Sahara, but it also is common in fairly dense Brachystegia woodlands. The Smaller Banded Snake Eagle is usually a bird of heavier woodland, with a special liking for the strips of forest along riverine floodplains. Its range is chiefly West Africa, but it comes to within two hundred miles of the East Coast in Kenya. The Southern Banded Snake Eagle is chiefly a bird of heavy woodland and forest on the eastern coastal plain of Africa from Zululand to Kenya; it is intermediate in size between the other two, and more strikingly barred than either. It would theoretically be possible to find all three species in the same general area, but in fact narrow ecological preferences seem to keep them separate. Between them they hunt snakes in all wooded and bushed country south of the Sahara, and replace the Serpent Eagle in this type of country.

Of these three, the **Brown Snake Eagle** is the only one that is at all well-known; it has been studied in Kenya and in Rhodesia. The two smaller species that live in denser woodland have not been much studied, and even some of the reputed cases of nesting may be doubtful. However, all three have one habit in common which makes them obvious once it is known. They all soar at a great height in nuptial display, uttering loud crowing calls, which sound like "Kok-kok-kok-kaauw" or "Ko-ho-ho". These calls are audible on the ground when the bird is a mere speck in the sky. Each of the three species has a slightly different voice, distinguishable by experts only. They would be difficult to identify with certainty, were it not for the fact that they have barred tails. The Brown Snake Eagle has three narrow pale bars in the tail, the Southern Banded two broader white bars, and the Smaller Banded one broad bar. With the aid of these tail markings it is possible to be certain of the identity of any of these little-known raptors.

Snakes are not safe from snake eagles even in the depths of tropical forests. Here occurs the **Congo Serpent Eagle**, a bird about which even less is known than the two small Banded Snake Eagles. It inhabits only the deepest forest, and has two races occurring in widely separated areas, one in upper Guinea (Sierra-Leone, Liberia and Guinea) and the other in the Congo–Gabon–Cameroon forest heartland. The habits of the two races do not seem to differ. They live in the dim moist gloom of the interior of the rain forest, and are very seldom seen. Their calls, which are deep-toned, may attract attention to them once known, and have been described as a nasal "cow-cow", which is similar to some sounds made by the Smaller Banded Snake Eagle. The eyes of the Congo Serpent Eagle are very large, probably an adaptation to life in the semi-dusk of deep rain forest, where an ordinary photographer's exposure meter will not register.

The most curious of all this interesting group is the **Bateleur**. Indeed it is one of the most remarkable of all birds and, if an emblem were required for African skies, the Bateleur would surely be chosen. Bateleurs inhabit all types of country from open plains to rather dense woodland, and occur from sea level to twelve thousand feet. They differ from all other snake eagles—and for that matter from all other birds of prey—in their exceptionally long wings which have twenty-five secondaries, more than in all but vultures. The very long wings combine with a very short tail in the adult Bateleur to produce the appearance of a delta-wing aircraft as the bird sweeps grandly across the sky. Add to this almost brilliant colouring, a black body contrasting sharply with a chestnut back, bright red legs and face, and silvery white underside of the wing in flight and one has a bird that is hard to beat, to many the most magnificent creature that flies in Africa.

Bateleurs are usually seen on the wing. Some people have never seen one perched, though as a matter of fact they do perch quite a lot. Bateleurs probably get on the wing as soon as the air becomes soarable—about nine o'clock each day, sometimes earlier—and they then continue to fly until the evening, about two hours before dark. They are probably on the wing for eight or nine hours on every fine day, and since they travel at a steady airspeed of 35–50 miles per hour, they probably cover between two and three hundred air miles on most days of their lives. They are grounded by wet weather, like most other large birds of prey, and will then often allow close approach rather than fly. They feed on snakes, small mammals, birds, and carrion, and are inclined to piracy, pursuing and buffeting vultures. One plausible theory is that their special habits of flight, traversing the sky at a rather low altitude and at a steady but fairly high speed, enables them to see small dead animals which escape the attention of the larger scavenging vultures. But they kill a good deal of live prey too, though the feats sometimes attributed to them, of killing good sized goats with a tremendous stoop that rips the luckless animal completely open, are highly improbable.

Although they seem very different to other snake eagles Bateleurs demonstrate their relationship in several ways. They have a taste for snakes as a start, including large puff-adders, which have been known to kill them. They share the hoarse crowing voice of the *Circaetus* species, and some calls of the Bateleur are almost identical with some of the calls of the Smaller Banded Snake Eagle. Lastly, the young of snake eagles, reared in extremely open situations, exposed to very strong hot sun, develop the feathers on the head and upper parts of the body while their tails and undersides remain downy. The Bateleur, though it usually nests inside a shady tree, shows the same mode of development of feathers in the young. It is reasonable therefore to conclude that the Bateleur is a specialised snake eagle related to the genus *Circaetus*, with the Smaller Banded as perhaps its closest relation.

Among their many peculiarities nothing is more extraordinary than the behaviour of Bateleurs near the nest. During the courtship and nesting period two males may be attached to one female—a very rare thing in birds of prey and recorded only among vultures apart from the Bateleur. One of these males seems to be the real mate, or "nest" male, who feeds the female and young during the breeding season, and the other is a mere hanger-on who appears whenever there is some excitement. A second peculiar feature of Bateleur behaviour is the rather frequent reports, once verified by myself, that immatures may incubate eggs. Immature Bateleurs tend to stay near the nest after they are fledged for an abnormally long time, perhaps because their highly specialised wings need more time to develop than among other raptors, but for a recently-reared juvenile to incubate an egg that it might not even have laid is very remarkable indeed.

Finally, Bateleurs have a habit of nesting quite close to well-frequented paths and roads. Here the sitting bird can observe people passing by, and will pay no attention, but should anyone approach and try to climb the tree the birds display tremendous agitation. They first treat the intruder to an impressive diving display, with loud wing-flapping, and when that does not work they will perch on a tree near by and utter loud sharp barks, accompanying the calls with shaking of the body and wings. One has the impression that one is in the presence of creatures beside themselves with fury, but this last display may actually be a sort of injury feigning, which is only recorded in one other diurnal raptor, and that a related species, the European Serpent Eagle. Bateleurs also perform bowing displays in greeting, either to their mates or to human captors, but this is rather rare, for despite prolonged study of Bateleurs I have only once seen this.

All snake eagles, including the Bateleur, eat some snakes and lizards, and most choose this form of food to the exclusion of almost all else, though occasional gamebirds and hares are killed by the larger species, and the Smaller Banded Snake Eagle also eats frogs. In captivity a snake eagle will not be much interested by a live rat in its cage, but becomes very excited at the sight of a snake, or even a belt or a piece of rope made to move about like a snake. Clearly they have a strong preference for snakes as prey, which could often place them in danger of their lives, for many snakes are highly venomous and snake eagles are not immune to their venom. In the case of the European Serpent Eagle, it appears that the commonest snake in the habitat, the adder, is not eaten, or is very seldom eaten, and one could conclude, probably wrongly, that the poisonous viper is avoided in favour of less common but not dangerous prey. However, the African race of this eagle, the Black-breasted Snake Eagle, does take some puff-adders which are far more venomous than European adders. Moreover it freely takes large and highly venomous cobras, as does the Brown Snake Eagle.

In Europe all slender snakes that are active by day are non-venomous, but in Africa such snakes include cobras and the even deadlier mambas. It seems therefore rather more likely that vipers are not taken so much because they are thick-bodied, cryptically coloured, and rather inactive snakes that do not move about much by day, than because they are venomous. However, habits can vary from place to place, and it is quite possible that some degree of selection is exercised by snake eagles, and that they take non-venomous snakes when these can be clearly and regularly distinguished, which they cannot in Africa. When killing venomous snakes African snake eagles seem to avoid harm either by speed, or because their legs are protected by heavy scales, or because the down on their thighs and underside is very thick so that a striking snake merely gets a mouthful of feathers and does not inject its venom into the eagle's body.

Although snakes are vulnerable to snake eagles in all types of country from dense forest to near-desert it is impossible to say whether or not snake eagles control their numbers. Certainly the eagles seem to be among the chief enemies of snakes. No reliable estimates exist of the numbers of snakes per square mile in any part of Africa, though it is known that they are sometimes very numerous. The carpet viper, *Echis carinatus pyramidum* is for instance very abundant in the deserts of northern Kenya, but is completely nocturnal, spending the day under logs and down rodent holes, so that it could not be captured by a diurnal snake eagle. Everywhere snake eagles seem to be rather rare birds, requiring a very large area of country to support a pair. Even the Bateleur, with more catholic tastes in food, needs fifty to seventy square miles of savanna to support a pair, and it is commoner than most snake eagles.

Men (herpetologists excepted) tend to think well of snake eagles because they kill snakes but actually a snake eagle that kills a puff-adder or a cobra may be doing man an ill turn. Such snakes feed partly or entirely on rodents that are crop pests, and are consequently friends of man, however much he may dislike them. Snakes are among the predators that can kill rats by day or night, above or below ground, or in long grass where they are not vulnerable to avian predators.

The typical snake eagles make very small nests, and unlike most other large birds of prey they do not regularly return to them year after year, though they may nest in the same general area. Bateleurs, which make solid nests in large trees, are again an exception to this general rule. The nest of the Congo Serpent Eagle has never been found, but those of the *Circaetus* species are usually flimsy structures placed right on top of a flat-topped Acacia or among the fronds of a *Euphorbia*, sometimes hidden in thorny creepers. These nests are very difficult to find, and even when found it is difficult to be certain that they are occupied. The sitting eagle will so flatten itself into the nest as to be nearly invisible, and will withstand a hail of sticks and stones without leaving. Even experts can be deceived. Recently in Rhodesia I had concluded after a prolonged scrutiny through binoculars that a nest on top of an Acacia was unoccupied only to see the adult leave it when a friend who wanted to make certain actually climbed the tree. Such behaviour probably has survival value, though it is difficult to see why men should want to climb thorny trees or euphorbias to interfere with snake eagles.

As stated fish eagles are not at all closely related to snake eagles. Their nearest relatives are probably the Asiatic and Australasian kites of the genus *Haliastur*. All the true fish eagles are included in the genus *Haliaeetus*, and there is only one African species, *Haliaeetus vocifer*. The Vulturine Fish Eagle or Palm Nut Vulture is a very strange, largely vegetarian raptor, that feeds chiefly on oil palm nuts. It may be nearly related to both fish eagles and vultures, but is so different in many of its habits from either, that the resemblances may be merely superficial. It is discussed in another chapter reserved for such oddities.

The **African Fish Eagle** would rival the Bateleur as the best known and most admired large raptor on the continent. It is a common and conspicuous inhabitant of all the larger lakes and rivers, is found also in mangrove swamps and on the sea coast, and penetrates the forest along waterways. Its loud ringing yelp, uttered either from a perch or in flight, and with the head flung upwards over the back, is one of the most characteristic and best-loved bird calls in Africa.

African Fish Eagles naturally eat fish, which they catch both in clear deep water or in turbulent rapids below waterfalls. They usually hunt from a perch, making short sorties out over the water, and returning if unsuccessful, but they will also parachute down from a height and snatch a fish from the surface, without plunging deep in the manner of an Osprey. The favourite food fishes are catfish, which are able to breathe air as well as absorbing oxygen from the water through the gills, and are consequently often on the surface. Fish Eagles sometimes fly straight out from a perch, catch a fish and return at once; when this happens they have probably detected the ripple of a surfacing catfish and flown straight to it, as a fisherman casts a fly to a rising trout.

Fish is not the whole of the Fish Eagle's diet, however. They eat many water birds, especially the young of cormorants, darters, and the more ornamental herons and Spoonbills. I have seen one visit a Spoonbill colony repeatedly till it had practically wiped out every brood. When Fish Eagles prey on such birds as cormorants they are being beneficial to the fishing industry, for cormorants are among the enemies of young *Tilapia* and other valuable food fish. This also applies in the case of catfish, which are carnivorous.

On alkaline lakes, such as Lakes Hannington and Elmenteita in the Rift Valley, Fish Eagles cannot eat fish, for there are none. They then make a staple of water birds, particularly flamingos, which occur in enormous numbers and are very easy to catch. A pair of Fish Eagles may kill a flamingo every two or three days, gorge upon it, and still leave enough to satisfy several other raptors such as Tawny Eagles and Marsh Harriers, which then do not have to kill anything themselves. Fish Eagles also eat some carrion, and I have found a Bateleur and a Fish Eagle together near the carcase of a waterbuck, some distance from any large river, and without any vultures near by. They are also given to piracy, robbing Ospreys regularly. I have seen one rob a Hammerkop and attempt unsuccessfully to rob a

Saddle-billed Stork, a much more formidable opponent, immediately after the stork had caught a Tilapia. Piracy may develop from the carrion-eating habit, for it occurs in such diverse birds as the Bateleur, the Fish Eagle, the Tawny Eagle, and Caracaras, all of which eat a good deal of carrion.

Where they are common Fish Eagles are semi-colonial in their nesting habits. I know of one island in Lake Victoria, only 500 acres in extent, which has nine pairs nesting on it; some of the nests are no more than 200 yards apart. At Lake Naivasha two nests, both occupied in 1968-9, are not more than sixty yards apart. The huge nests, usually built in fig trees or other large forest trees near the water's edge, are occupied by a succession of different eagles for many years. The haunts of a "pair" may continue to be occupied for half a century or more. In 1954 I knew of twelve nests belonging to seven pairs on one group of islands in Lake Victoria, one of which fell into disuse in 1955. Most of the other nests are still in use today, though several new adult Fish Eagles must have joined older birds among well established pairs since 1954.

The semi-colonial nesting habits of Fish Eagles tend to ally these birds with kites. However, it appears that some factor may sometimes operate to prevent Fish Eagles from nesting too close to one another, even where food is superabundant. Among those same seven pairs on Lake Victoria it appeared that the pairs which had nests on the outside of the group, with free access to open water, nested much more successfully than did those that had nests on either side of a channel between two large islands. Although there was no obvious competition, the four outside reared a total of eleven young in three years, while three "inside" pairs reared only one young one between them. The breeding success of the "outside" pairs was very significantly better than that of the inside pairs, though the figures are too small to mean much and more work needs to be done on this subject. However, it is possible that in such ways the total number of Fish Eagles is limited, even where food supply is superabundant and could not be a limiting factor on the eagle population. This result from Lake Victoria is not supported by more recent data from Lake Naivasha.

Even where they are common Fish Eagles obviously have little difficulty in getting their food, and cannot possibly have a limiting effect upon fish, though they are among the predators that severely limit the breeding success of other water birds. On Lake Albert the population of adult Fish Eagles on the southern shoreline has been estimated at about 167 in 207 kilometres. Counts show that there are about 24% of immature Fish Eagles in the total population, so that in fact there would be about one Fish Eagle per kilometre of shoreline on Lake Albert. Assuming similar figures for the northern shore, the total population of Fish Eagles on Lake Albert would be about 400–420. A Fish Eagle eats about half a pound of fish per day, so that in a year this population would account for about 36 tons of fish, assuming that they ate nothing else, which is unlikely. This compares with the estimated human catch of fish from the lake of 12,300 tons in a year, which is far below the estimated optimum yield of the lake. The Fish Eagles therefore consume at most 0·3% of the known human catch in the lake, and could not conceivably either compete with man or affect the population of fish in the lake. Of course one would hardly expect Fish Eagles to limit the population of fish in a large lake such as Lake Albert, for the only fish liable to be caught by eagles are those that come close to the surface or live in shallow water. It would be interesting to compare the total population of the favourite food fish, the catfish, with the food requirement of Fish Eagles. It might then be found that the Fish Eagle, besides being an ornament in the landscape, is on balance a very beneficial bird to mankind.

Chapter 7
Harriers

Although they are not usually common breeding birds in Africa (apart from the North-West) harriers, of the genus *Circus*, are among the most characteristic winter migrants to the continent. Harriers are related both to snake eagles and to the African Harrier Hawk, but their habits are very different to either of these. They form a very uniform genus of medium-sized, long-winged long-tailed hawks that quarter the plains, moors, or marshes they frequent with an easy, buoyant flapping flight unlike that of any other raptor. The quartering flight, to and fro, minutely searching an area of grassland, resembles the action of a hound seeking scent; hence "harrier". Their light bodies, low wing-loading relative to body weight, and easy flapping flight makes it as easy for them to fly over water as over land, unlike most birds of prey.

A harrier is almost instantly recognisable for what it is, though a large female Marsh Harrier can momentarily be confused with a Black Kite. To know one species from another, especially females and immatures, is much more difficult. On the rather rare occasions when they fly at more than 100 feet above the ground, or when they soar in spring in display, they are more difficult to recognise because they are then—like the Secretary Bird in similar circumstances—behaving in an unfamiliar manner.

Six species of harriers occur in Africa, of which three, the Marsh Harrier, African Marsh Harrier, and Black Harrier are resident, and the other three, Montagu's, the Pallid, and the Hen Harrier are migrants. Montagu's may possibly breed somewhere in the North-West, at least occasionally. Many would not accept that the African Marsh Harrier is a good species, and not a race of the European Marsh Harrier; but after giving it careful thought I have concluded that there are sufficient differences both in plumage and habits to merit keeping it as a good species—at least until a comparative behaviour study of the two proves that this view is wrong.

and white appearance has not meant—as has been the case in some species—that it has interested any bird of prey enthusiast and been carefully studied. It is the least known of any harrier that breeds in Africa, and has been far less studied at the nest than its much commoner relative the African Marsh Harrier. In this century it has probably decreased in numbers, if not to danger point in its limited South African haunts; yet there are probably farmers in the Little Karroo who shoot them because they might conceivably take chickens. A thorough survey of its status, and a full study of its breeding habits is urgently needed—and surely some enthusiast can be found to do it.

Of the three migrant species the **Hen Harrier** is a northern bird that does not migrate outside the Palearctic region, including Mediterranean Africa. The other two, **Montagu's** and the **Pallid**, are of special interest as among the commoner migrant hawks of savanna and grassland in Africa south of the Equator in the winter. Like the Hen Harrier they are both strongly dimorphic, with the adult males grey or blue-grey in strong contrast to the brown, ring-tailed females and young. In the "plains" harriers this sexual dimorphism is much more marked than in any of the marsh-breeding harriers, though in Morocco the male Marsh Harriers are striking enough as they soar and tumble in display.

It is very difficult to distinguish females and immatures of these two species with certainty. The only easily recognisable immature or female plumage is the unstreaked rufous-buff of the immature Montagu's Harrier; other distinctions are too slight to be useful in the field, at least at any distance, without very long experience. Even then, one would see individual females and young that could not be placed.

Males, however, are easy enough to tell apart, adult males especially, but also partly grey sub-adults. The male Montagu's is bluer-grey than the male Pallid (which sometimes seems almost white) and has a black wing bar, which can usually be seen in flight. A much better and more useful field distinction, however, is the chestnut markings under the wings. A hunting harrier often displays more of the underwings than of their upper surface, and the chestnut marking of the Montagu's are easily noted from some distance as the bird veers and banks.

Knowing these differences, it is possible to make comparative counts of male Pallid and Montagu's Harriers in different parts of Africa. Some rather extraordinary features would emerge from such counts. In Europe the Montagu's Harrier has a larger and more westerly breeding distribution than the Pallid, which breeds only in a relatively narrow band of steppe country in eastern Europe and central Asia. One would expect, therefore, that the total population of Montagu's Harriers would be the greater of the two, and that they would therefore be commoner in winter in Africa as a whole. One would also expect that (the migrant harriers entering Africa through Cape Spartel being mainly or entirely Montagu's) this species would be commoner in the savannas and steppes of West Africa than the Pallid. In both cases one would be wrong.

I have never found Montagu's Harrier more numerous than the Pallid. Even in East Africa, where Montagu's is fairly common, I would guess that there is one Montagu's for three or four Pallid. And in West Africa, where one would expect Montagu's to be relatively numerous, I have only seen the Pallid Harrier in the savannas of Northern Nigeria, and Montagu's, on the basis of other records, is decidedly less common and widespread. Both these species appear to be able to live together in the same sort of habitat, and hunt in the same way without competing. And, as has already been stressed, in winter they have a clear field, with no competition for their niche from any local raptor.

Yet anyone who has been to Cape Spartel in the migration seasons knows that, there at any rate, large numbers of Montagu's Harriers leave and enter Africa. On the days I have been there they have been the commonest migrant raptors passing over the straits to Spain. Formerly records from the savannas and steppes of West Africa were few, but in recent years Montagu's Harrier has turned up commonly N. of lat. 9° N. Migration right across the continent to East Africa would be extremely improbable. The Montagu's Harriers that visit East Africa may come from the central Asian and eastern European Steppe, where for all I know they may be much less common as breeders than are the Pallid Harriers, which seem the dominant species in all parts of Africa in winter.

It is, alas, becoming more difficult to make comparative counts of the numbers of any male harriers, as they seem to be becoming inceasingly scarce. Time was, when I was in Nigeria, when I thought little of seeing twenty or thirty harriers in a day, of which three or

1. *Above*, The Bat Hawk is a twilight hunter and feeds its young only in late evening or early morning. This young bird's nest is in a Eucalyptus in the grounds of a busy hospital.

Below, The Red Kite breeds only in North-West Africa and prefers deciduous woodlands. It is a larger but less successful species than the ubiquitous Black Kite.

2. *Above*, A Cape Vulture alighting at its nest. This species is typical of cliff-nesting colonial Griffons.

Below, Ruppell's Griffon and White-backed Vultures at a giraffe carcase freshly killed by lions. Subordinates await their turn.

four would be adult males. When I first went to Embu district in Kenya in 1946 I could write that they "literally swarmed" near the Nguka swamp in the evening. Nowadays I do not, on average, see twenty of either species in a season—October to March. I have little doubt that some disaster has stricken the populations that used to come to East Africa.

Whether this is increasing large-scale agriculture in the breeding range, with use of toxic pesticides and generally increased destruction of natural habitat, or whether it is because the country along the migration route through the Middle East into Africa is also becoming steadily more developed and contaminated with agricultural poisons I do not know. But I am sure the number of harriers, and of some other migrant hawks on the East African plains has decreased, and I fear that in some not too distant future time we may regard the sight of an adult male Pale or Montagu's Harrier as a real rarity. Whether this is true of other parts of the continent I know not; but I have seen harriers fairly commonly in the Ethiopian Rift Valley so that the situation may not be as bad everywhere as it seems to me.

The best place to make such comparative counts is near a communal roosting ground in the late evening. Harriers roost on the ground, in a sort of form in long grass or marsh vegetation, and they use the same roosting area for many weeks at a stretch. I have an idea that the same form may be occupied by the same bird each night for some time. Such communal roosting grounds have been reported in reeds on islands in the Nile, and I have seen them at the Nguka swamp in long bulrushes, at Lake Manyara in grass and at Ilorin in Nigeria in patches of stiff spear grass (*Imperata cylindrica*). During the northward migration season in March the number of unburned patches of grass or reeds is small, as most of the long grass has been burned, and this is therefore the best season to watch this habit.

Needless to say, the only good chance that I had of observing it closely I lost through ignorance, and because I thought it must be commonplace. At Ilorin, I used to sit on my verandah in the evening watching the Pallid and occasional Marsh Harriers going to roost in a patch of spear grass only two or three acres in extent and 100 yards away. It was perennially unburned, so I expect that it was particularly suitable for their purpose. Perhaps twenty or thirty of the birds would collect in the late evening and after flying about for some time would eventually settle. It was then that I watched where individual grey males settled and where it seemed to me that they used the same form nightly. Never since then have I had a really good chance to observe this curious activity. There I could do it on my doorstep, but every other such communal roosting ground I have seen has been more or less out of the way. And perhaps the time is coming when we shall see the habit disappear—from lack of sufficient migrant harriers.

Chapter 8
Sparrowhawks, Goshawks and their Kin

This chapter includes the genera *Melierax* (including *Micronisus*), *Accipiter* (including *Astur*), and *Urotriorchis*. I begin thus with Latin names because in discussing sparrowhawks, goshawks and their kin we deal with a splendid example of the sort of muddle that results from trying to give standard English names to a very widespread and varied group of related birds. Linnaeus sought to simplify and classify nomenclature, but in this case he would be bound to observe wryly "Idea good, execution poor". One is reminded of the White Knight, who madly tried to thrust a left-hand foot into a right-hand shoe.

The term "sparrowhawk" properly applies to the European Sparrowhawk *Accipiter nisus*, which breeds in North-West Africa and migrates sometimes about as far as the Equator—I have seen one in Kenya. "Goshawk" similarly applies to the European Goshawk *Accipiter gentilis*, formerly *Astur gentilis*, the largest and most powerful of the genus *Accipiter*, which includes most of the short-winged hawks. The genus *Accipiter* was formerly reserved to include only the so-called sparrowhawks, with thin legs and long needle-sharp talons, suitable for catching small birds. *Astur*, on the other hand, included the goshawk and its relatives, powerful birds with relatively thick strong legs which, in the case of the goshawk itself, can deal with animals as large as a hare and birds up to the size of a pheasant.

As time went on some very small hawks with thick legs, such as the Shikra, or Little-banded Goshawk (as they prefer to call it in South Africa) were placed in the genus *Astur*, and some very large hawks, such as the Black or Giant Sparrowhawk, were placed in the genus *Accipiter*. In the end the genera were combined in one, *Accipiter*, as there were many species with legs neither thick nor thin. Confusion is made worse confounded by the fact that in South Africa I have heard the Black Sparrowhawk called the Pied Goshawk while the Shikra's nearest relative is called the Levant Sparrowhawk. To further complicate matters, the three members of the genus *Melierax* include the two Chanting Goshawks, both large powerful hawks, and the Gabar Goshawk, a small species more like a sparrowhawk. It seems far better, excepting the Chanting and Gabar Goshawk and the Long-tailed Hawk, to call them all "Accipiters".

The short-winged hawks of the genus *Accipiter* are inhabitants of woodland or forest all over the world. They are not adapted to live in open country, for they do not normally catch their prey by speed, but rather by a quick dash inside cover, or by using cover to make a stealthy approach. There are exceptions to this general rule—for instance I have seen an African Goshawk fly down a Red-eyed Dove in the open, at some height above the forest near my home, in a manner that a falcon could hardly have bettered.

Eleven species of *Accipiter* occur in Africa, out of a total of forty-four species in the whole genus. Three of these are properly Palearctic, including the European Goshawk, European Sparrowhawk, and Levant Sparrowhawk; of these only the European Sparrowhawk breeds in Africa, and only in the Mediterranean North-West. The remaining eight species are all inhabitants of woodland and forest in Africa south of the Sahara, but one, the Shikra (or Little Banded Goshawk if you insist) is an African race of a small hawk widespread in the East. The Rufous-breasted Sparrowhawk of South Africa and the highlands of East Africa is the African representative of a superspecies (a term used to define a sub-section of a genus containing a number of very closely allied species) which also includes the European Sparrowhawk.

The African Accipiters include every variation from the very large Black Sparrowhawk to one of the smallest of all birds of prey, the Little Sparrowhawk, the size of an average thrush. They prefer, almost without exception, to feed on birds, though the larger members of the genus take a few mammals such as squirrels. Most are quite common in their range, sometimes the commonest birds of prey in their woodland or forest habitat. Yet they are, as a result of their very secretive nature, very difficult to get to know, and only two out of the eight truly African species have been thoroughly studied at the nest. Two, the Ovampo Sparrowhawk and the Chestnut-bellied Sparrowhawk (not to be confused with the Rufous-breasted) are rare and little known; the nest of the Chestnut-bellied Sparrowhawk has never been found.

The **Black Sparrowhawk**, the largest breeding African member of the group usually inhabits forest, and as a result is much commoner in West than in East or South Africa, where it is local. However, it has a liking for the neighbourhood of forest villages, where it becomes an accomplished and persistent chicken thief. If you try to keep chickens in a forest environment it is odds on that a Black Sparrowhawk will find them, and by degrees get most of them, unless they are enclosed in wire. Certainly there is no better method of showing that Black Sparrowhawks live in a certain area than to try to keep chickens; the hawk will surely appear. So bold is this bird that I once saw one, in Nigeria, snatch a chicken from between the knees of two old men who were chaffering for the fowl on the verandah of a hut. The expression of consternation on the faces of the old men, as they frantically reached after the disappearing chicken, was comic in the extreme. It was too big for the sparrowhawk to carry far, and was dropped in the bush never to be seen again. Perhaps the hawk retrieved it, but certainly the old men were cheated of their bargain.

Black Sparrowhawks have not been studied in full detail, though this is only a matter of time as they quite often breed in plantations of introduced Eucalyptus near human habitations—in Nairobi for instance. The best known of the African species is the **African Goshawk**, *Accipiter tachiro* (which really has thin enough legs to be called a sparrowhawk) and is very widespread in forest and heavy woodlands all over Africa south of the Sahara. It is usually the only "obvious" Accipiter in any African woodland or forest, though in some countries the Shikra is also very common. The two do not usually occur in the same area, however, as the Shikra is by preference an inhabitant of the more open woodlands and Acacia savanna.

African Goshawks draw attention to their existence by their nuptial displays. As already described the male—and sometimes the female too—fly in circles above the forest uttering a sharp rasping "*Krit*" or "*Kwit*" at intervals. This call is unusual in the genus, most members of which utter short, sharp, mewing calls like, "*kew-kew*" or versions thereof. This consistent call, uttered by all races of this species wherever it occurs, is one reason for rejecting the view of some systematists that the African Goshawks ought to be divided into at least three species, if not four—*Accipiter toussenelii*, *A. macroscelides*, *A. canescens*, and *A. tachiro*. I regard them all as racial variants of *tachiro*, since if one studies a series in a museum one finds intermediate types of plumage between all the extremes.

Typical African Goshawks are dark grey or grey brown above, and white or buff below with fine dark crossbars. The race *canescens*, inhabiting the densest forests, is so different in appearance that one could be forgiven for thinking it a distinct species. It is a very beautiful bird, dove-grey above, and pale chestnut below, with hardly any or no barring. But between these extremes there are chestnut-bellied types with barring, and they all cry "krit" as they soar of a morning above the forest, or from within the dense growth when they are not hunting.

African Goshawks are so extremely secretive that although several pairs nest in the forest opposite my home at Karen I have never managed to locate a nest in the early stages of the breeding cycle. They are more easily found when the young are large, for these then call from the nest. I walked almost daily right under the nest of one pair of this species until the young attracted my notice. Observation is complicated by the fact that they, in common with most of the smaller Accipiters, build a new nest each year. It is usually not very far from the old one, but well-hidden in a leafy tree, so that unless the parents give it away it remains difficult to find, even though one knows approximately where it ought to be. However, one observer, Dr. Van Someren, has studied nests in detail for several seasons, and from his observations we can reconstruct a typical Accipiter's nesting cycle.

From his records we learn that the nest is small, usually 1 foot to 18 inches across, with a deep cup in which the sitting female—who keeps almost absolutely quiet—is invisible. 2–3 eggs are laid, in the late dry season as a rule, at intervals of several days, which results in wide variation in the size of the young at hatching. There is here no suggestion that incubation proper does not begin with the first egg, as is claimed for some Accipiters in temperate climates. The female alone incubates for 28–30 days, and she is most unobtrusively fed at the nest by the male. The young hatch at intervals corresponding with the laying intervals and remain in the nest for about 32 days. In Kenya at least, they are often first on the wing at the beginning of a rainy season, and they may continue to be fed at the nest for some time by their parents. I have seen an immature in a nest almost two months after it made its first flight.

The only other sparrowhawk that has been properly studied is the **Little Sparrowhawk,** by R. Liversedge in South Africa. Although very much smaller than the African Goshawk, the combined incubation and fledging periods of this species (32 plus 26, or 58 days) is hardly different from the 60–62 days of the larger bird. This demonstrates what has also been found in some eagles, that small and large individuals of the same or closely related genera have about the same length of breeding cycle, especially in the incubation period. The fledging period, in smaller species, tends to be relatively the shorter; this we see also in the Little Sparrowhawk. This species has the distinction of being one of the very few birds of prey in which a male has been seen to incubate all night long.

The Little Sparrowhawk living in woodlands and savanna has a near relative, the Red-thighed Sparrowhawk, inhabiting dense forests. It might be thought, as in the African Goshawk, that this was only a race of the Little Sparrowhawk, and more study may show that this is so. However, although the type of plumage variation in adults is similar to that in the African Goshawk—dark above and barred below in savanna races and almost black above, chestnut below in the forest birds, the plumage of the immature Red-thighed is so different from that of the Little Sparrowhawk that it seems safer to regard them as distinct species. The **Red-thighed Sparrowhawk** is also markedly larger, and appears to occur, without interbreeding, in some areas also inhabited by normal Little Sparrowhawks. However, both the Red-thighed and the **Chestnut-bellied** Sparrowhawks are very little-known birds of dense forest, and when more is known about them this sort of conundrum may become easier to solve. Anyone finding either of these breeding would do a valuable service by making a study of their behaviour, and by leaving the eggs and birds alone.

The **Shikra,** and the very different **Ovampo Sparrowhawk,** are both inhabitants of woodland or of Acacia savanna and even thornbush. The Shikra is locally very common, but has not been studied in detail. I myself neglected opportunities to do so before I realised that the species had never been fully studied. The savannas of Nigeria where the Shikra is a dry season breeding migrant would be an ideal locality for such study. The Ovampo Sparrowhawk, easy to confuse with the Gabar Goshawk (which is not in the same genus) seems to be rare throughout its range, though it is commoner in southern Africa than elsewhere. One may fairly wonder why such a bird, which appears to be quite a typical member of a successful genus, should be so rare. It lives on birds, which abound in its habitat, yet it is rare and little known. This same feature of inexplicable rarity is also shown by Ayres Eagle and by the Teita Falcon.

Until 1968 I had seen only one Ovampo Sparrowhawk that I could certainly identify in a lifetime in Africa. However, in tha year a pair attempted to breed, unfortunately without success, in the forest near my house. Oddly enough they were both of the unusual slate-grey or melanistic phase, said to be very uncommon. They laid but failed to hatch eggs and disappeared after a couple of months. In that time I noted that they were very bold and confiding birds, quite unlike the African Goshawks common in the same forest. They attacked everything from these same Goshawks to Long-crested Eagles, and would perch in the same tree as I sat in to observe their nest at a level. Alas, these attractive little birds have not reappeared in 1969.

With the sparrowhawks proper we should include the **Long-tailed Hawk**, *Urotriorchis macrourus*. It is nothing but an aberrant forest goshawk—a large powerful black and chestnut species—with a long graduated tail. I once saw what could only have been one flit across a road in southern Nigeria and at first took it for a huge cuckoo of some sort. Later I realised that the hawk had not then been recorded in Nigeria. Little is known about its biology, though it is known to eat birds and forest squirrels. Again, it seems to be rare without any obvious reason for its rarity, and again, should any observer find one in circumstances suggestive of residence and nesting, let him spare the shot and watch it instead of making one more of the few known museum specimens. Young birds of this species reveal their close relationship to Accipiters by having a short tail; they are apparently very noisy when hungry, which may give a clue to anyone who might have a chance to observe them.

Three species remain, all called Goshawks, though one is a small species and the other two large. They are the two species of Chanting Goshawks, and the Gabar Goshawk. All three inhabit open savanna, thornbush, or sub-desert steppe, taking the place of Accipiters in such habitat. Two of them, the **Dark** and the **Pale Chanting**

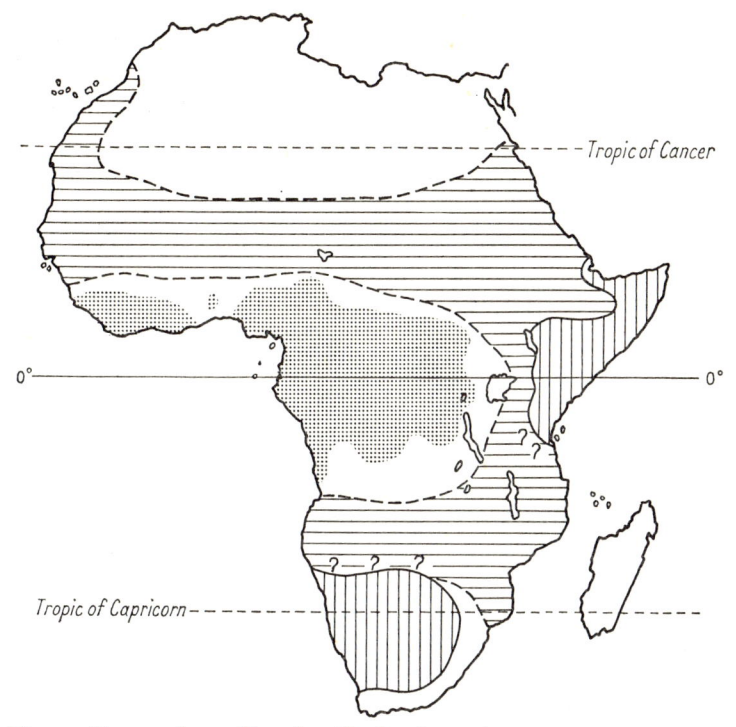

Fig. 5   Range of two Chanting Goshawk species.

≡ Dark Chanting Goshawk, *Melierax metabates*.

||||| Pale Chanting Goshawk, *Melierax canorus*. The two species are clearly separated in Kenya along the line of the Rift Valley, but farther to the south areas of overlap may occur, and need to be more clearly demarcated.

▦ Equatorial forest.

Goshawks, are so similar in all their habits that one wonders what, if anything, prevents them from interbreeding. Of the three, the Gabar Goshawk has been most studied, though the Chanting Goshawks are larger and easier to study.

In Kenya both species of Chanting Goshawks occur, and when one studies their distribution and habitat one is still more amazed that two such similar species can co-exist separately in the same country. The Dark Chanting Goshawk is more northern and western in its distribution, occurring in the Combretum savannas of the Lake Victoria basin, the Acacia thornbush of the Baringo Rift, and the dry deserts of Turkana. In most of North Africa and in West Africa it is the only species that occurs. Just east of the Rift Valley, in the desert of Samburu, and in the thornbush of Eastern Kenya and Tanzania, the Pale Chanting Goshawk is found. It is the Pale Chanting Goshawk that occurs in semi-arid country in South Africa, but a race of the dark Chanting Goshawk occurs in southern Tanzania, Angola, Mozambique and the Eastern Transvaal, cutting across the range of the Pale Chanting Goshawk.

One cannot even therefore say that one of these species is mainly northern and western, and the other southern and eastern, as is very often the case in Africa. Moreover both species, in one part of their range or another, inhabit much the same type of habitat. There is little ecological distinction between the sub-deserts of Turkana west of Lake Rudolf, and the sub-deserts of northern Samburu east of Lake Rudolf. Yet the one is inhabited by the Dark, the other by the Pale Chanting Goshawk. One can go still further, and observe that the Chanting Goshawks living in the Kenya Rift Valley south of Mount Longonot are all Pale, and those living north of it are all Dark. There is actually a gap, between Longonot and Nakuru, along about forty miles of the Rift Valley, in which Chanting Goshawks of either species are rare though the country should suit them. Is this a sort of cordon sanitaire, and does a similar gap exist, for instance at the north and south end of Lake Rudolf, two other areas where the species could mix, in suitable ecology for either?

Overlap is claimed in some parts of the range of these two species, for instance in N.E. Ethiopia, Baringo and S. Tanzania, but I would want to see that more closely substantiated by precise localities. From such studies as I have made the two are remarkably similar in appearance, habits, nesting, voice, and in all other ways.

Both are hawks that, although powerful, tend to feed much on ground animals such as lizards and large grasshoppers. To catch these they often walk about on the ground, aided by their very long legs, which make them resemble miniature Secretary Birds. But both can, on occasion, be swift and powerful predators. I have seen a Dark Chanting Goshawk, weighing just over a pound, catch and kill a Helmeted Guineafowl three times its weight, and I have seen a Pale Chanting Goshawk fly down and catch a Harlequin Quail in the open. Pale Chanting Goshawks, in the Kalahari, follow Honey Badgers on the prowl, in the hope of catching something the badger disturbs.

The Chanting Goshawks are sometimes thought to be a link between the harrier group and the typical Accipiters. Certainly the Gabar Goshawk appears to be the link between them and the true sparrowhawks. It is a small slim species and was formerly retained in its own genus *Micronisus*—an arrangement which in some ways I prefer. It is a bird killer, like many small Accipiters, but in its habit of sitting on a treetop and "chanting" at the beginning of the breeding season it shows its relationship to the Dark and Pale Chanting Goshawks. It has the interesting habit of camouflaging its nest with pieces of bark, and the webs of colonial spiders, which make the structure difficult to locate. Though it has not been proved, it is quite likely that the spiders' webs, with the spiders in them, are probably collected with the sticks used in building and the effect is apparently brought about more by accident than design. As the nest is, so far as is known, not used for more than one season, such elaborate camouflage must be rather quickly established.

The **Gabar Goshawk** has a melanistic or black phase, which in some areas is quite common. This is very similar to the black phase of the Ovampo Sparrowhawk, which is about the same size and often inhabits similar country. However, the red, not orange legs and the more strongly barred plumage of the melanistic Gabar Goshawk are adequate field marks, and the habits of the Gabar Goshawk are different, less bold and confiding; the call is also quite distinct. Several species of the true Accipiters have melanistic phases, including the African Goshawk and the Black Sparrowhawk. Without wanting to be dogmatic on the subject I would say that these melanistic variants are more likely to occur in dense moist forest country than in more open woodland. I have seen melanistic birds of all these species including the Ovampo Sparrowhawk, and the funereal black plumage makes them even more difficult to observe than is normally the case with this very elusive group of hawks.

Chapter 9
Buzzards and Small Eagles

In this group I include the mainly insectivorous Grasshopper Buzzard, the Lizard Buzzard, the typical buzzards of the genus *Buteo*, and certain small eagles of the genera *Aquila*, *Hieraaetus*, and *Lophaetus*. This is an arbitrary grouping based partly on order of classification and partly on the size of certain eagles, reflecting their function in the varied assembly of diurnal raptors.

The **Lizard Buzzard,** which is appropriately named, as it certainly eats many lizards, makes a nice link between the sparrow-hawks and the much larger buzzards. It is little larger than a sparrow-hawk, and can easily be mistaken for one, both by its shape and colour and in its mode of flight. It may be regarded as rather a specialised little buzzard which looks like a sparrowhawk, but still has some habits that link it with buzzards proper.

Lizard Buzzards chiefly inhabit broad-leaved woodlands but are also quite common in dense thornbush in, for instance, the Zambezi Valley or eastern Kenya. They are usually birds of the lowlands, but occur sporadically up to 6000 feet in East Africa. Locally, they are common, and they draw attention to their existence wherever they are by frequent calling. They have two main calls, a long drawn "Peeee-oh" which is decidedly buzzard-like, and not at all like the staccato calls of most Accipiters, and a very melodious whistled phrase "Kleeeoo-klu-klu-klu" which rather resembles the calls of Chanting Goshawks but is more buzzard-like in tone.

This call, curiously enough, is a great favourite as a subject for mimicry by Robin Chats (*Cossypha* spp). One may often learn the identity of a large bird's nest by sitting beneath it of an evening and listening to the calls of Robin Chats which will mimic the call of the owner of the nest. But they like the call of the Lizard Buzzard so much that they not only mimic it directly but also learn it from each other. Robin Chats in the Karen forest near my home regularly give the call of the Lizard Buzzard. But in ten years there I have only seen one of these hawks, and I have never heard one calling, so that the Robin Chats must have picked it up at some time and passed it on to one another.

Lizard Buzzards seldom soar, even as often as do some sparrowhawks. They perch for long periods on a vantage point and catch most of their prey from such perches. They specialise in lizards, as do Chanting Goshawks; but they also take small mammals, insects, and even some small birds, though birds are not alarmed by Lizard Buzzards as they are by sparrowhawks. The Lizard Buzzard is the only raptor that I have ever actually watched caching prey. In this case the prey was a white downy object, the body of a chick belonging to another raptor. After eating half of it the Lizard Buzzard laid the remains carefully over a branch, spreading out the legs so that they hung down either side and the prey could not fall off. The bird never returned to retrieve the body, for I climbed the tree to see what it was, and had to hook it off with a stick.

Lizard Buzzards are common, relatively tame birds that would be easy to study in many populous parts of Africa. They were very common in the broad-leaved savannas of Nigeria, for instance, and a pair well known to me nests annually in the garden of a hotel in Kenya—too far away for me to watch them regularly, though I always find them when I stop there for lunch. They make a small solid nest high up in trees, and give away its situation by much calling; in this and in some other respects they are more buzzard-like than Accipiter-like.

Grasshopper Buzzards are also locally very common birds, which have not been properly studied. A good deal will be said later about their regular migrations in West Africa. They do not occur far south of the Equator, but from November to February they are common in the thornbush near the coast in Kenya, for instance, in the Tsavo Park, and also further south in Tanzania. There is here a relatively arid belt of country which seems to attract the Grasshopper Buzzards. In this part of Kenya and northern Tanzania it is wet in November; but elsewhere, as in West Africa, they migrate south early in the dry season, and return northwards at the beginning of the rains, breeding at the end of the dry season in Acacia savannas further north but south of the desert proper.

Grasshopper Buzzards are another good example of the kind of angle that results from trying to think of an appropriate English name. They are also called Grasshopper Buzzard Eagles (though they do not resemble any eagle) and perhaps the most appropriate name is Red-winged Hawk. They are an African representative of the mainly eastern genus *Butastur*, with three other species ranging from India to Japan. The red or chestnut feathers in the wings are the best field guide and, in Africa, Red-winged Hawk would probably be the best name. It would not do for the eastern species, however, as all three have red in the wings.

The members of the genus resemble Chanting Goshawks in their habit of perching on treetops, telegraph posts, and other such prominent perches. When perched, the Grasshopper Buzzard resembles the Black Kite, but can at once be distinguished by the red feathers when it takes wing. The nest also resembles that of a kite. However, it is so little known and studied in its breeding quarters—though it must be locally common—that until very recently it was believed to be entirely mute. A captive individual in the London Zoo has shown that not only is it not mute but, like the other eastern members of the genus, is at times very noisy.

For the most part Grasshopper Buzzards eat insects. They will come to a grass fire in suitable country, gorging on the scorched grasshoppers with the Black Kites, rollers and other birds that congregate to share the feast. I would not ordinarily expect them to eat much else but insects, though their food in breeding quarters may be quite different for all that is known about it. I have only once seen a Grasshopper Buzzard eat anything other than an insect, and that was an immature that had caught a Sudan Dioch from among vast flocks of these finches drinking at a furrow in the Tsavo Park. We drove right up to the hawk, which sat there as if entranced, with its prey in its foot, and all feathers fluffed so that it looked quite unnatural. It still had not begun to feed ten minutes later, when we left. One was reminded of the delight of a small boy catching his first large fish.

Having dealt with these aberrant buzzards, we can come to the genus *Buteo*, of which there are five species in Africa, though only two, or sometimes three, will be found together in any part of the continent. Buzzards are a very numerous and successful group of medium to large-sized soaring hawks, with broad wings and usually rather short tails. In Europe, Asia, and Africa, there are comparatively few species, and in Australia none. The group is most varied

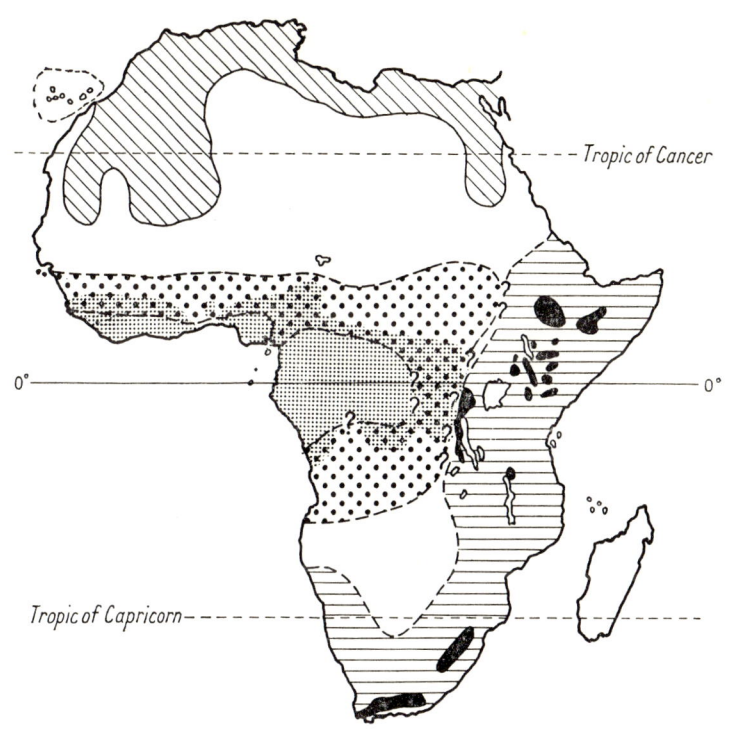

Fig. 6 Breeding distribution of five buzzard (*Buteo*) species in Africa, to show mutual exclusiveness. Circled with dotted line (Canary Islands): Common Buzzard, *B. buteo*.

⧗ Long-legged Buzzard, *Buteo rufinus*, predominantly desert.

⋯ Red-necked Buzzard, *Buteo auguralis*; uncertain how far within forest it may breed, or how wide is the area of division between it and *B. rufofuscus*.

═ Augur or Jackal Buzzard, *Buteo rufofuscus*; in highland grasslands and savannas.

■ Islands of Mountain Buzzard, *Buteo oreophilus*, in mountain forests within range of Augur Buzzard.

▦ Equatorial forest.

and successful in the New World, where there are species as small as a Lizard Buzzard while such giant birds as Harpy Eagles are no more than exceptionally large, powerful, and active buzzards.

The five buzzards that occur in Africa are the European or

Common Buzzard, a race of which, the Steppe Buzzard, migrates into southern Africa in winter; the Mountain Buzzard, which may be considered a race of the Common Buzzard and is certainly very like it: the Long-legged Buzzard, a race of which breeds in North-West Africa while another race migrates as far as Kenya; the Red-necked Buzzard, common in West African savannas and forest edge, and later discussed at some length under migration (page 201); and the Augur or Jackal Buzzard, the best-known African species, with three races in Somalia, East Africa and South Africa. To my mind, a comparative study of the behaviour of the South African race, the Jackal Buzzard, and of the East African race or Augur Buzzard might well reveal that they ought to be regarded as different species. Their plumages are very sharply distinct, and there are marked differences in their calls and behaviour, even on slight acquaintance. There is certainly as much reason to separate these two generally accepted races as species as there is to separate the African Mountain and Common Buzzards.

In the Old World buzzards are a very uniform group of hawks. They feed normally on small mammals, with some ground birds, but also eat many insects and small creatures such as young frogs. Normally they do not kill anything much larger than a mole-rat, but I have seen an Augur Buzzard grasping a still writhing three-foot puff-adder, and I suspect they kill young hyrax. The chief prey of all the African buzzards is probably rodents, with insects as the main alternative.

Buzzards live in either wooded or open country, and prefer fairly well-watered areas, though the Long-legged Buzzard is a bird of sub-desert steppe in its Asian range. In Morocco this species takes the place of the Common Buzzard in Europe. I have found a pair of the Moroccan race of the Long-legged Buzzard breeding on an ivy-covered cliff in the oak woods of the Rif Hills, exactly as one would find Common Buzzards in Devon. Common Buzzards do not breed on the mainland of Africa, except conceivably in the south. This thus seems to be an example in hawks where in two species with very similar habits, one keeps the habitat to itself, to the exclusion of the other.

In most parts of Africa one will likewise find only one resident buzzard species. The requirements of all are so similar that one succeeds in monopolising the available niche, as a predator mainly on

3. *Above*, A Black-breasted Snake Eagle with a Black-necked Cobra in its beak, alighting at its nest on top of a small acacia.

Below, The Secretary Bird paces steadily through the grassland preying on rodents, insects and snakes by stamping on them.

4. The African Fish Eagle is widespread and common in Africa. This nest, unusually situated in a Eucalyptus, contains two eggs.

small rodents and insects. In North-West Africa there is only the Long-legged Buzzard; in lowland West African savannas only the Red-necked; in Ethiopia, Somalia and East African savannas only the Augur Buzzard; and in South Africa only the Jackal Buzzard. In East and South Africa the Mountain Buzzard also breeds, but in East Africa it is confined to a rather narrow range of forest between 7000–9000 feet, which is *not* inhabited by the Augur Buzzard. The latter far better deserves the name of Mountain Buzzard, for it is the only species that occurs at great heights in East Africa and Ethiopia. I have seen an Augur Buzzard soaring round the summit peaks of Mount Kenya at 17,000 feet and I have found a nest with eggs in a giant groundsel at about 12,800 feet, in the crater of Mount Elgon, and others at 12,000 feet on the crest of the Arussi mountains in Ethiopia.

It is really a matter of opinion only (which I happen at present to share) as to whether the **Mountain Buzzard** is a good species. It does seem to me to be rather distinct in its plumage pattern, and to be a more active and dashing bird than the Common Buzzard of Europe, with which I am also familiar. But their voices are almost identical, and it is difficult to distinguish the South African race of the Mountain Buzzard from the migrant Steppe Buzzards. The easiest field distinction is, of course, the migratory habits of the Steppe Buzzard, which is absent from about the end of March to October. But even when Steppe Buzzards are present in Africa they are normally mute, while Mountain Buzzards, like most buzzards in their breeding areas, are much given to calling as they soar above the forest.

In South Africa there is even some doubt as to whether certain breeding buzzards are Mountain Buzzards or whether they are Steppe Buzzards that stay after the migration season to breed. A number of other European species, such as the Black Stork, occasionally the White Stork, and the European Bee-eater, breed in South Africa, and it is just possible that a few Steppe Buzzards may do the same. Only careful observation will prove whether these buzzards breeding in South African forests are Steppe Buzzards or Mountain Buzzards. At present this seems unlikely but if they prove to be Steppe Buzzards then I would agree with those who maintain that the African Mountain Buzzard is only a race of the Common Buzzard.

The **Augur** or **Jackal Buzzard** is the largest and finest of African

Buzzards and is a very fine raptor altogether. It is one of my favourites and I hope to make a fuller study of it in future, for it has hitherto been unjustly neglected. For many years it has been a familiar companion of mine on East African mountains and hills, and on the Ethiopian Plateau. Yet I, like others, have tended to neglect it, probably because it seems commonplace and easier to study than most eagles.

Augur Buzzards fly with remarkable control, and when soaring over a ridge top they are a joy to watch. They appear to be able to remain absolutely steady in turbulent air that would throw an aeroplane about, apparently by split second adjustments of the spread primary feathers. Once, on the summit ridge of Mount Nyiro in northern Kenya I watched an Augur Buzzard soaring in a very strong wind. Aligning the sights of a rifle on it and a point beyond it, I found that the hawk was steadier than the rifle sights, even when resting the barrel on a rock. Yet it was floating in a violent wind that thrashed the trees about, and in turbulence that would have caused an aeroplane to bump violently. It maintained its position, absolutely motionless, apart from a continual slight flickering of the wingtips, for minutes at a stretch, and I know no large raptor that can do this better.

Most buzzards often hover, and in open country the habit is used as a substitute for perching motionless on a dead tree, telegraph, or fence post, which is usually preferred when available. From such hovers or perches buzzards catch most of their prey by a short swoop, with wings raised above their backs, ending in a vertical plunge into the grass. At times the birds make a beautifully controlled descent from a hover, dropping a few feet, hesitating, dropping again, and accelerating for the final plunge only when a few feet above the ground. Most of the prey taken by buzzards is neither swift nor agile so this rather stealthy method succeeds. Mole rats, which are favourite prey of the Augur Buzzard in Kenya, cannot even see well, and may be caught as they tunnel near the surface. Buzzards may be unable to perform very striking aerobatics in pursuit of their prey, but they are most useful and generally very successful birds. What is rather astonishing is that no African species has been very thoroughly studied, the Augur Buzzard being better known than any, much better known than the Jackal Buzzard of South Africa.

All buzzards nest for preference in trees, even in odd sorts of trees such as the giant groundsels of the Mount Elgon crater. However, they will also nest in rock cliffs, and may tend to do so more in mountain country than in woodland in undulating country. Thus the Red-necked Buzzard breeds in trees in the lowlands of Nigeria, but in the highlands of Cameroon sometimes breeds on cliffs. The Augur Buzzard likes to breed in a tree growing on a steep slope or escarpment, but where there are no suitable trees, as on the moorlands of Mount Kenya or Arussi, it will nest on rock cliffs. Whether on cliffs or rocks the nests are substantial structures used year after year, like those of many eagles. Some breeding sites of the Augur Buzzard, and no doubt of other buzzards too, have been inhabited for very long periods. The actual nest site may be moved rather more often than is the case in eagles, but the pair of buzzards, or their successors, occupy the same general area year by year. Although in these respects buzzards may resemble eagles all, so far as we know, have much shorter incubation periods than eagles (30–35 days as compared to 45 days) again showing that the length of the incubation period is not wholly controlled by size.

Some of the small African eagles are, in their functions, no more than slightly more ferocious buzzards, living mainly on rats and mice easy to catch, with insects and a few birds as variation. Others are more predatory and the three small eagles of the genus *Hieraaetus* are, like goshawks, very swift or powerful for their size; hence the common name "Hawk Eagle". The largest of these, Bonelli's or the African Hawk Eagle is, weight for weight, probably the most potent avian predator on the continent. There is thus a trend, among these birds of rather similar size, to be more actively predatory than are buzzards.

The most buzzard-like of the small eagles is the **Long-crested Eagle**, an inhabitant of woodlands and the edges of forests, but not penetrating far into real forest and, in dry country, confined largely to the lines of taller trees along watercourses. It is a very striking black species with a long flopping crest, quite unmistakable wherever it occurs. Although it is relatively common in inhabited areas it has not been studied in full detail, though I have made enough observations myself to class it as well-known. These eagles will even breed in towns and can be decidedly social. Again, I suspect that they have been neglected because they are fairly common and familiar, perhaps also because they are, for an eagle, slightly "ignoble" and buzzard-like in habit, living mainly on small easily caught creatures and not hunting by dashing and spectacular methods.

Wahlberg's Eagle is another small eagle that lives mainly on small mammals and lizards, though it catches a fair number of gamebirds and often takes chickens. Though less striking to look at than the Long-crested Eagle it is rather more dashing, perhaps because it tends to inhabit more open savanna and thornbush, where skill and agility perhaps pay off, while in thick cover it may be just as useful to wait patiently to pounce from a perch on a rat or mouse.

These two little eagles, neither of them as big as an Augur Buzzard, are ecological counterparts in the parts of Kenya where I have studied them. The Long-crested Eagle inhabits the denser woodlands and forest edges, Wahlberg's the Acacia savannas and thornbush. Both may be found breeding along a watercourse running through light savanna but then the Wahlberg's Eagles hunt in more open country. Whether this ecological separation occurs in other parts of the continent where both are found I do not know, but on the eastern slopes of Mount Kenya it is very clearly marked.

It does not seem, however, that this separation is brought about by direct competition. I have watched a Long-crested Eagle breeding close to a pair of Wahlberg's Eagles, and neither appeared to compete with, or indeed pay any attention to the other. In this instance they both lived mainly on grass rats, which were probably abundant, so that fierce competition for the available food supply was unnecessary. We shall later see that there is likely to be a superabundance of such food in every Wahlberg's Eagle's territory. From what little I know there seems to be no effective competition for living space between these two eagles with rather similar needs. Yet they often seem to be mutually exclusive, just as two similar species of buzzards may be.

Wahlberg's Eagle has been very exhaustively studied at the nest, both by myself in Kenya and Peter Steyn in Rhodesia. Without any attempt at collusion the two of us obtained strikingly similar results in light savanna habitats, two thousand miles apart. I myself employed African observers to amplify my own observations. The close correlation obtained in our results indicated that well-trained African observers, properly supervised, can be effectively used to record much of the daily routine at nests. They have good eyes and remarkable patience, and I myself have found them invaluable.

With their aid we have shown that the nest, or nests, of a pair continue to be occupied for a number of years in succession. One egg is laid and incubated, normally only by the female but sometimes the male, for 45–46 days. The young fledges within 70 days and stays at the nest for a few weeks after making its first flight. The whole nesting cycle, from nest repair to departure of the young takes about 150–160 days and can therefore be completed partly within the Rhodesian dry season though in Kenya the young are in the nest at the height of the November rains. On average, only about one young survives for two eggs laid, and from this we may calculate that Wahlberg's Eagle must live on average about eight years as an adult for each individual to replace itself. This is the sort of result that can only be guessed at when one has a long series of observations at several nests. Although I class Wahlberg's Eagle as intimately known it is not quite as well known as some much rarer eagles. Little is known about it, for instance, in its non-breeding habitat in the savannas of northern tropical Africa.

The Long-crested Eagle is far less known. I would anticipate that the nesting cycle would be about as long as in Wahlberg's Eagle, or perhaps slightly shorter. However, the Long-crested Eagle is an African representative of the crested Hawk Eagles of the genus *Spizaetus* that are common in the east, so that there may well be some marked differences in habits. Certainly I have seen Long-crested Eagles do some very odd things. I have known one incubate the abandoned egg of a Wahlberg's Eagle (in the latter's nest) for 44 days; and I have seen one brooding day after day in a nest which, when I disturbed the eagle and climbed to it, proved to be empty. Their social tendencies, observed in Rhodesia, are also unusual. So whenever anyone has a good opportunity to observe Long-crested Eagles at the nest let him beware of such quirks of behaviour, which can be very misleading when one is trying to obtain accurate records.

One true member of the genus *Spizaetus*, **Cassin's Hawk Eagle**, inhabits the dense tropical forests, in this way resembling several species in the East. Its nest has never been found, and I cannot even find a good description of its habits. Like many forest raptors it seems both rare and difficult to observe. But it may well be fairly common in suitable haunts, though the nest is likely to prove very difficult to find and observe in tall primary forest—unless, as is quite likely, the birds give it away by uttering their (as yet undescribed) call. Since so little is known about this eagle we must leave it and pass on.

The three remaining small eagles in Africa are the Booted Eagle, Ayres Hawk Eagle, and Bonelli's or the African Hawk Eagle. The last is divided into two species by some authors, but having seen both the races and watched them for long enough to note the general similarity of habits, voice, and nesting behaviour I agree with those systematists who think that they should both be regarded as one species. All these eagles are the very reverse of buzzards, in that they are powerful swift predators. I include them here only because of their size, and because they indicate the end of the trend in eagles away from the sedentary hunting methods of buzzards, despite similar body size.

The dashing hunting methods of these little eagles are epitomised by both the Booted and Ayres Hawk Eagle, which are members of the same superspecies, and have very similar habits. I have watched Booted Eagles in Spain, where they are common, and in Kenya I have had a pair of Ayres Hawk Eagles under observation for 21 years. Both feed mainly on birds, and thus combine the functions of an eagle and a goshawk. Both take some mammalian prey and can on occasion kill birds, such as guineafowl, as heavy as themselves. I have watched both of them make kills, and have been amazed and enthralled by the headlong speed and dash of the attack. In fact, if I had to choose which was the most dashing predator in Africa I would probably choose Ayres Hawk Eagle, though I admit I am prejudiced in favour of these delightful little eagles.

Ayres Hawk Eagle, which is rare, and until recently was little known, can now be classed as intimately known, at least in the details of its breeding biology, as a result of my own studies over 19 years. For much of this time I have exercised my mind as to why they should be so rare, for they seem to be thoroughly capable predators, and there are plenty of doves and other suitably sized birds in their habitat. At first the pair I had been watching seemed to be very regular breeders, but in latter years a succession of disasters, with which they do not seem to be able to contend, has stricken them. A pair of Peregrines breeding on a cliff near them succeeded in preventing breeding for two years. Then part of the nest-tree fell down, exposing the nest to the sun. Instead of breeding in it, or making a new nest somewhere else, they have occupied the site for three years without breeding. They then appropriated the nest of a Harrier Hawk, and had a young bird in it in 1967, but it did not survive as the nest collapsed. In 1968 the tree died. At last, in 1969, they have built a new nest in a shady part of the old nest-tree but it also fell. Perhaps this inability to reproduce themselves, in the face of difficulties that other raptors would probably surmount by merely building a new nest, may be one reason why they are so rare. But until someone else in another part of Africa obtains confirmatory material over a good long time we cannot say whether Ayres Hawk Eagle is generally a shy breeder. And if it is not a shy breeder its rarity is all the more curious.

Booted Eagles, much commoner than Ayres in their European and North African haunts, are—perhaps needless to say—much less known. They breed rather late in the year so that there is no necessity, in their case, to start observations very early in the spring. I have reserved the Booted Eagle as a study for my retirement, if I am driven out of Africa. In Africa south of the Sahara the Booted Eagle is seldom noticed, but it could easily be confused either with Wahlberg's (in the dark phase) or with Ayres (in the light phase) and so can be overlooked. There are enough specimens to indicate that it is probably more common than one would think, and I myself have seen several little eagles that I thought were the Booted.

Bonelli's Eagle inhabits Africa north of the Sahara, and Southern Europe and Asia. The African Hawk Eagle is the race of this species that inhabits Africa south of the Sahara. It is much better known than its more northern counterpart, but not so well known as the very much rarer Ayres Hawk Eagle. This widespread species, for which someone once suggested the more appropriate name of Slender Hawk Eagle, is a very successful predator which in Africa kills almost the same range of prey as does the Martial Eagle, twice its weight and very much larger. For choice, it is a gamebird killer (and sad to say a chicken thief), but in North Africa Bonelli's Eagle kills birds as large as a stork and mammals up to the size of a rabbit. As in the case of Ayres Hawk Eagle, Bonelli's and the African Hawk Eagle are very aggressive near the nest. I have been more frightened by African Hawk Eagles than by any other species, for they attack with great vigour when one is trying to reach the nest on thin upper branches of a high tree. Bonelli's Eagle builds mainly on crags, the African Hawk Eagle in trees, but sometimes on crags.

No really good comparative study of Bonelli's and the African Hawk Eagle exists to help us to decide whether they are one and the same or two species. Each shares its range with a smaller fierce species—the Booted in one case, Ayres in the other—killing a rather different and smaller range of prey. In the case of the Booted Eagle and Bonelli's there must be some competition for the available gamebird prey. Perhaps this is minimised in Europe by breeding at different times. Bonelli's is a very early breeder, laying in February, the Booted much later, so that their times of greatest need are not the same; they also tend to occupy rather different habitats, the Booted living in heavier woodland. However, one may often see them in the same area, and in Africa I have known their ecological counterparts, the African and Ayres Hawk Eagles, to breed and live on the same hill for many years, apparently without conflict. Between them these eagles kill all sorts of small and large birds from passerines to guineafowl and storks, and of mammals from small squirrels to rabbits and hyrax. They carry on where the Goshawk of Europe leaves off and their presence in much of Africa may be one reason for the absence of powerful Goshawks from the unforested areas of the continent.

Chapter 10
Large and Spectacular Eagles

Among these I include six eagles of the genus *Aquila*, the Martial Eagle and the Crowned Eagle. These are all large, some very large, though the Lesser Spotted Eagle, the smallest, is not very much larger than Bonelli's Eagle. The largest eagle in Africa is the Martial Eagle, females of which can weigh up to 14 lb., with an eight-foot wing span. However, I would consider that the rather lighter and smaller Crowned Eagle is more powerful than the Martial Eagle, on the evidence of the size of prey regularly killed by this forest species. Appropriately enough the Crowned Eagle could therefore be called the King of African birds.

Large eagles are as a group better known than almost any other type of diurnal raptor, for the reason that they *are* large and spectacular and have accordingly been sought out by enthusiasts, some of whom have studied them for long periods. My own studies of the Crowned Eagle, extending over 22 years at one site are, so far as I know, the longest series of observations made of a particular pair of eagles and their successors at one nest site anywhere in the world. Generally speaking, the larger, the rarer, and the more spectacular the species, the more it has been studied.

It is therefore, perhaps, no surprise to find that two purely migrant African species, the **Greater** and the **Lesser Spotted Eagle**, have been less observed in Africa than any others. Both have been fairly thoroughly observed in their breeding quarters in the woods of Central Europe, and they have been watched and counted at such migration stations as the Bosphorus *en route* to Africa; but once in Africa they cease to be quite so remarkable and almost disappear from our ken. In part this is because they are very difficult to distinguish in the field from the Tawny Eagles that are permanent residents in Africa, and are augmented each winter by their migrant race, the Steppe Eagle from Europe and Asia. I have not found any very satisfactory field distinctions between these three species in adult plumage, though in immature plumage they are easily enough identified.

The main wintering ground of the Greater Spotted Eagle seems to be in the Sudan, Eritrea, and other areas of North-East Africa. They presumably enter Africa via the Bosphorus and Suez, and then move south-east to their winter quarters. They tend to winter in dry northern areas, whereas the Lesser Spotted Eagle certainly moves on further south and perhaps spends the winter in the Brachystegia woodland, where at that time of the year it is wet. However, as instanced in the chapter on migration, we know very little about either of these eagles in winter quarters. For the Lesser Spotted Eagle there is a suggestive record of migration through Kenya en masse and a resident of Francistown, in Botswana, told me that he had once seen many hundreds of small eagles round vleis on the edges of the Kalahari desert. They might have been Lesser Spotted Eagles, he thought, though in view of the difficulty of distinguishing the species the record needs confirmation.

The best field distinctions for the migrant Lesser and Greater Spotted Eagles, and the migrant Steppe Eagle, are in immature plumage. Both the Lesser and Greater Spotted Eagles are so called because immatures have white spots on the wing coverts; the adults are plain brown. The spots are small in the Lesser Spotted Eagle, but quite large in the Greater, half an inch or more across. The immature Steppe Eagle also has white markings on the wing coverts, but they are in the form of terminal bars or narrow edges to the feathers, so that the resulting effect is barred, or scaled, not spotted. These distinctions are shown better in a picture than by description. However, it should not be too difficult to identify any immature of these three species and, since all three tend to be rather gregarious in their winter quarters, there will probably be immatures along with any large number of adults that are seen. Accurate observations on the Spotted Eagles in their winter quarters are particularly needed.

The Tawny Eagle breeds all over the drier parts of Africa and has several races in Africa, eastern Europe, and Asia. It is probably the commonest, most widespread, and most adaptable large eagle in the Old World, inhabiting most types of terrain from semi-desert to woodland and from sea level to at least 8000 feet. Migrant Steppe Eagles are very common in the high Ethiopian mountains in winter at 12,000 feet and over, and have been found at 26,000 feet on the

South Col of Everest. In view of the numbers of migrant Steppe Eagles wintering in Africa it is very odd that this species is little observed migrating through Suez where Spotted Eagles, which almost disappear once they are inside Africa, appear to predominate. Is this mistaken identity, or does the Steppe Eagle really enter Africa by another route as yet unknown, say Bab-el-Mandeb, which no one has yet studied?

Probably one reason for the abundance and success of the **Tawny Eagle** and its various races is that it is partly a scavenger, partly a pirate, and partly an active predator on mammals and birds, and as such by no means the despicable bird that it is sometimes made out to be. We have here, in fact, another case, analogous to that of the Black Kite, where the species concerned has benefited from a catholic diet and an ability to associate with the habitations of man. The Tawny Eagle, it may be said, is the only large eagle that is regularly to be seen round slaughterhouses and such places in eastern or northern African cities. In Africa south of the Equator it has not yet acquired these scavenging habits to the same extent.

Because of its scavenging traits many people have regarded the Tawny Eagle as somewhat ignoble—not to be compared, for instance, with the Verreaux's Eagle, or even the Golden Eagle. However, a species should not be disdained because it is adaptable and successful, and some other more spectacular eagles will also eat carrion at times. As a predator the Tawny Eagle is not to be despised. It kills a surprising number of gamebirds such as francolins and guineafowl, and in Kenya some pairs live largely upon flamingos, which they sometimes kill in flight with a falcon-like stoop. I have seen a Tawny Eagle near the carcase of a Thompson's Gazelle calf, which I suspect it had killed, only to be robbed of it by a jackal. And in the Ethiopian highlands, at 12,000 feet, I have seen large brown eagles feeding on hares; they are either large and unusually predatory Steppe Eagles, or they are a hitherto undescribed and unrecorded population of Golden Eagles.

Essentially Tawny Eagles are killers of small mammals, such as mole rats, though at times they take larger animals and birds and also feed on carrion and scraps. In Kenya and Ethiopia where both resident and migrant races occur from October to March, mole rats appear to be favourite prey. In some parts of Kenya Tawny Eagles follow the plough, waiting for mole rats to be turned up. They do not, however, always, or even often, catch the mole rats themselves. Rather, they wait until either a European or a Marabou Stork has picked up a dead or injured mole rat, then rob the stork of its prize.

In fact, the Tawny Eagle is an accomplished pirate. I have seen it pursue and rob such other predators as Kestrels, Black-shouldered Kites, Martial Eagles and Lammergeiers. Size does not deter it, and it will attack and rout birds much larger than itself if it covets the prey that the other has caught. The piratical habit is shared by the Black Kite, the Fish Eagle and the Bateleur; and it is significant that all of these pirates do tend to feed upon carrion, or at least come to a carcase perhaps hoping to snatch something from a vulture by piracy. Again, a bird which will attack another, much larger and more powerful than itself, and rob it in fair fight, is not necessarily to be despised.

Some consider that the **Steppe Eagle** should be regarded as a separate species, on account of its greater size and the marked differences in the immature plumage. It is true that the Steppe Eagle has certain differences in habits; it is for instance, much more likely to perch on the ground than is the resident Tawny Eagle. However, this difference probably derives from its natural treeless habitat in the Asian and European Steppe, where the Steppe Eagle habitually breeds on the ground. The Eastern Steppe Eagle (*Aquila rapax nipalensis*) breeds on cliffs like a Golden Eagle, but does not commonly occur in Africa.

In Kenya at least the resident Tawny Eagles differ from most large eagles in that their nest sites are often not used for more than a year or two together. A nest I know of, which has been occupied for more than five years, is quite exceptional in this respect. Most of the nests I have known were built on the crowns of, or far out on a high lateral branch of an Acacia, but occasionally a Euphorbia or another tree is used. Tawny Eagles' nests on Acacias are large solid-seeming flat structures, but seem to fall down much more rapidly than do most other eagles' nests. It seems that this habit of frequently moving the nest site, or abandoning a nest after a few years also applies in South Africa; it may be brought about by the growth of thorny branches around the nest. We await a really full account of the breeding biology of this, the commonest and most easily observed of all the larger African Eagles.

The only other large brown eagle that could conceivably be confused with Tawny, Steppe, or Spotted Eagles is the **Imperial Eagle**. This is only a very doubtful breeder in Africa, there being one or two reported records from Morocco—presumably of the Spanish race *Aquila heliaca adalberti*. The nominate, eastern European race migrates to the North African tropics, wintering in much the same area as the Greater Spotted Eagle. Imperial Eagles in adult or immature plumage should be very easy to recognise. They are larger than any race of Tawny Eagles and they have white scapulars, forming an epaulette, clearly visible when perched. Unlike both Tawny and Spotted Eagles they also have a grey tail with a broad subterminal dark bar in adult plumage, while in immature plumage the underside is strongly streaked. Some Tawny Eagles also have a streaky phase of immature plumage, but the streaks are much less distinct than in the immature Imperial Eagle. There ought, therefore, to be little difficulty in identifying and observing a wintering Imperial Eagle. It will probably be seen in flat open plains, which is the preferred habitat in breeding quarters.

There remain four magnificent great eagles inhabiting different parts of Africa—the Golden Eagle, Verreaux's or the Black Eagle, the Martial Eagle, and the Crowned Eagle. The Martial Eagle, inhabiting savanna, thornbush, and open plains in Africa south of the Sahara, is a size larger than the other three, all of which are about the same size, weighing 8–12 lb. The Golden and Verreaux's Eagles are typical large members of the genus *Aquila*, but the Martial and Crowned Eagles are more specialised types, close to the *Spizaetus* group of Hawk Eagles. Their voices, for instance, are very different; they utter whistling or yelping calls, whereas all *Aquila* species (except the somewhat aberrant Wahlberg's Eagle) emit what the cognoscenti call a "typical Aquila cluck".

The **Golden Eagle** is a holarctic species which, in Africa, extends as far south as the Spanish Sahara and in America to Mexico. It is without doubt the most numerous eagle of its size in the world, with an enormous range in mountains of the Old and New World. It is not surprising to find that it has been very thoroughly studied in several parts of Europe and to a lesser extent in America. Many books have been written about it, and I therefore do not propose to go into much detail about it here. In the parts of Africa where it exists—mainly in the mountains of Morocco and Algeria—it has not been studied at all thoroughly, and here it is both a resident and a migrant. In some parts it is an inhabitant of desert mountains, where it demonstrates its adaptability by taking to a diet of large spiny-tailed *Uromastix* lizards. In most parts of its range it is a feeder on mammals, up to the size of deer calves, but especially on hares, rabbits, ground squirrels, and marmots.

It is for this reason that I have lately wondered about the identity of certain large brown eagles that I have seen in some mountain ranges of Ethiopia, on moorlands at over 11,000 feet. These appear to be too large to be Steppe Eagles, and are rather paler brown. They seem as big as the Verreaux's Eagles that inhabit the same mountain ranges, but are definitely not immatures of that species. I have, on a number of occasions, seen these big eagles feeding on hares, which are very common in some of the high mountains of Ethiopia. Their general mode of flight, habits, and food is so strikingly like the Golden Eagle, as I know it in my native Scotland, that when an opportunity occurs I shall have to try to collect one. First, however, I need to know whether they occur all the year round, for hitherto all my visits to Ethiopia have been made in the winter when migrant Steppe Eagles abound, even in high mountains, by feeding on rats. If, indeed, these large eagles prove to be Golden and not Steppe Eagles they will form a very nice faunal link with the Palearctic region in a country where there are already several other such links.

Verreaux's or the **Black Eagle** is the finest of the genus *Aquila* —a truly magnificent coal black bird with a white back and a white V on the shoulders. The handsome plumage is enhanced by consummate grace in flight, eclipsed only by the Lammergeier. Yet, apart from its colour, Verreaux's Eagle is very like the Golden Eagle, and replaces that species in Africa south of the Sahara. Like the Golden Eagle it feeds upon medium-sized mammals, chiefly rock hyrax of the genera *Procavia* and *Heterohyrax*—the conies of the Bible—varied by an occasional guineafowl, dikdik, or klipspringer. Unlike most members of the genus *Aquila*, Verreaux's Eagle very seldom or never feeds upon carrion; this "ignoble" habit has only been observed (rarely) in South Africa.

Throughout its range Verreaux's Eagle is a mountain bird, but it is as much at home on a rocky inselberg rearing out of the stark deserts of Kenya's Northern Province as among the heath-clad mountains of the Cape or the highlands of Ethiopia. In the more northern parts of its range, however, it seems to be more exclusively a mountain bird, and in Ethiopia I have not found it on apparently suitable inselbergs in the lowlands. In Kenya and in Ethiopia it breeds at very high altitudes, up to 11,000 and 13,500 feet respectively. Usually, however, one associates Verreaux's Eagle with rocky gorges and kopjes of rounded granite boulders, where rock hyrax normally abound.

Probably because it is so spectacular, and also because in some parts of its range it is rare, Verreaux's Eagle has been intensively studied. A classic study was made of a pair in Tanzania by E. G. Rowe, in 1944–45, which serves as a model for anyone else wanting to study a single pair. In one season Rowe learned more about the hitherto little-known Verreaux's Eagle than had up to then been properly recorded for any species of eagle in the world. Again, his work was a good example of the value of trained African observers, who may be illiterate but often are born field naturalists. Confirmatory studies should be made in South Africa, where it is quite possible that Verreaux's Eagle may not behave the same as in Tanzania. In southern temperate Africa, particularly, the fledging period may be shorter than it is near the Equator, where it is more than ninety days.

Reference is made, in the chapter on Territory (page 238), to the remarkable number of Verreaux's Eagles breeding in the Matopos Hills of Rhodesia, near Bulawayo. Although this would be an ideal locality in which to study certain aspects of the biology of this species it may not be entirely typical, since the Matopos are themselves a very unusual collection of boulder strewn kopjes swarming with hyrax. However, nowhere else that I know of could quantitative studies of a number of nests, their breeding success, and other such details, be made with as much ease as in the Matopos, where ten or more nests can be visited in a morning, and virtually all the sites are known. This community of Verreaux's Eagles is now being intensively studied and has yielded results of outstanding interest.

In South Africa Verreaux's Eagle is accused of taking lambs, but it does not seem to do this anywhere else, so that the reports need careful verification by capable naturalists. It has been repeatedly demonstrated that tales of lamb killing by Golden Eagles in Scotland and elsewhere are largely based on prejudice. Golden Eagles, and probably Verreaux's Eagles, too, either take no live lambs or very few; they may pick up some lambs when dead. They would perhaps be more inclined to attack lambs in a semi-desert environment where other food is short, such as the Karroo, but as long as the rock hyrax which are their staple prey are plentiful there would be little need for them to attack lambs. And in the Karroo rock hyrax are legion. In the territory of a pair of Verreaux's Eagles there may be from 2700–11,300 kgs. of hyrax per square mile, or a total of at least 67,500 kgs. in a home range of 25 square miles. To compare with this, the annual food requirement of a pair of Verreaux's Eagles and their offspring would be about 220 kgs., or 0·3% of the least possible total. In these conditions there is obviously no need for Verreaux's Eagles to eat lambs at all.

The preference for rock hyrax almost to the exclusion of other prey makes Verreaux's Eagle a very good subject for a close study of the predator–prey relationship. It is a relatively easy matter to locate the nests of every pair of Verreaux's Eagles in a wide stretch of country, for they are faithful for many years to the nest site, and the nest itself is usually easy to spot on a bare cliff ledge. Assessing the population of hyrax is more difficult, but can still be done. It should be possible to ascertain the total range of a pair, the approximate number of hyrax in that range, and the effect of the eagles upon the hyrax population, with a degree of accuracy which would be elusive with most species of eagles.

Verreaux's Eagle is a bird of open country, mountains and deserts with rocky hills, not of woodland or forest. The **Martial Eagle** is an inhabitant of woodland, plains, and savanna, entering forests only to find a suitable breeding site. The Martial Eagle is less well-known than the other two large and spectacular eagles in Africa, and its breeding biology has not yet been as thoroughly studied as that of either Verreaux's or the Crowned Eagle. This is not only perhaps, because the Martial Eagle, though the largest eagle in Africa, is somewhat less spectacular than either of the other two, but also because it is very much shyer than Verreaux's or the Crowned Eagle. I have had Martial Eagles under observation at one site for 21 years; but I have been unable to obtain the same sort of detail at that site as I have at the nest of the Crowned Eagle on the same hill, or even of the very much rarer Ayres Eagle. Thus we cannot class the Martial Eagle as intimately known, though a season's intensive observation would fill in most of the missing details of the breeding biology.

Martial Eagles are wide-ranging but nowhere common in Africa.

5. A Dark Chanting Goshawk hunting on the ground in Ethiopia. The erect stance and long legs are reminiscent of the Secretary Bird.

6. *Above*, A Black Sparrowhawk with its two eggs on a Rhodesian Eucalyptus plantation. The nest was originally built by a Gymnogene.

Below, An Augur Buzzard, common resident of East and Central Africa, brings a small squirrel to its ten-day-old chick.

A pair seem to require a large home range, even in savanna well stocked with suitable prey. In the Embu district of Kenya three pairs of Martial Eagles bred within my census area of 146 square miles, but one of the pairs certainly hunted for some distance outside the area, so that the average home range of a pair was more than 50 square miles. Again, it appears that within that range there was a super-abundant population of suitable gamebirds, such as Guineafowl, Yellow-necked Francolins, and household chickens, which the Martial Eagle finds easier than other "gamebirds" to catch. Why, or how, pairs of Martial Eagles manage to hold sway over such large areas is something of a mystery.

Perhaps part of the explanation is that Martial Eagles, of all the large eagles of Africa, tend to spend long periods soaring at great heights. The easiest way to see one in country where their presence is suspected is to search the sky minutely with field glasses, particularly over the summits of suitable hills. Martial Eagles undoubtedly have very acute sight, and they may, therefore, be able to see and repel other Martial Eagles at great distances, and at such heights that the action passes unnoticed by human beings on the ground below.

The acute sight of Martial Eagles was once graphically demonstrated to me in Embu district. I was watching an eagle as she soared over the summit of a rocky hill, and I saw her start off on a long slanting stoop. This took her straight to some farms where she attacked a flock of guineafowl and was seen to rise later with one in her talons. The distance between the hilltop and the farm where she made her kill was not less than four miles, yet there can be little doubt that she did see and attack the moving flock without hesitation from that distance.

Martial Eagles are chiefly gamebird killers, but they will kill mammals as large as Impala calves, often eat rock hyrax, and are accused, perhaps with some reason, of killing lambs. There may be more truth in this accusation than in the case of some other eagles, for it is made not only by large-scale farmers of European descent, who may be expected to be prejudiced, but also by Africans, who are generally acute observers. In Embu district the Martial Eagle was the only one of several large species that aroused any active animosity from the Mbere tribesmen, who knew the difference between the various species of eagles and were quite aware that some species were quite harmless to them.

A.B.P.

Among these species, oddly enough, was the Crowned Eagle, which, in the areas where I have studied them, habitually lives on small antelopes, hyrax, and monkeys, in that order of preference. They, of all eagles, could be expected to take an occasional kid wandering in thick bush, but apparently never do so even when they have the opportunity. In other parts of Africa they are said to live almost entirely on forest monkeys, and where these are very abundant that may be so. Certainly one or two pairs in Kenya, living in areas where rock hyrax abound, make use of the food that is most abundant, and there is no reason why this should not be so in tropical forests where monkeys are very common. But the monkeys in the forest near my home are seldom caught by the pair of Crowned Eagles that breed within sight of my house. They are very alert creatures, and I would expect that any Crowned Eagle would prefer to catch small antelopes on the forest floor.

The **Crowned Eagle** is slightly smaller but more powerful than the Martial Eagle, more spectacularly handsome in plumage, and very much bolder in demeanour. It is not to be trifled with and can be dangerous to a human climbing to the nest; I have been struck in the back myself. The Crowned Eagle is probably the best-known in the world. This is because I have had two pairs under continuous observation and record for, in one case twenty-two, and the other twelve years, the second being a pair that bred in sight of my study window at home. Daily observations of this pair, and long term observations of the other, has revealed facts about the lives of such eagles that have never been recorded or even suspected for any other species.

At Eagle Hill, for instance, I have been able to obtain a complete record over twenty-two years of the changes among the individuals of the pair. There have been three females and two males at the site since I discovered it in 1949. The middle one of these females, known as Regina II, arrived at the nest in 1952. She laid eggs five times, in 1952, '54, '56, '58 and '60, in each case rearing a young bird; sometimes she laid one egg, sometimes two, and there was a variation of more than two months between her earliest and latest laying date. She was replaced by a new female in 1961, Regina III, who may be still there, but who went blind in her right eye in 1967 and disappeared in 1969. We thus know the complete breeding lives of two wild female Crowned Eagles, nine and eight years. One male, Rex II, lived here from 1958-70, when he disappeared; he lived for at least twelve years as an adult. In each of these cases we may assume that they were young adults when they arrived, and that they only disappeared when they died. We may add at least four years to the adult life-spans to arrive at the true ages, which are 13-14 and 12-13 for the two females and 16-17 for the male. As far as I know, these are the only large wild eagles whose complete breeding lives have been thus recorded.

The reason for the curiously regular biennial breeding of this pair of Crowned Eagles eluded me until the pair at Karen built their nest in sight of my study in the same year as I built my house, 1959. They bred that year, and fed their young for 9 months after it made its first flight. Clearly, if the young has to be fed for a total of nearly four months in the nest, and as we now know, 9-11 months thereafter, Crowned Eagles cannot breed every year. They are only the second species in the world proved to have such a long breeding cycle that they cannot breed annually—the other being the Wandering Albatross. Subsequent observations have shown that they only breed in successive years when some mishap to eggs or young cuts short the normal course of events. The premature loss of a young one, at least 6 months out of the nest, has been in two cases followed by breeding again in the following year. In one of these cases Regina III also laid twice in one year at an abnormal time, some mishap having occurred to her first clutch.

The details of the Crowned Eagle's breeding biology are more intimately known than those of any other eagle, the length of the incubation period having been accurately recorded three times, that of the fledging period six times, while I have watched the post-fledging progress to independence of the five young that were reared near my house, in 1959 60, '61 62, '64 65, '66 67 and '68-69 respectively. The fourth of these young died before it became independent, but the other four all left of their own accord, thus disposing—at least in this case—of popular belief to the effect that adults will drive the young out of their home range. The loss of the fourth young deprived the Karen female of a unique record of breeding success— 100% of young reared to independence from five eggs known to be laid in the course of a decade. She can now only claim 80% success, which is still very remarkable.

In fact, the statistics from these two and several other nests tha

I have observed for more than two years show that the Crowned Eagle, besides being one of the most spectacular and powerful species in the world is also one of the most successful in its breeding economy. In the normal course of events, eggs are laid only in alternate years and in clutches of two the elder eaglet invariably kills the younger; no case of two young being reared has ever been recorded. Thus the "expected" maximum replacement rate would be 0·5 young/pair/annum. Observations at five nests totalling 37 nest/years have shown that the actual replacement rate, of eaglets reared to the flying stage, is 0·40/pair/annum, or 80% of the expected rate. The Karen observations indicate that perhaps 80% of the young that fly become independent, and this was probably the case also at Eagle Hill. Thus on average a pair of Kenya Crowned Eagles probably rears about 60% of the "expected" number of eaglets to independence, which is quite exceptionally successful for a bird. There are presumably further losses between independence and sexual maturity, which we have at present no means of calculating. But from the rate of change of mates at Eagle Hill and elsewhere we can calculate the mean life span of adults at about 10–12 years, and from this, in a stable population, we can reckon that at least half these young must survive to become sexually mature.

Incomplete as these results are they are a great advance on any other such records for large eagles anywhere in the world. They need confirmation and comparison with other eagles of the same species in, for instance South Africa, and with other species. In the Crowned Eagle's nearest relative, the Martial Eagle, which breeds on the same hill in Embu District, we already find some curious differences. In this case the young bird seems to move away from the nest site very much earlier, and to become independent before a year is out, so that there is no reason why the adults cannot breed in successive years. Records show that they do; yet in some peculiar and as yet inexplicable way the Martial Eagle arrives at about the same replacement rate as the Crowned Eagle, though evidently by quite different methods.

Although we know more in detail about some of these large African eagles than, for instance, about the Golden Eagle in Europe, we are not yet anywhere near a full knowledge of their economy. In the Crowned Eagle, for instance, it is relatively easy to watch this bold species at the nest, but not to study the relation between the numbers of potential prey and the predator. The common prey animal at Karen, for instance, is the Suni, a little antelope which is in itself very difficult to observe, study, or count in an area of thick forest, wherein it is both largely nocturnal and shy.

I have been told by at least one eminent ornithologist that birds of prey are "ornithologically unrewarding", meaning, I suppose, that it takes so long to study a few cases that many years of work are necessary before any even reasonably clear-cut results emerge. Nevertheless, such magnificent birds as the Crowned Eagle and other large African Eagles will always attract their enthusiastic following, and although difficult and exacting, the study of their habits in detail is a necessary exercise if we are to understand the function of such large birds of prey in nature.

Chapter 11
Falcons

All the true falcons are included in one genus, *Falco*, which is after *Accipiter* the largest of all genera of birds of prey, with 38 species of which 17, or nearly half, occur in Africa. With the true falcons in the family Falconidae are associated, in the Old World the Pigmy Falcons and Falconets, of which one species occurs in Africa, and in the New World a variety of very curious birds including the snake-eating Laughing Falcon, the bird-eating forest falcons of the genus *Micrastur*, and the carrion-eating Caracaras. The latter are the only group of the family which have been proved to build their own nests.

The 17 species that occur in Africa include three that are purely migratory, the Saker, the Red-footed Falcon, and the Merlin; the last only reaches North-West Africa on migration. Three species, the Lesser Kestrel, the Hobby, and Eleanora's Falcon breed in the Mediterranean countries or islands and migrate south of the Equator in winter. A fourth, the Sooty Falcon, breeds mainly in the North and East, on islands in the Red Sea, and performs similar southward migrations in winter. The remaining ten species are all resident south of the Sahara and some, such as the Peregrine and the Common Kestrel, are augmented by migrants during the winter.

Falcons are all long-winged, often rather long-tailed birds of powerful flight, including the swiftest fliers and most spectacular predators of all the birds of prey. Grand as may be the larger eagles, and agile as may be sparrowhawks and their kin, nothing equals the sight of a large falcon in full stoop, while the precision and grace with which Peregrines and Lanners execute aerial manoeuvres at speed is unequalled in the avian world. Potentially, such birds are capable of killing other birds very much larger than themselves, though usually they do not, as they cannot carry them.

Even small falcons may be very fierce and bold. I once saw a male Red-headed Falcon in Nigeria fly up behind a hovering Pied King-fisher, pause in flight, stretch out a foot and seize the kingfisher which promptly flew away dragging the little falcon with it. The Teita Falcon, a small species, apparently has the predatory habits of a miniature Peregrine. It is not only the large falcons that are worth watching in the attack, though they are undoubtedly the most spectacular. Some other small falcons, such as the Red-footed Falcon and the several species of kestrels are less actively predatory on other birds, and feed largely on small mammals and insects that they catch on the ground or in flight. But these make up in grace and beauty of flight for what they lack in speed and spectacular methods of attack.

The falcons form a much less uniform group than do the sparrowhawks and their kin, or the buzzards. They can be divided into a number of well-defined superspecies which by some authorities have been designated as genera. Most of these superspecies or groups are represented in Africa. The Gyrfalcon group includes the Saker and the Lanner; the Peregrine group the Peregrine and the Teita Falcon (and the Barbary Falcon which some consider a separate species); the Hobby group the European and African Hobbies, and so on. However, there are also a number of small or medium-sized falcons in Africa which do not fit very well with any superspecies, and probably, when their habits have been more intensively studied they may well not be regarded as closely related to more widespread forms. These would include the Fox Kestrel and the Greater Kestrel, neither of which seems to me quite like a typical kestrel; the Grey and Dickinson's Kestrel, which seem to me even less like true kestrels and are badly named; and the Red-necked Falcon, which is normally coupled with the European Merlin, but which seems to me rather distinct from that little bird.

Falcons differ in several respects from all the other birds of prey we have been discussing so far. They have certain anatomical peculiarities such as the serrations or "teeth" on the upper mandible, fitting into notches in the lower mandible, which are used to break the necks of their prey, and a different order of moulting the wing quills. These characters are reinforced by differences in behaviour. They allow their droppings to fall beneath them instead of squirting them well clear; they do not make nests of sticks but breed on cliff ledges or in the nests of other birds; head-bobbing and killing their prey by severing the neck vertebrae are other differences in which they are actually more similar to owls than to Accipiters. For these various reasons Dr. Amadon and myself do not consider that putting them in a family, the Falconidae, is sufficient distinction, and we place them in a suborder, the Falcones, all other Old World birds of prey (except the Secretary Bird) being in another suborder, the Accipitres.

The statement in the above list which will probably be regarded as most controversial is that the falcons do not make their own nests. We know that they often do lay eggs in stick nests, and many observers have assumed that these nests were built by the falcons themselves. But I do not believe this is so, and after careful study of available literature I have concluded that no good naturalist has ever seen a falcon building a substantial stick nest. Their behaviour is, for instance, entirely different from that of such birds as buzzards, which will also breed both on cliffs and in trees; in both such sites you will see the buzzard pair carrying sticks. But if a Lanner Falcon breeds on a cliff it uses the old nest of another bird, or a scrape in an earthy ledge, and in a tree it invariably finds an old or abandoned nest. This also applies to other species of falcons that nest in trees. The Greater Kestrel often uses the nests of the Cape Rook, and the Grey Kestrel—so far as is known—breeds mainly in abandoned or commandeered nests of the Hammerkop.

The Pigmy Falcon, the only African member of the family not in the genus *Falco*, is another good example of this habit. It is quite a common bird in thornbush and sub-desert country both in North-East and South-West Africa. In Kenya and Somalia it uses the thorny nests of Buffalo Weavers, and may perhaps wait until they have been lined by another bird, such as a Waxbill or a starling, before it finally takes over. In South Africa it lives in the huge colonial nests of the Sociable Weaver. Buffalo Weavers are as large as or even larger than the Pigmy Falcon, so that it is normally forced to live on amicable terms with them. But, although it makes use of Social Weavers' nests, it occasionally abuses their hospitality by eating them.

Most falcons eggs are much admired by collectors because of their handsome appearance, the ground colour often being nearly obscured by dark red-brown spots and freckles. The Pigmy Falcon, which breeds in dark enclosed spaces, lays nearly white eggs, though they are not as pale as those of the still smaller Far Eastern falconets (*Microhierax* spp.), which breed in barbets' holes. In most other respects the Pigmy Falcon is a quite typical if tiny falcon. It feeds largely on insects, but it will certainly catch small birds when it can and I have seen one eating a mouse. In the Kalahari it eats many reptiles in summer. In appearance it is strikingly like the White-crowned Bush Shrike, an insectivorous species very common in north-eastern thornbush, but not in the south. In eastern Kenya one can often see both perched on tops of trees, and it is sometimes not until they fly that one recognises the Pigmy Falcon for what it is. I have felt that mimicry may here be at work, but no one has watched Pigmy Falcons enough to prove the point.

Among the smallest of the true falcons are the **Common** and **Lesser Kestrels**, and they are also the most inoffensive, feeding largely on insects and small mammals caught in the grass. They are inhabitants of open plains, and are often to be found together in the same flock, which makes identification very difficult. As in harriers, there are some curious features of their distribution as migrants and as breeding birds. I shall later comment on the lack of breeding kestrels in what would seem to be perfect kestrel habitat, such as the Rift Valley of Kenya, where insects and grass mice abound, where there are plenty of cliff ledges or other birds' nests, but no, or very few, resident kestrels. Here is a case where an ecological niche exists, apparently unfilled by any predator.

The Lesser Kestrel breeds in Morocco, where I have seen them at breeding stations in a gorge near the Rif Hills. They breed commonly in the countries of the western Mediterranean, and in winter large numbers must enter Africa from these countries. Yet they are rare in West African savannas, and in four years in Nigeria I saw only three among many hundreds of Common Kestrels. In savannas of East Africa, on the other hand, they appear to be the commoner of the two. Lesser Kestrels also appear to be rare in the more arid northern parts of Nigeria, in the type of open grassy country where they are common in Kenya so that this appears not to be a matter explicable by ecological preference. The Lesser Kestrel appears to winter mainly south of the Equator, especially, as the counts have shown, in South Africa. Do they travel all the way from Morocco and South Spain to South Africa, and if so how and why—when there is plenty of suitable habitat in the steppes of West Africa south of the Sahara?

Lesser Kestrels are regularly gregarious at their nesting grounds, and Common Kestrels, particularly the resident races in Africa, are normally solitary. In some parts of the world, however, Common Kestrels are also colonial nesters. Both tend to be gregarious in winter quarters though the Lesser is the more gregarious of the two. Although they are regularly found together in the same flock there are probably slight ecological differences in their habits. The Common Kestrel, slightly larger and more powerful, may kill more mammals and birds, and the Lesser Kestrel more insects. In areas of long grass savanna Common rather than Lesser Kestrels are likely to be found, and in drier areas of short grass vice versa. These are only my general views, but I believe they would be supported by quantitative data related to habitat and prey preferences.

Nearest to the Common and Lesser Kestrels are the **Greater** or **White-eyed Kestrel** and the **Fox Kestrel**. Neither has been much studied, but I am quite familiar with both. Both are solitary nesters, usually rather rare and local, though there are places in Kenya where one can guarantee seeing the Greater Kestrel and in northern Nigeria every rocky hill had its Fox Kestrels. Broadly speaking, they divide the continent between them, the Fox Kestrel being northern and western in its distribution, and the Greater Kestrel a bird of the semi-arid grasslands and steppes of the south and east. To me they do not appear to have very similar habits, for Fox Kestrels live on rocky hills and Greater Kestrels on plains, breeding in the nests of other birds, especially those of the Cape Rook. There therefore seems no very good reason why they should be mutually exclusive (as are, for instance, the two closely allied Chanting Goshawks and the Red-necked and Augur Buzzards) and perhaps this separation in range is merely coincidence. There are places in Kenya where both occur quite close together, but where they are both so uncommon that it is difficult to believe they could compete with or exclude each other.

Of the two the Greater Kestrel is more kestrel-like, flying over open plains, sometimes hovering, and dropping on prey in the grass. Yet it seems to me a swifter, more typically falcon-like bird than the Common Kestrel. It seldom hovers, whereas the Common Kestrel very often does. In the Rift Valley near Nairobi the Greater Kestrel prefers to perch on telephone posts and dead trees whence it preys upon small mammals and insects. Unfortunately we know too little about it.

The same is true of the Fox Kestrel, and again, when I was in Nigeria, I had splendid chances of watching it but never seized them because I thought the bird commonplace. A pair nested each year on Sobi Hill, near Ilorin, and I found them on many other rocky hills in that area. I believe they only nest on rocky hills or cliffs, never in the nests of other birds, whereas the Greater Kestrel always chooses other birds' nests, and never rocky hills. Other birds' nests are more likely to be widely available than a particular type of rocky hill or a cliff, so the rarity of the Fox Kestrel is more easily understood. But these two species do not appear to be able to adapt to other situations, which may be the basic reason why they are rare and local. From the viewpoint of food supply there seems no reason why either should be.

I have only once seen **Dickinson's Kestrel** but have seen many **Grey Kestrels.** These two species also seem to divide up the continent of Africa between them, and again, it is difficult to understand why. The Grey Kestrel is northern and western, while Dickinson's essentially inhabits the great belt of Brachystegia woodland in south tropical Africa. There is a considerable area of overlap in these two species, in the southern part of the Grey Kestrel's range. But for the most part they seem to keep separate.

Again, neither is a very common bird, and both are more falcon-like, killing more mammals and birds, than are Common Kestrels. I dislike applying the name kestrel to either for they are not red-brown like the true kestrels, and neither of them regularly hovers. They ought to be called the Grey and Dickinson's Falcon.

The Grey Kestrel is said to nest in other birds' nests, hollow trees, and in Hammerkops' nests. Although some reference works give the first two sites, all recent records that I have come across have been in Hammerkops' nests. Does the Grey Kestrel only breed in Hammerkops' nests or does it not? And if it does, and if it eats (as it appears to eat) insects, small mammals and bats, why on earth is it so uncommon on a continent where there are certainly more Hammerkops' nests than rocky hills, and any amount of insects and small mammals?

Dickinson's Kestrel is also rather rare and local, also apparently without very good reason, for its prey, birds, small mammals, and insects, is abundant. One possible reason for its local distribution is that for reasons which are likely to remain obscure for many years it prefers to live in the vicinity of Borassus palms, tall palms with fan-like leaves that occur mainly in low-lying rather wet savannas. It does not occur everywhere with Borassus palms, and it sometimes occurs in areas where there are no or very few Borassus palms, but there is a fairly close connection between the two. It nests either at the base of the Borassus palm fronds—as inaccessible a site as can be found in Africa—or in the hollow on top of a dead stump of a coconut palm, also very inaccessible. Consequently, the breeding habits are relatively unknown. Dickinson's Kestrel (or Falcon) has perhaps greater reason for its local distribution and rarity than the Grey Kestrel, which breeds mainly or exclusively in Hammerkops' nests. But again, from the viewpoint of food, neither should be rare.

Red-necked Falcons are also, for some reason or another, associated with Borassus palms and with the rather similar but branching Doum Palm *Hyphaene thebaica*. They are small but rather fierce bird-killing falcons, prepared to tackle birds as large or larger than themselves. Although they are classed as being near to Merlins I cannot see that their habits resemble those of Merlins and I prefer to regard them as something of an enigma. Red-necked Falcons also occur in India; among African raptors they have a distribution similar to that of the Shikra or Little Banded Goshawk; but they are everywhere very local, and there is a big gap in their range between India and tropical Africa. Yet they are undoubtedly the same species, with, in India, the same taste for living near Borassus palms—why, no one can say.

The Borassus palm is a tall, rather stately palm with a stem of up to 70–80 feet, narrow at the base, and swollen into a bulb at the top, smooth, not ridged like a coconut palm and virtually unclimbable. At the top there is a tuft of broad fan-like leaves; the Indian Palmyra Palm, also a species of *Borassus*, is similar but smaller. What the attraction of these palms may be is obscure, but the little falcons are not the only birds attracted by them. In parts of Africa they are the main haunts of Speckled Pigeons and Piapiacs, or Black Magpies. And for some reason also there are parts of Africa where the Red-necked Falcon does not frequent palm areas.

Such a place is the Kalahari Desert, where the falcon is quite common in low Acacia scrub with a few larger trees, without a palm within hundreds of miles. Anyway there the falcon is, apparently living quite happily on birds, whereas elsewhere in Africa it is rare unless it has its favourite palms and is not always found where they occur. With the pair breeding near my office in Nigeria I lost a golden opportunity to study a rare species, through ignorance, and because I was not at that time specially interested in birds of prey.

Thus we have three little falcons, the Grey Kestrel (a sort of kestrel?) Dickinson's Falcon, and the Red-necked Falcon (a sort of merlin?) which are rather rare and curiously restricted in habitat for reasons which are obscure. The most extraordinary example of all, however is the **Teita Falcon**. In its anatomical characters and mode of life this is a miniature Peregrine, living on passerine and other birds, breeding on cliffs and apparently well-fitted for life in many parts of Africa. Yet its range is discontinuous, and it is exceedingly rare within that range. In museums it is known only by a handful of specimens, and I have searched for it in vain in its type locality, the Teita Hills of Kenya. It occurs in Southern Ethiopia, the highlands of Kenya and northern Tanzania, but is absent from a vast stretch of country between the Crater Highlands of Tanzania and the Zambezi Valley. Why, heaven knows.

I shall never forget the dramatic discovery of the Teita Falcon in the Zambezi Gorge in 1957 during the course of the first Pan African Ornithologists Congress at Livingstone. I was out for an evening stroll with the late Dick Herbert, and we saw and heard a little falcon on the basalt cliffs not far from the Victoria Falls Hotel. We looked at one another and said, unlikely though it might be, that it looked to both of us like a Teita Falcon. And it was. From then on a procession of distinguished ornithologists went to look at the little falcon, and what little is known about the species has been learned in this same spot, where several pairs nest on the walls of the gorge above the rushing Zambezi. They seem perfectly well able to look after themselves, and why they should be so rare and so scattered as they are is a complete mystery.

The other places in which I have seen the Teita Falcon have been on rather high mountains in rather dry localities, and I suspect that this is their true East African habitat. They usually share it with much larger and more powerful highly predatory falcons, the Lanner and the Peregrine, and this is a possible reason why the Teita Falcon is rare, for these are very aggressive birds. However, no one so far has been able to gauge the possible interactions of Teita Falcons and their most likely competitors, Lanners, so it is impossible to say whether there is anything in this idea at all. The best place in which to study the Teita Falcon as such is undoubtedly the Zambezi Gorge, and it is surprising that the 1957 discovery has not been followed up by some enthusiast or group of enthusiasts. I myself, living in Kenya, would look for Teita Falcons not on the very big cliffs of the higher Teita Hills, but in the thornbush at their foot, ecologically similar to the Zambezi Gorge, and with plenty of good cliffs. But I haven't found one yet.

The remaining smaller falcons in Africa are all either hobbies or birds rather like them. To start with the **African Hobby,** here again we have a small and apparently efficient species which is rare for no apparent reason. It is not as rare as some of the other species we have been discussing, and it is quite common in well-watered savannas in some parts of Africa. But I usually see less than six in a year in Kenya, so that there is no doubt that it is rare. Once more, we know little about its breeding biology, but not because it does not nest in accessible places. A pair breeds, or bred, outside the library of Makerere College in Kampala, but appears to have been regarded by ornithologists there as part of the landscape, much as I neglected the Red-necked Falcons at Ilorin. Naturalists at Makerere please note.

African Hobbies are very similar to European Hobbies in their habits, but are smaller and almost incredibly swift and graceful in the hunt. In eastern Kenya I chiefly come across them near highland forests, and this is probably why I do not see many. When I lived in western Kenya I found them quite common; and the best way to see them was to be out and about at dusk, when they would often come to hunt the flying termites that emerged after afternoon showers.

It may be that a regular supply of flying termites is the key to the distribution of the African Hobby. In arid areas, such as eastern Kenya, termite swarms are only common for perhaps three months in twelve, at the height of the rainy seasons, when they are, as we shall see, also of use to migrating European Hobbies. In western Kenya, in much higher rainfall, flying termites would regularly be available during five or six months of the year, and occasionally in almost any month, so that the African Hobby has a far better chance of feeding on them. But although a great many birds make use of termite swarms it will not do for any to be entirely dependent on them, for they are of irregular and sometimes infrequent occurrence. Like the European Hobby, the African Hobby also feeds on birds, and tends to feed the young in the nest mainly on small birds. Small birds are legion in Africa; African Hobbies, Teita Falcons, and some others are not.

The **European Hobby** is a larger and more powerful bird than the African Hobby. It breeds in north-western woodlands, and has been well studied in Europe. In most of Africa it is only seen as a migrant, and here again we encounter the curious feature that although the bird breeds in north-west Africa and migrates to the tropics it does not, or only very rarely, migrate through West Africa to its wintering grounds. According to Bannerman only one Hobby has been obtained in West Africa, catching a fowl—presumably on the ground, an unlikely thing for a Hobby to do, for small birds and insects caught in the air are their normal food. What happens to hobbies which leave Morocco and Algeria in the winter we do not know, but perhaps they move eastwards along the Mediterranean seaboard, join with many others coming across the Mediterranean from Europe, and then down the eastern side of Africa, where they are at times numerous. Why they should do this, if they do it, is obscure.

The **Red-footed Falcon**, of which there are either two distinct races or two species—the Eastern and the Western, according to whether one is a splitter or a lumper—winters in much the same area as the Hobby, the southern part of the African tropics. In some of its ways the Red-footed Falcon is more like a kestrel than a hobby and in North Africa in spring the western race is seen migrating in flocks with Lesser Kestrels. In their breeding haunts they are colonial, nesting in the abandoned nests of rooks and other corvids. They hunt low over open country, catching their prey as much on the ground as in the air, and in this way resembling kestrels more than hobbies. However, in Africa we see them only as migrants.

Very few Red-footed Falcons seem to pass through Kenya, even of the Western race, which is odd because they winter to the north and west of Kenya in the Sudan and Congo–Katanga savannas. On the occasions when I have seen them they strike me as like kestrels in their habit of perching on posts and dead trees, but like hobbies once they are in the air. They do not hover, and they have graceful gliding and swooping flight, unlike that of kestrels. On one occasion, when I came on a group near Naivasha, they were in company with Lesser Kestrels and Hobbies which were hawking in the air while the kestrels and the Red-footed Falcons sat on posts. However, both Hobbies and Red-footed Falcons eventually soared to great heights and disappeared into the base of a thundercloud. I estimated that they could have gone out of sight of the naked eye at about 2000 feet and out of view with × 12 binoculars at well over 20,000 feet. Once into the base of the cloud, they could be carried up to a very great height without effort, as glider pilots know. Perhaps most Red-footed Falcons, both Western and Eastern, pass thus over the North African tropics, where it is dry in October–November, with very few termites, en route to their southern wintering grounds where it is wet from November on and there are plenty of termites and other insects.

The most remarkable habit of the Red-footed Falcon in southern Africa is the gregarious roosting prior to northward migration. They tend to be gregarious at all times in their winter quarters, hunting in flocks, but collect in thousands to roost. One such roost, near Dedza, described by C. W. Benson in 1951, was in gum trees and had been occupied each winter for about a decade. It was shared by Pied Crows. Benson estimated that it contained four to five thousand falcons, which used the roost regularly from December to March, when they departed on northward migration. Other such roosts are known. The falcons did not settle until it was too dark to count them in a tree, but collected near the roost in the evening. They left within ten minutes as dawn was breaking, and made a deafening clamour in their communal excitement. More needs to be known about these roosts, which are evidently characteristic of this species in the winter. For instance how far away do the falcons forage each day, and are the roosts spread over the country in suitable places at regular intervals as are, for instance, rook roosts in Britain in winter?

Two other remarkable small or medium-sized falcons remain, the **Sooty** and **Eleanora's Falcon**, both strongly migratory, and similar in that they breed at a time when small migrant birds are passing south on their way to Africa and migrate to Madagascar for the winter. Eleanora's breeds on islands in the Mediterranean and in the Canaries, and has been intensively studied by R. Vaughan and others. The Sooty Falcon, on the other hand, has been until recently more a bird of mystery. Long ago it was reported breeding on the Dahlac

7. *Above*, A female Ayres Hawk Eagle with its downy chick. The long legs assist in capturing small birds, this rare species' main prey.

Below, A Wahlberg's Eagle with its downy chick. This small eagle feeds mainly on lizards and rodents.

8. *Above*, Two Tawny Eagles contesting prey on the ground. Both migrant and resident races are catholic feeders, preying on everything from termites to dead elephants.

Below, The African Hawk Eagle is perhaps the most potent predator, size for size, among African birds of prey. It feeds mainly on Guineafowl and smaller gamebirds.

Archipelago in the Red Sea, but this was not properly confirmed until 1964, by C. S. Clapham, who found them quite common with up to 100 pairs on large islands. The only other nest that has recently been found was in the depths of the Libyan desert, under a cairn of stones where the temperature was 108°F. In their breeding grounds Eleanora's Falcons are gregarious, Sooty Falcons more solitary, though several pairs may breed well spaced out on the same island, in a sort of loose group. Both breed in July–August, and so have their young in the nest or getting on the wing when small passerine migrants from Europe and Asia are abundant.

Neither of these falcons winters on the mainland of Africa, though some are seen on migration. Some Sooty Falcons probably come down the Nile, and the Great Rift Valley, presumably from the inland deserts, and I myself have seen a pair at Lake Nakuru, 350 miles inland. Most, however, seem to pass southward through the eastern thornbush of Kenya where, on the lower Sabaki river, they may at times be quite common, feeding on small weaver birds roosting in the reeds. Eleanora's Falcon is seldom seen inland, but migrates through Somalia in company with Hobbies and is difficult to distinguish from them, perhaps bypassing the Horn of Africa overland. One place far inland where it has lately been reported is the Ruaha National Park in Tanzania, as a passage migrant. This is about 250 miles from the coast, and far further inland than anywhere else that Eleanora's Falcon has been seen. In November, when the falcons would be likely to arrive, early rains would have fallen here, and it is not impossible that this is what brings them to ground, just as the rains in Kenya attract Hobbies on passage.

Both Sooty and Eleanora's Falcons winter in the savannas of Madagascar. Even the Eleanora's Falcons breeding in the Western Mediterranean migrate to Madagascar, on the evidence of one bird ringed in Morocco. One wonders why Madagascar, and not somewhere on the mainland of Africa, in company with similarly insectivorous Hobbies and Red-footed Falcons. Both species, bird eaters in their breeding grounds, feed mainly upon insects in Madagascar. The total world population of Eleanora's Falcon is fairly well known, and may be only about 4000 birds. That of the Sooty Falcon is not known but is probably greater than this, as it breeds on numerous islands in the Red Sea, and has a more extensive breeding range than hitherto supposed. In Madagascar, according to A. L. Rand, it is the Sooty Falcon which is the commoner species. As they both winter in the same area, the proportions seen there are probably a good index of total numbers. Perhaps there is another wintering ground of Eleanora's Falcon, as yet not known, or else the numbers of Sooty Falcons are far greater than we suppose.

The similarities in habits of these several migratory small falcons, the Lesser Kestrel, Red-footed Falcon, African Hobby, Eleanora's and the Sooty will by now be obvious. All winter mainly in the southern part of Africa or in Madagascar, at a season when it is wet, and insects appear to be abundant. Probably this is the key to their winter distribution and the reason for otherwise apparently inexplicable movements, explaining for instance, the absence of Hobbies from West African savannas in winter, when it is dry from October–March north of the forest belt. What seems likely is that all of these birds, excepting the Lesser Kestrel, carry out most of their migration at a great height where they are invisible or unnoticed by humans, coming to ground only to roost, catch a late finch or a bat, or to get a feed of flying termites after a shower.

There remain the three large powerful falcons, the Peregrine, Lanner and Saker. The third of these is only a migrant to northern Africa, though there is a suspicion that some may breed somewhere in the deserts south of the Atlas. It is difficult to distinguish Sakers from Lanners in the field, and Meinertzhagen, for instance, combined them with Gyrfalcons in a single species. But if one studies the races of the Lanner and Saker living adjacent to one another in eastern Europe it seems fairly clear that they are different species.

The **Peregrine** and the **Lanner** may be both found in many parts of Africa, but it is the Lanner that is the characteristic, successful, and common species; the Peregrine is normally rare. In Morocco, where both occur, the Peregrine is mainly a bird of sea coasts and the Lanner of the inland deserts. However, the situation is complicated by the presence of the Barbary Falcon, which some consider to be a race of the Peregrine, *Falco peregrinus pelegrinoides*, and others a different species, *F. pelegrinoides*. The controversy has been partially cleared up lately by K. D. Smith, who found the Barbary Falcon on the cliffs of the Atlantic Coast and the Mediterranean Peregrine *F. p. brookei* on the Mediterranean Coast, neither occurring commonly inland, where the Lanner is the common falcon. The two races or species of Peregrine cannot thus be said to share a range in

Morocco, and it seems more likely that they are races rather than species; but the question is still open, and could be effectively studied by someone in Morocco with a summer to spare.

Barbary Falcons appear to be able to breed commonly on the cliffs of Morocco along with Lanners, though doubtless they occupy different stretches of cliff. In Kenya I have found that Peregrines and Lanners are mutually exclusive, the Peregrine being rare or absent where the Lanner is common. This appears to be partly an ecological separation, but not entirely. On the eastern slopes of Mount Kenya west of the Tana River the Peregrine was the common, indeed the only species on the rocky hills. But east of the Tana, in similar thornbush and savanna country in Kitui district the Lanner appears to be the common large falcon and to exclude the Peregrine, though I knew of one pair of Peregrines on a high forested range of hills. In Teita district, further to the east, and on the slopes of Mount Elgon in western Kenya, I found only Lanners in the type of cultivated, formerly forested, and well watered country favoured by Peregrines in Embu district. I have occasionally seen Peregrines in western Kenya and know of odd places where they may be seen within the main haunts of the Lanner, but usually if there are Lanners there are no Peregrines. The obvious reason for this is that one species is able to monopolise the large bird-killing falcon niche. But then one has both Lanners and Barbary Falcons as common residents on the Atlantic seaboard of Morocco. Is this another reason for supposing the Barbary Falcon to be a good species?

It is a pity that the Peregrine is so rare, for it is the finest flier of all the large Falcons, and to my mind has a presence, partly the result of its deep harsh voice, that the screaming, keening Lanner lacks. Nevertheless I do not agree with those who say that the Lanner is a much poorer performer in the air than the Peregrine. I have seen Lanners perform evolutions that a Peregrine could not have bettered, and I have seen them hunting everything from flying termites to large gamebirds. The Lanner may kill a few more birds and mammals on the ground than does the Peregrine, but both are quite magnificent.

The Peregrine has been exhaustively studied in Europe and America, and on that account may be classed as intimately known. However, no very good breeding study of the Lanner has been done, the best being from Sicily, by T. Mebs. The bird has hardly been studied at the nest in full detail in Africa, though several photographers have made preliminary observations in Rhodesia and elsewhere. It should not be a very difficult bird to study, though it does nest very often on fearsome cliffs where the nest is practically invisible and inaccessible in a deep cranny. But the same is often true of the Peregrine, yet easily accessible nests have been found and studied in places, including one in Embu district by myself.

I have gone into so much detail about the falcons because they seem to me to be among the most interesting of African birds of prey, as well as one of the most beautiful and spectacular of the main groups. I have posed a number of curious conundrums that puzzle me—rarity without any apparent reason, odd migration routes and habits—in the hope that others may be stimulated to probe into these questions, which seem more characteristic of the falcons than of any other group of African birds of prey—except some of the owls which, unlike Falcons, are very difficult to study.

Chapter 12
Oddities

Four species of birds of prey in Africa do not fit well into any of the recognised groupings, and their affinities are still somewhat in doubt. They are the Osprey, Vulturine Fish Eagle (or Palm-nut Vulture), Harrier Hawk and Secretary Bird, which last may not be a true Falconiform at all. Of these, all but one—the Osprey—are found only in Africa or Madagascar, and the Secretary Bird belongs to an exclusively African family. Of these three only the Secretary Bird—the largest and most spectacular, but by no means the commonest—has been thoroughly studied. The Osprey has been very well studied in Europe and North America, but little in Africa itself.

In most classifications the **Osprey** is placed close to Falcons (suborder Falcones) with which it agrees in many respects. However, it is not like any of the true falcons, and does not even bear much resemblance to the Carrion Hawks and Caracaras, which are normally regarded as being the most primitive types of the family Falconidae. One authority has said that the Osprey ought to be placed with the New World vultures, and there seems general doubt that its nearest affinities have been established. Dr. Amadon and myself have felt that it is perhaps more nearly related to kites than to falcons. The Osprey, for instance, lacks a bony shield above the eye (as in kites) has rounded rather than grooved undersides of the talons and lays an egg which, when held up against the light, shows green, like those of eagles, hawks, kites and Old World vultures, instead of reddish, as is the case with all falcons' eggs. It has a shrill whistling voice, kite-like, but quite unlike that of any falcon. All that one can really say is that no-one is quite clear as to the affinities of the Osprey, but that most agree that it deserves a family to itself—the Pandionidae—and that this family should either be placed near to falcons or alternatively, much earlier in the normal classification sequence, near the New World vultures or the kites.

Leaving aside questions of classification, for which there is no good answer at the moment, the Osprey is a well-known, relatively common large raptor confined exclusively to the neighbourhood of water and feeding, for practical purposes, entirely on fish. The feet of the Osprey are lined with sharp spicules which enable it to grasp the fish, and the outer toe is reversible (as in owls), perhaps also an adaptation to enable it to grasp and carry slippery prey. The basic method of fishing is to fly at a height of 100–300 feet above the water —lake, river, or coastal lagoon, but preferably fairly calm—and, on seeing a fish, check, perhaps hover briefly, and then plunge with a great splash into the water. It appears sometimes that the Osprey dives head first, but in fact, when close to the water, the feet and long legs are thrown forward in front of the head and the fish is grasped with the talons. The Osprey is unique among fish-eating birds of prey in that it plunges right in, disappearing in a cloud of spray. When it rises with the fish it at once shakes itself free of water in flight, and makes off to a perch to eat. The fish is always carried fore and aft, like a torpedo slung beneath an aircraft, a method of reducing air resistance also used by Fish Eagles.

Ospreys build very large nests in trees, on cliffs, on buildings, or even on the ground in a salt marsh or on a beach. Most of the Ospreys that breed in Africa live on the Red Sea Coast, and their nests are on low bushes or on the ground, but I have seen an Osprey's nest on a rock stack off the Mediterranean Coast of Morocco and in the Cape Verde islands they nest on cliffs. The nest is repaired and resorted to year after year. Over a period of years it becomes enormous in proportion to the size of the bird—larger even than those of large eagles. In America Ospreys can be induced to breed on cartwheels placed for them, and may make themselves a nuisance by trying to build nests on power installations. Their most common breeding sites are, however, tall trees or low islands offshore.

In Africa we at once run up against a curious feature in the Osprey. One would think that all that would be necessary to attract a permanently resident pair of Ospreys would be a good supply of fish, and a tall tree or an offshore rock or sandbank to breed on. This is what seems to be necessary to Europe, North America and Australia. But the fact is that south of Somalia and Morocco (excepting for the Atlantic islands) Ospreys are either absent as breeding birds or extremely rare. They do not appear to take advantage of the abundant fish supply and suitable tall trees that occur in and around many African lakes or coastal lagoons. Thus here again, as in harriers and some kestrels, there is an apparently available ecological niche which is not filled. This cannot be because of competition from Fish Eagles, which do harass and rob Ospreys of their prey, for Ospreys live and breed successfully among several other species of Fish Eagles and Sea Eagles elsewhere in the world. All one can say is that it is inexplicable.

As a matter of fact, Ospreys are practically absent as breeding birds in the whole southern hemisphere, except in Australasia—where they are common enough for instance along the Great Barrier Reef. I am entirely unconvinced that they breed in Kenya, though claims have been made to that effect. I have never seen a nest myself, but have heard quite competent ornithologists observe that they have seen Ospreys nesting at Lake Naivasha. On investigation I have always found that the Osprey was using a Fish Eagle's nest as a feeding platform. There are records from South Africa, and some authentic eggs are listed in Roberts' *Birds of South Africa*. But even here it is obviously a rare breeding bird, for reasons which are very obscure, for there are abundant dams and coastal lagoons, which would be ideal for Ospreys. If such coastal marshes existed in, for instance, North-East America, Ospreys would breed in colonies.

In North-East Africa Ospreys breed in Somalia in December and rather later in February or March on islands in the Red Sea proper. In Morocco I saw a pair breeding in April; in other words in the Palearctic spring. Thus most of the resident continental African Ospreys conform broadly to Palearctic breeding seasons starting in late winter or early spring except for those few cases in South Africa, where the eggs were reported in November—which is actually the Austral Spring. But, since Ospreys are able to breed around the Equator in Australasia there seems no good reason why they should not breed in tropical Africa—for instance on the islands in Lake Rudolf, which teems with fish and is inaccessible and undisturbed. We shall have to leave at that the mysterious breeding distribution of the Osprey—inexplicable.

There is no mystery about the distribution of the **Vulturine Fish Eagle**, or Palm-nut Vulture, but it is undoubtedly peculiar. Essentially, this strange bird is a vegetarian, feeding largely or exclusively on the ripe fruits of the Oil Palm, *Elaeis guineensis*. Thus its main distribution is in the tropical forests and the better watered savannas, where oil palms may be expected to occur. The species does occur uncommonly away from areas where oil palms are abundant. For instance it is regularly seen in the ground-water forest at Lake Manyara and in mangrove swamps of the Kenya Coast, where oil palms are certainly rare. In such situations it feeds to a considerable extent on crabs, small fish snatched from the surface, either alive or dead, and even on molluscs and other invertebrates.

Vulturine Fish Eagles, as I prefer to call them, are large, clumsy looking black and white raptors, which yet can soar nicely on occasion. I used to see them soaring round the tops of mountains in West African savannas, often in company with other eagles. Again, it is far from easy to say where they should be placed. They resemble Fish and Sea Eagles in having the adult plumage largely white, with a very different brown immature plumage. But they also resemble in this respect the Egyptian Vulture. One thinks of them as a nice link between Fish Eagles and vultures. But they may be quite wrongly placed here, and they need close study in order to see where their behavioural affinities, if any, lie.

I personally think of them as being much more like Fish Eagles in their habits than vultures. Hence I dislike the name Palm-nut Vulture, which is suggested mainly because the face is partially bare. So is that of the New World vultures (which everyone admits are in no way closely related to Old World vultures), of some Caracaras, which are even less closely related, and of the African Harrier Hawk. The bare face is the result of feeding frequently on oily and messy food; the Harrier Hawk also often eats oil palm nuts.

It is a very curious sight to watch a Vulturine Fish Eagle eating oil palm fruit. The bird visits certain trees regularly every day as long as the fruit is ripe, alights on a frond, and walks or sidles up it to the base, whence the fruits can be reached. It bends and deliberately pulls out the fruits one by one, swallowing them, or tearing off the pericarp and rejecting the hard kernel. When I had really good opportunities to watch this process, in Nigeria, I let it pass, and now that I live in Kenya oil palms and Vulturine Fish Eagles are scarce, chiefly confined to the coastal strip, and uncommon even there. The wilder savannas of central Nigeria, about the junction of the Niger and Benue rivers, would be a good area to study these birds in relatively pleasant surroundings.

When nesting, Vulturine Fish Eagles seem fairly typical of any medium-sized eagle, making a large nest in a tall tree, and using it for a number of years in succession. No good study of the breeding behaviour has been done, but from what little is known it certainly appears peculiar in some respects. One pair, observed by Dr. W. M. Serle in the Cameroons, made three attempts to breed within eighteen months. They laid in January, but lost their young one, and bred again that year, this time successfully. The long fledging period —90 days—resembles vultures rather than Fish Eagles. Their nest was blown down, but they built a new one and were sitting again in the following January. Such frequent breeding is very unusual in a raptor of this size. I suspect that it is even unusual for the Vulturine Fish Eagle which, in Nigeria, breeds mainly in the dry season, October–March. Perhaps it was in response to an almost perpetual abundance of ripe oil palm fruits in the Cameroons.

Other peculiarities of this odd bird are a curious growling voice —it makes a double-syllabled call like "pruk–kurr" or "wuk–keh", and contented duck-like quacking sounds (unlike the calls of either fish eagles or vultures)—and a very powerful grip. A friend who looks after them in the London Zoo fears them more than most of his charges for this reason. Why a bird that lives on fruit or small, unresisting fish and molluscs should require a powerful foot is obscure. It has been suggested that the diet of oil palm nuts is because the species has a very high need for Vitamin C; but it turns out that oil palm nuts are just a favourite food and that the bird can do without them quite well. This is no doubt why it can survive in areas where oil palms are scarce or absent; but it does not colonise every such place, and evidently does not like living far from its favourite food.

Harrier Hawks are less odd then are Vulturine Fish Eagles, but they are nevertheless extraordinary birds. There are two species, one on the African Mainland, the other in Madagascar, which appears to differ only in colour from its mainland relative. In their case there is no special difficulty in placing them near obvious relatives. Anatomically they make a fairly clear link between the snake eagles (of the Asiatic genus *Spilornis* rather than the African *Circaetus*) and harriers. However, their habits do not closely resemble either of these groups and their most obvious close relatives are the South American Crane Hawks, genus *Geranospiza*.

Harrier Hawks are inhabitants of forest or woodland. They occur in deep forest but are less common there than in country of mixed clearings, cultivation, and forest. Where they occur in semi-arid country they are associated with relict forest patches on hills and along watercourses, and do not go very far from big trees. They are much less common in East and South than in wooded or forested West Africa, where they are one of the more commonplace raptors.

The Harrier Hawks are recognisably hawks, and they have only one striking peculiarity. They have very long legs which can bend either way at the tibio-tarsal joint, whereas the legs of all other raptors can only bend one way. This, together with the short outer toe, is probably an adaptation to their way of life. They feed upon any small creature they can catch or hook out of a cranny in a tree, from grubs and insects to lizards and attain extraordinary postures in their efforts. They make a speciality of visiting colonies of weaver birds where, hanging upside down with flapping wings, they extract the young from the nests. They also eat palm fruits at times, and perhaps because of this, and also because of their way of pushing into crevices, their faces are partially bare of feathers.

In Africa they occupy the same niche as the South American Crane Hawks—preying upon small, helpless or inactive creatures which can be found by patient search rather than by speed or stealth. One may watch a Harrier Hawk spending as much as fifteen minutes or more, methodically searching among the bases of the fronds of a palm tree, or working among the epiphytes on a rotten bough. Essentially they fly only to move from place to place, or to soar in display. I suspect that their wing loading is very low, and that, partly for this reason, they can fly very slowly, which could be an aid to methodical search. The structure of their wing quills, which are flexible, not greatly emarginated, and rather soft, may also aid in this respect. This character, together with the short outer toe, they share with the aberrant Indian Black Eagle, which some have thought more like a kite. The Crane and Harrier Hawks, and the Indian Black Eagle, all fill roughly the same ecological niche in the moist tropical regions they frequent—feeding on small animals, birds' eggs and nestlings, rarely killing anything very large. It is of interest therefore that they seem to have developed similar features, though the Indian Eagle is not apparently closely related to the other two.

A pair of Harrier Hawks bred in the forest near my home at

Karen, and I have watched them when I could. Nothing in their breeding behaviour differentiates them from many other raptors that make large nests in trees, though they are not really like either snake eagles or harriers. They have a typical Accipitrine undulating display, accompanied by calling, performed at a height above the forest. Like many small eagles and buzzards, they occupy their nest for at least several years; the one in our forest was occupied for four years, and then abandoned. Occasionally they breed on cliffs, or at least in a tree or bush growing out of a cliff face. They lay 1-2 eggs, and the course of the incubation and fledging periods could be duplicated in many other medium-sized raptor species. Both sexes share the duties at the nest. When changing over, at feeding time, or when the male brings a stick the bare greenish-yellow facial skin glows red or pink—blushing in fact, like the Hooded Vulture and one or two other species. Their main peculiarity is in the ecological niche they exclusively occupy, and to which they appear to be specially adapted by certain anatomical features.

There remains the **Secretary Bird**, the oddest bird of prey in Africa, if only because it alone is mainly terrestrial. Secretary Birds are familiar enough creatures in East and South Africa but are rare in West or North Africa. They are inhabitants of grassland and semi-arid open steppe, avoiding woodlands and real desert as a rule, though they are common in some rather dry places such as the Kalahari. Here they stalk about the plains, feeding on rodents, grasshoppers, and snakes—in my opinion in that order of importance. It is their snake-killing habits that have attracted most attention, but they kill far fewer snakes than is generally supposed.

We consider the Secretary Bird to be a bird of prey for various reasons. It has a hooked beak, feeds on flesh or insects, builds a large stick nest in a tree and—unlikely enough—soars high in the air in display, like a big eagle. But it differs from other Falconiformes in a good many anatomical peculiarities, and superficially resembles the Crested Cariama from South America. The egg-shell is green inside, like that of eagles and hawks, but the egg white, on electrophoretic analysis, in one case resembles that of a bustard and in others that of an eagle. Bustards are near relatives of Cariamas and, like Secretary Birds and Cariamas, are terrestrial, with long bare shanks and short stubby toes. So although we say that the Secretary Bird is a Falconiform, and think of it as a sort of terrestrial eagle, it may be more closely allied to other types that are not birds of prey, and not closely related to the Falconiformes at all.

Secretary Birds require about 10–13,000 acres of short grassland to support a pair, and a larger home range in desert areas. They can adapt to mixed wheatfields and pastures, and have so adapted to such areas in Kenya and South Africa. But they quickly seem to disappear when grasslands are invaded by small-scale peasant farmers, probably because such people interfere with the Secretary Birds' nests. Twenty years ago, when I worked on eagles in Embu district there were several pairs of Secretary Birds in the same area, which was not ideal, being largely open woodland; now it is difficult to find one.

Hunting on the ground as they do, Secretary Birds cannot exist satisfactorily in areas where the grass grows tall. They are not common in places where the grass is more than, say 16–20 inches high, and usually they like it shorter. Equally, since they cover their hunting ground daily on foot, and not from the air, they require a fair density of grasshoppers, mice, and the like to be able to catch enough food. In real deserts where they would have to walk a mile or two to find a beetle they could not thrive. So, although their terrestrial habits bring them some advantages, in effect they also deny Secretary Birds existence in the richest and most productive African habitats, woodland and forest, and severely limit their existence in very dry areas.

Secretary Birds roost in trees, often in the tree where they nest. When the sun has been up for some time, and the day is warm, they jump to the ground and start foraging. They continue for most of the morning, but may rest in the shade in the heat of the day. In the evening they return to roost, an hour or two before dark.

So far as I know no one has ever followed a Secretary Bird throughout the day, but in some areas this would not be specially difficult. The bird walks along steadily through the grass, its head nodding in a manner that has earned for it the name of "He goat of the plains" among some East African tribes. From time to time it snatches an insect with its beak, or stops and stamps rapidly with both legs, either to drive out a mouse or to kill a snake. Sometimes a pair runs over the grassland with wings held above the back; this may perhaps be in pursuit of a large snake, or may be merely a form of display.

Should a pair of Secretary Birds meet a neighbouring pair on the boundary of, or in their home range they will pursue the interlopers, jump over them, and strike downwards with their feet; the intruders usually run away. When the victor returns to its partner it will run round the other in circles, with crest erected. These various movements are unlike those performed by other birds of prey, but since no other is so exclusively terrestrial, we have nothing to compare them with. They do put one in mind of the dancing of cranes, rather distant relatives of the Cariamas.

Oddly enough, Secretary Birds fly quite a lot, and not merely to get from place to place. I have seen them soaring on thermals like vultures and a friend of mine in a small aircraft met with one, at a height of over 12,000 feet, near Dar-es-Salaam. I doubt if he could have been mistaken. Some of the curious running about on the ground may be nuptial display, but equally, Secretary Birds do perform a vigorous, typically undulating display flight, high in the air, similar to that of many other large raptors, and accompanied by loud hoarse groaning calls. The voice is unusual, but the performance is typically Accipitrine. So are the nesting habits, as the Secretary Bird builds a large stick nest on top of a tree, usually thorny, and often one which has been pruned into an impenetrable tangle of topiary work by giraffes. This nest may be used for several years, and each pair has several nests in its home range. Two or three eggs are laid, and one to three young usually reared. At first they are fed a liquid by regurgitation, but in the later stages the adults disgorge a mass of grasshoppers, mice and the like into the nest and leave the young to it. There is really nothing in this nesting cycle to distinguish the Secretary Bird from many other diurnal birds of prey.

Secretary Birds are normally resident in their home ranges, but the numbers of breeding pairs may fluctuate considerably from one year to the next. In one year in my Embu census area of 146 square miles there were five pairs, the next only one, and that nowhere near the haunts of the other five. In the Nairobi National Park there seem in some years to be numbers of nests, in others few; and in exceptionally good years for rodents the Secretary Birds may be double-brooded—as one pair certainly was in 1962. This adaptation to an environment which has a widely fluctuating food potential is also shared by the Black-shouldered Kite, which is undoubtedly a Falconiform.

Only a really detailed study of habits will demonstrate whether we are right in regarding the Secretary Bird as a true Falconiform, or whether it ought to be regarded as a predatory sort of bustard or Cariama. The latest indications are that it is a true bird of prey, though very specialised. I have not read much about Cariamas, but from what little I have read they seem to have some similarities of habit, as well as of appearance and anatomy, with Secretary Birds. Moreover, Cariamas may possibly be akin to formidable extinct terrestrial predatory birds, *Diatryma*, which may have hunted in a manner not very unlike that of today's Secretary Bird. At one time I used to regard it as scarcely possible that the Secretary Bird could be more closely related to Cariamas than to eagles; but that one case of egg white analysis suggests that the matter should be pursued further, and I am bound to say that I now have my doubts that the familiar Secretary Bird is actually the terrestrial eagle that we usually think it is. Meantime we must leave it, as a familiar, but a very odd bird of prey indeed.

Chapter 13
Little Owls, Scops Owls and Owlets

Owls, as already stated, are far less well known than are the diurnal raptors of Africa—or for that matter of most other places. This applies in particular to the small owls of Africa, none of which have been thoroughly studied within the continent. In fact, one could say that the only one of the small owls of Africa that is at all well known is the Little Owl of Europe, which migrates to and breeds in North and North-West Africa, and is not properly a bird of the Ethiopian region.

The other small owls of Africa include five tiny, insectivorous, Scops Owls, one of which, Bruce's Scops Owl, is only a very rare vagrant and may be neglected. Whether the White-faced Owl, or White-faced Scops Owl as it is sometimes called, should be regarded in the same class is open to question; it is considerably larger than the Little Owl, but smaller than the smallest of the owls in the next chapter. Since it is sometimes included with Scops Owls it seems best to discuss it here. Then there are five species of Owlets, of which the Pearl-spotted is among the smallest of predatory birds, little bigger than a sparrow; others are larger. One or other of these small owls occurs in most parts of Africa, but seldom more than two together in any area.

The **Little Owl** is one of the commonest, if not the commonest of all owls in Europe, a successful and efficient little bird that hunts mainly by night, but also to some extent in daylight, and has the facial disc less developed than in purely nocturnal owls. It is also common in the Mediterranean countries of North and North-West Africa. Within tropical Africa it is only common in northern Somalia, the former British Somaliland, where it is the commonest owl. It is numerous here in thornbush but, as usual, we run into an ecological problem almost at once. The Little Owl does not occur in the southern part of Somalia, or further south, in country very similar to that in northern Somalia. There is no obvious reason for this, since it appears to have no competitor and no counterpart. In Somalia it occurs alongside the White-faced Owl, which is somewhat larger, and the smaller Scops Owl and Pearl-spotted Owlet. Yet in thornbush in northern Kenya one may find these other three, but no Little Owls. One just has to leave it at that—inexplicable.

In Europe there is much controversy over whether or not the Little Owl damages human interests by consuming the young of gamebirds. In Africa it seems, like most small and some large owls, to be chiefly insectivorous. It is all the more inexplicable, therefore, that it should not have colonised other parts of Africa, south of the Horn, where there are plenty of insects. It is difficult to believe that this can have been because of competition from any other species, for the Little Owl seems well able to look after itself elsewhere.

The smallest African Owl, the **Scops Owl**, occurs in much the same area as the Little Owl in Europe, though not so far north. In Africa it is much more widespread, found throughout the continent outside forests but rather local. In North Africa the European Scops Owl breeds, and is augmented by migrants in winter. In Africa south of the Sahara the African Scops Owl, now regarded as only a race of the Scops Owl, is common in woodland and thornbush all through the warmer lowlands, avoiding forests and mountain ranges, where the night temperatures are low. Like the Little Owl it is a successful and efficient little bird, but occurs wherever conditions suit it, and is not inexplicably absent from apparently suitable areas.

One does not see Scops Owls by day, for they then hide in leafy trees. Their small size makes them very difficult to detect in such cover; if they are found at all it is by chance, or because they may be mobbed by small birds. When observed by day they remain quite still, but compress the feathers and stretch upwards so that they look thinner than they really are, and more like a bit of dead stump. The only other birds that I know of that do this are some small bitterns that live in reeds and some nightjars; presumably the object is concealment.

At dusk the presence of the Scops Owl becomes evident, for it calls before the last of the daylight is gone and usually continues to call for much of the night. Unlike Nightjars, which call only in moonlight, or at dawn and dusk, owls continue to call at intervals for much of the night, and Scops Owls are no exception. For me this

9. *Above*, Although the largest African Eagle, the Martial Eagle is not the most powerful and feeds mainly on gamebirds. This female attends, but does not brood, her small downy chick.

Below, A Verreaux's Eagle feeding its young on hyrax. This magnificent eagle lives on rocky hills and preys almost exclusively on the local hyrax.

10. The African Hobby is a small, very swift falcon that feeds mainly on insects and small birds. This one is in first year immature plumage.

Little Owls, Scops Owls and Owlets

call—a short melodious, somewhat ventriloquial trill, "trr", has been characteristic of every district I have lived in in tropical Africa, and of every good camp in the bush. It is a sound I love to hear, and it can also be heard in towns as long as these are well enough wooded. The call is heard round the campfire at dusk, accompanies one to bed, and if one wakes in the still small hours the Scops Owl probably will still be calling, though all else may be silent.

Having heard the call it is still far from easy to see the tiny bird that makes it. It is impossible for a human being to see well enough by night to pick out the owl as it perches high up in a tree, and when a torch is used the owl usually falls silent and cannot be located at all. When it re-starts it will probably be found to have flown to another perch. Moreover, the call has a ventriloquial character making it difficult to locate precisely, so that even with a torch the bird is hard to find. That, at least, has been my experience. Others say that it is tame and easy to approach on a perch at night. In Nigeria I found that it was commoner near the haunts of men than it was in uninhabited woodlands; but in East Africa it has appeared to call just as commonly in uninhabited as in inhabited country.

The Scops Owl is an entirely nocturnal hunter with a large facial disc and prominent ear-tufts. The latter are presumably nothing to do with hunting, and may be ornaments used in nuptial display, though I know of no good explanation for their occurrence in some owls, but not in others. At any rate they result in the imaginative name "Petit Duc" or Little Duke being applied to the Scops Owl in France, as opposed to the "Grand Duc" or Eagle Owl. I once handled a Scops Owl caught in a mist net set for migrants in the Camargue, and the name is apt, for this exquisitely made little bundle of feathers had all the snapping ferocity one would expect of a much bigger predator, and its yellow eyes, finely veined and marbled with red, were no whit less beautiful than the great glowing orbs of the Eagle Owl itself. Many owls have these brilliant yellow eyes, others having soft, liquid, dark brown eyes. What advantage there may be between one and the other is not clear.

Although the African Scops Owl is found everywhere in lowland Africa, apart from forests and deserts, it has no widespread counterpart in forests. Three other little Scops Owls occur, the **Cinnamon Scops Owl** in West Africa, the **Russet Scops Owl**, or Pemba Scops Owl, on Pemba Island (and also Madagascar and the Comoros), and **Morden's Scops Owl** in a few square miles of the Arabuko–Sokoke Forest in Kenya; but they are all very local. Inside lowland and highland forests alike no owl takes the place of the Scops Owl that is so common in thornbush and savanna. Perhaps a species that is strictly nocturnal outside forests would find it impossible to hunt successfully in the deeper gloom of the tropical forest itself.

Morden's Scops Owl of the Arabuko–Sokoke Forest (which is not very dense forest) has only been discovered within the last five years, and as yet has been little studied. Its nest is unknown, but its voice, a repeated melodious tenor toot, is totally different to that of the Scops Owl. The nest of the Pemba Scops Owl is also unknown, and the inhabitants of Pemba think the bird is viviparous! Otherwise its habits seem similar to the Scops Owl; it calls much of the night, with a single monotonous note, "hu", perhaps not unlike that of the mainland Scops Owl. It lives in thickets of clove plantations on Pemba. It is of interest to observe that it occurs on Pemba, and the Oceanic islands, but not on Zanzibar, sharing this peculiar distribution with fruit bats or flying foxes of the genus *Pteropus*. One would think that if it could colonise the volcanic Comoro Islands it could fly across to Zanzibar and the mainland, but apparently not. Pemba is separated from the mainland of Africa by a deep channel, whereas Zanzibar is on the Continental shelf. All the same the sea crossing is far less than that undertaken annually by European Scops Owls such as the one I handled in the Camargue, which had presumably flown direct from the North African Coast. Why the Pemba Scops Owl, and much more so the Flying Fox, have not made it is obscure.

Several Scops Owls, including the Pemba Scops Owl, occur in more than one colour phase, a normal and a rufous or russet phase. The Cinnamon Scops Owl of West Africa is all russet; no grey or brown phases are known. It is found in two small areas of forest in West Africa, one in Cameroon and one in Ghana. Nothing has been learned of it in recent years, and it is known only from a few specimens in collections. Its voice is undescribed, and its nest has never been found. Thus, although it cannot be said that much is known about the common African Scops Owl, the other members of the genus are real birds of mystery, inhabiting only very small areas, only recently discovered, or not heard of for many years. Of the three, Morden's Scops Owl, which lives in a relatively accessible small area, is most likely to become well known within the near future.

The **White-faced Owl**, or White-faced Scops Owl, which is sometimes included in the genus *Otus* with Scops Owls, is considerably larger than any true Scops, and in my opinion is better left in a genus of its own, *Ptilopsis*. Its voice is quite different to that of any Scops Owl, a clear distinct "Cuck-oooh" uttered especially at dusk, but also at other times during the night. I have not heard it since I left West Africa twenty-three years ago, which will indicate that the species is not very common in most of East Africa, where I have camped out extensively. In Nigeria I had a pair in my garden at Lagos, and often heard them at other places though they were less common than Scops or Pearl-spotted Owlets. In Kenya they occur in the arid bush of the northern part of the country, not in the thornbush further south. There seems to be a gap in the range astride the Equator; they reappear in Tanzania about lat. 4°S. Why such a gap should occur is obscure; but there it is, and the only explanation I can think of concerns this owl's nesting habits.

The nesting site appears to be usually in an old or abandoned nest of another bird of prey. Some authorities say it breeds in shallow holes in trees, but the modern records indicate that it mainly uses other birds' nests—in other words, sites that are not sheltered from the rain. It is also reputed to make a flimsy nest of its own, but no modern naturalist has seen any such thing, and as it would be a habit quite unique among owls I believe the statement can be discounted. If, as I suspect, this owl breeds in the nests of other birds or in open situations such as a hollow or fork of a tree, then it would be an advantage to be sure of a longish dry season in which to breed. Long dry seasons are characteristic of the northern and southern tropics, and in north Kenya this owl inhabits only arid regions.

It is, however, impossible to say whether this suggested explanation for a problem of distribution has any weight, for no one has studied this owl in detail. What little is known indicates that it breeds towards the end of the dry season. At Ilorin, in Nigeria, where I was once stationed, it breeds in February and March, so that the newly-fledged young would be well placed to take advantage of the flush of insects appearing with the early rains in late March and April. In Darfur, where the rains are later, it breeds in May and June, and in the southern tropics mainly from August to October, likewise late in a long dry season. In South-West Africa and Natal it breeds from July to February. Maybe this means nothing at all, but there does appear to be an otherwise inexplicable gap in this owl's range, from a few degrees N. to about 4°S. of the Equator, which corresponds roughly with the area in which rains come in two seasons of the year, with shorter dry seasons between. This owl is not the only species of animal or bird that is absent from apparently suitable country in this belt; it also affects, for instance, the Common Kestrel, the Roan Antelope, and the Greater Kudu, to name a few. Anyway—it is a pity again that I did not study the pair I had in my garden at Lagos within a few weeks of reaching Africa for the first time.

The Owlets of the genus *Glaucidium* are among the smallest of African Owls. Two species inhabit savanna—the **Pearl-spotted** and the **Barred Owlets**—and three forest, the **Red-chested** and **Sjostedt's Barred Owlets**, the latter being larger than the others, and a new, as yet unnamed species just discovered in Liberia. Needless to say the savanna species are better known than the forest species, though none have been thoroughly studied. The best known is the Pearl-spotted Owlet, which is the most widespread, occurring in savanna and thornbush almost throughout Africa south of the Sahara, much as does the Scops Owl. The Barred Owlet inhabits the southern part of this range, but is larger than the Pearl-spotted, and much less common.

For all their diminutive size Pearl-spotted Owlets are not to be despised. They are nocturnal or crepuscular equivalents of the Pigmy Falcon, aggressive, partly diurnal birds that feed on small birds, lizards, and mammals in addition to insects, which are probably their main food. They are even piratical—a very rare thing in owls as far as is known. My brother was once stationed on the Yatta Plateau in Kenya and had a pair of Wood Hoopoes nesting in a hole in a tree in his garden. A Pearl-spotted Owlet, much smaller than the Wood Hoopoe, waited on a perch 15–20 ft. away for the Hoopoe to come to the nest with food, then dashed at it, knocked it over, and made off with the prey. It did this repeatedly but had to take the Wood Hoopoe by surprise to be successful.

Pearl-spotted Owlets are more diurnal than any other of the small African species of owls. One often sees them active long before dark, and I have recently watched one sitting on a bare bush in the Tsavo National Park at ten in the morning, apparently not discommoded by strong sunlight. They call by day as well as by night, but most usually make their presence known by calling an hour or so before dark. The call is a series of mews, first rising in pitch to a crescendo, then falling again. It is unmistakable, and enables one to locate an otherwise elusive little bird. The Pearl-spotted Owlet is not deliberately elusive or shy; it just happens to be very small and brown (smaller, for instance, than the White-crowned Bush Shrikes which shared its perch in the Tsavo Park) and does not move much by day unless pushed. It will then fly off with an undulating thrush or woodpecker-like flight.

Pearl-spotted and Barred Owlets breed in holes in trees, often those of barbets or woodpeckers which have been occupied or commandeered (which, we do not know). Other than this nothing is known of their breeding cycles, though probably there are places where they breed in gardens. The nest of two of the three forest-loving owlets, the Red-chested Owlet and the new species have never been described. That of the other, Sjostedt's Barred Owlet, is known from two records, both in holes in trees; in both cases the eggs, young, or the adult were taken by the collectors concerned. Apparently this larger owlet is likely to attract attention through the small birds that mob it. It is confined to the forests of Cameroon, where it is said to be not uncommon. But no one seems to have recorded the call, so that the standard method of locating owls (and nightjars) by night to study their activity is missing.

I once spent a night in a forest in Ankole, Western Uganda. It was a beautiful moonlight night, and I strolled along forest paths before going to bed. In the tops of some tall trees I heard a mewing call which reminded me of that of the Pearl-spotted Owlet, though fainter. When I turned a powerful torch on the treetops the calling stopped and I could not see the author. The Red-chested Owlet is not recorded from that locality, but it struck me as possible that this mewing was made by it. I have since listened to the recorded call of the red-chested Owlet and have confirmed that it was indeed that species that was calling. It also makes a soft fluting, or ringing "*hoo-hoo-hoo*" rather like the calls of the Boubou Shrike. These clues are offered to anyone able to study these small forest owlets, which will remain unknown long after the habits of larger owls have been fully studied.

Chapter 14
A Variety of Middle-sized Owls

In between the very small Scops Owls and Owlets and the large or very large Eagle and Fishing Owls are a number of owls that are neither big nor small, and which live mainly on small mammals and insects, seldom exclusively one or the other. They include the Barn Owl and the Cape Grass Owl, which have very different habits but are closely related to one another; two Long-eared Owls; Short-eared and Marsh Owls; the Tawny Owl and Woodford's Owl; and two extraordinary forest oddities, the Congo Bay Owl and the Maned Owl. From this it will be seen that although they prey on similar-sized animals and are in the same range they are not a homogeneous group like Eagle Owls or Scops Owls. I discuss them here mainly for convenience.

In practice one finds that the ten species of middle-sized owls can be split up into closely related pairs, some of which are ecological counterparts of one another, dividing the continent of Africa between them. Ecological pairs of this kind include the Short-eared and Marsh Owls, the Tawny and Woodford's Owl, and perhaps also the European and Abyssinian Long-eared Owls. The Barn Owl and Cape Grass Owl do not lend themselves to this arbitrary treatment, while the two forest oddities are (as usual) so little known in the field that they must be treated separately.

The **Barn Owl** could almost be described as the world's most successful bird, a title that it would contest with the Peregrine Falcon. It occurs on every continent, has found its way to many oceanic islands, and is widespread and common in many of the areas where it occurs. It is therefore all the more remarkable that there should be areas, such as southern Somalia and much of Ethiopia, where it does not occur, or is rare.

At first sight it would seem that this curious fact is explicable on the ground that the Barn Owl undoubtedly is largely commensal with man. It is not called the Barn Owl for nothing, and it is common in towns and even large cities in Europe and America. It likes to live and breed in old abandoned or ruined buildings made of permanent materials and has colonised the mine-dumps of Johannesburg. Over much of tropical Africa, and particularly perhaps in a place such as Somalia where the inhabitants are nomadic, living in small temporary dwellings that offer no secure nesting place for even the most opportunist barn owl, the type of permanent building that the Barn Owls like to live in is a feature of the very recent past. For practical purposes there were no permanent dwellings between the Limpopo and the southern Sahara at the beginning of this century, save perhaps in some of the towns of West Africa where the houses, though of mud, were rather more substantial than the thatched huts occupied by most African peasants.

It is very likely that since the colonisation of Africa, bringing with it the development of towns and permanent buildings, the Barn Owl has greatly increased its total numbers as a breeding bird within the tropics. In this it would simply repeat the example of several other species of birds that make use of human dwellings and structures, for instance most species of swallows, several species of swifts, and Red-winged Starlings (*Onychognathus morio*). The area where I live in Kenya is a residential suburb of Nairobi, and supports several pairs of Barn Owls; I would wager that in 1900 there were none.

However, this is not the whole explanation. The Barn Owl, in places, breeds in holes in trees or in the nests of Hammerkops, which are common birds over most parts of Africa south of the Sahara. Each pair of Hammerkops usually has several nests, only one of which they actually use, either for roosting or breeding. Even if they were powerfully possessive over this one, Barn Owls could get into and use the others. In the Baringo district—where there were no permanent buildings at all until well after the turn of the century, and are not many now—Barn Owls commonly use Hammerkops' nests for breeding. Even if Africa were totally uninhabited this type of desirable residence, together with holes in trees, would be available to the Barn Owl. Though there may not be very many Hammerkops' nests in Somalia, there are some; the Barn Owl does not seem to use them. There are certainly plenty in Ethiopia where, despite what Von Heuglin said long ago, I have found the Barn Owl rare or absent from most highland districts. In all these places the rats and mice on which the Barn Owl preys are abundant; it seems inexplicable that Barn Owls do not occur.

Do we see here an example of a bird that is spreading and increasing because of the increased human population of Africa, and especially because of the development of permanent structures? Has it only recently taken to using Hammerkops' nests, or did it use them before man came on the scene in any numbers, as seems more likely? We cannot know the answers to these questions, but the bird population of Africa is changing as a result of man's impact upon natural environments, and the Barn Owl is one species that tends to flourish as a result. It is not yet adversely affected, in most of Africa, by the toxic chemicals that may have reduced the population in civilised Europe.

I do not think the Barn Owl has been intensively studied anywhere in Africa, but several good studies of its behaviour have been made in Europe and America. So far as I can see, its behaviour differs little in Africa from that in these other areas. As with many other birds in tropical Africa the clutch and brood size is probably smaller than in temperate latitudes. In South Africa clutches vary from five to nine, whereas in tropical Africa they are usually two to four, occasionally up to seven. They are laid at intervals, as in all owls, so that in a large clutch there is a very great size difference between the youngest of the brood and the eldest. If mice continue to be abundant during the breeding season most or all of the young will be reared, but if a shortage develops the eldest will get the food and the youngest will die. It seems to me that there is a greater likelihood of breeding being successful in a secure nesting site, such as that afforded by a hollow in a tree, a Hammerkop's nest, or a cranny in a building, than could be expected by any owl that breeds on the ground or in the open on another bird's nest. That may be one reason for the Barn Owl's notable success.

The **Cape Grass Owl**, which is the Barn Owl's nearest relative, is a very different bird. It does not live in towns or buildings, but in long grass, especially in rather damp situations, and breeds on the ground. It is confined largely to the southern third of Africa, but occurs in grasslands near Nairobi, and in the grasslands of Cameroon, the only locality in West Africa which is much like southern or East African highland grasslands. This is another proof that belts of similar vegetation have at one time or another extended right across Africa from East to West. The Cape Grass Owl probably spread to Cameroon in one of the glacial periods, when vegetation typical of much higher altitudes in East Africa occurred at lower levels. With the general retreat of the ice in the northern hemisphere it has been isolated in patches of highland grassland both in East Africa and Cameroon.

In such areas one would think that the Cape Grass Owl ought to flourish, for such grasslands abound in the rodents on which it feeds, and since it is one of the few owls that occur in grasslands it has little competition. Yet it appears to be rather rare and local in most of its range, though there are places in South Africa where it is the commonest owl. Probably it is often overlooked or misidentified, but nevertheless rather little has been recorded of its habits.

From what I have seen of the Cape Grass Owl, and from what is recorded elsewhere, it appears to be the nocturnal alternative of the harriers that are common on the dry grass plains in the European winter by day. The owl is present all the year round so far as we know, but certainly undertakes local movements and may suddenly appear relatively common in areas where rodents are temporarily abundant. It is well named, for it lives in long grass and is seldom seen unless one stumbles across it. If it were common it would be an important predator on grass mice and rats, but except in some parts of South Africa it scarcely can have much overall effect on rodent populations.

The Grass Owl rests in a form by day, like that used by harriers when on migration. This resting place resembles the nest, which is a slight structure of grass on the ground. Little in detail is recorded of its nesting habits, but it lays three or four white eggs, at varying intervals, and in the dry season, as one would expect. The young apparently use the old nest as sleeping quarters after they can fly, only later taking up a form of their own in the grass. Anyone who finds a nest of this species would do a service by watching it carefully over a period of time.

In habits the Grass Owl is very much more like the Short-eared and the Marsh Owl than it is like its relative the Barn Owl. It does not occur in areas inhabited by the Short-eared Owl, but occurs alongside the Marsh Owl. The latter, however, is a much more widespread and common species as a whole in Africa, and though one cannot say that there is direct competition between Grass Owls and Marsh Owls this could be a contributory reason for the scarcity of Grass Owls in some parts of the continent.

The **Short-eared** and **Marsh Owls** are birds of a feather. In Africa they live in grasslands, marshes, and in low shrubby vegetation, but frequently prefer to feed near swampy or marshy areas. The Short-eared Owl is a European species that is reputed to breed in Morocco, though this is contested. It visits the northern part of tropical Africa in winter, but not in large numbers. The Marsh Owl, often called the Algerian Marsh Owl, breeds from North Africa to the Cape, and is locally common. It replaces the Short-eared Owl in Africa, especially south of the Equator, where the Short-eared does not occur.

The Marsh Owl is not confined to marshy places, though it may prefer to hunt and breed in the longer vegetation associated with such places. It occurs commonly in the grasslands of the Rift Valley and elsewhere. On the Bauchi Plateau of Nigeria its local movements are seasonally controlled by rainfall. In the wet season it is widespread, but in the dry season concentrates in swamps and bogs, where it breeds. Here it is relatively very common, and a large swamp will hold several pairs.

Observations of the Marsh Owl in this area—far more comprehensive than for most African Owls—show that the pairs begin display as soon as the country dries in October. The owls call, and also clap their wings, flying around in wide circles, and defending their territory against neighbouring pairs, except when a greater danger threatens, when several adjacent pairs may combine to mob the intruder. Eggs are laid (three to six per nest) from October onwards, and by January the latest clutches have hatched. All young would be on the wing and able to fend for themselves before the following rainy season began.

From what is known about this species at the nest and elsewhere it seems to be an ecological counterpart in Africa of the European Short-eared Owl with very similar behaviour. The latter also performs circling and wing-clapping nuptial displays, calling as it does. Both species, when disturbed at the nest, perform injury-feigning displays, which are often seen in owls but very seldom in diurnal birds of prey. In the Marsh Owl the birds fly in tight circles, then crash to the ground and flap about, squealing. It is most likely that this device would serve to attract some such possible predator as a dog or jackal away from the vulnerable young or eggs in their nest on the ground. Such displays are also seen, however, in some other owls where their usefulness is more obscure. This may be a type of behaviour evolved in ground-breeding owls, persisting in some that breed in trees.

Although the Marsh Owl is locally common, even semi-colonial, it is not universal. It likes areas where the grass is relatively short, knee or thigh rather than head or shoulder high. In Nigeria, for instance, it was rare or absent from the long grass savannas of the areas south of the Niger; I only once saw one, and that was on an island in the Niger itself. It is common in the Sudd of the Sudan, and in parts of Kenya and South Africa. But it does not by any means inhabit all grassland areas, and is not to be found in well wooded savannas, unless these are interspersed with wide expanses of swampy ground and short grass, as sometimes happens. Probably, although it likes to roost and nest in the tall coarse vegetation of swampy areas it prefers to have available areas of short grass or cultivation in which to hunt. Roadsides are a favourite area for hunting, no doubt because the road itself is an open place where mice can easily be caught. This results in heavy mortality, at least in Kenya, where many of the Marsh Owls I have seen have been corpses, killed by cars at night. Despite its name, areas covered with a uniform stand of tall marsh grasses, or the type of long grass associated with certain savannas, would be unsuited to this owl. But not enough is known or recorded of its habits and habitat preferences to be certain of this.

Long-eared Owls belong to the same genus as the Short-eared and Marsh Owls, but are very different in habits. They are birds of woodland or forest, and the European Long-eared Owl prefers coniferous woods, though where it is common it occurs also in broad-leaved woodlands. In Europe one would tend to find Tawny Owls the common species in broad-leaved deciduous woodland, Long-eared in coniferous woods. In such woods it usually breeds in the abandoned nests of other birds, rarely on the ground. It feeds on small mammals, birds, and insects, taking more birds than do most owls.

In Africa the two species, the European and Abyssinian Long-eared Owls do not occur in the same part of the continent. The European Long-eared Owl breeds from Morocco to Tunisia, frequenting the mixture of pines, cedars, and oak woods that clothe the slopes of the Rif and Atlas. The only other owl that occurs here and might compete with it is the Tawny Owl, and there are probably ecological preferences on both sides that prevent excessive competition. Long-eared Owls hunt over open country as well as in woods, but are less obvious and less vociferous than are Tawny Owls in most places where the two occur together.

The Abyssinian Long-eared Owl occurs only in the highlands of Ethiopia, Mount Kenya, and in the high mountains of the Eastern Congo. It is practically speaking unknown over the whole of this range, but it is likely that it is largely confined to highland forests of cedar and *Podocarpus*—primitive conifers—that occur in these mountainous areas. In Ethiopia it is said to occur in bushy ravines, but in the last few centuries practically all forest on most of the Ethiopian plateau has been destroyed by human cultivation, even on the very steepest slopes. These owls may formerly have been more common in extensive cedar woods, but may now be reduced in numbers and confined to the scrub-covered gullies with occasional cedars, which are too rocky and steep for even Ethiopians to cultivate. In travels in Ethiopia I have never seen it, nor heard any owl at night that might be it, but a friend has seen a number in Giant Heath is the high Bale Mountains.

The remaining ecological "pair" is composed of the Tawny Owl and Woodford's owl. They are actually in different genera, but have rather similar habits. The **Tawny Owl** is another Palearctic bird that occurs only in North-West Africa, where it breeds from Morocco to Tunisia. It is unlikely that it has been studied in great detail in these countries but by reason of studies made in Britain and Europe it is probably the best known of all owls after the Barn Owl, perhaps even better known. Since its occurrence in Africa is only an extension of its Palearctic range, and as it does not migrate further south, those who are interested may consult the European studies for details of its habits.

Woodford's Owl is a widespread species, occurring wherever there is forest south of the Sahara in Africa. It is nocturnal, entirely resident where it occurs, and very secretive, so that little in detail is known of its habits despite the fact that it is the commonest forest owl in Africa. Its tastes in habitat are catholic; I have seen it in coastal bush in Kenya, at 11,500 feet in the Ethiopian Highlands, and have heard it or seen it at various altitudes in between. It does not appear to be confined to either broad-leaved or coniferous forest, though it seems commonest in mixed broad-leaved woodlands of no great height, such as the olive forests of Natal or the Kenya Highlands. However, it also occurs in dense tropical forest in much hotter and wetter climates.

A pair of Woodford's Owls lives in the forest opposite my house, and I hear them calling almost every night. However, it is so difficult to find and observe them in the forest at night, and they are so disinclined to move by day, that I have failed to learn much about them. They resemble Tawny Owls in that they have favourite roosting sites to which they return day after day, even in a forest where there is an almost unlimited selection of apparently suitable roosting places. The pair in the forest opposite my house roost regularly in a creeper-covered tree, deserting it only when the creeper loses its leaves in a drought. I found this roost by chance some years ago, and now have a path to it; the owls sit there and gaze at me when I visit them, and are disinclined to fly. But there our acquaintance stops, and I have not found where they nest, though I know that they nest in the early part of the year, for I have seen young with the parents in March.

Like the Tawny Owl, Woodford's Owl nests in holes in trees. Few nests have been found or are recorded in the literature, but they are usually not very high up in trees, and are in hollow branches or an open cavity—the sort of site that is most often used by the Tawny Owl. Woodford's Owl lays a very small clutch of eggs for an owl of its size, one or two, and there is the usual interval between the eggs, so that the young differ markedly in size. In hollow branches the growing owlets come up to the entrance of the nest to receive prey.

Woodford's Owl may always be located by its call, which is unlike that of any other African Owl. One call is a high pitched but rather melodious howl "oowaaow", another a sort of deep chuckle "whu-uh-uh, whu-uh". In suitable forest country, where one has no inkling of this owl's presence by day, it will be found far more common than expected by night, starting to call soon after dark. After dawn, however, it might take weeks to find the roosts of the pairs that live in quite a small patch of forest, so that anyone who knows a regular roost will be well advised to watch it keenly.

The remaining owls of this group are the two oddities, the Congo Bay Owl and the Maned Owl. Only one specimen of the **Congo Bay Owl** is known; another in captivity proved only a rumour. The single specimen came from a forest at 7500 feet north-west of Lake Tanganyika, in an area unlikely to be visited by ornithologists for some time. So it will probably remain a bird of mystery as far as Africa is concerned. It is worth noting, however, that the only other species of Bay Owl occurs in India and the Far East. The African Bay Owl therefore probably represents a relic of some long past time when Asian and African forests were connected. A similar case is that of the Congo Peacock, *Afropavo congensis*. Perhaps, like the Congo Peacock, the Bay Owl will be found more commonly than is supposed when anyone gets a chance to study that area again.

The **Maned Owl** is a unique bird, not closely related to any other African Owl, and in a monotypic genus. It occurs only in the forests of Cameroon and Upper Guinea, and there is a gap of 1500 miles between the extremes of its range in Liberia and Cameroon. It does not seem to occur in any of the country in between, though as it is a secretive and nocturnal species it could be overlooked. However, the Upper Guinea Forest and the Cameroons represent two areas that probably remained forested in periods when the climate was much drier than it is now, when they were separated by savannas reaching the sea. Several other raptors have a similar distribution; one may mention the Congo Serpent Eagle and Cassin's Hawk Eagle. All the same, one wonders why, when forest now extends over much of the ground in between, the owl and the other raptors do not apparently reoccupy more territory.

Little is known about the Maned Owl. Its calls and breeding habits are quite undescribed, and the collectors who obtained most of the examples that have been found shot it at once and did not bother to watch it. Although quite a large bird, larger than the Barn Owl, it has weak feet and all the known specimens that have been examined had eaten nothing but insects, and a substance like squashed green peas—perhaps some sort of forest fruit. Attention is attracted to this bird sometimes by the small birds that mob it, apparently without real reason if it eats only insects. To the next person who finds one by this means I suggest that he does not shoot it for a museum, but observes it carefully. Many owls are very sedentary, and if their daytime roost is once discovered it will quite likely be used again. It is only by such forbearance, followed by observation, that we have any real chance of learning more about this mystery bird.

Chapter 15
Eagle Owls and Fishing Owls

Eagle Owls, all of which belong to one genus, *Bubo*, are the largest and finest of owls and are spectacular and powerful birds of prey. Seven species occur in Africa, of which only one, the European Eagle Owl, occurs outside the continent. Three of the species, Shelley's, Fraser's (or the Nduk Eagle Owl) and the Akun Eagle Owl are little known inhabitants of dense tropical forest, rare without apparent good reason, as is so often the case among forest-loving owls. The other four are probably better known than most owls in Africa, though only one, the Spotted Eagle Owl, has been exhaustively studied; the results of this study await publication.

Among the four species that occur in Africa outside forests there is little or no competition for living space. Each occurs only or mainly in one habitat, and securely fills the eagle owl niche in that habitat. In North-West Africa, and in the deserts of the Palearctic region, the **European Eagle Owl**, with its desert race, sometimes regarded as a separate species, *Bubo b. ascalaphus*, occurs. This is the largest of all the world's owls, and is a magnificent creature, seldom seen by day. It is appropriately named "Grand Duc" by the French, but is put to despicable use by them and by some other continental people. Tethered, it is used to attract other birds of prey to mob it, or small birds, which are then shot. Usually, however, smaller owls are used for this purpose, particularly in Italy—a country which is a conservationist's nightmare, infinitely less conscious of its heritage of wildlife than most so called primitive African countries.

The European Eagle Owl has been quite extensively studied in those parts of Europe where it occurs, but it has not been studied in detail in Africa. Morocco or Algeria would be interesting countries in which to study this grand bird, for there both the typical and the desert races occur. It may seem surprising that such a large bird can exist at all in true desert. However, in many deserts there are surprising numbers of small nocturnal rodents and in the very open terrain the owl probably has little difficulty in catching them. Like the rodents themselves the owl can avoid the scorching heat of the desert summer at midday by roosting in the shade, and at night the desert is seldom really hot. The owl obtains the water it needs from the bodies of its prey; in any case, how many people have ever seen a wild owl of any species drinking?

Personally I wonder whether the Desert Eagle Owl really occurs in the heart of the starkest desert. I say this because I once spent some time in the deserts of Arabia, on the edge of the Empty Quarter. Here, although I hardly expected to find many diurnal birds of prey active, I did expect to find owls at night. Yet I saw none, nor did I ever hear the deep hoot that would signal the presence of an eagle owl. In the dead stillness of a quiet desert night, which is equalled only in the lifeless wastes of the Arctic or Antarctic, such a hoot would carry a long way, and a listening man would detect an eagle owl in suitable country with ease. But I heard nothing at any of several camps, usually in rather well vegetated valleys flanked with cliffs, where one might have expected eagle owls to occur.

The **Spotted Eagle Owl** is the smallest, the commonest, and the most widespread of the genus in most of Africa. It occurs in thornbush, savanna, and even inside forested areas where there are rocky hills. It usually inhabits rocky terrain, but quite a small pile of rocks will serve its purpose, and it will sometimes be found in country without any rocks at all, as in the Kalahari. However, where there are many small rocky kopjes in savanna, this owl is likely to be much commoner than it is elsewhere. It avoids completely open grass plains.

The Spotted Eagle Owl is the African representative of a type of eagle owl found over much of the Old World. I have flushed similar eagle owls in India from rocky hills, where they appear to behave in just the same way as they do in Africa. Usually the Spotted Eagle Owl nests on the ground, under a rock or on a ledge of a cliff, rarely in hollow trees. In most of Africa it does not use other birds' nests, though it must use these when no rocks are available. Particular areas harbour a pair of Spotted Eagles Owl year after year. What little study I was able to make of them in Embu district years ago indicated that they bred in the dry season, laying usually about August, and produced one or two young from clutches of two or three eggs. These young usually got on the wing about October–November, when the first rains had brought out a flush of insects. Although it can

11. *Above,* The Peregrine Falcon is uncommon or rare throughout the continent. This unusually accessible nest site is on a hill in Kenya.

Below, The Harrier Hawk or Gymnogene preys on small creatures living in holes, under bark, etc. Nest sites are usually in trees, although this bird has chosen a cliff face to rear its young.

12. Four African owls. *Above*, Pearl-spotted Owlet and Barn Owl; *below*, Spotted Eagle Owl and Woodford's Owl.

and does kill quite large prey on occasion the Spotted Eagle Owl is probably more dependent on insects than some of its larger relatives.

In the Kalahari I have seen the Spotted Eagle Owl in broad daylight accompanying a honey badger on the prowl, presumably in the hope of catching some mice that the badger might disturb from burrows. The badger was alternately followed by the owl and a Chanting Goshawk, and there was no doubt that both came to the badger from some distance away. Usually, however, this eagle owl is not very active by day, though it will fly more readily than will some of the more strictly nocturnal owls, and can evidently see quite well enough in broad daylight. Its behaviour in the Kalahari is another example of how life in the desert forces a species that usually inhabits some less rigorous environment to be more enterprising. In the Kalahari also this species has been known to kill so formidable a bird as an adult Lanner Falcon, presumably catching it unawares on the roost at night.

The **Cape** or **Mountain Eagle Owl** is another species that nests on the ground. It is, however, confined to mountainous habitat where no other species of eagle owl occurs, so it has the field to itself. It has a discontinuous distribution in mountains from South Africa to Ethiopia, with races in South Africa, East Africa and Ethiopia. Its altitude range appears to vary and it occurs at lower altitudes in South Africa than elsewhere. In Kenya, where the resident race is known as Mackinder's Eagle Owl (after Sir Halford Mackinder, who made the first ascent of Mount Kenya), it does not occur much below 7500 feet above sea level (though I have seen one at 6000 feet). In Ethiopia, where the race *B. capensis dilloni* occurs in high mountains, I have not seen or heard it below 9500 feet, though this is not to say that in that little-known country it may not occur at lower altitudes.

In the high mountains of East Africa and Ethiopia there are often very abundant small rodents, which honeycomb the ground with their burrows. However, the fact that the rodents are present in numbers does not necessarily mean that the Mountain Eagle Owl has plenty of available food. The climate of these heights has been aptly described as "summer all day and winter all night" and in Ethiopia at least I found that upland pastures at 13,000 feet, swarming with active rodents by day, showed little or no movement by night;

the rodents had gone below to keep warm. Yet the hooting of Mountain Eagle Owls among the giant crags of Semien, or the lava flows of the Mendebo Mountains of Bale, showed that the owls were there and were active. Perhaps, in such situations, they eat young hyrax, which may be more active at night; or perhaps they do much of their hunting at dusk before the rats have finally gone underground—though I myself have seen nothing to suggest this.

At altitudes where the nocturnal cold is not so extreme, as on the Mau Narok plateau of Kenya, at around 9000 feet, every little valley seems to hold a pair of Mackinder's Eagle Owls. They breed on the ground in situations where they would seem very vulnerable to attack, in country where jackals, mongooses, wild cats and other nocturnal mammalian predators, including the leopard, are common. The owls must be able to defend themselves against interference by any such, probably by threat display, which in an eagle owl can be quite terrifying, and will disconcert much larger creatures than the owl itself, or by distraction displays, which have not been described in this species.

In these areas the main prey of the Mountain Eagle Owl is the mole rat, *Tachyoryctes*. The mole rat apparently has a thin time of it, in danger from Augur Buzzards and Tawny Eagles by day, and the Mackinder's Eagle Owls by night. Yet in this area it has increased, largely because ploughing up the ground for wheat has almost exterminated the mole snakes that used to eat the young rats in their burrows, where no owl or buzzard could take them. The owls and buzzards, though they can be regarded as beneficial, maintain such large territories that it is unlikely that they could make any real impact on the very large population of mole rats.

In the Bale Mountains of Ethiopia the multitudes of rodents are preyed upon by day by several raptorial birds, also by the Thick-billed Ravens that are common there, and by an unusual mammalian predator, the Semien Fox, found only in Ethiopia. In an attempt to find out what the owls were eating I sought nest-sites and roosts, which I found on ledges at the base of low cliffs. Such places are usually strewn with castings, from which one can deduce what the owl eats. In Bale, at 9500 feet in cedar forests, I found that the castings of the owls contained an extraordinary number of skulls of bats, alternating with those of mole rats in almost equal proportions. One can understand that a mole rat, which is not a fast mover, has poor eyesight, and which makes quite an appreciable noise as it burrows close to the surface, is easily caught by an eagle owl. But quite how an owl would catch large numbers of bats is not so easy to understand; one would suppose them to be flying about actively at night, and not at all easy to catch. All the Bale bats' skulls were of a frugivorous species, however, so perhaps they were surprised in trees where they were feeding. I could not identify the species, for at the time of year I was there there were no trees in fruit, and no fruit bats to be seen.

The Mountain Eagle Owl is the only species of eagle owl which normally occurs in the terrain it frequents. Here and there, on the lower fringes of its altitude range it may occur together with the Spotted Eagle Owl or with **Verreaux's** (or the Milky) **Eagle Owl**, the largest owl in tropical Africa and one of the largest in the world. Verreaux's Eagle Owl is a bird of riverine Acacia forests, and of broad-leaved woodlands or forests interspersed with grassy glades. It is not by any means universal; but a few pairs will be found in many types of habitat. It lives alongside the Spotted Eagle Owl in many areas, but scarcely competes with the latter, for the Spotted Eagle Owl likes open ground and rocky hillsides while Verreaux's for choice inhabits any patches of woodland there may be. Verreaux's is also a very much more powerful bird than is the Spotted Eagle Owl, habitually taking quite large mammals, whereas the Spotted Eagle Owl is more dependent on small mammals and insects. In the tropical African savannas there are often so many insects that it is inconceivable that either species could ever experience a shortage that would lead to actual competition for available prey.

Verreaux's Eagle Owl is the only species I have studied in any detail, and that not as much as I would like. It differs from all other eagle owls in Africa in that its eyes are dark brown, not brilliant yellow or orange, like the great glowing orbs of Mackinder's Eagle Owl. What may be the reason for this difference is impossible to say at present, but one may at least conjecture that it has nothing to do with actual eyesight, which appears to be as acute as is necessary in Verreaux's Eagle Owl. Verreaux's Eagle Owl has, however, upper eyelids which are rather bright orange or pink on their outer surface, an adornment not so far as I know possessed by other eagle owls. From this one may perhaps conjecture that the bright orange colour may be used in some form of display as yet undescribed, and which could perhaps best be observed in captive birds. I have never noted any possible reason for it among wild Verreaux's Eagle Owls.

Verreaux's Eagle Owl nests high in trees, in holes or more often in the old nests of other birds of prey, or of Hammerkops. It takes over the latter in the course of construction, for once the Hammerkop's nest is complete the owl could not get into it at all—though Barn Owls can and do. The Hammerkop first fashions an ordinary basin-like structure, over which it later builds a roof. The eagle owl appropriates the nest before the roof is put on, and I have watched one sitting there unperturbed while an enraged Hammerkop made repeated passes over its head. The owl laid in the nest a few days later, and the Hammerkop had to start all over again elsewhere.

Usually I have found Verreaux's Eagle Owls nesting in unoccupied or abandoned nests of eagles and vultures. The first that I watched was in an old Wahlberg's Eagle's nest, one which was successively occupied by the original owner, the owl, and a Long-crested Eagle. The nest was fifty feet up in a slippery-barked fig tree, and when I went to watch the owl at night from a hide I had one arm in plaster. As I was climbing the tree the owl came and sat on the topmost branches, and mindful of the possibility of attack I was very alarmed indeed. Had she attacked me it is doubtful whether I could have held on and defended myself, and I could either have been seriously clawed by the owl or have fallen from the tree, probably killing myself. I was still more alarmed when, after midnight, and stiff after a long sit, I had to descend the tree in pitch darkness. Again the owl, which had not fed her young one all that time, probably because she knew I was there, came and perched a few feet above me, snapping her beak and grunting in the dark. Fortunately she did nothing. The nest was near a swamp, and I was bitten badly by mosquitoes. My observations were later curtailed by a sharp attack of malaria, after which I gave the old bird best.

The second nest was in a garden not far from my home, in an abandoned Hooded Vulture's nest in a dead and rotten fig. It was completely open by day, and the single young one it contained was persistently attacked in the nest by Augur Buzzards and Pied Crows until it finally fell out. In trepidation lest the tree would collapse, we returned it, and constructed a sort of fence round it which kept off the buzzards and crows, but did not hinder the owl when it came to attend and feed its young one.

Although I made no really sustained observations, for I was very hard-pressed with other affairs at the time, we obtained quite a lot of data on the food of this owl. The old birds used to perch in two tall leafy trees thirty yards from the nest, and beneath these trees they strewed the remnants of their prey. They fed on mammals as large as a cane rat and bushbaby—the latter an animal that could only be caught at night. They also ate snakes, frogs, many insects, and some birds, including such unlikely types as sunbirds. which they presumably caught in their nests or on roosts. But especially they ate hedgehogs, again a species of prey that could hardly be taken by day (though I have known a Bateleur bring one to its nest, probably picked up dead). The hedgehogs were neatly skinned by the owl, and the prickly skin dropped from the perch, while the body was fed to the young. It was a good example of how it does not necessarily serve an animal to be nocturnal; if immune from avian predation by day it is in danger by night.

I later mention the extraordinary mutual display of a pair of Verreaux's Eagle Owls, facing each other on a perch and grunting a duet for half an hour on end. At this nest we also saw remarkable distraction displays, by the male only; the female merely sat close by and snapped her beak in anxiety. When we approached the nest the male would fly across our front from his perch in nearby Eucalyptus trees, falling and flopping in flight, and eventually landing, apparently with difficulty, in the lower branches of a tree, where he would hang upside down. He accompanied this performance with an extraordinary raucous scream. It was certainly eye-catching, and it diverted any dogs that happened to be near. He would only do it once; if he failed, he did not try again. Presumably such distraction displays, which are not seen in diurnal birds of prey, but have been observed in the Marsh Owl and in the European Eagle Owl, may help to draw off nocturnal predators from nesting sites on the ground, though it seems to me doubtful if they would delude any determined predator that had once set out to climb a tree.

Eagle owls of several species are known to be predators on the young of other large birds of prey. In this Verreaux's Eagle Owl's nest we found the feathers of Pied Crows and of a Barn Owl, and in several cases where young eagles have disappeared from nests without trace we have suspected attack by an eagle owl, either a Spotted or a Verreaux's. In America the Great Horned Owl is known to take the young of buzzards (*Buteo*, spp.) and in Europe a Golden Eagle has been known to kill an eagle owl. The vicious attacks of the Augur Buzzards on our young Verreaux's Eagle Owl would undoubtedly have meant its premature death if we had not saved it. Here is one area where large birds of prey actively prey upon each other.

Of the three species of forest eagle owl there is little to say. They are so rare, and so little known in the areas where they occur that no good account of their habits can be given. One of them, the **Akun Eagle Owl**, appears to be mainly insectivorous, and to have small weak feet as befits a bird that does not ever kill anything very large. The other two appear to be powerful predators that can kill quite large mammals. The East African race of *Bubo poensis*, the Nduk Eagle Owl, *inter alia* eats bats, but this is not so surprising in view of the fact that at least two others species of eagle owls also eat bats. In the absence of any detailed knowledge on the habits of any of these three large forest owls we must just assume that they will be rather similar to those of other members of the genus, and leave it at that.

With these three owls we again find the extraordinary feature of very local distribution and rarity within a restricted range—so far as is known. Two, the Akun Eagle Owl and **Shelley's Eagle Owl**, are confined to the dense forests of West Africa. The third species, **Fraser's Eagle Owl**, has one race there and another living in a small isolated forest area in the Usambara Mountains near the East Coast of Africa. This race, the Nduk Eagle Owl, is sometimes regarded as a separate species, and one would think it isolated enough to have developed specific rank. Its presence in the Usambaras is one link in a chain of evidence to show that at one time forest extended right across Africa from West to East, separating the northern savannas from the southern. This, according to some authorities, was the case in comparatively recent geological times. If that is so it is curious that the Nduk Eagle Owl has not occupied forests on, for instance, Kilimanjaro, Mount Kenya, or in the Uganda–Congo border highlands. Perhaps this is because most of the forests in this region are at fairly high altitudes. It may be that only in the Usambaras, in East Africa, is there tropical forest sufficiently dense to support an owl that has its centre of distribution in the heartland of the vast tropical West African forests.

Fishing Owls are much less well known than eagle owls. There are three species, two of which occur only in the West African forests and must be dismissed at once as scarcely known at all. They are rare, local and have normally been shot as soon as seen. Young birds have occasionally been obtained, but the nests from which they came have not been described. One species, the Vermiculated Fishing Owl, is known to eat small fish, prawns, and an occasional bird. The third, Pel's Fishing Owl, is better known because it is more widespread, but even at that it is very little known. It is known to nest in other birds' abandoned nests, or perhaps in holes in trees, but no one has ever to my knowledge watched a nest for any length of time. It is known to eat both frogs and fish, on the evidence of stomach contents, but so far as I know no one has watched it hunting for long or observed how it catches these. It, and other fishing owls, like the Osprey and Fish Eagle, has sharp spicules on the underside of the toes to help in grasping the prey. The facial disc is less developed than in some owls, and the wings are not modified for silent flight. From this some have deduced that Pel's Owl is probably diurnal, but observation of its habits shows that it is strictly nocturnal.

I have seldom come across any of the fishing owls. Once, in Nigeria, I was lying very ill with malaria in the Niger flood plain. However, I thought interesting birds might be found there, so I sent my very intelligent house servant Momo, with a shotgun and two cartridges, to go and bring back any unusual large birds he might see. He came back with two, one of them a Pel's Fishing Owl with the head completely blown off, the other a Tiger Bittern, *Tigrisoma lineatum*, the only one that I ever saw. He was apologetic about the fishing owl's head but explained that the bird would not fly away, and that he could not see it in the very thick cover if he backed away far enough to kill it without destroying it. He said he thought it better to blow off its head than to blow it in half.

Another place where I found have Pel's Fishing Owl is along a tributary of the Omo River in South-west Ethiopia. Camping there with my brother I was intrigued by the hooting of a large owl along the river, which was dry except for a few pools in which fish and frogs were concentrated. The rather sonorous and unusually musical hoot did not resemble the call of any owl I knew, and the unmistakable grunt of Verreaux's Eagle Owl was also to be heard in the same area. I sought the bird by day, but could not find it. Later my brother, who is Game Warden in that area, both heard the hoot and saw the bird near his house. He found them not uncommon in forest along the Omo River. My own curiosity was eventually satisfied on a later visit, when I heard and saw the owls along the river. They roosted in pairs in great fig trees by day, and at evening came out and perched on snags above the river apparently fishing. Exploring further up river I found several other pairs, and concluded that there was one pair to 3-4 miles of tortuous river bed. Fish abounded in the pools and were probably easily caught in the shallows, though I did not see the owls succeed. The hoot is audible at least a quarter of a mile away, so that adjacent pairs could hear each other without coming too close. It is a double note "Hooomm-hut", with a slight pause between the two, and the male has a higher pitched call than the female. Although not strictly a forest bird Pel's Fishing Owl is not found away from forested riverine strips, though the river could be passing through very dry country without making any difference. The owl inhabits the river, not the surrounding country.

None of these fishing owls appears to occur along any highland forested river. They are all lowland tropical species. Perhaps this is because along lowland rivers, in the dry season, there are often expanses of sandbanks and stones, with a small trickle of water connecting large pools. In the rainy seasons, when the river comes down in flood, frogs and fish may be found in shallow water on the flood plain or in oxbow lakes, and are probably hunted there. What little is known of the breeding of these owls (and the nests of two have now been found) indicates that they breed in the dry season, when fish and frogs in isolated pools should be relatively easy to catch. But there are so few records that this may not always be the case.

When Professor Broekhuysen's studies of the Spotted Eagle Owl are published we may expect to have a model on which anyone can base comparative studies of other species of eagle owl. But the rare and elusive forest eagle owls, and the fishing owls, large and spectacular as they are, may well remain birds of mystery for many a year yet.

Part III
The Life of African Raptors

Chapter 16
Some Ecological and Distribution Problems

The facts given in Chapter 3 show that the size range, in both the diurnal Falconiforms and the nocturnal owls, is almost as great within Africa as it is for the world as a whole. The largest common resident raptor is the Lappet-faced Vulture, a huge bird weighing fifteen pounds or more with a wingspan of eight feet or more. Only the two American Condors, the European Black Vulture (which visits North Africa occasionally and may breed in Morocco) and perhaps the Himalayan Griffon, are larger. At the other extreme are the tiny Pigmy Falcon, barely bigger than a shrike and weighing 50–60 grams, and the thrush-sized Little Sparrowhawk. In between there is every variety of diurnal birds of prey from several large powerful eagles through buzzards and smaller eagles, kites, falcons, harriers, and sparrowhawks of various sizes, capable of taking a wide range of prey.

Among owls, a similar size range occurs. The largest typically African species, Verreaux's Eagle Owl, is one of the largest owls in the world and the smallest, the Scops Owl (with its near relatives) is one of the smallest. In between there are medium-sized owls such as the Spotted Eagle Owl, Woodford's Owl, the Barn Owl, Grass Owls, and the White-faced Scops Owl. Here too the variety and capacity for predation on various animals is great.

This variation is not only true for Africa as a whole, but it is also true of any habitat in Africa where a large variety of species occurs. If, for instance, we consider the richest habitat for both owls and diurnal raptors, woodland, we find that large vultures occur (though the woodland is not their favourite habitat). There are large eagles such as the Martial Eagle; snake-eating eagles, bird-eating eagles and hawks, rat-eating small eagles and buzzards, and various specialised types such as the Harrier Hawk, living upon nestlings, oil palm nuts and insects. Shrikes, rather fierce insectivorous birds which kill a variety of small lizards and young birds as well (and even on occasion birds as large as themselves), take on where the smallest predators, such as the Little Sparrowhawk, leave off. Among owls, the range is as great. Verreaux's Eagle Owl, and the Scops Owl both occur commonly in woodlands.

This may also be true of some less favourable habitats, with a smaller variety of species, such as mountains, deserts, or forests. Mountains have their large eagles, large vultures, bird-killing falcons, and smaller birds of prey. Though there is only one large owl in most of mountainous Africa, the Mountain Eagle Owl, Woodford's Owl occurs also in Giant Heath at 11,500 feet. Likewise in deserts there are diurnal raptors from large vultures to small falcons—though for only a few of these is the desert preferred habitat. In forests there are large eagles and small sparrowhawks, large eagle owls and owlets. Large vultures are excluded from the forest habitat only because any carrion there may be is lying on the forest floor, where they cannot get it. They hunt by sight, and are commonest in mountains, Acacia woodland, or semi-arid steppes where, although the number of large dead animals may actually be fewer than in forest or woodland, they can see them and find them. The only vulture that occurs in any numbers within forests is the Hooded Vulture, which is a scavenger on man's remains in the neighbourhood of villages, and will not come to a dead buffalo inside the forest canopy.

Thus, in theory at least, for the continent as a whole, or for any habitat within it, one can draw up charts showing the types of prey available and the raptors, diurnal or nocturnal that ought to or do feed upon these animals. Think of an animal or bird, in fact, and within limits there is a raptor potentially capable of killing it. One or two are even partly or wholly vegetarian. It all seems very well arranged by Nature.

However, when one comes to go into it in detail, as in the study of the community of raptors living in particular areas, some very surprising contradictions to this general idea present themselves. Quite often one finds that there is a potential food supply available in abundance, but the raptor that ought to be there to make use of it is not. Although, in general terms, it is true to say that various types of prey animals are exposed to risk at all hours of the twenty-four, there are some notable exceptions, quite inexplicable in terms of what is known about the habits of the raptors concerned.

Take, for instance, the case of the small mouse and insect-eating falcons such as the Common Kestrel, Lesser Kestrel, Greater or White-eyed Kestrel, and Red-footed Falcon. The Fox Kestrel might also be included, though it is larger and more powerful than these others. Of these the Common and Lesser Kestrels, and the Red-footed Falcon are largely or entirely migratory. Certainly, in almost every part of the continent, their numbers in the European winter would be greatly in excess of any resident numbers of the local races of the Common Kestrel. The Greater or White-eyed Kestrel is resident, but very local, and the Fox Kestrel is by no means abundant, occurring only near rocky cliffs or hills, where it can breed.

When one goes into the distribution of these little falcons in detail one finds that their prey—small mice and insects—while very abundant in most woodland and savanna in Africa—is either largely or entirely free of risk from them during the northern spring and summer, from say mid-April to mid-October. Common Kestrels, of the resident races *F. tinnunculus rufescens (carlo)* and *rupicolus*, inhabiting northern and southern Africa respectively, are in places quite common, but they are seldom nearly as common as their near relatives would be in the breeding season in Europe, and there are large tracts of apparently suitable country where they do not seem to occur at all. *F. t. rufescens*, in N. Nigeria, does not appear to have learned to use the old nests of other birds, such as crows, kites or herons, in which to breed, as *F. t. tinnunculus* has in Britain. And although the East African grass plains near Nairobi would appear to be ideal kestrel habitat, and is preferred habitat for the migrant races in winter, they appear to have no resident kestrels despite plenty of suitable cliffs, quarries, or abandoned or old nests of other large birds, in which the kestrels could nest. It is true that in this habitat the mouse-killing kestrel niche is to some extent occupied by the resident Black-shouldered Kite; but equally there are areas on the continent, such as South Africa, where the resident kestrels and the Black-shouldered Kite live side by side, so that the absence of resident kestrels from the East African plains can hardly be explained by possible competition with the kite.

An examination of this situation will show quite clearly that an abundant food supply, in the shape of mice or insects, goes practically scot-free of predation by day, and is certainly not preyed upon in relation to its abundance, except during the European winter, when the migrant raptors come in to take their toll. This can scarcely be explained by season for in some parts of East Africa it is dry, and grasshoppers and mice are abundant, from June–August, when one would expect any local resident kestrels to breed. Equally, in almost every part of the continent, counts would show that migrant small falcons in winter greatly outnumber any small falcons that are resident locally, irrespective of whether the weather is wet or dry. Some small falcons appear to be dependant upon insects swarming in wet weather, especially termites, and these include the European Hobby and Red-footed Falcon, which for preference winter in the southern third of Africa where it is wet in the period November–February.

A somewhat similar case concerns the harriers. Pallid and Montagu's Harriers are very abundant—or used to be twenty years ago—in many African savannas and grasslands during the winter, from October to March. They occur more or less irrespective of wet or dry weather as far south as the Cape, but winter in greater numbers in Nigeria, where this period is dry, than in Rhodesia, where it is wet. They prey on the abundant mice and large insects, with some small ground birds.

In Africa, apart from North-West Africa, which is properly a part of the Palearctic region, the only resident harriers are the rare Black Harrier of South Africa and the African Marsh Harrier of East and South Africa. West Africa has no resident harrier at all, though there are marshes there just as suitable for the African Marsh Harrier as those of Uganda or Katanga. In some other continents, such as N. America or Australia, where only one species of harrier is common, the species concerned has learned to make use of a wide variety of breeding habitats, wheatfields, grasslands and marshes. This has not happened in Africa. The resident harriers breed only rather sparingly in marshlands in the eastern half of the continent. The grass mice, and for that matter the West African frogs, do not have to worry about harriers.

This type of problem becomes even more puzzling when one encounters it in what appears to be a ubiquitous and highly successful bird, such as the Barn Owl. This species has managed to find its way to every continent, and to many oceanic islands, not even colonised by the almost equally cosmopolitan Peregrine. It is, as stated, common in many African cities, and also breeds in woodlands or Acacia savanna in various places. It feeds upon rats and mice, abundant everywhere, to a greater or lesser degree. Yet there are large areas of apparently suitable country where it is either absent or very rare. One such is Somalia, where it is very seldom recorded, though there are plenty of suitable breeding places. Why one should find Barn Owls breeding commonly in Hammerkops' nests in the Acacia woodland of Baringo district and not in Hammerkops' nests in almost identical woodland types along the Webe Shebeli river in Somalia is not easily explicable by anyone.

One may even find this sort of thing cropping up in what appears to be a very clear predator–prey relationship. Take, for instance, Verreaux's Eagle, a magnificent black bird that preys almost exclusively upon rock hyrax. Anyone who studied this eagle in the Matopos of Rhodesia or in Baringo district of Kenya would be justified in assuming that where there were hyrax to eat and rock cliffs to breed upon there Verreaux's Eagle would be as common as, in the nature of large eagles, it could be. But he would be wrong. There are places I know of in Kenya and Tanzania where the two apparent essentials—a supply of hyrax and a good nesting cliff occur—but no Verreaux's Eagles. I even know of one which is directly in line between, and in sight of two other breeding localities, but certainly far enough away from both not to be disturbed by the Verreaux's Eagles living on either. And this is an area of thornbush and savanna where the occurrence of most other eagles can be plotted on a map at a certain distance from one another with almost mathematical exactitude.

When one looks at the distribution of owls in forests it appears at first sight that their nocturnal habits and ability to see in poor light have favoured them in comparison to the diurnal raptors. Among the latter 29 species occur in forests, but only 13, or about 45% prefer it as habitat. Most of these, however, are rather widespread, and often fairly numerous in forests throughout the continent south of the Sahara. The Crowned Eagle, for instance, is relatively more numerous in many forests than is the Martial Eagle in savanna. There are a few species that are confined to the deepest and densest forests of the Congo and Upper Guinea, such as Cassin's Hawk Eagle and the Congo Serpent Eagle, but within these forests they probably have a rather wide range. Thus it seems that those diurnal raptors which have adapted to forest have become quite well suited

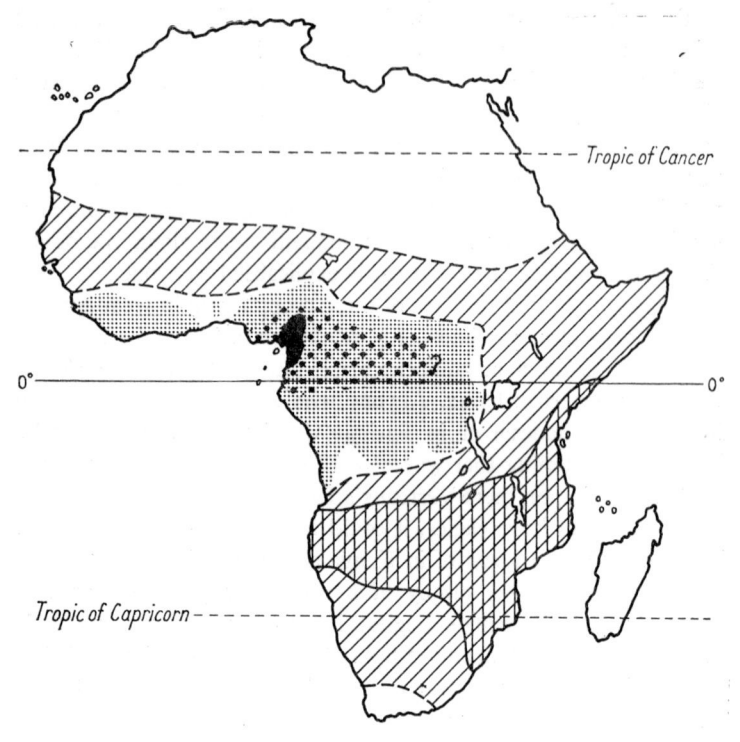

Fig. 7 Genus *Glaucidium*, Owlets.

- Pearl-spotted Owlet, *Glaucidium perlatum*; in open savanna all over Africa south of Sahara.
- Barred Owlet, *Glaucidium capense*; occurs within the range of *G. perlatum*, perhaps in different habitat.
- Red-chested Owlet, *Glaucidium tephronotum*; in West African forests and on Mount Elgon; distribution irregular and inconclusive within this general area.
- Sjostedt's Barred Owlet, *Glaucidium sjostedti*; only in Cameroon and Gabon.
- Equatorial forest.

Fig. 8 Some members of Genus *Bubo*, Eagle Owls.

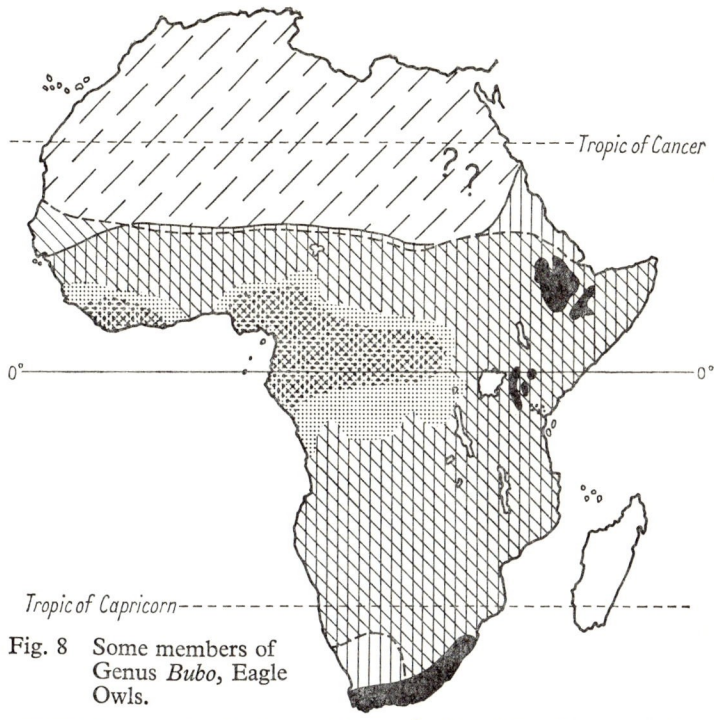

- ▨ Eagle Owl, *Bubo bubo* including the desert race *B. b. ascalaphus*.
- ▧ Verreaux's Eagle Owl, *Bubo lacteus*; in heavy woodland, forest patches, and riverine forest.
- ▥ Spotted Eagle Owl, *Bubo africanus*; range almost coincident with that of *B. lacteus* except in Eritrea, Mauretania, and Western Cape, but found in different country, open savanna and rocky hills, not heavy cover.
- ▦ Fraser's Eagle Owl, *Bubo poensis*; in West African forests extending in race *B. p. vosseleri*, the Nduk Eagle Owl, to the Usambara Mountains in Tanzania.
- ■ Cape or Mountain Eagle Owl, *Bubo capensis*; three races *B. c. capensis*, *B. c. mackinderi*, and *B. c. dilloni*, found respectively in mountains of Cape and Natal, East Africa, and Ethiopia within the range of *B. africanus* and *B. lacteus*.
  N.B. Shelley's Eagle Owl, *B. shelleyi* and Akun Eagle Owl, *B. leucostictus* have a more restricted distribution in forest within the range of *B. poensis*, but do not extend to the East Coast.
- ▒ Equatorial forest.

to this environment, and may be expected to be effective predators within it.

Among the owls, 13 species occur in forests and of these 11, or 85%, occur only in forests. If one includes the Fishing Owls the figures are 16 species of which 13 are confined to forest. At first sight this looks as if owls, with their vision adapted to poor light, and their stealthy as opposed to speedy or agile hunting habits, have taken over a more important section of the function of predation in forests than have the diurnal raptors. The number of owls that prefer the forest environment is 39% of all the owl species in Africa, whereas among diurnal raptors it is only 14%. Owls appear better adapted to life in forests, and a glance at Tables 10 and 11 (see pp. 296, 300) would lead one to expect to find owls, large or small, hunting in forests throughout the continent.

Although, however, it appears that the diurnal birds of prey have adapted reasonably well to the forest habitat in the cases where they have adopted it for preference the same cannot be said of owls. The distribution of most of the forest owls is so local as to be quite inexplicable. One is properly an island species, occurring only on Pemba island (and on the oceanic Madagascar and Comoros Islands), but another is confined to a few square miles of coastal forest in Kenya, and several others have an extraordinary restricted distribution. *Bubo poenis vosseleri*, the Nduk Eagle Owl of the Usambara mountains, is a good example. From what little is known, it eats mammals, including galagos and bats, and ought to be able to make shift to catch its prey in a wide area. Yet it seems quite remarkably rare even in the Usambaras. Its nearest relative, Fraser's Eagle Owl, inhabits forests in upper Guinea and Cameroon, over a rather larger area, but still apparently very rare and little known. Shelley's Eagle Owl, a large powerful species that ought to take the place of the widely distributed Verreaux's Eagle Owl within forests (just as the Crowned Eagle replaces the Martial Eagle) is apparently still rarer. Thus, we have the paradox that although more species of owls, in proportion, prefer to live in forest, they are rarer, and probably less effective as predators in that environment than are the diurnal raptors, which theoretically should be less suited to life in the poor light of forests.

One ought to qualify this statement by saying that forests have not been very extensively studied by ornithologists at night. Thus owls of one sort and another may be commoner and more widespread than appears. But owls are, on the whole, much more noisy birds than are diurnal raptors, and in savanna they advertise their presence readily enough. I have spent a good many nights in forests, under fine moonlight conditions when savanna owls would be calling, without hearing a single hoot. If a hoot is heard, it is as like as not that of Woodford's Owl or Verreaux's Eagle Owl, both widespread woodland species which also occur in some types of forests.

These puzzles, not explicable by anything we know of the species concerned at present, may well be solved when the behaviour and ecology of each species has been studied in greater detail. Meanwhile they add to the interest of the study of raptors in Africa, and provide a challenge for anyone who happens to be able to attack them. They do not wholly invalidate the general idea that the distribution of predators and their prey is exposed to risk from one or other of them at most or all times of the day and night.

Chapter 17
Migrant African Birds of Prey

As shown in Table 13 (see p. 304), a proportion (11 species) of the diurnal birds of prey in Africa are purely migratory, visiting the continent only in the northern winter. A further 21 species are both resident and migratory, having races which breed in some part of Africa and other races breeding further to the north, in Europe and Asia, which visit the continent only in winter. Then there are 5 species which perform regular migrations entirely within the continent south of the Sahara, and one species which is only a vagrant.

The diurnal birds of prey that visit Africa only in winter are the Honey Buzzard, the Hen Harrier (North-West only), Pale Harrier, Levant Sparrowhawk, Common Buzzard (which breeds on islands off the north-western coast but not on the continent itself, unless the Mountain Buzzard is included as a race), Lesser Spotted Eagle, Greater Spotted Eagle, Imperial Eagle, Red-footed Falcon, Merlin (North-West only) and Saker Falcon. Of these, two, the Hen Harrier and Merlin, do not penetrate south of the Sahara, and three others, the Greater Spotted and Imperial Eagle and the Saker, do not normally occur as far south as the Equator. The remainder reach the southern third of Africa where they may be the commonest of all raptors present between October and March.

The 21 species which have races or individuals resident on the continental mainland but which are greatly augmented by migrant individuals from further north in winter include the Osprey; the Red and Black Kites; the Egyptian Vulture, European Griffon, and Black Vulture; the European Snake Eagle, the Marsh Harrier, and Montagu's Harrier; Goshawk and Sparrowhawk; the Long-legged Buzzard; the Tawny, and the Booted Eagle; the Lesser and Common Kestrels, the Hobby, Eleanora's Falcon, the Sooty Falcon, the Lanner and the Peregrine.

Among owls, six species, the Barn Owl, Scops Owl, Eagle Owl,

Little Owl and Long-eared and Short-eared Owls all migrate to some extent to Africa. Among them only the Short-eared Owl has no races resident on the continent. Migrant Eagle Owls and Barn Owls are rather rarely seen in Africa, and the most conspicuous and common migrants are the Little, Scops, and Short-eared Owls. The Little Owl and Scops Owl have races resident in tropical Africa, but only the Scops Owl is resident south of the Equator. African Scops Owls used to be regarded as a separate species but are nowadays included with the European *Otus scops*. None of the owls which migrate regularly from Europe occur south of the Equator, and several (Barn Owl, Long-eared and Eagle Owls) occur as migrants only in North and North-West Africa, though they may have races breeding further to the south. Much less is known about the movements of owls than about those of diurnal birds of prey for obvious reasons; they migrate at night and are probably overlooked in their winter quarters unless collected.

The vagrants, which can be ignored hereafter in this chapter, are the European Sea Eagle and Bruce's Scops Owl, which many would regard as a race of the common Scops Owl. The other migrants are more or less regular, some of them in great numbers.

The first thing that will strike anyone who studies these lists is that the population of migrant raptors is made up very largely of kites, harriers, buzzards, eagles, and falcons. Three out of four kite species are migratory and the fourth performs marked local movements. Of the six harrier species occurring in Africa four are either purely winter visitors or have migrant and breeding races. Three out of five buzzard species, and one close relative, the Grasshopper Buzzard, migrate either within the continent (two) or from Europe in winter. Of the ten species included in the eagle genera *Aquila* and *Hieraetus* (which some combine with *Aquila*) six are migratory, one of them entirely within the continent. Of 17 falcons 11 are known to perform more or less regular migrations, and probably several of the others perform local movements which may prove to be regular and quite extensive when they have been more carefully studied.

This situation may be contrasted with 15 species of sparrowhawks and goshawks (*Melierax*, *Accipiter* and *Urotriorchis*) of which only four are more or less regularly migratory, none to the southern half of the continent, and ten species of vultures of which three are migratory, two only to the North and North-West of the continent. Kites, harriers, buzzards, eagles and falcons would be regarded by any observer in Africa as the most characteristic migrants, their arrival being expected and anticipated in much the same way as that of the swallow or cuckoo in Britain.

The remaining migrants, the Osprey, the Honey Buzzard, Serpent Eagle, Black and Egyptian Vultures are, like the above, all birds of powerful or soaring flight. In fact, the majority of the migrant species are capable of soaring on thermals, even the smaller falcons such as the Red-footed Falcon and Hobby. Evidently the development of strong flight and the ability to soar may tend to make a species migratory. However, this is not the whole story. No-one would accuse the Lammergeier, Nubian Vulture, Black Eagle, Crowned Eagle, or Martial Eagle of being other than magnificent and powerful fliers, but they are, so far as we know, sedentary. Some other species of very powerful flight, such as the Bateleur, which perhaps travels 200 miles every day, would evidently be able to migrate if there was any advantage in it for them. Although relatively weak flight, and specialisation to fit a woodland or forest habitat, as is seen in some of the sparrowhawks, seems to reduce the proportion of species that migrate, it does not follow that birds of very powerful or rapid flight will be migratory.

The study of migration in Africa is far from complete. The approximate ranges of most of the more regular migrants, with their times of arrival and departure are known, but little is known as to their numbers relative to resident species, or of the causes of big local movements, perhaps connected with weather changes. There are some outstanding mysteries—for instance, how does the Eastern Red-footed Falcon reach Africa and return to its breeding haunts? And in the case of what seems to be the commonest, most widespread, and successful large bird of prey in Africa, the Black Kite, the migration pattern of the various races is still very far from clear.

The reason for this, of course, is that hitherto all ornithologists in Africa have been European. Only some of the colonising powers, notably the British, and to a lesser extent the French, the Portuguese and Spanish much less, have produced individuals interested in birds. And of these individuals a comparatively small number have been able to make the regular records over a long period that are necessary for the understanding of migratory movements. Rural

Africans, who have the best opportunities for observing migration, do note these movements, but neither comprehend them nor record them.

I know from my own experience how difficult it is. For the four years I lived in Nigeria, mainly in the savannas of Ilorin and Kabba provinces where the Niger and Benue join, I was able to keep good and regular records of migration. I did it again for four years when I was at Embu, on the eastern slopes of Mt. Kenya. But from then on I was never sufficiently long in one place to make recording worth while until I came to Nairobi, by which time I had specialised in other interests, or was so office-bound that I could not easily observe the arrival and departure of migrants with any certainty. But I was luckier than many other officers, who were transferred from place to place with such bewildering rapidity that sustained observations of any sort were denied them.

It is mainly in South Africa and Rhodesia, and perhaps to a lesser extent in North and North-West Africa, that many sustained observations have been made. Certain places in Nigeria have been fortunate, through the observations of J. H. Elgood and others. But our knowledge of the movements of migrants within Africa is at best scrappy and incoherent. A co-operative study of movements of, for instance, the Black Kite, has been and is almost impossible to organise.

However, we know enough to be able to make some sort of sense out of the movements of certain species, particularly the common and more noticeable migrants such as harriers, kestrels, buzzards and eagles. One thing that is obvious is that in the northern winter the migrant Palearctic raptors are relatively more numerous, sometimes very much so, than are their nearest relatives in their wintering quarters. Essentially this is because the breeding range, comprising much of Europe and Asia, which together total 20·8 million square miles, is very much larger than the potential winter range in Africa. Africa's total area is 11·7 million square miles but a vast extent of this is desert, where few raptors attempt to winter.

It would, perhaps, be fair to estimate that for every square mile of winter habitat in Africa south of the Sahara there may be 2–3 square miles of breeding habitat in Europe and Asia. Hence the migrants would, in winter, be two to three times as numerous as their resident relations even if these were equally common as breeding birds. And, as has been discussed in Chapter 16 (page 173) residents of the same genus or family are frequently unaccountably rare, so that the migrants often outnumber them to a greater degree than one would expect. Whether this is because the residents cannot compete, in winter, with a very large influx of related migrants, is another matter.

The harriers perfectly illustrate this point. The four migrant species, the Marsh Harrier, Hen Harrier, Pale and Montagu's Harrier all have extensive breeding ranges in Europe and Asia. Of these the two which breed in Africa, the Marsh Harrier and Montagu's Harrier, breed only in the North-West, which is properly part of the Mediterranean basin or Palearctic Europe. When they migrate to Africa they encounter no rivals at all in the western and northern parts of the continent. Only in East and South Africa do they meet any resident harriers, the African Marsh Harrier and the rare Black Harrier of the Cape. Both of these are rather restricted as to habitat or range, so that even in their range the Pale and Montagu's Harriers have the grasslands to themselves. The rather inadequate figures given in Table 9 (page 294) show that in East and South Africa migrant harriers, with 35 individuals in the counts, outnumber the resident African Marsh Harrier in the proportion 6:1. In West Africa, where there are no resident harriers at all, and where, 25 years ago at least, Pale Harriers seemed to me far more common than they are in Kenya in 1969, the difference in favour of the migratory species would be infinite.

It would not surprise me to learn that the savannas and steppes of West and Western Central Africa, from Gambia to the Sudan, were the main wintering grounds of all Palearctic Harriers, and that those which penetrate into Kenya, Tanzania and further south are only a small proportion of the main body. However, until we have some quantitative data from West Africa and Sudan we cannot say whether this is so or not. What is clear is that migrant harriers are not very common south of the Equator, and that they become rare and irregular in such places as the Kruger Park or Cape Province.

This is certainly not true of some other Palearctic migrants. From Rudebeck's South African figures, given in Chapter 19 (page 209) it is clear that Lesser Kestrels in 1950–57 enormously outnumbered all resident species combined, let alone their near relatives such as the resident Common (Rock) Kestrel, or possible competitors such as the Black-shouldered Kite. It is true that these figures have not been confirmed in the same degree by any later observer, perhaps indicating that Rudebeck went out of his way to find and record Palearctic migrants. But still the figures for Common and Lesser Kestrels on the East African plains and in the Uganda National Parks, Tables 6, 8, where they are certainly migrants, are much higher than for their near relatives and possible competitors, the Grey Kestrel and Greater Kestrel. The Black-shouldered Kite here appears relatively more numerous than in South Africa, but the Common and Lesser Kestrels with 35 individuals (cf. 10 Black-shouldered Kites in the migration season), still outnumber their possible rivals. A longer series of counts, in the course of which a large flock of at least several hundred kestrels would sometime or other be encountered, would probably demonstrate the much greater numbers of kestrels than Black-shouldered Kites.

Here I must say that in recent years there has been disquieting evidence of a decline in the numbers of migrant harriers and kestrels visiting East Africa. In 1947–52, when I lived at Embu, migrant harriers, chiefly the Pale Harrier, but with some Marsh and Montagu's Harriers, used to be very common on the plains east of Mount Kenya. At a place called the Nguka swamp they roosted communally in rough grass and reeds, and my notes of the time record that they "literally swarmed". They were certainly in scores, if not in hundreds. In 1967, twenty years later, I see only the odd harrier quartering the very similar grass plains near Nairobi and I am quite sure I could never write that they "literally swarmed" anywhere. Likewise Common and Lesser Kestrels were at times very numerous in lower Embu district, particularly in March 1948; but it is years since I saw a big flock of Lesser Kestrels anywhere in Kenya, the last being in 1961.

Whether this apparent decline signifies a real reduction in numbers in the breeding areas (as could have been brought about by increased use of persistent toxic chemicals in agriculture) or whether it indicates changed habits, perhaps on account of above-average rains in East Africa in and after 1961, is impossible to say. Counts will doubtless show whether the numbers decline still further, and though there is nothing that can be done about it in Africa we may at least be able to say that harriers and kestrels *are* declining and alert people in the breeding areas.

Lesser Kestrels probably visit East Africa mainly as passage migrants; most of them probably pass on to the South. This is also true of several of the falcons, notably the Hobby and Red-footed Falcons, while both Eleanora's Falcon and the Sooty Falcon winter in the savannas of Madagascar. The same habit of wintering mainly or entirely in the southern third of Africa is probably shared by the Honey Buzzard and the Lesser Spotted Eagle. In fact rather a large proportion, about half, of all the Palearctic migrant diurnal raptors that visit Africa regularly winter in the southern tropics and further south.

In some of these, notably the small insectivorous falcons, the Hobby and Red-footed Falcon, it is not difficult to see why. In the southern third of Africa between November and February, the rains are at their height. Consequently insects are very abundant, particularly flying termites which swarm with the onset of heavy rain. Presumably this also applies in the savannas of Madagascar, where Eleanora's Falcon and the Sooty Falcon winter. These two species feed on birds during the breeding season, but mainly on insects in their winter quarters. Hobbies eat some birds in breeding quarters, but in Africa feed mainly on insects, while Red-footed Falcons and Lesser Kestrels are mainly insectivorous in both breeding and wintering quarters. There can be little doubt that the wintering quarters of these small falcons are influenced by the availability of insect food.

It is extremely striking to watch Hobbies on migration through Kenya. They appear at two times of the year, late October–November going south, and in late March going north. Both are periods in which the first storms of a rainy season are likely to fall. Late October is the onset of the short rains, which last from then to mid-December, and late March of the long rains which continue to late May. The passage of Hobbies through Kenya is hardly observable except when one of these storms has fallen, bringing out swarms of alate termites. Hobbies then appear, often in numbers, as if by magic, feed greedily on the termites for a time and disappear again. In dry weather they are simply not seen. Presumably they are then so high up as to be invisible, and it is likely that they go from rain-front to rain-front, feeding on the abundant termites before moving on. In September–October the rain-fronts in the northern tropics gradually move southwards. The Hobbies take advantage of this to make the passage without experiencing any hunger until they reach their southern winter quarters when the rains have set in in November. When the rains there begin to die off, in March, they move back northwards, and eventually follow the northward moving fronts in March and April en route to their breeding quarters.

The Red-footed Falcon, at least the Eastern race *amurensis*, appears to have adapted to this situation in a still more striking way. It is a gregarious bird at all times and roosts communally in enormous numbers in its winter quarters in Malawi, Zambia, and Rhodesia. But its route from Eastern China to Southern Tanzania, where it first becomes numerous, is still not understood. There are no records of large numbers being encountered crossing Afghanistan and Arabia, so that there is no evidence that they come overland. One must presume that they cross the Indian Ocean from North-East to South-West, arriving on the African coast at some part south of the Equator, when the rains are about to start or have started. A few are sometimes seen on the Kenya coast, and I have seen them myself in the Rift Valley; but there are no records of movements correlating with the vast congregations—thousands together—of these falcons that roost in certain places in Zambia or Malawi in March before departure for the North. We must again presume that they make the journey at a great height, where they are invisible, and that unlike the Hobby they do not regularly descend for a termite snack en route.

Common Buzzards (mainly the Steppe Buzzard *Buteo buteo vulpinus*) migrate to South Africa in large numbers, in this respect resembling the Lesser Kestrel. This has given rise to controversy over the identity of buzzards that breed in the mountains of Cape Province. These are either a local race of the Mountain Buzzard, *Buteo oreophilus*, or they are genuine Steppe Buzzards that stay to breed in South Africa, just as the European Bee Eater and European Stork sometimes breed there. Fair numbers of Steppe Buzzards winter in wooded country in Kenya and Uganda, but the majority pass on south. One migration route followed is over the summit of Mount Elgon and around the Kavirondo Gulf in West Kenya, avoiding a crossing of Lake Victoria just as buzzards avoid flying over the sea.

Some of the other species that winter in the south are also attracted to this area by the wet weather, and abundant insects or frogs. The Honey Buzzard is probably one of these, and the Lesser Spotted Eagle another. Neither of these raptors is seen in any great numbers on passage through West Africa or East Africa; in fact in thirty years' residence I have never seen a Lesser Spotted Eagle. But Honey Buzzards migrate out of Africa in some numbers in March-April through Cape Spartel, Malta and other places, and Lesser Spotted Eagles come into Africa through the Bosphorus and Suez in large numbers. They manage to travel from these observable extremities to their wintering quarters largely unobserved and unrecorded, and their main wintering areas are still not clearly defined. One must conjecture from what little is known.

If Lesser Spotted Eagles enter Africa through Suez—as they are known to do—their obvious route is through the Sudan and East Africa, avoiding the forests of the Congo. They are very rarely observed or collected. There are no known specimens from Kenya. But in November 1966, Dr. R. Bowles, a good observer, found a large flock of eagles feeding on termites beside the main road from Mombasa to Nairobi. He identified them as probably Lesser Spotted Eagles. I have also been informed that Lesser Spotted Eagles may be seen in numbers in Botswana in winter, though good records are lacking, and that they pass through Northern Tanzania. The evidence, though fragmentary, points to a scarcely observed or observable migration from north to south, descending only occasionally to feed, similar to that of the Hobby, and for the same reasons—that the insects and frogs on which this species feeds are abundant in the rains there during the northern winter.

Most of the other eagles which migrate into Africa do not travel so far to the south. They winter chiefly in the grass plains and savannas of the northern tropics, or in East Africa as far south as Tanzania. These include the Tawny Eagle (including the Steppe Eagle as a race of that species), Imperial and Greater Spotted Eagles. The Booted Eagle goes further south than these, but its movements are so indefinite and it is so easily confused with, for instance, Wahlberg's Eagle or Ayres Eagle, that it is best not to be dogmatic about it.

Steppe Eagles are the most obvious of all these migrant eagles, at least in East Africa and Ethiopia, where I have seen them commonly. The adult Steppe Eagle is only distinguishable from resident Tawny Eagles by darker colour, larger size, and a greater tendency to perch on the ground. Immatures are much more easily distinguished, having broad whitish tips to the wing coverts forming a clear wing bar. Thus it is possible to determine when the Steppe Eagles arrive by noting these immatures. They normally arrive in Kenya in October.

In Table 6 (page 290) I have analysed the counts I have made of Tawny Eagles and other species to compare the numbers present within and outside the main migration season. Tawny Eagles are more than three times as numerous in Kenya between 1 October and 31 March, in the migration season, as they are between the beginning of April and the end of September, which period includes the breeding season for residents (June–October). Thus, since the residents are also present at that time augmented to some extent by the young that were reared, we can deduce that about two-thirds of the Tawny Eagles present from October to March are of the migrant races normally called Steppe Eagles, and sometimes distinguished as a separate species.

In South Africa, in the Kalahari National Park, a Tawny Eagle was recorded once every 60 miles outside the Palearctic winter migration season and about twice as often, once every 30 miles, during the season. As, however, the Steppe Eagle has very seldom been collected in southern Africa we must deduce in this case that if a migratory concentration occurred the birds were all of the resident race. The resident African Tawny Eagles (*Aquila rapax rapax*) and *A. r. raptor*) certainly do move about, just as their northern cousins do. But on the Equator in Kenya it seems that the proportions of the two are just about what they ought to be taking into account the fact that most migrant Steppe Eagles appear to concentrate in East Africa. In Ethiopia I would guess that, in the high mountains at least, where they feed on abundant rodents, as they must on the Siberian steppes, the migrant Steppe Eagles are far more common.

Imperial Eagles are too scarce to be able to say definitely what controls their migrations, but Greater Spotted Eagles are better known. They winter mainly in the Sudan and Eritrea, though stragglers have been observed further south. They are said to feed greedily on locusts, in company with other large raptors from big vultures to Lanner Falcons. Their choice of wintering grounds is very different to those of their nearest relatives the Lesser Spotted Eagles—dry rather than wet. It is possible that the choice of wintering ground may have been partly influenced by the availability of locusts. It is only within the last twenty years or so that the Desert Locust

Schistocerca gregaria, which is the species involved, has been brought under control. In former times, when the migration pattern of the Lesser Spotted Eagle became established, the frequent abundance of this insect in North-East Africa during the Palearctic winter might well have been one of the main factors influencing the extent of the winter range.

As a general rule it seems that those species which feed mainly or entirely on insects, particularly those insects such as flying termites which are associated with wet weather, tend to migrate as far as the southern part of the continent. Those, such as harriers and eagles, which feed largely upon small mammals caught in the grass, or larger mammals such as mole rats (Tawny Eagle and Steppe Eagle) tend to go no further south than the southern parts of the East African grassland in Tanzania and Uganda. They do not, at least in numbers, pass on into the Brachystegia woodland to the south and remain generally north of the area which receives rain from November to April.

As and when we know more about it, we may find that local weather conditions affect the movements of Palearctic migrants within Africa. I have often observed in Kenya that large soaring species such as the Steppe Eagle and Common Buzzard are grounded by an unexpected rainstorm. Then one sees the Hobbies hunting happily near to the ground while the Tawny Eagle sits hunched and draggled on a fence post. The main cause of migration to Africa is undoubtedly to avoid the Palearctic winter. But the migrants, once there, may be controlled and guided to wintering areas by the shift of local rainy seasons which, with visibility of 100 miles or more quite common, they may easily be able to see and interpret from long distance.

Chapter 18
Migration within Continental Africa

Migration within the continent of Africa is little understood. Several workers, notably the late Dr. J. P. Chapin in the Congo, R. E. Moreau, J. H. Elgood and myself in Nigeria, and others have recognised that intra-continental migration exists and have studied it for a period. Recently, Moreau has discussed it in his monumental work on the Bird Faunas of Africa. However, most works on migration as such dismiss African intra-continental migration in a few paragraphs, as if it was an irregular feature attributable merely to local variations of food supply.

When speaking of African intra-continental migration we mean a journey regularly and seasonally performed by some numbers of birds, of at least 250 miles either way, often much more, as defined by Moreau. It is certain that if the movements performed by certain birds of prey (and some other well-known species such as Abdim's Stork) took place in Europe or North America they would be recognised for what they are—regular seasonal migrations. But observers in Africa are scarce. Not all of them take any interest in migration, and of those that do most live in temperate South Africa where intra-continental migration is not easily observed. Consequently, no co-ordinated study of intra-continental migration in Africa exists. Since so little is known about it in general it is worth discussing it in some detail as it affects African birds of prey.

Five species of diurnal raptors migrate regularly within the African continent. They are (a) The Grasshopper Buzzard and Swallow-tailed Kite, which breed in the northern part of their range and migrate southwards during the dry season, from October–March; (b) The Shikra and the Red-necked Buzzard which breed, at least in West Africa, in the southern, better watered parts of their range, and migrate out of this northwards in the wet season; (c) Wahlberg's Eagle, which migrates into the southern third of Africa, breeds there in the dry season, and moves out again in the wet season. In addition, several other species, such as Fox Kestrels, Lanner Falcons, Tawny Eagles, and the resident races of the Black Kite perform more or less regular movements within the continent. Some populations of the species concerned may be migratory, others not: e.g. there is no good evidence for regular movements by the Shikra in the savannas of southern tropical Africa. This, however, is comparable to the European Common Buzzard which in Britain is resident all the year round, but in Scandinavia is migratory.

These movements show a variety of patterns but they share the common feature that they are all related to the seasonal alternation of rains and drought which is such a characteristic feature of tropical Africa, and which results in sudden and far more dramatic changes of weather than, for instance, the gradual transition from winter to spring or summer to autumn of temperate latitudes. The phrase "the rains broke" has real meaning in tropical Africa. The start of the rains is usually heralded by the catastrophic passage of violent thunderstorms, sluicing water on parched earth and on savannas which have been blackened and stripped of their vegetative cover by fire. The result, within a few days, is a great upsurge of plant and insect life, while all sorts of small birds start nesting; there is, for instance, an immediate increase in the volume and intensity of the dawn passerine bird chorus.

In the case of birds of prey the sudden onset of the rains, heralded by the development of enormous thunderclouds, may well be taken both as a signal to vacate the area and a convenient means of doing so. In cold areas the southward movement is often initiated or accelerated by snowfall, and there seems no reason why, in the tropics, unfavourable weather, in this case heavy rain, should not similarly initiate or accelerate widespread movements. Heavy tropical rain soaks many large soaring birds so that they are hardly able to fly. But at the same time big thunderclouds may enable them to rise to great heights and move quickly away from an area which is about to become inhospitable. I have observed large soaring raptors and storks using thunderclouds to gain great height, and Honey Buzzards have been seen doing the same over Malta.

Recent climatological studies have shown that in tropical West Africa this alternation of the seasons is particularly clear cut and regular. In East Africa, on the other hand, it is less clear cut. This is

Migration within Continental Africa

partly because much of East Africa, lying athwart the Equator, has two rainy seasons and two dry seasons annually, associated with air movements which, essentially, are connected with the twice-yearly passage of the sun north and south across the Equator. Also East Africa is mountainous, with huge masses such as the Ethiopian plateau, Kenya and Kilimanjaro, and the Ruwenzori–Virunga highlands of the Congo helping to disrupt any weather patterns there may be. To the south, again, the alternation of the seasons again becomes clear, with one rainy and one dry season, in some ways even more clear cut and definite than in tropical West Africa, but also affected by high plateaux and mountain ranges, especially from Rhodesia to the Cape of Good Hope.

If the seasonal migrations of birds of prey are connected with weather phenomena we should therefore expect that they would be more clearly and regularly observed in West Africa and the southern Tropics than athwart the Equator. In West Africa this is the case. It is no coincidence that most studies of this phenomenon come from Nigeria or the Congo. There are good reasons for the lack of data from the southern third of Africa in that several of the migratory species do not occur there at all while others that do do not migrate.

Weather phenomena can also be connected with observed movements of birds of prey in Equatorial East Africa, but here the weather is notoriously "unreliable". There is no such thing as a "normal year" in Kenya. The relation between movement of birds of prey and weather is less clear cut, and observations must be interpreted with insight. If one attempts, for instance to correlate observed movements with a single recorded fact of climate, for instance total rainfall, the answer is not likely to be clear. This does not mean, however, that good and valid observations of the effect of rainfall cannot be made.

In the last chapter I did not discuss the movements of the Black Kite, although it is a species which migrates from Europe to Africa. This is because the resident African races, notably the Tropical African Yellow-billed Kite, perform regular migrations within Africa which are similar to those of some of the migrant African Hawks. It is therefore useful to discuss the migrations of the Black Kite in the context of intra-continental migration.

The races of Black Kite which occur in Africa are: (i) The

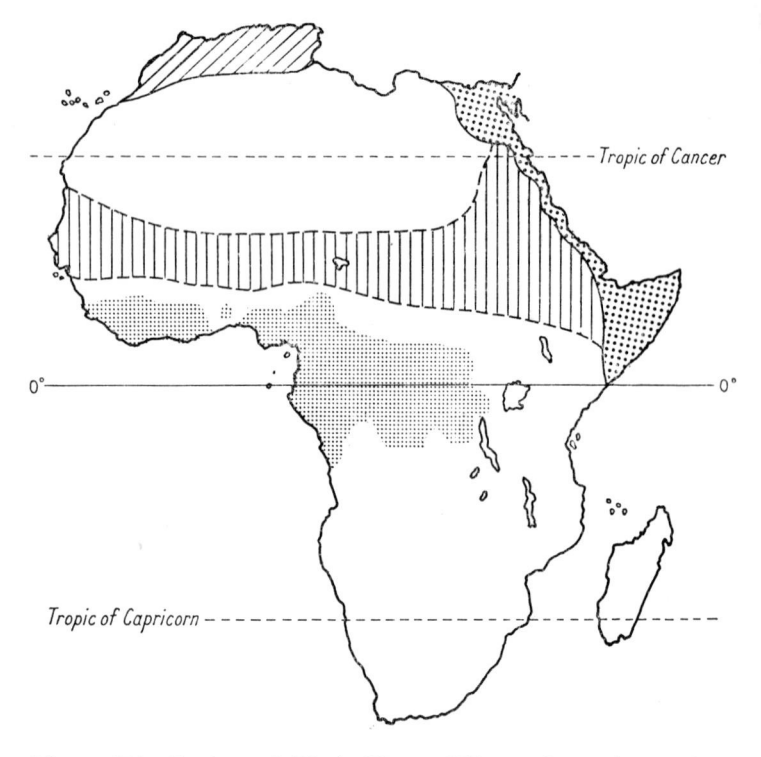

Fig. 9 Distribution of Black Kites, *Milvus migrans* in northern summer, May–June.

▨ *M. m. migrans*; in breeding areas in Morocco and Algeria.

▨ Breeding range, *M. m. aegyptius*.

▥ Probable area of concentration of non-breeding *M. m. parasitus*; only stragglers farther south.

▨ Equatorial forest.

nominate European Black Kite *Milvus migrans migrans*, which migrates into much of Africa in winter; (ii) The Egyptian Kite *M. m. aegyptius* (including *M. m. arabicus*) of North-East Africa, which migrates south to East Africa, especially coastal areas, in winter; (iii) The Tropical African Yellow-billed Kite *M. m. parasitus* (including *M. m. tenebrosus*, which is indistinguishable) which

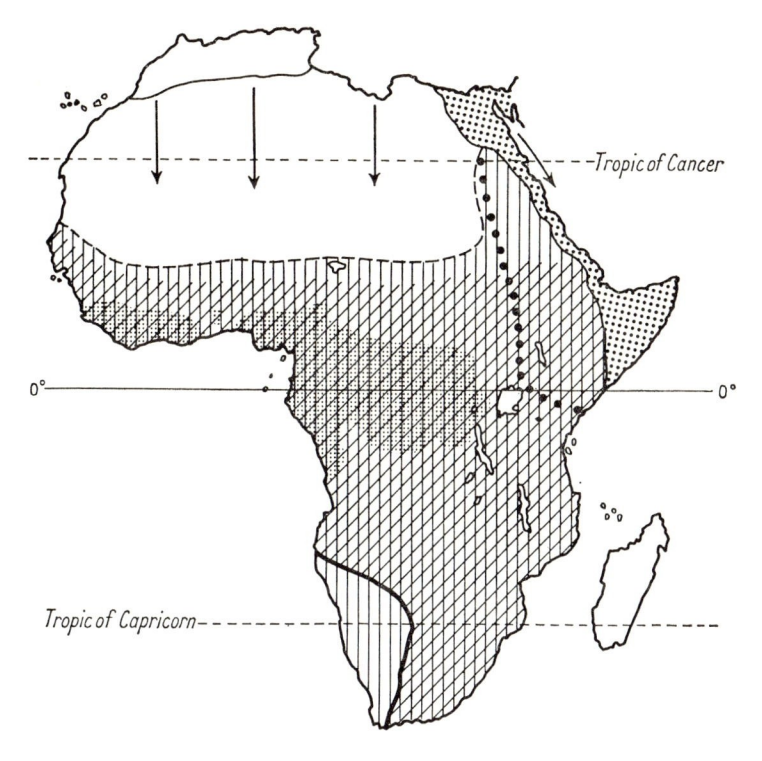

Fig. 10 Distribution of Black Kites in southern summer, November–December.

▨ *M. m. migrans* has left breeding area in N.W. Africa (outlined) and is spread through much of the range of *M. m. parasitus* and part of the range of *M. m. aegyptius*; arrows indicate southward movement on broad front, heavy black line limit of distribution in S.W. Africa.

▨ *M. m. aegyptius* is mainly sedentary, but with some movement south, especially along coast.

••••• Black Circles: Probable westward and southward limit of migration.

▨ *M. m. parasitus*, either breeding or about to breed.

▨ Equatorial forest.

performs regular migrations entirely within Africa south of the Sahara. The movements and relative numbers of all these races are not fully understood, since they are difficult to distinguish in the field with certainty: adults of both the Egyptian and Tropical African Kites have yellow bills, while the immatures have black bills, like the European Black Kite. It would be difficult to distinguish some in a museum, let alone in a circulating migratory flock, or among kites soaring over a town. Thus, although the Black Kite is the commonest and most easily observed raptor in most of tropical Africa, we have still much to learn about its movements, which would be an ideal subject for a co-operative study.

So far as they are known, the movements of kites within Africa are set out in the maps and Fig. 11, which also gives details of the main rainfall seasons and the breeding seasons of kites. It is clear at once that south of the Sahara the only kites likely to be present during the North Temperate summer are Tropical African Kites. The European Kites are then breeding in Europe, and the Egyptian Kite is breeding in its North-East African range. Possibly a few stragglers of these races remain in tropical Africa but even in the main migration season they may often be less numerous than Tropical African Kites.

The Tropical African Kite in West Africa performs regular north to south movements in October–November, breeds, and retreats northwards with the start of the rains in March—the same type of migratory movement seen in the Shikra and Red-necked Buzzard. During this time it mingles with migrant European Kites. In Kenya and Uganda, athwart the Equator, a few kites are present all the year round, but the species is only common from October to March–April; during this period the residents breed and are augmented by migrant European and Egyptian Kites. There may even, then, be some visiting *M. m. parasitus* from the south avoiding the South African winter, though this cannot be proved without extensive ringing.

In the southern tropics, when the rains fall during the northern winter, the kites breed August–November, and fledge their young before the rains become heavy. They remain common however, perhaps partly because of an influx of European Kites, between November and March. In South Africa itself kites are present in spring and summer, from September–March, breeding in spring and

MOVEMENTS OF KITES IN AFRICA

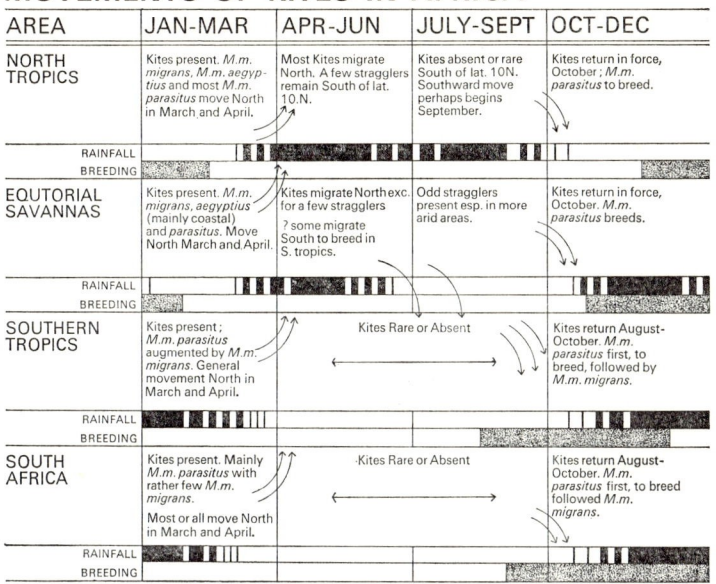

AREA	JAN-MAR	APR-JUN	JULY-SEPT	OCT-DEC
NORTH TROPICS	Kites present. *M.m. migrans*, *M.m. aegyptius* and most *M.m. parasitus* move North in March and April.	Most Kites migrate North. A few stragglers remain South of lat. 10.N.	Kites absent or rare South of lat. 10N. Southward move perhaps begins September.	Kites return in force, October; *M.m. parasitus* to breed.
RAINFALL / BREEDING				
EQUTORIAL SAVANNAS	Kites present. *M.m. migrans*, *aegyptius* (mainly coastal) and *parasitus*. Move North March and April.	Kites migrate North exc. for a few stragglers ? some migrate South to breed in S. tropics.	Odd stragglers present esp. in more arid areas.	Kites return in force, October. *M.m. parasitus* breeds.
RAINFALL / BREEDING				
SOUTHERN TROPICS	Kites present; *M.m. parasitus* augmented by *M.m. migrans*. General movement North in March and April.	Kites Rare or Absent		Kites return August-October. *M.m. parasitus* first, to breed, followed by *M.m. migrans*.
RAINFALL / BREEDING				
SOUTH AFRICA	Kites present. Mainly *M.m. parasitus* with rather few *M.m. migrans*. Most or all move North in March and April.	Kites Rare or Absent		Kites return August-October. *M.m. parasitus* first, to breed followed *M.m. migrans*.
RAINFALL / BREEDING				

Fig. 11

early summer September–December, and again mingling at this time with smaller numbers of European Kites. In March–April there is a northward movement of resident South African kites to escape the winter, at least into Rhodesia, and perhaps further north. This movement, out of the breeding areas in the austral autumn, takes place at the same time as the northward movement of European Kites back to their breeding areas. Some of the kites have finished breeding, others are about to start.

This attempt at a summary of the movements of Black Kites in Africa serves to show how much work needs to be done before they can be properly understood. The outstanding mystery is—where are all the Tropical African Kites between May and August–September? This is a dry season in East Africa, but kites are certainly then uncommon in all parts of East Africa, and do not become common until October, when they arrive from the north.

Between June and September kites are absent from or uncommon in almost the whole of Africa south of say 8°–10° N., and it seems likely that they are concentrated in the northern parts of the African tropics where, though it is raining from June–September, the climate is still relatively dry. Monthly counts from such places as Khartoum and Fort Lamy might well establish the point.

What can, perhaps, be said with fair certainty, is that kites avoid those parts of the continent where it is, for the time being, very wet or cold; that they usually breed in the latter half of the dry season, and often leave the area with the onset of the rains soon after breeding (exceptions being in Kenya where kites breed in the short rains October–December, and perhaps in the South African summer rainfall area); and that, all over the continent and among all races there is a strong tendency for southward movements from September to November and northward movements from March to May.

In West Africa, and also in Kenya, where I have studied the movements of Black Kites, they are clearly associated with weather. In West Africa, at Ilorin and Okene (both stations in broad-leaved savanna woodland about 8·5° and 7·5° N. respectively) I kept careful records of arrival and departure dates, and related these to weather. Although some of the migrant kites may have been European *M. m. migrans* the majority were the Tropical African Kite, migrating to the forest edge and further. It was the movement of these which seemed clearly allied to weather phenomena.

The outstanding feature of the West African dry season is the prevalence of a dry dust-laden north-east wind, known as the Harmattan. In far northern Nigeria it blows most of the time, but at the latitudes of Ilorin and Okene it comes in blasts or waves, each of the early waves being usually preceded by a thunderstorm or series of storms. In effect, it has been shown that the Harmattan is a layer of dry air from the Sahara, which overlays the moist air coming inland from the Gulf of Guinea. The nearer the coast, the more the moisture predominates, and the less sharp and frequent and prolonged the blasts of Harmattan. Following heavy rain from thunderclouds, the dry layer is able to descend to ground level and persists for a few days until again forced upwards by incoming moist air from the ocean. A wave or blast of Harmattan is immediately accompanied by increased dryness (the relative humidity drops sharply) and by a reduction of visibility from, say 20–30 miles or more, to less than one mile in the dust-laden air.

The kites, and several other dry-season migrants (which included, for instance, kingfishers and hornbills) seemed to me to arrive on the early blasts of Harmattan. Thus, on 16-18 October, 1943, near Lokoja, there was Harmattan, and Black Kites, Shikras and Grey Hornbills appeared within two to three days, in numbers. On 22-23 October there was another stronger blast, and these same migrants then appeared at Okene, 40 miles south-west, and a thousand feet higher up. On several other occasions flocks of Black Kites appeared with the Harmattan though the effect was not always so clear cut. It seemed probable that the kites were moving south in or at the edge of the dry air, which itself advanced in fits and starts. Once there, the kites and other migrants that came on the Harmattan stayed, though the intensity of the Harmattan died away. In those days I never thought to make counts to establish these facts, but I am confident that regular counts in October correlated with weather would prove the point.

In Kenya, on the eastern slopes of Mt. Kenya, there is a dismal season of the year, locally known as *Gathano* in which sopping wet mist hangs on the mountain slopes above 5000-5500 feet. At lower levels this mist is a continuous layer of cloud, which extends usually to within 100 miles of the Coast. In September the mist lifts, and gloomy cloudy weather is suddenly replaced by bright sunshine. The lifting of the mist, at Embu, often brought in the kites. For instance, their arrival coincided with the start of sunny weather on 6-8 September, 1947. Perhaps more striking still, in Machakos district in 1950, weeks of gloomy cloud were broken by a few days of unseasonal sunshine on 21 July; kites appeared in some numbers on that day where on the previous week's touring I had not seen one in the same area.

These and other observations have convinced me that in Kenya kites generally avoid wet, cold, or heavy cloud. A few kites are, as stated, present in Kenya the year round, but I have observed that they may be more numerous in a "dry" year, and in Embu they occurred in years of below average rainfall (such as 1948-49) in parts of the district where none were seen in wet years, such as 1947, or 1950-51. My conclusions were that local movements of kites were connected with weather changes from year to year or season to season, just as more extensive migrations were in Nigeria. Once the kites had really come in, in the dry weather of September–October, they stayed through the short rains, and had begun breeding

MOVEMENTS AND BREEDING SEASONS
(Rainfall shown in breeding range)

SPECIES	JAN-MAR	APR-JUN	JULY-SEPT	OCT-DEC
SWALLOW-TAILED KITE *Chelictinia riocourii*	Migrant in savanna to 8 N in West, to near Equator in East. Leaves March, going North.	Moves to desert fringes 15-20 N. Breeds.	Remains in Breeding areas.	Returns southward reaching 8 N in late November or December.
GRASSHOPPER BUZZARD *Butastur rufipennis*	Migrant to southern savannas to near forest fringe. Leaves late March going North.	Breeds in northern savannas just before rains.	Remains in northern savannas.	Returns southward in late October or November.
RED-NECKED BUZZARD *Buteo auguralis*	Breeding in forest and southern savannas.	Moves North in early rains, May onwards.	Non-breeding, presumably in more northern savannas.	Migrates South, reaching savannas and forest fringe at 7 N in late October or November.
SHIKRA *Accipiter badius*	In savannas; breeds February-March.		Some remain in savannas. Others migrate North.	Migrates South reaching savanna at 7 N in October.

Fig. 12 NOTE. In this figure rainfall is shown in the breeding areas, clearly indicating that the species (Swallow-tailed Kite and Grasshopper Buzzard) that breed in drier areas or which are insectivorous prefer to breed in the rains, while those that breed in wet southern areas prefer to breed in the dry season.

before the heavy rains came in November. Even during the short rains the weather is predominantly sunny in Embu district, and once the kites have begun breeding they can hardly leave.

I have gone into all this detail about the Black Kite to show, not only how little we know about its movements in Africa but also to indicate (as I firmly believe myself) that these are probably related to weather phenomena. West Africa would be the best area in which to study this problem, for there the weather changes are well marked and regular, while at least four other species of diurnal raptors are regular north-south migrants at the beginning of the dry season, retreating northwards with the coming of the rains.

In Nigeria, the four other species which made regular dry season movements to areas south of $8°-10°$ N. were the Swallow-tailed Kite,

Shikra, Grasshopper Buzzard, and Red-necked Buzzard. These four illustrate two different types of movement: (a) migrating into the southern areas in October–November (Shikra and Red-necked Buzzard), breeding there, and retreating northwards after breeding (as does the Black Kite); (b) breeding somewhere far to the north (Swallow-tailed Kite and Grasshopper Buzzard) and visiting these southern areas only during the dry season. The movements of these species related to rainfall and their own breeding seasons are set out in Fig. 12.

The Shikra and the Red-necked Buzzard migrate to the edge of the forest belt, or into it (the Buzzard breeds in the forests). Shikras were absent from the savannas of Ilorin and Kabba, apart from an odd straggler, between June and October, sometimes not returning till November. In 1944 at Okene I observed that the main influx occurred immediately after a blast of Harmattan, on 17–18 October, but in the previous year, when the rains continued rather longer, Shikras were not common until after 2 November. They bred much later than did Black Kites, breeding in February–March, having eggs in March, and fledging young in April, after the first real storms of the year had occurred. They were less common in the forest belt than in the savannas, but bred in extensively cultivated and consequently open areas near Ibadan and Lagos. Elgood at Ibadan has also observed that they are dry season migrants arriving in November and breeding before departure in April–May. Shikras also breed much further to the north, but their migration behaviour is unknown or unobserved there.

Red-necked Buzzards were another clear case of the same sort. They passed through Okene on their way south in late October, and especially November, thereafter decreasing in numbers, though a few remained round forest patches on hilltops, doubtless breeding there and also, occasionally, in the savannas, as I found one nest 50 miles north of any real forest. When on southward passage they travelled in small flocks, calling to one another as they went, in very much the same way as, for instance, Honey Buzzards travel on migration in Europe. They bred in the forest belt, in the late dry season, in January–March, and after breeding remained into early May, after the rainy season proper had started. They were absent from the forest belt from June to November, but were not observed on northward passage—for reasons unknown, but again possibly connected with the weather. The southward passage took place at a time when the thunderclouds were absent and the air generally thick with Harmattan haze. The birds must have gone north when monsoon thunderstorms were frequent. Perhaps these enabled the buzzards to mount to a great height and pass northwards unobserved —as Hobbies would pass unobserved over East Africa if they did not come down for a termite snack from time to time, and as some other species such as the Lesser Spotted Eagle evidently do.

The other two conspicuous dry season migrants, the Grasshopper Buzzard and the Swallow-tailed Kite show exactly the reverse pattern. They visit the savannas around latitude 8°–10° N., but do not breed there, and depart to breed somewhere to the north. Very little is known about the breeding habits of either, but the Swallow-tailed Kite appears to breed in deserts or at their edges, while the Grasshopper Buzzard breeds in the drier Acacia savannas. There are only a few records from northern Nigeria of the Grasshopper Buzzard breeding, in March. In Sudan and Somalia it breeds from March to May.

Swallow-tailed Kites breed in drier areas than do Grasshopper Buzzards. They nest in May and June in the Southern Sahara and in the deserts of northern Kenya. Thus both these species actually breed just before the main onset of the rains in their breeding haunts, and to this extent resemble the kites, Shikra and Red-necked Buzzard though they breed after moving north, not before. As might be expected from their northern breeding distribution in arid areas, they are less regular migrants to southern savannas than are those species which breed there. The Swallow-tailed Kite, in fact, does not occur every year as far south as 8° N. in Nigeria, and the numbers of the Grasshopper Buzzard vary greatly from year to year—abundant in some years, scarce in others. Probably the weather conditions and the ecological conditions resulting from them affect these movements and more detailed studies would be needed before they can be understood.

It is possible that these differences in migratory patterns may be due to the type of food eaten by each species. The Shikra is a bird-eater, and the Red-necked Buzzard lives—presumably—on rats and mice, with frogs and insects as a sideline. The Grasshopper Buzzard and Swallow-tailed Kite are both almost entirely insectivorous. They may find insects so abundant at the break of the rains in their northern breeding haunts that they are able to breed successfully in the short time available, whereas the bird-eating Shikra and the mouse-eating Red-necked Buzzard may find the more stable southern areas much more favourable for breeding.

In the southern third of Africa, and also in Kenya, Wahlberg's Eagle is a migrant, breeding in the dry season to the south and during the short rains in Kenya. The movements of Wahlberg's Eagle are not very clearly understood, since it is both much rarer and less easy to observe and identify with certainty than are, for instance, Grasshopper Buzzards, or Red-necked Buzzards. Nevertheless it is quite clear that in Rhodesia near the southern limit of this eagle's range it arrives in the latter part of the dry season in August or September, laying in September and October, and disappearing before the main rains have ended. In Kenya it is commonest from August–December, breeding through the short rains from October–December. A few are seen at all times of the year, and these may be residents that have not migrated or visitors from further south. Southward migration is seen in Kenya and Tanzania in August–September. It is a common migrant through Darfur in the Sudan, and apparently spends the non-breeding season somewhere to the north. Apparently it does not breed much north of the Equator. When we know more about this eagle it will probably prove to be a regular trans-equatorial migrant, moving over greater distances than most of the species discussed so far. Its movements may perhaps give us a clue as to the behaviour of the Tropical African Kites which breed in the southern third of Africa.

There are many other species of diurnal raptors which perform considerable movements, perhaps more or less regular. Besides species already mentioned, such as the Tawny Eagle and Fox Kestrel, it would be worth studying even such apparently sedentary creatures as the Bateleur and the Crowned Eagle. I have been noting the sexes and ages of Bateleurs for years in East and South Africa and in the course of this study have found that I see very few or none in areas where rain is falling or imminent, and most in dry areas. And once, after a violent thunderstorm in Nyanza Province, I found a Crowned Eagle perching near a hilltop many miles from any possible breeding area. It had been on the move, with a large number of Kites, Steppe Buzzards and Tawny Eagles, and like them it had been grounded by the storm.

So far as we know, the type of migration shown by a good many diurnal birds of prey is not performed by any owls. In Nigeria the five owls commonly inhabiting the woodland areas where I lived, the Barn Owl, Spotted Eagle Owl, Scops Owl, White-faced Owl and Pearl-Spotted Owlet were all sedentary, for I was looking out for the possibility of movements and would have noted them had they occurred. One owl which might be migratory within the continent is the Marsh Owl, though most records indicate that it is sedentary. It would, at least, be the most likely species as a near relative of the migratory Short-eared Owl. But when we know so little about the migrations of the common obvious diurnal Black Kite it will evidently be a long time before we can understand those of a rather local species of owl.

Chapter 19
The Numbers of African Birds of Prey

In most of Africa the birds of prey are not only found in great variety but strike many people as being very common. Again, this observation applies more to diurnal than to nocturnal birds of prey. But although one certainly sees more diurnal birds of prey than in, for instance, civilised populated Europe, little has been recorded as to the *actual* numbers of the various species involved. And without an exact knowledge of the actual numbers present in any given area it is impossible to arrive at any true idea of the real effect of the birds of prey upon any prey animals in the area. We can guess, in broad terms, what is likely to happen, but that does not mean that this is actually what happens.

I do not know of any part of Africa where the population of nocturnal and diurnal resident and migrant raptors has been accurately and completely estimated, even for one year, much less over a series of years. I myself have estimated the population, of eagles only, in certain areas of the Embu district of Kenya, and so far as it went that census was quite accurate, over a period of two to three years, in an area of 146 square miles of savanna. But I studied only the breeding eagles of the area, and the Secretary Bird, of which there was a total of 31 pairs of 11 species in 146 square miles. I did not attempt, at the same time, to record, other than in a general way, the numbers and habits of other birds of prey occurring in the area. At one time and another these included members of another 23 species of diurnal raptors and six species of owls. Nor did I ever try to estimate in any detail the numbers of prey that might be available in the area, though I made rough estimates of relative abundance.

The reason for this was simple enough—it would have been a physical impossibility for me to achieve such a task. I was at the time a hard-working Agricultural Officer, and I had evenings and weekends only in which to gather my information. So I stuck to the birds that interested me most at the time—the large eagles—and tried to learn as much as I could about their breeding behaviour, then largely unknown. I was assisted by two Africans, Njeru Kicho and Ireri Mungato, the second of whom still works with me. Even with their assistance it was as much as I could do to visit, several times a year, every eagle's nest in this comparatively small area of 146 square miles.

There were 31 pairs in the area, and to visit one of them could involve a walk of anything from 2 to 10 miles. I could usually make a round trip including several pairs, but I walked about 4 to 5 miles for every nest I visited, and usually had to drive for 10 to 40 miles to reach my starting point. Call it 200 miles' walking to visit all of them once, or 800 miles to visit them four times a year—barely often enough to be certain myself what happened, but sufficient to check up on my observers' reports. 800 miles' walking in a year may not seem much—it is the distance from Land's End to John o' Groats, which any able-bodied man should be able to cover along roads in six weeks flat. But add to that the difficulties imposed by heat, thornbush, rough ground, torrential rains and mud, the fact that not every evening or weekend was available, and the need to spend long hours observing breeding behaviour at each nest, and it is not difficult to see why I stuck to one objective that I could do reasonably well, neglecting others except in a general way.

I do not cite these facts in order to excuse my own failure to achieve more (for one has only to say to carping critics, "Go and try—I'll watch you", to bring about a rapid change of manner) but to stress the reasons why we know so little about the actual numbers of birds of prey. The fact is that the physical demands on the investigator, particularly perhaps in tropical Africa or similar parts of the world, are such that few attempt it.

To this day I know of no other such estimate except the count of Verreaux's and other species of eagles which has been done by Val Gargett and others in the Matopos Hills of Rhodesia. The area covered was larger (220 square miles) than my Embu census but was very much better served by roads and tracks. In 1968 it supported at least 93 pairs of seven species of eagles and at least 21 pairs of Augur Buzzards and Kites. Among these, 52 pairs of Verreaux's Eagles are a particular feature and represent the greatest population density of any large eagle known. But no real attempt has been made to count the small diurnal birds of prey in the area, or the owls, nor have the numbers of eagles been adequately related to the numbers of the main food animals—rock hyrax—in the area. However, there is hope that more detailed study of this area now in progress will provide some of the answers needed.

We remain, therefore, with no accurate count of *all* the birds of prey, diurnal and nocturnal, resident and migrant, over a single decent sized area of Africa, even in one year. This need not inspire any sense of guilt, for the same is true of most of Europe and North America, where ornithologists are much more numerous. But it is a pity, because it is only in such places as tropical Africa, where nature is still more or less in the raw, that it is possible to arrive at an idea of the true ecological effects of birds of prey. In Europe and North America, where most such studies have been done to date, man interferes with, or manages the environment to such a degree that the results of a study relating birds of prey to their food animals cannot bear much relation to what might be called " unspoiled" countries. Such conditions are still found in Africa, and the chance should be taken to study birds of prey, in detail, in a natural environment, before it is too late.

In recent years observers have counted birds of prey seen from cars, as they drove about the country. Research of this sort has been stimulated by the general alarm caused by the reduction or disappearance of certain birds of prey in Europe and North America, such as the Peregrine in Britain or the Bald Eagle or Osprey in America. Counts made from cars can be useful in assessing the relative abundance of birds of prey from year to year, but they can never give a really accurate idea of the numbers of each species in a particular area of country.

I have done a good many such counts myself, and as a result I know that the picture they give is inaccurate. To start with, one tends to see the large and obvious species, and to overlook the small species, particularly those that live in woodland or bush, such as various species of Accipiters. One tends to get an exaggerated idea of the numbers of the species, such as the Augur Buzzard, Black-shouldered Kite, and Long-crested Eagle, which habitually perch on roadside telegraph poles or fence posts as convenient places from which to catch their prey. The time of day at which the count is made also affects the issue. In Kenya I have broadly found that one sees a maximum between 9 and 11 a.m. when the day has warmed up enough to enable the larger soaring species to get on the wing, but is not yet too hot. The same birds disappear later in the day—either soaring so high that one does not see them when one is driving along, or perching in shade. They may reappear in the late afternoon and evening, but are still less active then than earlier in the day.

Weather affects them too; they dislike dull and cold weather and prefer it sunny and warm. In dull wet conditions or great heat it is possible to drive through an area such as my eagle census area in Embu without seeing a single raptor, though from experience I know perfectly well that they are there. However, the effects of weather and time of day tend to be fairly constant for all species. There are no species that are more active in wet or dull weather, and most species are most active at certain times of day. One sees fewer birds of prey at 2 p.m. in the heat of the day than at 9 a.m., but they are of the same species that one would see at other times. So, by making enough counts, one tends to get a figure which, at least in large measure, eliminates the effects of time of day and weather.

This method of counting is really only applicable to diurnal birds of prey in fairly open country. It cannot be effectively used in thick woodland or forest, or at night, to estimate the numbers of owls. In the headlights of a car one sees an owl only briefly and often cannot identify it. If one can, one finds that it is a species like the Spotted Eagle Owl that likes perching on roadside fence posts and catching mice or insects on the convenient open surface.

Roadside counts are thus of limited value, and their drawbacks have to be borne in mind. Nevertheless, they are the only easily available method of making a quick estimate of the different species living in an area of country and, intelligently used and interpreted, they can be of some real value.

Most such counts have been done in South Africa, an area where the farming population is as bigoted and ignorant on the subject of birds of prey as are people in Europe, North America and Australia. Birds of prey, particularly the larger species such as Verreaux's and the Martial Eagle, exist there in a beleaguered state, shot or poisoned all too often by sheepfarmers who have never once attempted to assess objectively the overall effect, beneficial or otherwise, of such predators and probably would not listen to a biologist who did.

The Numbers of African Birds of Prey

Other species, not obviously regarded as harmful, or even known to be useful, may not be deliberately persecuted, though they may be shot wantonly by a boy to test his new ·22 rifle. All the bird of prey counts from South Africa outside National Parks must be examined with this qualification in mind.

The earliest South African counts were done by G. Rudebeck, in the course of an expedition from the University of Lund, Sweden, in 1950–51, the results of which were not published until 1963. He was chiefly interested in Palearctic migrants, and did his counts in the northern winter. He also included all the Lesser Kestrels found in one huge roost (about 6000) so that his counts give a quite disproportionate idea of the numbers of some species. However, they are summarised in Table 1 (see page 284).

Rudebeck's figures, taken twenty years ago or more, show that in the winter of 1950-51 Lesser Kestrels enormously outnumbered all other species, and that migrant raptors greatly outnumbered any residents—8477 to 130. However, this figure is greatly swollen by including the huge roost of Lesser Kestrels, and does not mean that there was a Lesser Kestrel for every half mile of road. If the first count containing the roost figure is omitted the distance travelled per Lesser Kestrel seen is about 15 miles, which compares more reasonably with the other figures. The rarity of the resident raptors, even then, is striking by comparison with other figures given for the Kruger Park and East Africa later in this chapter. It was necessary for Rudebeck to travel more than 30 miles for the sight of one resident raptor, of any species, and hundreds or thousands of miles to see a bird like a Crowned or a Martial Eagle from the road.

In more recent times Mrs. M. K. Rowan and W. R. Siegfried have counted raptors seen along roadsides in various parts of Cape Province. Their results are given in Table 2. These figures are less detailed than Rudebeck's but they indicate quite clearly that there had been no serious decline in the numbers of resident raptors in the Cape and Karroo. Rudebeck in 1950–51 found it necessary to travel about 32 miles for every resident raptor he saw in those areas, while Rowan and Siegfried, fifteen or more years later, after the ravages of DDT, Dieldrin and poisoning campaigns based on strychnine, saw an average of one resident raptor per 11·4 miles, indicating that there had been no decline in the population of resident raptor species since 1951, perhaps even some increase.

This is the sort of useful general result that can emerge from such counts, done over a long enough period.

Rudebeck likewise found that in the Orange Free State and Transvaal, over 4365 miles in the winters of 1951–55 and February 1956, that Palearctic migrants greatly outnumbered the resident species (3417 to 231), and that a resident raptor was seen every 19 miles. Ten years later, in July and August 1965, Cade and Prozesky counted one resident raptor to 18·5 miles in the Transvaal and Orange Free State. In 1956 Rudebeck saw only five resident raptors in 392 miles between Pretoria and Pietermaritzburg, Natal, and over a similar route, but longer (590 miles) Prozesky and Cade saw one resident raptor every 11 miles. Thus it would seem that in this area at least, if anything there has been an increase over the last decade. (See Table 3, p. 286.)

Thus far all the counts have concerned those areas of South Africa where the raptor fauna has been impoverished, directly or indirectly, by the action of man, either by shooting, or by damage to the whole environment. To find any areas in South Africa which have not been so affected by man we must go to the Kruger or Kalahari National Parks. Both of these are in environments very different to those of Cape Province or the Highveld or the Transvaal or Orange Free State, being thornbush and very dry Acacia steppe respectively. The results are not, therefore, directly comparable. They are given in Tables 4 and 5 (see pp. 288, 289).

These counts from the uninhabited, "unspoiled" areas show quite a different pattern. The distance travelled per resident bird of prey seen becomes much less, and large eagles persecuted in inhabited areas become relatively common. The Bateleur even becomes the commonest of all birds of prey in Kruger Park, followed by the Tawny Eagle. It is difficult to believe that this is actually the case, and it is more likely that these two species, especially the Bateleur, appear as common as they are simply because they are the most obvious. In Kruger, some such small species as the Gabar Goshawk or Shikra is likely to be actually commoner than the Bateleur and, at a different time of year, the migrant Wahlberg's Eagle would have appeared relatively more numerous.

The counts in the Kalahari are affected by the fact that they are all made along the courses of the Auob and Nossob rivers. In fact these are dry watercourses subject to occasional floods in the rains, where large trees grow and wild life tends to congregate. The density of the population of birds of prey appears still higher than in Kruger Park, though I doubt if this would be true of the Kalahari Desert as a whole.

It comes as no surprise, to anyone who has visited that area, that the commonest raptor is the Chanting Goshawk, though it is somewhat surprising to find the Pigmy Falcon second. In this area, however, the Pigmy Falcon breeds in the numerous nests of the Sociable Weaver *Philetairus socius* and is therefore unusually common. These species are followed by the Secretary Bird, Tawny Eagle, and Bateleur in that order. Again, while I would suspect that this count gives a reasonably true picture of the numbers of various species seen along the Auob and Nossob rivers, I doubt if the same results would be obtained by repeatedly making a census of, say 500 square miles of Kalahari Desert, in which the favourable environment typical of the Auob and Nossob valleys would be only a small fraction. I would, however, expect to find the Chanting Goshawk still considerably the commonest species.

All the counts given to date were collated by Professor T. J. Cade and he excluded vultures. They were probably included in some of the original counts but because of their scavenging habits have not been regarded as "birds of prey". In the Kalahari Desert and Kruger National Parks the White-backed Vulture would probably be as common as any of the large eagles, and the Lappet-faced and other vultures would be seen more rarely. Vultures may not be active predators, but they are certainly part of the population of Falconiformes, depending upon flesh which is available in any area.

In my own counts in East Africa I have included vultures, and as a result they appear among the commonest of the large birds. The counts for East Africa have the advantage that, whether they were made in inhabited or uninhabited areas, they have been done in country where scarcely anyone interferes with birds of prey—at present. The majority of the inhabitants of the country are small farmers who do not own powerful guns, and who often have a better idea of the functions of birds of prey than have people from Europe, North America, South Africa, or Australia. European farmers in Kenya usually have a tolerant attitude towards birds of prey. Thus the counts represent, fairly accurately, the relative numbers of different species that would occur in different parts of East Africa.

I have divided the counts into three tables. Table 6 covers a total of 25 counts, aggregating 2403 miles, in the mixture of grasslands, Acacia woodland, and thornbush which is characteristic of much of the country of eastern Kenya and northern Tanzania, including parts of the Rift Valley. This total includes 1613 miles outside the main migration season October–March, and 790 miles within it. For several species I have further analysed results in the next chapter. I have eliminated some counts that appear to me unrepresentative (done in wet weather or late in the evening) and I have lost some counts when a field notebook was stolen from my car at a petrol station. But the result appears to me a reasonable representation of the population of raptors over a wide area including rather varied habitat.

It averages out at about one raptor seen for every 2·7 miles travelled. To compare this figure with, for instance, the Kalahari and Kruger Parks it is necessary to exclude all vultures and migrants—the latter comprising about 40 Tawny Eagles and all of several other species, but not Black Kites, which come into this area to breed. This eliminates 321 out of 874 birds counted, and leaves a figure of one resident raptor, not a vulture, per 4·1 miles covered. This is almost the same as the most favourable of all South African environments, the Auob and Nossob valleys in the Kalahari Park. Moreover, as it is derived from a longish series of counts on bush tracks as well as on main roads, it gives a truer picture of the general population of birds of prey in the area as a whole. In fact, though it is undoubtedly biased, as all such counts are, in favour of large, easily seen species, I think it is quite a fair estimate of relative numbers, over the course of two to three years.

Such counts, individually analysed, also help to bring out how widespread a species may be. In my East African counts summarised in Table 6 only one species, the Augur Buzzard, was seen in 20/25 counts. It is, therefore, both the commonest and the most widespread species in this area: I should be surprised if further counts did not confirm this, at least among the larger species. The Augur Buzzard, given trees or crags to breed on, is ideally suited to living on plains with plenty of rats and mice. White-backed Vultures are next, but appear in only 10/25 counts indicating that they are met with in fairly large numbers—as one would expect—on the occasions when they are encountered. Then comes the Black Kite, but being a local migrant it appears in only 16/25 counts. Tawny Eagles, with 97 individuals in 18/25 counts, are more widespread than either of these two, and as in Kalahari are the commonest large eagles in this rather dry open grassland.

The second main group of counts (Table 7) is of 13 covering 625 miles of inhabited and cultivated country, including Kikuyuland near my home and parts of Uganda. The species composition revealed by these counts is quite different, partly because the areas in which they were made were originally either forest or woodland, not open grassland or thornbush, and partly because of the attraction of inhabited areas for certain species. The Black Kite is by far the commonest and most widespread species, with 211 individuals in 9/13 counts. 207 of these were seen in the season when Black Kites migrate into this area, either to breed or from the north, and only four at other times. The Augur Buzzard, with about one-eighth of the numbers of the Black Kite, is as widespread, and the scavenging Hooded Vulture, while it appears in less than half the total number of counts is the most numerous after the Black Kite. Large eagles such as the Tawny Eagle and Martial Eagle, characteristic of the drier savannas and steppes, are either rare or absent, but the forest-loving Crowned Eagle replaces the Martial Eagle. Smaller eagles, such as Wahlberg's and the Long-crested Eagle are, on the other hand, relatively common by comparison with their occurrence in more open uninhabited country.

A quite different environment is presented by the counts made over 430 miles of Uganda National Parks and thinly uninhabited country in Ankole. (Table 8.) Here again the Black Kite is the commonest species, with the White-backed Vulture second. The combined total of carrion-eating vultures exceeds that of kites. Fish Eagles are unusually common because of the proximity of all parts of these parks to the Nile or to other waters, and the commonest of the eagles are, once again, the Bateleur and the Tawny Eagle. What is rather surprising is the small number of Palearctic migrants (38/356) seen in this open country at the height of the northern winter.

If the density of population is calculated in the same way as for the South African areas, eliminating migrants, intra-continental migrants, and vultures, the Uganda National Parks come up with a figure of 1 raptor/3·0 miles, slightly better than the best South

African area. More surprising, it appears that the inhabited environment of East Africa gives a figure of 1 resident/4·5 miles, almost as good as in uninhabited areas and many times better than the inhabited areas of South Africa where birds of prey are persecuted. To be fair, the figure is biased by the number of Black Kites, but even eliminating all Black Kites, it is still about 1/10 miles. In other words, the man-made or man-affected environment can still support a good population of birds of prey provided that they are left alone.

It is possible to put all these counts together, and arrive at some sort of aggregate figure for the relative abundance of birds of prey in East and South Africa—for we have few counts for West or North Africa. This is perhaps worth doing in the case of the National Parks and the relatively undisturbed East African grasslands, and has been done in Table 9. I would certainly deny that this is a true representation of the relative abundance of various species of birds of prey in uninhabited or sparsely populated areas of East and South Africa, for the figures for Pigmy Falcons and Chanting Goshawks, for instance, are exaggerated by their abundance in the Kalahari and for the Augur Buzzard by the East African figures. But it does point to certain species as being unmistakably successful and widespread or abundant.

On the basis of these counts the Black Kite is probably the most abundant, widespread and successful bird of prey in Africa, doubtless because it can adapt to many environments; we have seen that it is relatively still more abundant in inhabited areas. The Bateleur and the Tawny Eagle are partly scavengers and both widespread and successful, each much commoner than their near relatives—the Snake Eagles and, for instance, Wahlberg's Eagle. The Martial Eagle is a widespread and successful species, rare mainly because it is so large and powerful that each pair requires a large range. The Lanner is the common, widespread large falcon in Africa south of the Sahara. And so on. The relatively very low numbers of migrants, such as Common or Lesser Kestrels, and of harriers, is a surprise, for most of us who have lived long in Africa would think of them as being among the commoner birds of prey in grasslands and plains during the European winter.

It is impossible, from the evidence available, to arrive at any sort of sound estimate of the total, or even the relative numbers of Africa's birds of prey from these figures. But perhaps they are useful in that they put into rather better perspective such general terms as "abundant, common, rare, very rare" etc. Many more counts over longer periods are necessary before more accurate ideas of the shifting fluctuating population in any particular area are possible. But before anyone can do a count he must be able to identify his species with fair certainty as he drives along.

Chapter 20
The Effects of Predation

The birds of prey are only one of a number of different classes of predators affecting the lives of other African animals. Excluding insectivores such as shrews and hedgehogs there are, for instance, mammalian predators from the lion to small mongooses; reptiles, including crocodiles, snakes and large lizards; and perhaps occasionally such creatures as crabs or large spiders. In considering the effect of any individual bird of prey, or any group of birds of prey, upon their food animals one must not forget that these other animals exist, and that they too demand a share of the available food supply. They complicate a situation which is complicated enough when only the birds of prey are considered. The raptorial birds are, as it were, one section of a very large orchestra.

Even among birds of prey one may elect to study the effect of a mixed population of diurnal and nocturnal species, hawks, owls, and vultures, on the potential population of their prey as a whole, or one may pick out a particular species and study that in detail. This is actually an essential preliminary to any fuller study, for only by understanding how one species acts upon its prey can one hope to understand the combined effect of a number of different species. Before attempting to conduct the whole orchestra it is as well to learn to play a particular instrument.

The effect of any particular species of raptor on its food animals depends on the interaction of a number of different factors, such as:

1 The size of the raptor concerned.
2 Its daily food requirement, which is actually related to size; small active species eat a greater proportion of their own weight daily than do large species such as big vultures or eagles.
3 The temperature of the air. Birds of prey eat more in cold weather than they do in warm climates. The effect of variations in temperature in most of Africa is not likely to be great.
4 The amount that each raptor has to *kill*, in order to obtain its

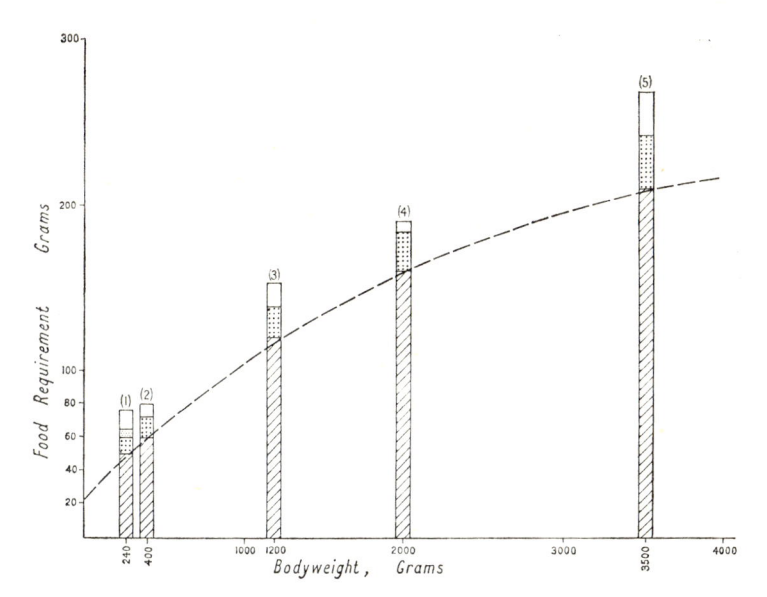

Fig. 13 Estimated Food Requirements of some African Raptors.

▨ Actual daily food requirement.

▨ Allowance for exercise in normal hunting.

▨ (Sparrowhawk only) allowance for cold weather.

☐ Waste factor.

The graph of actual food requirement is similar in form to that for actual food consumption of American raptors. (Fig. 14)

(1) Sparrowhawk, *Accipiter nisus*, bodyweight 240 gr., food requirement estimated 50 gr. daily, kills about 77 gr.

(2) Harrier, *Circus pygargus* or *C. macrourus*, bodyweight 400 gr., food requirement 60 gr., kills 80 gr., nearly the same as Sparrowhawk

(3) Buzzard, *Buteo rufofuscus*, bodyweight 1200 gr., food requirement 120 gr., kills ca. 152 gr. daily.

(4) Snake Eagle, *Circaetus cinereus*, bodyweight 2000 gr., food requirement 160 gr., kills ca. 190 gr. (very low waste).

(5) Crowned Eagle, *Stephanoaetus coronatus*, bodyweight 3500 gr., food requirement about 210 gr., kills about 270 gr. Actual field observations indicate this estimate is too high.

actual daily ration to *eat*. Every raptor kills more than it actually eats, and the amount of a kill that is wasted depends on the type of kill. But to the actual food requirement one must add perhaps a fifth by weight to arrive at the amount that must be killed to enable a raptor to live.

These four factors combine as shown in Figure 13 to produce a reasonably accurate idea of the raptor's daily food need, from which one can calculate the amount required in a year by a pair of raptors and their descendants. To obtain this latter figure one must know, from study of breeding success and similar aspects, how many birds of the species concerned, besides the original pair, must live in any breeding territory to enable the species to survive. In Wahlberg's Eagle, for instance, each pair's territory must support about 3·2 adult equivalents, and in the much larger Martial Eagle this figure is 2·8.

Having arrived at a reasonably sound figure for the total food requirement of a single raptor, or a pair and their descendants, one must consider several other facts to assess the effect on the prey, for instance:

1 The area of the home range of an individual raptor or a pair of raptors. This is another fundamental starting point. It can only be determined by trying to count all the raptors that occur in a large area of country. In some cases, such as big eagles that make conspicuous nests this is fairly easy; in others, like small owls that live in holes in trees, or small skulking sparrowhawks such as the Little Sparrowhawk, it is exceedingly difficult.
2 Knowing the area of the home range one must then determine, as far as possible, the number of possible prey that exist in it; this requires a detailed knowledge of the food preferences of the raptor concerned.
3 The vulnerability of the prey animals to attack depends on their habits, the amount of cover available, and so on. A strictly nocturnal animal, for instance, however abundant and conspicuous by night, is quite safe from a diurnal raptor.

If the interactions of all these various factors are studied carefully over a period of time one may arrive at a fair idea of the effect of any single raptor or group of raptors on their prey. But it is quite useless to make wild guesses or rough estimates, and the study of even the

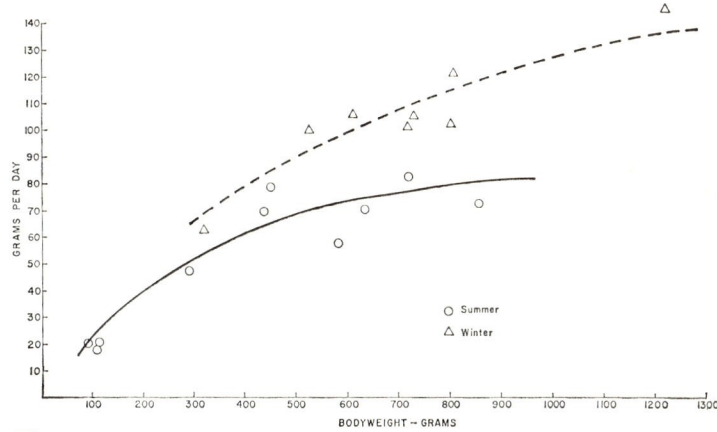

DIURNAL RAPTORS - FOOD CONSUMPTION AND BODYWEIGHT

Fig. 14

simplest case is a prolonged and difficult exercise which has yet to be thoroughly accomplished for any African raptor. What follows is therefore little better than an informed estimate.

As yet we know very little detail as to the amounts of food actually eaten by wild raptors in Africa. It is exceedingly difficult to gauge the amount eaten by a wild bird, even if it is watched daily with the greatest diligence. In the case of Crowned Eagles that nest near my house in Kenya, I know from direct observations that on one occasion a female ate about 1lb. 4oz. of a Suni at one meal, and that a Vervet Monkey, weighing 5lb. 14oz. once apparently sufficed the adult pair for 28 eagle days, an average of 110 grams, or ¼lb. per day each. In general the observation of wild birds gives an idea of the type of prey eaten and the general numbers of each, but little that is certain on their daily ration, though this can be inferred from the recorded kills. The amount eaten by any raptor is far better studied with the aid of captive birds, which are weighed accurately before and after feeding. Again this has not been recorded with African raptors, but a good deal is known about it in other parts of the world, and it seems pretty certain that African raptors are not extraordinary in their food needs. Thus, by studying a buzzard in America or an eagle in the London Zoo one can get a fair idea of how much a buzzard or an eagle will eat in Africa.

The available information shows that small active species eat a greater proportion of their own weight per day than do large and relatively sluggish species. The food requirement is increased by cold weather, and by the amount of exercise that must be taken to capture the prey. Thus a small active sparrowhawk will eat about 25% of its own weight per day, while a very large and powerful eagle or owl will eat less than 10% of its own weight, and the very largest vultures might well need even less than that. In Fig. 14 is set out a graph showing the food requirements of certain American raptors as known, and the sort of food requirements that might be expected of African raptors of comparable size, making allowance for the warm climate of most of the continent. The food requirement of tropical raptors is not likely to be very much less than those of temperate zone species in summer.

When assessing the proportion of any particular kill that is wasted we have very few specific facts, but we can infer a good deal. The amount that is wasted depends chiefly on the size of the animal killed in relation to the size of the killer and the latter's ability to carry the prey away. Most small kills can be swallowed entire, and the waste is then only what cannot be digested, which is cast up as pellets. Large kills, however, may have to be dismembered before they can be lifted, even by a large and powerful eagle, and the major portion may have to be left lying about, perhaps to be recovered later, but more likely not in a country swarming with other scavengers.

As an example of one extreme, it is known that the wastage of snakes and fish is often very small. When a Snake Eagle eats a six-foot snake it swallows it whole, bones, scales and all. All that does not actually pass through the digestive system is a few scales that are cast up as leathery pellets at long intervals. Likewise when a Fish Eagle eats a small *Tilapia* it consumes the whole fish, bones and skull included, at one sitting, and most of this is digested and not even cast up.

In contrast to this complete utilisation, I once saw a Dark Chanting Goshawk kill a guineafowl within fifteen yards of my camp. The guineafowl, probably about three times the Goshawk's weight, took some subduing and could not be lifted. Nevertheless the hawk dragged the bird out into the open and killed it by tearing at the neck. It then ate to satiety and flew away with a full crop. When I went to examine the guineafowl I found that the hawk had only consumed the flesh of the neck, and had not touched the breast or intestines.

The Effects of Predation 221

Since the prey would probably have been eaten by something else perhaps ants, before the satiated hawk would return, I took it and ate the rest myself. In this particular case the waste involved was at least 90% of the weight of the kill—though as must often happen, another predator benefited from the Goshawk's work.

Such apparently abandoned prey is not always, however, consumed by other predators. Near my home I once found a Suni, a small antelope weighing about six to eight pounds, lying part eaten on a forest track. It had evidently been killed by an immature Martial Eagle which was perched near by. Although the prey was lying in the open on a track frequented by hyenas and other nocturnal scavengers none found it. The Martial Eagle returned to it each day for four days and eventually consumed all but the skull, the skin, some of the larger bones, and the stomach. Here was a situation where potential waste of about 80% had been reduced to about 20%. The Crowned Eagle that lives in the same forest, regularly dismembers its Suni kills and certainly caches them in trees, as does a Leopard with an antelope it has killed. In such ways waste may be reduced, and it may vary from almost nil in the case of frogs, fish, or snakes, which are almost all digested to about 30% by weight of the larger mammals killed by big eagles. As a whole one may conclude that a raptor will require to *kill* from 10 to 20% more prey by weight than it actually will *eat* to obtain its full food requirement.

If we use the example of such a species as Wahlberg's Eagle, which preys largely on gamebirds, lizards, and small mammals, we can conclude that the waste factor is not likely to be more than 10%. Wahlberg's Eagle is known to eat, in captivity, about 10% of its own bodyweight, or about 80–100 grams per day according to sex. If it eats about the same in the wild state the amount that must be killed will be 90–110 grams per day, or an average of about 100 grams per adult. In a territory that must support 3·2 adult equivalents to keep the population static the daily food requirement that the territory must produce is 320 grams. Over a full year this amounts to about 117 kg. but since Wahlberg's Eagle is a migrant, resident in its breeding haunts only for about half the year, we can say that an average home range will have to produce about 58 kg. to maintain its Wahlberg's Eagles.

According to available data, Wahlberg's Eagle feeds upon reptiles, gamebirds and small mammals roughly in the proportions: 50%

reptiles, 25% each of mammals and gamebirds, in terms of *numbers* killed. By *weight*, however, these proportions differ, and would be about 50% gamebirds, 30% reptiles, and 20% mammals. As weight is the important factor in assessing what an eagle eats we can conclude that half a Wahlberg's Eagle's daily ration will be provided by birds (including young domestic chickens), a third by reptiles, and the rest by mammals. Allowing for waste, which will only be considerable in the case of an occasional full-grown francolin, the requirement resolves itself into about 100 small gamebirds, perhaps 200 lizards and small snakes, and about 120 small grass rats.

We now know approximately what a Wahlberg's Eagle pair and their descendants will need to survive in their territory. To assess the effect on the prey we must know the size of the territory, or home range. It is only possible to discover this by prolonged study and great exertion over a big area of country. One takes an area, enumerates the number of eagles in it, and then calculates the average home range. In the case of Wahlberg's Eagle there were 11 pairs in about 146 square miles in Embu district in 1950–52 and, allowing for certain areas which were not suited to this eagle, the average home range worked out at about 7,680 acres. This is the next piece of vital information on which we can base an assessment of the effect of the raptor on its prey.

Even then the situation is complicated by unknown factors. A pair of raptors, or an individual, may live roughly in the same area the year round, but there is little to prevent them straying outside it into the home ranges of neighbouring pairs. It is also unlikely that the whole of a home range is effectively and regularly hunted; each pair will have favourite areas where they often hunt while other areas are neglected. However, one must assume that a pair can and will at intervals hunt over the whole of their home range.

The home ranges of some African raptors are reasonably well known. In 146 square miles of Embu district in 1950–52 there were an average of 2 pairs of Secretary Birds, 1 pair of Verreaux's Eagles, 11 pairs of Wahlberg's Eagles, 2 pairs of African Hawk Eagles, 1 pair of Ayres Hawk Eagles, 3 pairs of Maritial Eagles, 1 pair each of Crowned Eagles and of Long-crested Eagles, 2 pairs of Bateleurs, and 1–2 pairs of Brown Snake Eagles. 2 pairs of Fish Eagles inhabited the rivers on one boundary, and there were besides vultures, buzzards, goshawks, falcons and others not enumerated.

Using these figures, and considering those species which hunt over large areas of country as opposed to particular places such as patches of forest or rock outcrops one arrives at an average home range of about 13 square miles for Wahlberg's Eagle, almost 50 square miles for Martial Eagles, and about 70 square miles for Bateleurs. Most of the Verreaux's Eagles' hunting was done on one hill in about 2 square miles, but they ranged altogether over at least 80 square miles. In the Matapos Hills of Rhodesia, an area of 220 square miles contains at least 52 pairs of Verreaux's Eagles, 17 pairs of African Hawk Eagles, 15 pairs of Wahlberg's Eagles and four of Crowned Eagles. These figures give an average home range of Verreaux's Eagle of 4.2 square miles, and nearly 13 square miles for African Hawk Eagles. In Cape Province, South Africa, a pair of Verreaux's Eagles may need 25 square miles.

Working from such figures one can assess fairly well the effect of the raptor on its prey. To continue with the case of Wahlberg's Eagle we know nothing in detail of the populations of gamebirds and reptiles in the type of country they frequent. It is clear, however, that lizards are very abundant, and probably easily caught as they bask on rock outcrops. Gamebirds, including domestic chickens as gamebirds, are also abundant; there could be 2–3000 young chickens of the right size in the territory during the breeding season. In the case of rodents such as the grass rats eaten by these eagles (*Arvicanthis* and *Mastomys*) populations may vary from 20 per acre in periods of low numbers to as many as 200 per acre in peak population years; the whole country then seems alive with rats. Anyway, using such figures one may calculate that an average home range of Wahlberg's Eagle is unlikely to maintain less than 5000 poultry and gamebirds of suitable size, at least 150,000 small rodents, and an unknown but very large number of suitable lizards. It seems quite obvious that Wahlberg's Eagle alone, with a total requirement of about 100 gamebirds, 200 lizards, and 120 grass rats could not have any appreciable controlling effect on the numbers of prey living in an average home range.

There is, however, one other factor that has to be considered, and that is the vulnerability or availability of the prey to the eagle's attack. In this particular area Wahlberg's Eagle breeds during September–January, and the food requirements of a pair are at their maximum about December, when there is a large and voracious young bird in most nests. It so happens that cover, at the end of the short rains in Kenya, is then at its maximum, with the grass long, the bush in full leaf, and field crops tall and still green. In Rhodesia, on the other hand, Wahlberg's Eagle, also breeding in September–December, nests in the dry season and at the time of maximum need the cover is sharply reduced. If, in both areas, Wahlberg's Eagle lives mainly on gamebirds and grass rodents, or reptiles that bask on rocks it would appear that in Kenya these would be less vulnerable than in Rhodesia because of the density of the cover in Kenya.

Some study of the habits of the prey, however, shows that there are compensating factors that may operate to complicate the situation further. On wet mornings in long grass, gamebirds, and such rodents as ground squirrels, tend to stay out in open patches of ground longer than they would on a hot day. In Embu Wahlberg's Eagle fed to a considerable extent on plated lizards (*Gerrhosaurus major*), a lizard that lives in holes in the ground and probably basks more outside its hole on a wet morning than on a hot dry day. Hence wet weather and thick damp cover, though apparently disadvantageous to the Wahlberg's Eagle, may actually be something of an advantage by forcing the prey to stay in the open longer. It is however clear that Wahlberg's Eagle can breed as successfully in dry conditions as in wet, and this is another reason for supposing that it can live successfully on only a small proportion of the total food available in its home range. If this is so, then it is again improbable that the eagles have any considerable effect on the population of their prey.

To obtain a clear idea of the effect of a raptor on the prey population in its area it is necessary to pick a fairly simple case, and using these principles, work out a reasonably sound result. An ideal bird to study is Verreaux's Eagle—a large and conspicuous eagle that hunts in the open and lives on rocky hills where its total range, lines of flight and the like can be readily observed. Moreover it lives almost entirely on rock hyrax with some tree hyrax, and small antelopes, gamebirds and poultry occasionally taken. The main drawback is that it is difficult to arrive at a good estimate of the population of hyrax in their rock piles.

However, one can compare this situation with, for instance, Verreaux's Eagle Owl, also a large raptor but a much less conspicuous one because it is nocturnal. This owl has a very catholic taste in food, eating everything from mammals such as hedgehogs, bushbabies, and bats, to rats, snakes, frogs, some birds, and many small night-flying insects. In the first case the observer has only to master the intricacies of behaviour of a large and conspicuous eagle and a fairly large and conspicuous mammal by day. In the second, with the additional difficulty of working in the dark, the complications become almost endless. In such cases one can only make an informed guess at best as to the effect of the raptor on its prey, but the principles set out in the preceding paragraphs are the best method of arriving at that informed guess.

The probable effect of Verreaux's Eagle on hyrax has been roughly computed in parts of the Karroo, Cape Province, where hyrax, as a result of the destruction of predators, have become serious competitors with sheep. The biomass—the weight of living animals—of hyrax in the Karroo varies from 2,700–11,300 kg/square mile. The estimate is obtained by counting the number of rocky kopjes on farms and estimating the average population of hyrax per kopje. Thus, in an average home range of 25 square miles, a pair of Verreaux's Eagles and their young have *at least* 67,500 kg. of live hyrax available, and probably much more. The daily requirement of 3 adult equivalents (necessary to maintain the population) is about 700 grams, or about 300 kg./year, allowing for wastage. In other words, at the present population level, the Verreaux's Eagles of the Karroo might consume from 0·1 to 0·45% of the hyrax available in each home range. In such circumstances it is obvious that their effect on the hyrax problem will be negligible, and it is incredible that in the midst of such abundance of their favourite prey they would kill many or any sheep.

Thus far we have considered only the effect of a single species of raptor on the population of its prey, often complicated enough. We now have to consider the combined effect of a varied population of raptors on their prey. Even using the principles which seem to be sound in assessing the effect of a single raptor this is obviously a much more complicated business.

In Table 10 (p. 296) the range of prey available, and the nocturnal and diurnal raptors that prey on it in Africa is set out diagrammatically. It is obviously impossible to take into account all the minor variations in diet that a particular raptor may show in a table of this sort, and the main prey only has been considered. The Egyptian Vulture is for instance an important predator on the eggs of some colonial birds such as flamingos and pelicans, but is here shown as a carrion eater only. Even simplifying the tastes of the birds concerned in this way the table shows the formidable complications that must be faced in assessing the overall position.

From the table one can see that virtually all possible prey, from large mammals (as carrion only) to insects is preyed upon or eaten by some form of raptorial bird either by day or by night. In practice, it turns out that carrion is only eaten by day, by large vultures and such birds as Tawny Eagles and Bateleurs. Since it does not move, and since birds have very little sense of smell, it cannot normally be located by night by owls that hunt chiefly by ear. But virtually every animal less than 5 kg. in weight is theoretically in danger from some avian predator at some point in the 24 hours. Each of these creatures must move about to feed sometime. A nocturnal grass rat that is not vulnerable to the attack of a buzzard or small eagle by day becomes vulnerable and is in danger by night—even in quite thick long vegetation where an owl can locate it by ear.

In most of tropical Africa the resident birds of prey, varied enough, are greatly augmented during the northern winter by migrants from the Eurasian landmass. Eagles, harriers, buzzards, and small falcons such as kestrels, are all conspicuous common winter migrants to Africa, and are often relatively much more common in Africa than they are as breeding birds in Europe. They may thus have, as migrants in Africa, a greater proportionate effect on potential prey than they do as residents in their breeding haunts, in, for instance, the northern Taiga zone.

Such migrant hawks in certain areas greatly outnumber the resident birds that are present all the year round. There might be six to ten times the number of migrant harriers that there are of resident African Marsh Harriers, three or four times the number of Tawny Eagles, maybe a hundred times the number of resident kestrels. For the period that they are in Africa therefore, the migrant hawks are likely to have a greater effect on the prey than are the resident species. This is particularly true of the great southern savanna belt, or Brachystegia woodland of south central Africa. Because this area is wet during the northern winter (the northern tropical belt is dry at this time) it receives the great majority of the Hobbies, Red-footed Falcons, and perhaps Honey Buzzards and lesser Spotted Eagles that winter on the African Continent. It also receives certain migrant birds of prey during the other half of the year, which is the South African winter. This region thus supports a remarkable variety and number of raptors and would be specially interesting to study.

The total effect of such a mixed population of raptorial birds, resident and migrant, diurnal and nocturnal, cannot be properly assessed without repeated counts over a long period of time in quite a large area. Some raptors hunt over great expanses of country, and hence an area of a few hundred acres, which might be a manageable size for a single observer, is quite useless for a study of this nature. Even in 146 square miles of Embu district, with the assistance of many Africans and a reward system, I found it difficult enough to enumerate more or less exactly the numbers of the largest and most conspicuous of diurnal resident raptors. This makes it almost impossible to assess the combined effect of all available birds of prey in Africa, on the basis of Table 10 (p. 296), except on theoretical grounds. Just so may one enjoy the pleasant sound made by a full orchestra without having more than a vague knowledge of the score.

However, in practice it is possible to split up this rather formidable Table into component parts which can be studied in isolation. This can be done in two ways. In the first method, the birds of prey are segregated according to the habitat they live in. There are birds that live exclusively in forest, savanna, desert, or on high mountain tops. A bird that lives in dense forest will not be found in desert country. Even some classes of birds may be confined to particular types of country. Vultures, for instance, are commonest in open plains or semi-desert, both because there is usually a high death rate among the large mammals that inhabit such inhospitable areas and because the denser the vegetation the more difficulty they have in seeing carrion when soaring at two or three thousand feet. In dense forests vultures are excluded because they cannot see any carrion that might be available.

Table 11 sets out the sort of differences that might be expected to occur among nocturnal and diurnal predators inhabiting forest, savanna, and sub-desert scrub respectively, using some of the same groups of prey as illustrations. This simplifies the situation with regard to prey preferences, and it will be seen that while there is considerable overlap between the species living in savanna and in

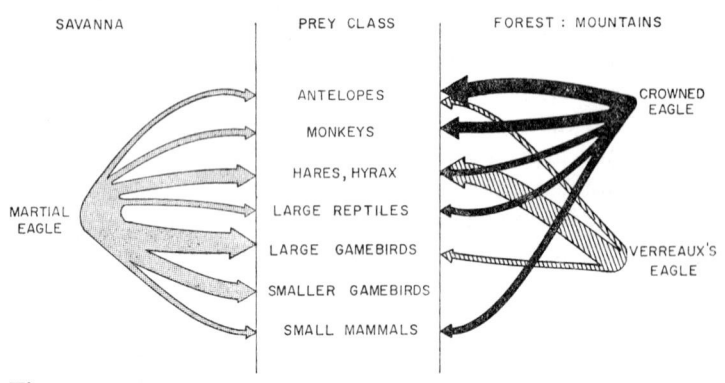

```
           SAVANNA        |   PREY CLASS      |   FOREST : MOUNTAINS

                                ANTELOPES                        CROWNED
                                                                 EAGLE
                                MONKEYS

                                HARES, HYRAX

           MARTIAL              LARGE REPTILES
           EAGLE
                                LARGE GAMEBIRDS                  VERREAUX'S
                                                                 EAGLE
                                SMALLER GAMEBIRDS

                                SMALL MAMMALS
```

Fig. 15

deserts there is little between savanna and forest and none between forest and desert. Thus of a total of 89 species of diurnal raptors occurring in Africa only 29 are found in forests, and the corresponding figure for nocturnal raptors is 13 out of 31. In savannas the position is a good deal more complex, but even here considerable simplification is possible in any given locality.

In practice this ecological separation of raptor species becomes still clearer in the field. One very seldom finds the two large falcons, the Peregrine and the Lanner (both of them bird killers and likely to compete for a possible range of prey), living together in the same area. In Kenya the Peregrine is normally found in rainfall of more than 35 inches per annum while the Lanner is an inhabitant of semi-arid country. Thus, though in Table 11 (p. 300) these two species occur together as possible competitors in savanna and desert, in practice they usually seem to avoid each other, and in any given area one finds the Peregrine or the Lanner but not both. Likewise, in the case of the two large Chanting Goshawks, there is hardly any overlap in their range. In most parts of Africa they are mutually exclusive, even though the type of country inhabited by either may be strikingly similar. In practice, this sort of separation has quite an effect on the number and variety of raptors one might have to study in any area of country.

Fig. 15 shows how prey preferences may act to prevent competition between different species. Here we have three large eagles, all powerful and rapacious birds living entirely on living prey which they kill. There is some overlap in the prey species taken, especially hyrax, but this overlap does not lead to competition because the three species inhabit different types of country. Verreaux's Eagle lives on rocky hills, the Martial Eagle in open plains or savanna, and the Crowned Eagle in forest. Hyrax occur to some extent in all these habitats, wherever there are rock piles. Verreaux's Eagle makes a staple diet of hyrax, and hunts chiefly where they are abundant. The Martial Eagle picks up a few hyrax when hunting near rock piles in open country, but seldom minutely quarters rocky hillsides as does Verreaux's Eagle. The Crowned Eagle probably kills its hyrax within forest, where they often move about by day but would be invisible inside the forest canopy to a Verreaux's Eagle. Thus one may find that all or some of these large and powerful birds live close together. On one hill in Embu district all three bred, usually without coming into conflict with one another. However, on one occasion I did see a Verreaux's Eagle launch an attack on a Martial Eagle from a distance of about two miles; the disputed prey was probably a hyrax, and the Verreaux's Eagle, the smaller bird, got it.

Another way of simplifying the study of the effect of raptors on their prey is to start from the prey species and work back to the birds that feed on it. In some cases the prey species is very specialised, for instance in the Bat Hawk. This is a wide ranging but very local raptor that lives almost exclusively on small bats (not the large fruit bats) which it captures by very swift flight in the last of the daylight and dusk. The Bat Hawk catches most of its prey in about a quarter or half an hour each day. Moreover, it cannot always succeed, as it must have a clear open space, such as a river pool, railway station platform, beach, or large lawn against which to sight and catch its rapidly moving prey. In such a case, when one compares the numbers of bats and of Bat Hawks it becomes perfectly plain at once that the Bat Hawk can have little effect on the numbers of the bats. Owls and falcons only kill bats as a sideline, and are not important overall predators.

Another good example is provided by fish. There is only one species of eagle, the African Fish Eagle that regularly eats fish, and the only other raptor that does is the Osprey. The Vulturine Fish Eagle takes some fish, and so do kites, but as a sideline only. It ought therefore to be fairly simple to relate the numbers of Fish

Eagles to the numbers of their prey, and this has been done on Lake Albert. Here it appeared that the total known population of Fish Eagles accounted for only 0·3% of the known catch of fish by human fishermen, and of course for a far smaller percentage of the total fish population in the lake. Even that figure of 0·3% was probably too high, and it is safe to conclude that the Fish Eagle has little overall effect on the numbers of fish in African rivers and lakes and that it is not a danger to fishery interests.

In some classes of prey, notably the small mammals such as rats, squirrels, shrews and the like, the situation is much more complex. Even here, however, in any part of Africa one will find actually fewer species preying on such mammals than would appear from Table 10 or 11. There are, for instance, two species of resident buzzards in African savannas, but there is little if any overlap in their ranges, and in any given area the rat population is probably only attacked by one species of resident buzzard and migrant races of the European Buzzard. Thus, on the plains near Nairobi in Kenya, rats and mice might be attacked by about 10 species of diurnal raptors—the Tawny Eagle, Bateleur, Augur Buzzard, Black-shouldered Kite, Secretary Bird, and White-eyed or Greater Kestrel, augmented in winter by migrant Steppe Eagles, Common Buzzards, and Pale and Montagu's Harriers. This reduces the list of about 36 species potentially able to attack this class of prey in Africa as a whole to less than a third. In such ways the problem if still difficult and complex, can be reduced to manageable proportions.

Unfortunately no quantitative studies of the full effect of any population of raptors on their prey has yet been attempted in Africa, on the lines of the studies undertaken by the Craighead brothers in the United States. Were they to be undertaken I believe that the answer would be that no class of avian predators, efficient though they might be, would have anything better than a local effect in controlling the numbers of their prey. It is possible that Tawny Eagles and migrant harriers, passing down the Rift Valley in October and November, may congregate here and there in such numbers as to have a marked temporary effect on the population of their potential prey. But as a whole it seems more likely that the raptor population has little overall effect on the major population fluctuations that are brought about by droughts or diseases. They may possibly smooth out the curves of these fluctuations to a minor degree, but that is all.

Chapter 21
Territory and the Regulation of Raptor Numbers

Ornithologists can claim to have been among the first scientists to recognise the true importance of territorial behaviour—to be followed in these days by mammalogists and even anthropologists. So far as birds of prey are concerned the idea goes back at least to Aristotle, who observed that one does not find two pairs of eagles in the same wood. His observation was not strictly correct, for some birds of prey nest in colonies or in loose groups, but he was broadly right for the species he could have known. Birds of prey may thus have been the first group of birds in which the phenomenon of territory was recognised. Serious study of territory in birds dates from Eliot Howard, in 1920.

At the present time a territory is defined as "a defended area", one from which the owner excludes other individuals of its own kind, and perhaps of other species. From early observations on birds of prey have sprung a good many misconceptions, repeated from book to book without critical examination. Many think of birds of prey as fierce and aggressive, defending their territory from others of their kind by violent fighting, sometimes to the death, and mercilessly expelling their own young to starve if necessary, when the time comes for them to be independent. Only recently, I have seen it written that the Golden Eagle (an African species in the Palearctic northwest of the continent) fiercely defends its very large territory. In fact, from a long experience of Golden Eagles, it has seemed to me clear they do not defend their territories by acts of overt violence, even when a rather dense population of eagles is living permanently in an area where natural food is very scarce. Many other eagles, including the closely related Verreaux's Eagle, likewise do not defend their territories by obvious battle. The idea of a territory as a defended area needs some re-thinking as far as birds of prey are concerned.

In Africa, where birds of prey can often be studied in unusually undisturbed conditions, they appear to behave much as they do

EMBU DISTRICT, CENSUS AREA 1949-52   146 Sq. Miles

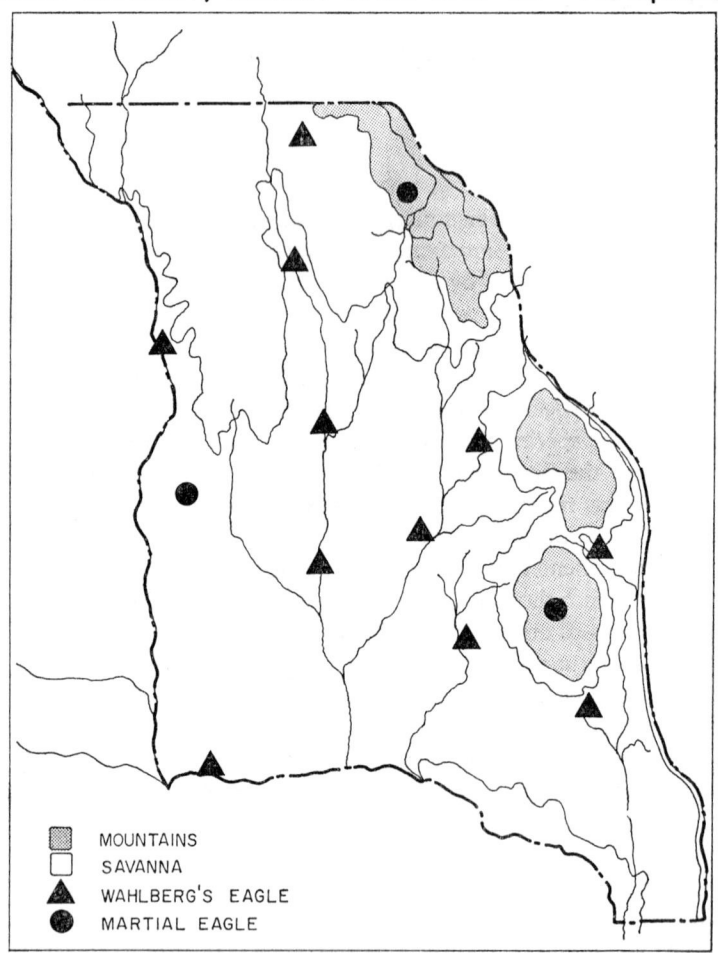

Fig. 16

elsewhere. Some species, especially the large falcons, buzzards, and some kites, unquestionably defend their territory by vigorous attack, not only against their own but other species. Others, equally well-equipped for attack, allow intruders to pass through or over their territory unmolested. Violent defence of a territory is by no means the rule. Some species are definitely colonial, such as the

Territory and the Regulation of Raptor Numbers

four species of Griffon Vultures, the Swallow-tailed Kite, and the Lesser Kestrel. In these, any territorial defence is reserved for a few square yards or feet round the nest itself. Others, such as the Fish Eagle, sometimes seem to breed in loose groups where the individual pairs, although some distance apart, seem too close for the situation to have come about by chance.

Territories are, in fact, sometimes vigorously defended, sometimes not, and whether the area is defended or not depends more upon the individual behaviour of the species concerned than its power, speed or offensive equipment. The largest and most powerful eagles in Africa, for instance, are not normally aggressive. The area that is defended may vary from a few square feet in the case of a colonial vulture to a large area of several square miles, in the case of some large falcons or buzzards. Yet pairs of eagles, which are not obviously aggressive to others, seem to be able to hold influence over a very large area which, in a species such as the Bateleur or Martial Eagle, may be as much as 50–70 square miles. Evidently, an area of this size cannot be patrolled and defended all the time by any raptor, however keen-sighted and swift. In theory a Martial Eagle, the possessor of a territory perhaps 8–10 miles across, may be able to see another Martial Eagle the instant it crosses the boundary, but in practice it could hardly do so. Yet such very large areas do remain, from year to year, the domain of particular pairs, with no other pair of the same species attempting to nest therein.

In such cases it is probably desirable to abandon the term "territory", at least implying a defended area, and substitute the term "home range", meaning the area hunted over at one time or another by an individual or a pair. Raptor "territories" in Africa, as elsewhere, can in fact be divided into three types. First, the actual nesting territory, which is often or usually defended against all comers, and may be a few square yards of cliff or quite a large area, depending on the inherent aggressiveness of the species concerned. Secondly, the much larger "home range" including and surrounding the nesting site, but not defended in its entirety or consistently; this is what most people actually think of as the "territory" of a pair—the ground over which they may hunt. And finally, some species of migrant birds of prey may perhaps take up and defend a temporary winter territory, where they hunt for the time being.

This last type can be dismissed with a few words, although more observations are needed on the point. I have not observed that temporary winter territories are important, and a good many migrant birds of prey feed in company when they find a good area for food. Steppe Buzzards, belonging to a strongly territorial genus, sometimes appear to take up a temporary hunting ground for a few weeks together. However, although I sometimes find the same Steppe Buzzard in the same place for some time in the forest near my house at Karen I do not believe they defend this temporary hunting ground against others. I do not, therefore, think that winter territories among migrant birds of prey are important in tropical Africa.

In many African birds of prey, owls and diurnal raptors alike, the actual vicinity of a nest is either defended from intruders, or is the centre of anxiety when danger threatens. In my experience, the species most likely to defend their nests vigorously are kites, buzzards and falcons. I have been struck by both Black Kites and Peregrine Falcons, but ordinarily I do not feel any anxiety in the presence of much more powerful and potentially dangerous species such as Verreaux's or the Martial Eagle. Some eagles, however, are aggressive, including Ayres and the African Hawk Eagle, and the very powerful Crowned Eagle. But vigorous or violent defence against a human intruder is shown only by a minority of species, and by many not at all.

Many species do, however, show anxiety near the nest, and in owls this may result in distraction display. The male Verreaux's Eagle Owl flies from a high perch at an angle towards the ground, then clings to a low branch upside down, flopping about and shrieking. This does not deceive a human being who knows what he is about, but does deceive a dog (which will pursue the owl, but could not in any case climb the tree to get at the nest). Bateleur Eagles, which often nest close to a path or road, will pay very little attention to passers by but demonstrate violently if one actually climbs to the nest. The eagle first dives at the intruder with loud flapping noises of the wings and, if that fails, perches on a tree nearby and barks, jerking itself up and down. This creates the impression that the bird is beside itself with fury, but could well be a form of distraction display. These rather violent displays contrast with the low anxious barks emitted by a Fish Eagle near the nest, or the soaring overhead at a safe distance of many other species.

A raptor which produces such a defensive reaction to a human being may be expected to react vigorously to other raptors or to other potentially dangerous animals. Augur Buzzards show anxiety by flying close by and calling, though they are not aggressive to human beings near their nests. They are, however, among the most aggressive of all to other birds of prey, or to such birds as ravens that live in the same area. I have seen a spectacular "dogfight" in which a pair of Verreaux's Eagles first attacked an adult Lammergeier that passed near their nest, all three being then attacked and routed by a pair of Augur Buzzards, much smaller than either the eagles or the Lammergeier. Black Kites and Peregrine Falcons are aggressive alike to humans, cats and dogs, and to other birds near their nesting sites, and although Crowned Eagles are not normally very aggressive in this way I have seen one strike a Hooded Vulture close to the nest. It is these relatively rare violent displays which scarcely ever result in physical damage that have led many people to think of birds of prey as aggressive, defending their territory against all comers. In fact, such aggression is less common than usually supposed, and there are many species that do not behave aggressively at all.

We must assume that aggressive demonstrations of this sort would be of greater value and importance in preventing other raptors, especially of the same species, from approaching the nest site than against humans or other animals. Since breeding pairs of a species are usually well-spaced over a large area of country actual conflict with an individual of the same species is rather seldom seen. The situation can be artificially contrived by, for instance, placing a stuffed specimen in the occupied territory, or by capturing and releasing a live bird. But as far as I know little or no experiment of this sort has been done in Africa with birds of prey, either diurnal or nocturnal.

In natural conditions some species in which such reactions might often be observed are the Tawny Eagle, Black Kite, and Fish Eagle. In the first two, migrant adults from Europe and Asia mingle in winter with adults of the resident races. The Tawny Eagle is a solitary breeder, while both African Yellow-billed Kites and Fish Eagles often breed so close together that the adults of adjacent pairs must see each other constantly. Among kites I have seen breeding adults attack and pursue each other for a short distance, but seldom for long. Tawny Eagles, in Kenya, do not usually breed while migrant adults are present, and a better area in which to observe possible reactions of this sort would be in the northern tropics, where Tawny Eagles breed during the European winter.

In the Fish Eagle and the Black Kite, both of which tend to be semi-colonial, breeding in loose groups, frequent violent aggression towards their near neighbours could be disadvantageous to successful nesting. The need to drive all comers away from the nest site could lead to the egg or small chick being exposed too often to sun, wet, or to enemies such as crows. Kites are quite likely to steal sticks from the nests of other kites if they get the chance, and some aggression and pursuit is seen. However, although there was no obvious aggression, some results seemed to indicate that pairs nesting close together might have more subtle antagonistic effects upon each other.

Among seven pairs of Fish Eagles that I studied on Lake Victoria I never saw any overt aggression between adjacent pairs, though in some cases the nests were only two hundred yards apart, and the owners often flew over each other's nest sites. They appeared to have no effect in arousing defensive reactions from their near neighbours.

In the three years of the study the overall breeding success was 0·66 young per pair per annum. However, the seven pairs could be divided into two classes: four " outside" pairs breeding around the perimeter of the island group, and three "inside" pairs breeding along a channel between the two largest islands. The outside pairs were more successful, rearing 11 young in the three years, an average of 0·92 young/pair/annum. The inside pairs reared only 1 young or 0·11/pair/annum between them. One pair bred twice and failed once, one pair did not breed in any year, and the third broke up or disappeared in the third year of observation. I found other suggestive cases of the same sort on other neighbouring islands, where pairs that bred close together seemed less successful than those which bred apart. For what that is worth in such a small sample, the figures are statistically significant. Although then, Fish Eagles may be very tolerant of near neighbours, and may not actually attack them, some other influence, perhaps frequent calling, may prevent them from breeding successfully if too close to one another.

However, later results obtained at Lake Naivasha conflict with these indications. There is a very large population, about 70 pairs, on Lake Naivasha, and 54 of these can be viewed from a boat in

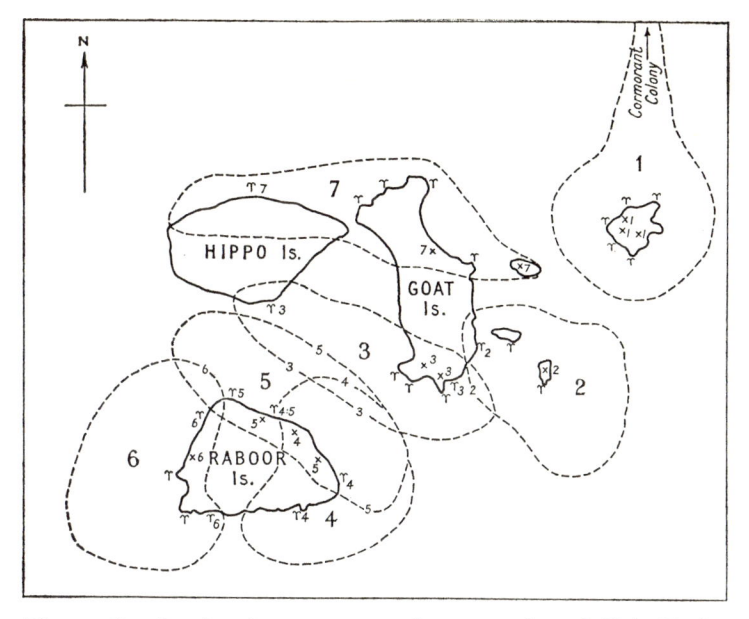

Fig. 17 Overlapping home ranges of seven pairs of Fish Eagles
Haliaeetus vocifer, Kaloka Islands, Kavirondo Gulf.
Islands.
Boundaries of normal ranges of each pair, dotted lines.
γ or γ4: trees on which eagles habitually perched. x3: nest sites of individual pairs.
In the pairs concerned, pairs 1, 2, 6, and 7 (outside pairs) in three years made 9 attempts to breed, laid 19 eggs and reared 11 young (0.92/pair/annum). Pairs 3, 4 and 5 (inside pairs) made only 3 attempts to breed, laid 6 eggs and reared 1 young in the same time (0.11 young/pair/annum). Breeding rate of outside pairs is very significantly better than that of inside pairs. ($p = .001$)

two days. Close neighbours do continually call at one another, and demonstrate to or attack others that pass over their territories. At Lake Naivasha, however, there is no clearly defined breeding season, some pairs breeding in every month. Possibly if all the pairs bred at the same time of the year, territorial conflict might be more likely to occur.

The Fish Eagle is evidently a good species in which to study this type of effect, for it is very common in places, and largely unmolested. Another case now receiving close study is the remarkable group of Verreaux's Eagles that breed in the Matopos Hills of Rhodesia. In an area of 220 square miles here, there are at least 52 pairs of Verreaux's Eagles, with an average "home range" of 4.2 square miles. Some of the home ranges, however, are much smaller than others and some of the pairs are no more than one and a half miles apart. One may sit on top of a hill in the Matopos and see four or five pairs of Verreaux's Eagles in the air at the same time. If a human can see them they can evidently see each other, yet they do not obviously fight. A superabundance of the food animal, hyrax, may here result in an unusual degree of mutual tolerance; but it will be worth comparing the breeding success of pairs that are very close to one another with that of pairs that are further apart.

Most of the birds of prey in Africa do not have the semi-colonial or colonial habits of Fish Eagles or kites. Any careful surveys that have been done indicate that they are spaced out remarkably evenly over a large area of terrain. Fig. 16 shows the distribution of Wahlberg's and Martial Eagles, for instance, in 146 square miles of Embu district in 1952. It can be seen that although there is some variation in the distance between individual nesting sites there is no tendency to nest in groups in for instance, the rather common Wahlberg's Eagle. This regular espacement from pair to pair is typical of a majority of the birds of prey that have been closely studied in this way (which do not include any owls at all—in Africa). If, as appears to be the case, it is not usually brought about through overt aggression between adjacent pairs, then how is this regular division of the available ground achieved?

Passerine birds, and a good many other species such as grouse or, in Africa, francolins, advertise their position by singing or calling from regularly used song-posts. It is likely that the same means of advertisement is used by a great many birds of prey, including owls. Some birds of prey are more vociferous than others, and, as a general rule, the most vociferous appear to be those which live in thick woodland, dense thornbush, or forest. Species that live in open plains, such as the Tawny Eagle or the Black-breasted Snake Eagle, are much less vociferous. The calling of birds of prey probably serves the same purpose as passerine song, and in some cases must help to establish the ownership of a home range. But voice as an

Territory and the Regulation of Raptor Numbers 239

advertising medium is more important in some species than in others.

Opposite my house at Karen there is a patch of forest which is inhabited by a pair of Crowned Eagles and several pairs of African Goshawks. Both of these species would be difficult to find and observe if they remained within the thick growth, and they would likewise find it very difficult to observe any neighbours. Both perform striking and noisy aerial displays. The Goshawks fly high over the forest, with slow and regular wing beats, uttering a loud rather rasping "krit", like two stones being sharply rubbed together. The male of the pair that lives near my house does this over a considerable area, within half a mile or so of the nest site, and also perches on top of trees, often on a bare branch, and calls. In either event he is many times more obvious, not only to me, but presumably to other Goshawks in the forest, than when he is hunting or perching within the canopy. These displays usually take place on fine mornings when the air is soarable, and they are noted outside the breeding season as well as when nesting. They cannot fail to advertise the male in his breeding area.

There is only one pair of Crowned Eagles in this patch of forest, which is small and isolated. However, in more extensive forests such as those on Mount Kenya or Mount Elgon there are many pairs. Essentially, they appear to behave in just the same sort of way as the Goshawk. The male Crowned Eagle's display is particularly striking, and at once draws attention to the bird. He soars high up, performing vigorous dives and upward swoops, and uttering a continuous loud whistling "kewick-kewick-kewick" for minutes at a stretch. Although one at once hears this sound the bird is often so high up as to be quite invisible with binoculars, but audible at $1\frac{1}{2}$-2 miles range. Loud sound is reinforced with vigorous aerobatics, so that any other Crowned Eagle in the area would almost certainly see and note these actions. Within the forest canopy either Crowned Eagles or Goshawks could come to very close range before they could see one another; but the aerial noisy displays probably help to prevent such encounters, and ensure that the individuals of the species are regularly spaced through the available habitat.

Many other species of African raptors display in the same way, for instance the Long-crested Eagle, Brown Snake Eagle, the Augur and Red-necked Buzzards, the Lizard Buzzard, and Chanting

Goshawks—which usually emit their regular series of melodious calls from a perch. Even the terrestrial Secretary Bird, which hunts exclusively on the ground, performs a spectacular soaring and diving display, accompanied by loud growling groans. At night the same process can be noted at work with owls. One assumes that owls cannot see each other in the dark at a range of even a quarter of a mile, and calling serves to establish their position. Even small species, such as the Scops Owl or Pearl-spotted Owlet, can emit loud or very far-carrying calls, while the deep hooting of such species as Mackinder's Eagle Owl reverberates about the high mountain valleys where they live.

These methods perhaps serve to ensure that a home range, much larger than the actual nesting area, is demonstrably occupied, if not defended by the individuals of particular pairs. In the case of the Crowned Eagles I know well, at Karen and at Eagle Hill in Embu district, the male seldom displays directly over the nest site. He is usually a mile or more away from it. In both these pairs the nests are isolated from those of other Crowned Eagles, but the behaviour does not seem to differ from that of forest pairs, and one must assume that it works for the species as a whole. By displaying at some distance from the nest, but not necessarily right on the boundary of the home range, the male is enabling any other Crowned Eagle in adjacent ground to know where he is without approaching to such close range that contact occurs. In this way fighting, which could be disastrous in such powerfully armed birds, may be avoided.

However, the use of voice as a method of advertising the owner in its home range is far from universal. Some large species still manage to maintain control over a big area while scarcely uttering a sound. As a general rule, among closely related species, it has seemed to me that the more vociferous types are those which live in thick cover, where sound might be expected to be more effective than sight. Thus, in the Martial Eagle, which is the Crowned Eagle's nearest relative, but is an inhabitant of plains and savanna rather than forest or woodland, calling is quite loud, but is confined to a rather short period and usually near the breeding site; no vigorous noisy displays of the type performed by the Crowned Eagle are seen in the Martial Eagle. The Brown Snake Eagle, which lives in woodland and thornbush, is likewise very much more vociferous than is the Black-breasted Snake Eagle, which lives in open plains.

However, one must be careful about such generalisations for one of the noisiest species in Africa is the Fish Eagle—in which pairs often nest so close together that they cannot avoid seeing each other. Calling, in this species, is stimulated by the calling of neighbours, and apparently establishes territorial rights. It seemed to me that the "inside" and less successful pairs at Lake Victoria were more vociferous than the more successful "outside" pairs, and at Lake Naivasha adult mated birds call constantly at neighbours or any strangers passing over or near.

How a bird that makes hardly any noise in the ordinary course of events makes its presence felt over as much as fifty square miles of country we do not know. However, we must take into account the superior eyesight of such birds. A Martial Eagle, which can see and attack a flock of guineafowl at an estimated range of four miles, can probably also see its neighbour at least five or six miles away. Given to flying at great heights, Martial Eagles may well make soundless demonstrations to others of their kind which are unobserved by human beings on the ground.

On rare occasions it does happen that two eagles or other large raptors do approach one another in a situation where conflict is likely. The available evidence for what actually happens then is very slender, but on a few occasions I have seen what I believe is a threat flight. In this the aggressor flies deliberately and straight at the intruder, with head up, rather measured wingbeats, sometimes calling. It is as if the bird were trying to fly forward in a heraldic attitude—which is the standard form of threat display when on the nest or on a perch. On the occasions when I have seen this performance the intruder has immediately withdrawn without a fight. Something in the other bird's attitude seems to warn it that to remain is undesirable.

Too little is known about this whole subject, but once the erroneous idea of constant fierce territorial fighting between adjacent pairs of raptors has been discarded, we may find that such symbolic behaviour, which makes clear the situation of the owner within its home range, is the more usual method of ensuring adequate espacement.

In some birds of prey it is not necessary for the individuals to maintain either a large inviolate nesting territory or a home range. These include the colonial vultures, and few other truly colonial species such as the Swallow-tailed Kite and Lesser Kestrel. In these, the individuals of a colony forage without conflict over a very large area and defend from each other only a few square feet near the nest, if that (there is no evidence, from what little is known, that the Swallow-tailed Kite does defend its nest). Griffons and other large colonial vultures enforce a dominance hierarchy when at a carcase; but this has little to do with the normal concept of a territory or home range, as an area defended or occupied by an individual or a pair, to the exclusion of others of the same species.

In every territory or home range the resident pair of raptors has a nest site. In most of the species that have been studied for any length of time it is this that tends to be permanent, while the individuals of the pair occupying the area change. This may not, of course, be the case in all species. However, it has been true for all of the large species I have studied, even in migrant species such as Wahlberg's Eagle. I know one pair of Wahlberg's Eagles in which the male was of the pale phase while the female was dark brown. They were mated together for at least four years and, though absent from their breeding area from about February to about August, they reappeared at the beginning of each breeding season. I can recognise the individuals of the pairs of Crowned and Ayres Eagles that I study from year to year; and one female Crowned Eagle went blind in her right eye so that I was able to recognise her successor with certainty as soon as she appeared.

Although much more study is needed I would expect this principle to apply to almost all birds of prey, including owls. In smaller species changes of mate would occur more often than in larger, longer lived species. In all the species I have studied for more than a few years, when one individual disappears the survivor remains at the site and acquires a new mate. In practice this means that the prey in the territory or home range is preyed upon by a pair of individuals, their offspring before independence, and their successors. The hunting pressure exerted by resident species on particular prey animals is likely to be relatively constant from year to year.

There are some species, however, in which the raptor population seems to fluctuate more widely than usual. Such would include the Secretary Bird and the Black-shouldered Kite which, in the Nairobi area, seem to be more numerous in some years than in others. These are inhabitants of the grass plains, feeding chiefly on a variety of large insects and small grass rodents, which are subject to cycles of abundance, not necessarily regular, probably in response to climatic conditions. After the exceptional rainy season of 1961, for instance, grass mice and insects both became unusually abundant, and in 1962–63 both Black-shouldered Kites and Secretary Birds were more numerous than they have been since. At least one pair of Secretary Birds in the Nairobi National Park reared two broods in that season. The fluctuation in numbers of such arctic and temperate species as the Snowy Owl, Short-eared Owl, and Rough-legged Buzzard in response to lemming or vole cycles is quite well documented, and it is not surprising to find that something of the same sort occurs on the plains of East Africa, an environment in which fluctuating abundance of mice and insects would be likely to show such an effect. Even then, I had the feeling that the home ranges of the pairs of Secretary Birds remained more or less constant; more of them were occupied by breeding pairs and some of these pairs bred more successfully than usual. Unfortunately I was so hard-worked at the time that I was only able to make very general observations.

One would expect food supply to have an overall effect in controlling the numbers of raptors in any area. In areas with abundant food supply a particular raptor species should have a smaller territory or home range than in an area where food is scarce. There is probably a general broad correlation between food supply and the size of home range, but it also seems that even in areas where food supply is very abundant in relation to the requirements of the resident pair of raptors, home ranges do not fall below a certain minimum size. In the discussions on the predation effect of African birds of prey it seemed clear that pairs often appropriate and occupy a much larger area, in terms of the biomass of probable prey within it, than is strictly needed for survival.

Little if any good quantitative work has been done in Africa on this subject, though a competent observer can form a general idea of the relative abundance of possible prey animals from one year to another. However, there are pertinent examples from other areas. The Golden Eagle has not been extensively studied in Africa, but in Scotland the home range of a pair does not fall much below 11,000 acres whatever the abundance of suitable prey animals within it. In parts of the country where food is very scarce, the eagles could exert a limiting effect on their favoured prey; in others they could hardly have much effect. Likewise, in an area of savanna with a few widely scattered pairs of Martial Eagles and African Hawk Eagles the numbers of the latter remained more or less constant while the numbers of guineafowl and francolins (gamebirds rearing relatively large broods) varied a good deal from one year to another.

Evidently more quantitative work should be done in Africa, relating the numbers of food animals to the numbers and breeding success of the raptors that prey upon them. If and when such work is done, however, I would expect it to support in most cases, the general conclusion arrived at by observation, that it is behaviour and not the available food supply that controls the size of a raptor's home range or territory, and hence the total population of raptors that can exist in any stretch of country. We do not, as yet, fully understand what sort of behaviour this is, but it seems plain that in some way a pair of Martial Eagles or Bateleurs manage to exclude others of their species from a 50 square mile stretch of country, which may contain enough food of the right sort to suffice many members of the same species and which, in the European winter, supports other apparently competitive raptors. Only time and prolonged observation will provide the necessary clues to answer such puzzling questions.

Chapter 22
Breeding Seasons and Food Supply

In cold or temperate climates in high latitudes the breeding season of raptors of all kinds is mainly dictated by the weather conditions. They cannot breed in winter, and often migrate right out of their breeding areas, though a few hardy species such as Gyrfalcons remain. The breeding season is thus concentrated in the warmer months of the year. This happens also to be the time at which all probable prey species, insects, small mammals, frogs, reptiles, and birds, multiply: fish may sometimes be an exception to this rule of summer breeding, but then they cannot be caught by a bird of prey under ice.

Most of Africa, with relatively small exceptions, in the mountains of the Cape and the Atlas, is warm enough at all times of the year for the prey to be active, and for raptors to breed. Wet and dry seasons here take the place of winter and summer. Variations of temperature, while still considerable, are certainly not of the magnitude observed in high latitudes. Moreover, very low temperatures, in which breeding could scarcely succeed, are rare. In tropical Africa it ought, therefore, to be relatively easy to decide whether breeding seasons are controlled by weather conditions or by abundance of food supply. In temperate climates the generally held view is that the breeding seasons are so timed that the young are being reared when food supplies are maximal, in mid and late summer, though low temperatures in any case prevent breeding in autumn and winter. In the tropics we might perhaps expect to see the effect of fluctuating food supplies dominant over weather influences in regulating the time of year at which breeding takes place.

In northern and southern temperate Africa the raptors tend to breed in the late winter or very early spring. Breeding is usually over by the beginning of the hot dry summer characteristic of Mediterranean climates. In the tropical zones north and south of the equatorial two-season rainfall belt there is one long dry season and one long rainy season. Here all records indicate that raptors, diurnal species and owls alike, tend to lay eggs in the dry season, often towards the end of it, so that the young get on the wing in the early rains. There thus appears to be a strong preference for breeding in cool and/or dry seasons in most of Africa, and it has often been suggested that this is because, at that time, cover is at a minimum and prey easy to catch.

In the belt on either side of the Equator, where the rains either come in two seasons separated by well marked droughts or, in forest areas, occur in every month of the year, with peaks of higher rainfall at certain times, there are a suggestive number of exceptions to this general rule of dry-season breeding. In Eastern Kenya, where the two rainy seasons are both short, occurring from mid-March to late May and late October to mid-December, there is a strong tendency for many species to lay in June–August. However, a good many species may lay later, and so find themselves breeding through the Short Rains—October–December—which may be the wettest time of the year. Breeding in the Long Rains, April–May, is exceptional. It thus appears here that the birds of prey start to breed during the longer and cooler of the two annual dry seasons, but are often caught in heavy rain and the resulting conditions of thick cover in the latter part of the breeding season. So far as I have been able to observe, this is little disadvantage to them, and they succeed in rearing young.

Some specific cases may better illustrate the point. Wahlberg's Eagle lays in August–October, especially September, throughout its breeding range. With a 45-day incubation period and a 70-day nestling period this means that the young are first on the wing in mid-November to mid-January, chiefly in December. In Rhodesia, where the species is a definite migrant, this breeding season begins in dry weather, but ends after rains have started. In eastern Kenya the breeding begins towards the end of the longer dry season (and in the hottest part of it), continues through the Short Rains, and the young get on the wing in the first part of the December–March dry season. In Western Kenya breeding begins in the latter part of a long rainy season, and ends in the dry season. However, Western Kenya may be a rather marginal habitat for Wahlberg's Eagle, which is not common there. Since Wahlberg's Eagle is no more successful as a breeder in Rhodesia than in Kenya (in fact the reverse according to the few available records: 0·62 young per annum in Kenya as cf.

0·38 in Rhodesia) we must assume that there is no disadvantage for this species in breeding through the wet season.

Black Kites, a species for which a large number of records are available, lay in December–January in the northern and West African tropics (mid dry season, young on the wing early rains); in eastern Kenya chiefly in October (early rains, young on the wing in the following dry season); in western Kenya, January (mid dry season, young on the wing early rains) and in the southern tropics of Zambia to Transvaal in August–September (mid or late dry season, young on the wing after rains have started.) There are no quantitative data on breeding success in a number of pairs of the Black Kite in different parts of Africa, but there is no reason at present to suppose they are more successful in one area than another, or to show that it matters whether the young get on the wing in a dry or a wet season.

It has usually been considered that the tendency to breed in the cool dry season is explicable on the ground that cover is then at a minimum and prey is therefore easier to catch, while the advantage of coolness is that the young can be left for considerable periods in the nest without being scorched by the sun. The latter point is incorrect. In the whole of the northern tropics, the young in most species are in the nest at the end of the dry season, when the heat is at its most extreme, in February and March. There is no reason at present to indicate that this is any particular disadvantage, though again we need those quantitative studies on breeding success—with, for instance, notes on whether successful nests were in shady or leafless trees. I doubt, personally, whether the prevailing temperatures have much effect in controlling the breeding season or affecting breeding success.

Any intelligent discussion on this subject must take into account the behaviour and the needs of the parent raptors and their young on the one hand and the behaviour of the prey on the other. A good deal is now known about the behaviour of a variety of raptor species, especially the larger and more spectacular. But we are lamentably ignorant about the behaviour and cyclic abundance of prey animals and birds, at least in relation to the raptors that might prey on them. I have been as guilty of this failing as any, and I merely observe that what is needed now is correlated study of the abundance of prey in relation to the breeding seasons and success of raptor species.

However, in the absence of really reliable data, we can attempt an analysis of some of the factors that might be involved. The discussion will have to centre upon diurnal birds of prey for the reason that only in these have any very detailed observations been made, with one as yet unpublished exception, in an owl, in South Africa. Sufficient is now known about the breeding cycle of many diurnal raptors—even in one case about the post-fledgling period, where most observers give up—to permit an intelligent discussion.

So far as the parent raptors are concerned one may consider the possible effect of weather first and food supply second. With regard to weather, only one effect is really noticeable to anyone who has studied a number of breeding pairs. It is that wet weather retards and delays hunting, and sometimes seems to make it impossible. Large soaring species, in particular, are effectively grounded by a tropical rainstorm, and may even be killed by heavy hail.

Therefore, we could expect that, if a supply of fresh food is needed daily for the young, it would be a disadvantage for the pair to have young in the nest in times of heavy rain. Yet, as we have seen, a number do have to feed young in the nest in rainy weather. Although, in Kenya, breeding in the Long Rains April–May is exceptional, this does not mean that periods of heavy rain are avoided, for in some parts of eastern Kenya the October–December rains are the heavier and more reliable of the two seasons. Black Kites and Wahlberg's Eagles still breed during August–December in these areas. I have also known an Ayres Eagle to breed successfully during the Long Rains March–July though the normal breeding season is July–November. From such facts one can perhaps conclude that though the wet weather may be a disadvantage it is not necessarily crucial.

Very hot weather is an inconvenience and a discomfort to a bird of prey such as a Tawny, Snake, or Fish Eagle, that may nest in a very open site, on the crown of a Euphorbia or an Acacia. In the Fish Eagles of Lake Victoria already mentioned I observed that the females with young in very open nests spent more time on the nest sheltering the young than did those that had young in big leafy trees. Prolonged exposure to very strong sun may kill small raptor chicks in the nest, but apparently exposure to sun is physiologically beneficial to older young, though they too experience discomfort.

From such facts we may perhaps conclude that although wet or hot weather may be a disadvantage and a discomfort it is not necessarily fatal. Indeed, it is possible that the behaviour of prey may compensate, to some extent anyway, for the shorter available hunting time resulting during spells of wet weather. Weather, in short, is in itself less likely to be of importance in controlling breeding seasons than its probable secondary effect—the development of vegetative cover and the abundance of prey living in that cover.

So far as the parents and young in the nest of a raptor are concerned there appear to me to be three points, which can be termed "points of strain", at which a shortage of food might have an important effect on the breeding cycle: (i) when the female is about to lay, (ii) during the first half of the fledgling period and (iii) when the young is about to become independent. The first could have an effect on initiating breeding, the second on brood survival, and the third on survival of the young to sexual maturity. We cannot at present say which, if any of these, is likely to be most important in its effect on the population as a whole, but probably their effect would in any case vary according to different conditions.

In a number of large raptors the male feeds the female before and during the incubation period. Before the eggs are laid this corresponds to the familiar "courtship feeding", well enough known in some smaller birds. It is associated with nest-building and copulation. If the male is unable to catch enough food for the female she will probably go off and try to catch her own, and may thus lose interest in the nest site or be unable to convert food energy into an egg.

I have observed only one case which suggests that this may possibly have happened—in the Crowned Eagle near my house in Karen in 1963. In that year, there was a new male at the site, perhaps young and inexperienced at hunting in this home range, and there was also an apparent shortage of the favourite food animal, a small antelope, the Suni, *Nesotragus moschatus*. It appeared that the male was unable to feed the female often enough, in June and July, to prevent her from going off hunting on her own, which she did. In this same pair, in 1967, by which time the male seemed to have become more expert at catching prey, the loss of a young one nearing independence in August triggered off a new breeding cycle at an abnormal time of the year. The male fed the female at the nest during October and November and repeatedly copulated with her, often when he brought prey. The female remained at the nest site and finally laid in the latter half of December. It is noteworthy that the same individual birds were concerned, and that this particular female has laid eggs in June, July, August, and December. In such a case one may reasonbly wonder what the term "breeding season" really means.

Once the young have hatched the female usually remains at the nest with them, and the male feeds not only himself but the whole family. His rate of killing, in the Crowned Eagle, is about doubled as soon as the young hatch, and the same seems to hold good for other raptors. The demand on the male's killing powers increases as the young grow until they are partly feathered, when the female can leave them alone in the nest and assist her mate in hunting. Just before this occurs the male may find himself killing for two adults and the equivalent of one to three more in the shape of the voracious young. If shortage of food during the breeding season is going to have an effect it ought to appear here, where strain on the male is at a maximum. Shortage of food at this stage could reduce brood survival, from two or more to one, or none.

Finally, it will be very little use to the species if the female lays a full clutch of fertile eggs, and the young that hatch are all reared to their first flight if thereafter they cannot find food when they become independent. An abundance of easily caught food for the newly independent young may be as important as either of the other two possible "points of strain", for the survival of the species as a whole.

Breeding seasons of African raptors should be analysed in this sort of way as well as in relation to obvious features such as rainy or dry seasons and the state of the cover. In only one African species, the Crowned Eagle, can the effect of all three of these possible points of strain be assessed, as far as I know. In this species the pre-laying period in Kenya is normally May–June, when the vegetation is long and lush following the Long Rains, the weather is cool and, in western Kenya, actually wet, and the staple food animals (so far as is known) are relatively abundant following breeding during the Long Rains. Dense vegetation might make Suni difficult to catch, but on the other hand cool moist conditions undoubtedly make them more active through the day, so that these two effects could cancel each other out. If the female is fed sufficiently, and lays her egg normally in July–August, it will hatch during September or early October, and the next point of strain, when the male has to feed himself, his mate, and a voracious growing young one comes in November. In eastern Kenya this is one of the two wettest months in the year, but in western Kenya it is the start of a dry season. Further south, eggs which have been laid in the late dry season would produce voracious young in the early rains.

It is only in the Crowned Eagle, and only in Kenya, that we know that the young one finally becomes independent of its parents 9–11 months after making its first flight. Before then it has certainly killed for itself, perhaps more often than has been observed. For a young one hatched in September from an egg laid in July of one year, and making its first flight about four months later, independence comes in September or October of the following year—at the end of a dry season when food supplies are likely to be minimal, but when cover is relatively thin. Thus, in the Crowned Eagle the two possible points of strain for the hunting male both tend to come in wet, lush conditions, and that for the newly independent young in hot dry conditions, when food supplies may be poor.

This sort of analysis can be done for any raptor in any part of Africa provided that the full details of the breeding cycle are known. Egg-laying dates, incubation and fledgling periods are accurately or approximately known for a good many species, and their near relatives can be expected to behave in a similar way. The post-fledging behaviour of the young is relatively unknown, and is most difficult to study, but it is likely that after their first flight the young may be dependent on their parents for much longer than is often thought. At any rate, to assume that birds of prey breed during the dry season because at that time cover is minimal and prey consequently easiest to catch may be to underestimate several other factors of equal importance.

A further factor which is obviously important is the behaviour of the favourite prey. Thus far, studies of breeding behaviour and seasons have not taken this into account in Africa, except in a very general way. Seasons and breeding cycles of particular species have never been properly correlated with the behaviour and abundance of the prey. This badly needs doing, for at least some of the commoner species, and I hope to work on this problem myself in future years. We need to know, of course, the type of prey taken by the species of raptor concerned, its appetite, and so on. Perhaps an ideal species to study is Verreaux's Eagle, where the food animal is almost exclusively rock hyrax; but rock hyrax are very difficult to count with any accuracy among boulder piles.

One general comment is that it appears to me an unwarranted assumption to say that in all cases food is likely to be easiest to catch in the middle of the dry season when the cover is at a minimum. Whether a food animal is easy to catch or not will depend, first on its relative abundance, and secondly on its behaviour. Even relatively scarce animals might be easier for a raptor to catch if active and mobile in the open during the day, while much more abundant species might never be caught at all if they skulked persistently in thick cover. My general impression is that the height of the dry season, after the grass has been burned off, or the leaves have fallen off the trees, is a time of little diurnal activity among many possible prey animals, while some of them, including insects, are actually less abundant then than they are in tall green cover. This varies from animal to animal, and from place to place. But in many areas birds, small mammals, snakes, frogs, and insects are all more obvious and active in the open during the first half of the rainy season than at any other time.

I have not, here, attempted to explain why breeding seasons in African raptors have evolved so as to occur at certain times of the year, for I personally feel that we do not as yet know enough to attempt any such explanation on satisfactory grounds. What does seem plain, however, is that there must be some factor that initiates the breeding season. This can scarcely be a foreknowledge of the probable abundance of prey and the cover conditions several months later. It is possible that the main reason why raptors breed in the dry seasons is that the changes in weather are obvious and clear cut phenomena which birds of prey can observe as well as we can. The onset of the dry or wet season which, as we have seen, tends to influence migrations within the tropics, could also be the most important factor in initiating the breeding cycle, irrespective of the relative abundance of prey, or of how easy the animals may be to catch.

Once again, some support for the idea that seasonal weather changes are the "trigger" for the breeding cycle comes from the Crowned Eagles I have studied so long at my house and at Eagle Hill. In both these places the "normal" course of events is for breeding to commence in earnest in May–June, about 7–8 months after the last young bird became independent the previous September–November. Sporadic building may have occurred just after independence of the young, but is usually discontinued in the wet weather of November–December. The fine sunny weather of late May and June, with the air soarable for the male in display, and perhaps an abundance of Suni after the Long Rains, so that feeding the female at the nest may be easier, may help to initiate a chain of events which, if successful, will only be concluded 500 days later. Equally, however, as the observations at Karen show, the mere physical absence of the young bird, through a premature accident, can initiate the whole cycle in the Crowned Eagle at an abnormal date. The fact is that although there are some pointers, we are not able to say yet whether weather, food supply, or some quite different factor initiates the breeding seasons of African birds of prey.

Chapter 23
The Breeding Cycle

In some African raptors the breeding cycle has been studied as intensively, if not more so, than anywhere else in the world. In others, nothing at all is known, no nest ever having been found. Between these two stages of knowledge there is every variation, from a few known nests to a thorough knowledge of behaviour which yet leaves some details missing. It is convenient here to summarise what is known so that those who find themselves with an opportunity to study a little known species may do so, and not repeat the mistake I made twenty-seven years ago at Ilorin in Nigeria, in 1940–42. I had a pair of Red-necked Falcons breeding in a Borassus palm outside my office, and paid little attention to them; I have never seen another. Admittedly I was under grave suspicion from my superiors for being interested in birds at all, and might have got the sack for watching the birds instead of turning over files, but the fact remains that I have ever since regretted the loss of that opportunity.

So far as the knowledge of the breeding cycle is concerned, I divide the African birds of prey into five broad classes. (1) Unknown; the nest has never been found. (2) Little-known; a few nests have been found and the eggs described, but no sustained observations on behaviour have been made. (3) Well-known; a good general idea of the type of nest and nest site, clutch size etc. derived from many nests, and a few sustained observations covering part of a breeding cycle in at least one case. (4) Very well known; the general nesting behaviour is understood and detailed accurate observations are available throughout most of the breeding cycle for at least one nest, leaving only a few details to add. (5) Intimately known; observations in detail made over many years or at many nest sites, including such advanced detail as changes of mates among adults and survival rates of young.

It does not matter, of course, what one calls these various classes but it is useful to subdivide the available knowledge in this way as it

The Breeding Cycle

can help to direct future research. As will be seen to date, there has been an understandable tendency to study the finest and most spectacular species (of which I have been as guilty as anyone) and to neglect commoner species, which would be both easier to study and perhaps more rewarding in terms of biological knowledge. Thus I class Ayres Hawk Eagle, a rare species, as intimately known, from my own studies at one nest for the last 21 years, while such much commoner species as the Harrier Hawk and Augur Buzzard are only well-known, and even the Black Kite can only be called very well known, although it is the commonest and most obvious large diurnal raptor in Africa.

It is again no surprise to find that far less is known about owls than about diurnal raptors. Those that are in the better known categories usually have not been studied in Africa, but are Palearctic species. So far as I know only one species of owl has been studied thoroughly in Africa, the Spotted Eagle Owl, by Professor G. J. Broekhuysen. His results have not been published, though he hopes to do so shortly. There is a complete lack of information on a much greater proportion of owls than of diurnal raptors.

Omitting the purely migratory species that do not breed in any part of Africa, the following is a summary of our knowledge, as it is known to me in October 1969. If I have omitted any enthusiast's work it is because it has not been published in a widely known journal or because I have not heard of it or him.

1 *Unknown.* The nests of four species of diurnal raptors, the Congo Serpent Eagle, Chestnut-bellied Sparrowhawk, Long-tailed Hawk, and Cassin's Hawk Eagle have never been found. All of these are inhabitants of the depths of Equatorial forest, and are nowhere very common therein. Anyone finding a nest of any of these would be well advised to stay and observe it if possible rather than merely collect the parents and the eggs as has so often been done in the past. It is quite possible to describe and measure eggs in the nest and colour photography is perfectly good documentary evidence.

Among owls the nests and eggs of the Bay Owl, the Abyssinian Long-eared Owl, the Russet, Cinnamon, and Morden's Scops Owl, the Maned Owl, the Red-chested Owlet, Sjostedt's Barred Owlet, (and, of course, that of the as yet unnamed owlet) Fraser's Eagle Owl, Barred Eagle Owl, Akun Eagle Owl, and the Rufous and Vermiculated Fishing Owls have never to my knowledge been found. Fourteen species, or almost half the owls occurring in Africa. Again, virtually all of them are inhabitants of dense tropical or montane forest, and usually rare even there. Once more should anyone have the luck to find a nest he should, if possible stay and watch it rather than destroy it immediately for the sake of a skin and a clutch of eggs in a museum.

2 *Little known*. In this class come the Cuckoo Falcon, Swallow-tailed Kite, Smaller Banded Snake Eagle, Southern Banded Snake Eagle, Ovampo Sparrowhawk, Grasshopper Buzzard, Mountain Buzzard, Red-necked Buzzard, Greater Kestrel, Fox Kestrel, Dickinson's Kestrel, and Red-necked Falcon. Many of these are quite common birds occurring in open country, and for some a season's observation in a good area for the particular species would advance our knowledge into the "Very well known" class. On this group, above all, there is a case for the egg-collector to hold his hand and become a steady observer for a few months. The eggs are well known and no more need to be taken.

In owls, I class here the Cape Grass Owl, Woodford's Owl, White-faced Owl, Pearl-spotted and Barred Owlets, and Pel's Fishing Owl. Again, some of these are common species living in open country—even in gardens. It is a reflection of the relative state of our knowledge of owls as compared to diurnal birds of prey that 19/29 species of owls are breeding in Africa, either unknown or little known whereas only 16/78 diurnal breeding species fall in these two categories.

3 *Well known*. Diurnal species include the Bat Hawk, Black-shouldered Kite, Vulturine Fish Eagle, Egyptian Vulture, Lammergeier, White-backed Vulture, Ruppell's Griffon, Cape Vulture, European Black Vulture (doubtfully admissible as a breeder in Africa), White-headed Vulture, Lappet-faced Vulture, Harrier Hawk (not published) African Marsh Harrier, Black Harrier, Dark Chanting Goshawk, Pale Chanting Goshawk, Gabar Goshawk, Rufous-breasted Sparrowhawk, Shikra (or little Banded Goshawk), Lizard Buzzard, Long-legged Buzzard, Augur Buzzard, Tawny Eagle, Booted Eagle, Long-crested Eagle, Pigmy Falcon (unpublished South African data), Lesser Kestrel, Grey Kestrel,

African Hobby, Sooty Falcon, Lanner, and Teita Falcon. One may comment on the fact that the Teita Falcon, whose nest had never been found until 1957, and the Sooty Falcon which breeds only in extreme desert conditions, are in this category while the abundant Tawny Eagle and all African vultures except one are also here. To my present shame I have never made the same effort over the Long-crested Eagle as I have over rarer and more spectacular species.

The number of owls in this category is small, including the Long-eared Owl, Marsh Owl, Scops Owl, Eagle Owl, Mountain and Verreaux's Eagle Owl. Of these most have been studied in their European breeding quarters, and the African species that have been observed have only been observed at one or two nests for part of a cycle. Great advances could be made in this group also.

4 *Very well known*. Here are included the Osprey, Red Kite, Black Kite, Hooded Vulture, European Griffon, Short-toed or Serpent Eagle, Brown Snake Eagle, Bateleur, Marsh Harrier, European Sparrowhawk, Little Sparrowhawk, African Goshawk, Bonelli's or African Hawk Eagle, Martial Eagle, Secretary Bird, European Hobby, Eleanora's Falcon, and Peregrine Falcon. Some of these are better known than others, including the Eleanora's and Peregrine Falcon and the Black Kite. But I know of no case among these where the entire details of a single breeding cycle have been studied and then coupled with prolonged observation over a series of years. I have watched a pair of Martial Eagles for 21 years myself, but have never yet recorded the incubation period accurately—it is still unknown. For several of the species our knowledge comes from European studies, but these are useful as comparative data for African studies yet to be done.

I do not class any owls in this category.

5 *Intimately known*. These include the African Fish Eagle, Wahlberg's Eagle, Golden Eagle, Verreaux's Eagle, Ayres Eagle, Crowned Eagle, and European Kestrel. Two of these, the Golden Eagle and European Kestrel have mainly or entirely been studied in Europe, and there may be some differences in their behaviour in Africa. The Crowned Eagle, as a result of my own prolonged studies over 22 years, is probably the best known eagle in the world, and the rare Ayres Eagle, in which I have studied one nest over 21 years, is a

good example of the value of leaving a pair alone instead of shooting them or robbing the nest—which would have nipped in the bud a valuable series of long-term observation.

Four owls, the Barn Owl, Tawny Owl, Little Owl, and Spotted Eagle Owl come in this category. Of these all but the Spotted Eagle Owl have only been studied in detail in Europe or America, and the results of Broekhuysen's long-term studies of the Spotted Eagle Owl are eagerly awaited.

It is really only in this last category that we can say that we know enough of the biology of any species to understand it properly, though even here there are of course gaps in the knowledge that can be filled by the use of more advanced techniques, or confirmatory study in different parts of Africa. We do not know, for instance, whether the Crowned Eagle behaves in the same way in southern Africa as it does in Kenya, where it normally breeds only every second year, feeding the young one after it has made its first flight for 9-11 months; observations indicate that it does not.

The details given here may perhaps serve to indicate where research on the breeding cycle may be most usefully pursued. One great gap is in the common colonial vultures, which have been neglected hitherto for probably obvious reasons; for some reason these useful and sometimes spectacular birds are thought repulsive by many. Anyone who wishes to undertake detailed research on any of these species would be well-advised to select an area where one or more is common, study at least one nest in detail throughout a season, with some confirmatory observations at other nests, and then continue over a period of years to ascertain the population over a larger area, the size of home range, breeding success and other such details. This is actually being done at present in the Serengeti National Park. A good study of the Black Kite, breaking new ground, could be made in many towns by someone with no transport. Keeping captive birds to see how much they eat is also a valuable line of research, for this is a point very difficult to establish in the wild state even by prolonged observation.

Further research on the breeding cycle in the various species will probably reveal a certain sameness in behaviour, which has appeared from the studies which have so far been done, of large and small species alike. There is a general pattern which is followed by most birds of prey that have been watched and a summary of the events likely to be observed may be helpful to others in fitting together what is seen.

In the diurnal species breeding begins with more or less spectacular display, which is often observed outside the breeding season as well, especially in those species which occupy the same home-range all the year round. Displays are mainly performed by the male, but in some species the female also displays, and often joins with the male in mutual aerial displays. The commonest forms of display are:

(i) Perching and calling. The male sits on top of a commanding perch and emits a display call, which is usually loud and far-carrying. Sometimes the species performs no other sort of display, but usually aerial displays are also performed. Females, and even immatures, may also sometimes perch and call.

(ii) Soaring and calling. The bird soars high up, or flies in circles and figures of eight, vigorously diving and swooping, attracting attention to itself by loud calling. Sometimes the vigorous flight manoeuvres are performed without calling (as for instance in the Golden and Verreaux's Eagles) but more commonly it is the loud voice that first attracts attention.

(iii) Mutual displays, in which the male flies above the female, often calling, then dives towards her; she then turns on her back and presents her feet to his. There is every variation on this theme from the slow and majestic paired circling of large vultures to the spectacular cartwheeling fall of Fish Eagles, with feet locked together. Black Kites pursue each other in weaving twisting flight and here, as in many other cases, it is easy to mistake a display for a fight, and vice versa. Most of such aerial manoeuvres, if carefully watched, will be seen to be performed by birds of different sexes, the female being larger than the male, who usually flies above and behind the female.

Owls are much less known and observed than diurnal species but doubtless the repeated calling of owls from well-used perches serves the same function as the perching and calling of the diurnal birds of prey. I have not heard any owl calling in flight, and evidently spectacular aerial manoeuvres would be very little value in birds that could not see each other in the dark half a mile away. Hence among owls voice should play a more important part in display than sight.

However, I have once seen a most extraordinary display by a pair of Verreaux's Eagle Owls, which sat in the top of a big tree and called to one another for a long time. The male jerked himself up and down, calling "Uh-uhu-uh-uh" to which the female responded with a still deeper-toned "Uh-hu". This amounts to the use of the voice in a mutual display, as opposed to aerial manoeuvres, but it does not appear to be common, though Verreaux's Eagle Owls frequently call to one another when perched in thick woodland.

Display is followed by nest building and copulation. As is well-known a nest site may be occupied for many years by the larger diurnal raptors, which repair it each year. Among smaller species the same general area may be used again and again, but the nest is annually built afresh. This accounts in part for the difficulty in finding the nests of some secretive small Sparrowhawks, or even of Snake Eagles, which build a very slight nest and usually make a new one each year.

The major part in nest building is, in most species, taken by the female. The male frequently brings sticks in the early part of the construction or nest repair and the female stays in the nest and works them into place. This varies a great deal between individuals, however. During nest-building the male is likely to feed the female at or near the nest; and feeding is sometimes accompanied by copulation, which may also take place after the bringing of a stick, or even without such preliminaries, on a branch or treetop some distance from the nest.

Feeding serves to anchor the female—who would otherwise hunt for herself when hungry—near the nest, and also probably provides her with the extra energy required for egg production. Copulation—at least in large species—does not necessarily mean that eggs will shortly be laid; I have seen successful copulation in the Crowned Eagle more than a year before egg-laying.

Owls, and all falcons also, do not build their own nests, but breed on a bare rock ledge, under a big stone, in a hole in a tree or a building, or in another large bird's nest, including the special behaviour of the Grey Kestrel which, so far as is known, breeds mainly or only in the nests of Hammerkops—as does the Barn Owl also, though not exclusively. In these there is of course no nest-building. It has often been stated that falcons build their own nests, but after an extensive study of the literature on the subject I remain unconvinced that any careful observer has ever seen this process.

The Breeding Cycle

The eggs are laid in the completed nest or scrape, and in both owls and diurnal species a clutch of several eggs is laid at intervals of several days between each egg. In cases, such as the ground-nesting harriers and some owls, where a large clutch of four or five, or even more, is laid, egg-laying may take 10–14 days. The end result of this is that, since incubation begins with the first egg, the young hatch over a longish period and the smallest is much weaker than the largest, which hatches from the first egg laid.

Usually the female incubates alone or takes the major share. The male in some diurnal species relieves her at intervals by day, but seldom even sits for half the daylight hours, so that the total share of the female is 75% or more. Even in the same species this varies between individuals. The female Crowned Eagle at Karen sits alone, but each of three females at Eagle Hill has shared these duties with her mate by day. In one recorded case, the little Sparrowhawk, a male has been known to sit all night. In diurnal species the bird that is sitting in the evening will usually continue to sit till about the middle of the following morning, but in the nocturnal owls we should expect this process to be reversed. The male would be inactive during the day on some perch, and might relieve the female on the eggs by night. Only protracted watching at night can demonstrate what occurs.

Clutches of eggs are usually small. In the better known diurnal African raptors about 11 species regularly lay only one egg; 21, one to two; 35, two to three; and 10, three or more, of which a few may sometimes lay more than four. In those species where there are enough data for a valid comparison, such as the Common, Rock, or European Kestrel (*Falco tinnunculus*) the races breeding in the tropics lay on average smaller clutches than those that breed in temperate climates. This may also apply to such large species as the Crowned Eagle, which in Kenya lays one egg about as often as two, but in South Africa normally lays two. In tropical environments there is a potentially lower breeding rate from the start, and we do not know the reason for this, though we may assume that the survival of fledged young in the tropics is easier than in temperate latitudes.

In owls clutches are usually larger than in the diurnal species, but again here we know so little of the nesting habits of many African Owls that it is difficult to generalise. However, the average clutch size of the Little Owl and the Barn Owl in Africa is less than in temperate environments. Large Eagle Owls, such as Verreaux's, lay 1–2 eggs, and usually produce only a single young one.

Incubation periods are usually quite long, varying from about 27–30 days in the smallest species (kestrels and the Little Sparrowhawk) to 49 days in the Crowned Eagle and probably even longer (50+ days) in such large vultures as the Lappet-faced Vulture or Lammergeier. It is likely that related species will have similar incubation periods irrespective of size. Ayres Eagle, weighing less than 1000 grams incubates for 45 days, the same as a Golden or Verreaux's Eagle twice the size and four times as heavy. In owls, size for size, the incubation period is relatively shorter, from what little is recorded on the subject.

In all birds of prey, owls and diurnal species alike, the eggs hatch at intervals. In the sparrowhawks, which lay rather larger clutches, the hatching period is sometimes shorter than the laying period, and it has been claimed in some European species of the genus *Accipiter* that incubation proper does not begin till the penultimate or the last egg has been laid. However, in all young African sparrowhawks and goshawks I have seen there has been a marked size difference between the eldest and the youngest, indicating that this may not be true in Africa.

Among those large eagles that lay two eggs there is generally a violent battle between the elder and the younger chick (which on hatching is only a third of its sibling's weight) which usually ends in the death of the younger chick. This does not apply so much in the case of Fish Eagles or in the Secretary Bird, which sometimes rear 2–3 young although there is a large size difference at first between the eldest and the youngest nestling.

The purpose of what has been called "the Cain and Abel battle" in the large eagles is still obscure; I have seen no explanation of this apparent biological waste (which can be avoided by laying half the number of eggs) which satisfies me. One suggestion is that fighting for food would tend to make the larger and older chick more vigorous and better able to fend for itself after independence, but no really good evidence has been put forward in support of this view. In times of food shortage the youngest and smallest of any brood, of owls and diurnal species alike, tend to succumb, for the largest and most vigorous chick will normally solicit its parent first, and be fed. The parents exercise no discrimination, but feed the chick that wants to be fed, even if smaller and weaker chicks are then ignored to starve. During the Cain and Abel battle the larger eagles watch the strife quite unconcerned. Any dead young are either thrown out of the nest or sometimes eaten by parents or, if large, left to putrefy where they are.

The end result is that invariably fewer young are reared than eggs are laid. The potential rate of breeding success is the full number of eggs in the clutch, 1, 2, or 3 or more according to species. Some eggs are inevitably infertile, which causes the first reduction. Some young that hatch are eaten by enemies, succumb to the Cain and Abel battle, or die in the nest from starvation or other causes. Study of a long series of cases will establish an average rate of breeding success, which can be defined as the number of young fledged from each nest. Generally it is necessary to have at least 20 complete records before this can be established, and this does not only mean records from successful nests. It means studying every pair in a considerable area and recording their results. Some pairs will be found, especially in many large species, not to lay eggs at all, others to lay and fail to hatch, others again to rear some young. Thus, on average, 7 pairs of Fish Eagles on Lake Victoria over three years reared 0·66 young/pair/annum, while results from the nests which actually reared young averaged 1·6 per successful nest. These pairs included every variation from one which did not lay in any of three years to one which reared four young in three years. At Lake Naivasha 53 pairs in 1968-9 averaged 0.53 young/pair and varied from two pairs that each bred twice in the course of the year to several pairs who did not breed at all, including some that regularly occupied a stretch of shoreline but had no nest.

As a rule, the larger the species, the fewer young it rears. The breeding success of the two largest eagles in Africa, the Crowned and Martial Eagles, is about 0·4 young/pair/annum, in both cases based on more than 20 records. That of small falcons and sparrowhawks, or even such species as the Black Kite and Augur Buzzard, may be more than 1·5 per pair/annum. In owls, Verreaux's Eagle Owl, the largest, rears on average less than one young per occupied nest (based on scanty records) and the Barn Owl two to three. In smaller owls we simply do not know the answer.

This replacement rate may be achieved by different means in closely allied species. In the Crowned Eagle in Kenya, for instance, the birds breed on average every second year; they only lay in consecutive years if something happens to eggs or young in the nest, or perhaps occasionally when the young has left the nest but has not become independent. In the Martial Eagle nest records show that the number of young fledged per nest is about the same, but Martial Eagles breed successfully for several years in succession and appear to alternate this with several years in which they do not breed. What process causes such variation we do not know.

The first flight of the young one is not, of course, the end of the story. We need to know how many of these young survive to independence, and thereafter to adulthood, in the case of those species such as large eagles which spend several years in immature plumage. The post-fledging period, when the young are free-moving but are still being fed by the adults, is very difficult indeed to study, and I think the only species in which it has been well observed are the Crowned and Verreaux's Eagles. In the former the young, after making its first flight, continues to be fed by the parent in the nest, or very close to it, for 9-11 months. It then leaves of its own volition, and is not driven away by the parents, as popular opinion might suppose. It, in fact, releases the parents from their duty of feeding it, simply by not being there and responding when they come with food. Perhaps this happens more often than we suppose.

At any rate, in the Crowned Eagle that breeds near my house at Karen five eggs have been laid by the same female, in 1959, '61, '64, '66 and late '67. She hatched all these eggs and reared each of the subsequent young ones to their first flight, after 110–125 days in the nest. The first three and the fifth became independent 9–11 months later but the fourth died seven months after it left the nest, from causes unknown, but probably natural. This particular female eagle, therefore, is known to have been 100% successful over a decade up to the point of fledging young, but has only reared 80% of these young to independence. Obviously, it takes many years to accumulate enough data of this sort to establish what happens in these large, slow breeding, uncommon species, but commoner species of smaller size, such as the Black Kite and Augur Buzzard, should give reliable results in three or four years' watching.

One possible method of assessing the number of young that eventually arrive at maturity is by counting accurately the proportion of immatures in the total population. Ringing results have been used in Europe and America to construct age tables showing the mortality rate of the young, but they suffer from several disadvantages, the chief being that very large numbers must be ringed before enough returns come in, and the fact that most recorded deaths are usually from unnatural causes, chiefly shooting. In some African raptors the immature and sub-adults can be easily recognised in the field, even at some distance. Such include the Fish Eagle, Bateleur, and Lammergeier. Counts show that in these species, in Kenya and Ethiopia, the proportion of young in the total population over a period of years is about 24, 31 and 23% respectively. At Lake Naivasha a year's counts gave an average of 134.4 Fish Eagles, of which 22.4 or about 17% were immature. If we assume (from inadequate evidence) that Fish Eagles are mature at four years, Bateleurs at seven years, and Lammergeiers at five or more, and that (based upon evidence from elsewhere) 75% of young raptors are bound to die before reaching maturity, we can roughly calculate the average wild life spans of adults at 16-17 for the Fish Eagle, 16-28 for the Bateleur, and about 20 for the Lammergeier.

When we reach this sort of stage we are beginning to understand the biology of the birds of prey, as opposed to merely photographing them or collecting their eggs. However, so much remains to be done on the simpler aspects of the breeding cycle in most species that it will be many years before the population structure of such species, based on enough accurate data, can be properly calculated. This brief summary of the events of the breeding cycle may help those who are interested in more than a superficial study of African birds of prey to direct their efforts to those points most in need of detailed study. And strange as it may seem, gathering accurate data on population dynamics by studying many nests over a big area can be just as interesting and less frustrating, or even boring, as trying to photograph a Martial Eagle that will not come to the nest.

Chapter 24
Birds of Prey and Man

(i) Fables, Fiction and Prejudice

Birds of prey have for centuries attracted both attention and enmity from mankind. I was surprised not long ago in Britain, to be told that there were still people who considered that there was something inherently revolting about a bird that ate the raw flesh of other animals. There is still too little general understanding of the role of predators in nature, and birds of prey are often subject to unreasoning prejudice, sometimes leading to their destruction.

At the same time there is a sort of love-hate relationship between birds of prey and man. Even though one may deplore the result it is difficult not to have a grudging admiration for the skill and speed with which a bird of prey often carries out its attack. Grumble they might, but I will wager that those two old men on the verandah in Nigeria would never forget the sparrowhawk that took a chicken from between their knees. And I have often heard people close to nature, both African and European, speak with wonder of some feat of flight they may have observed as a falcon or an eagle makes its kill.

This feeling of wonder is one factor that has led to the development of the sport of falconry. Falconry is a sport that can only be pursued in open country, and by people who have plenty of leisure, or who have enough money to command the services of full-time falconers. It originated in the East and may have been practised by the ancient Egyptians, who certainly held certain birds of prey in awe. In North Africa it was and no doubt still is practised by Arabs, always among the premier practitioners of falconry. But in tropical Africa, even in open country where falcons occur, and where they might successfully be used, I have never come across any tribe who had any knowledge of falconry. The idea that one could train a hawk to do one's bidding has always seemed totally strange to them. In tropical forests, or in the rather dense woodland that covers much of Central and West Africa, falconry is scarcely practicable, for the hawk is likely to be lost in a short time. In Africa there are ecological and social reasons why falconry has never been extensively used as a means of food getting or a sport of kings.

There are, however, a number of African species of hawks that have been used successfully in falconry. They include races of the Peregrine Falcon, the Lanner and other falcons such as Kestrels and the Red-headed Falcon, while I have heard of a trained African Hobby. Several short-winged hawks, the Shikra, the African Goshawk, Black Sparrowhawk, Ovampo Sparrowhawk, and the Chanting Goshawks have been tried, and several African eagles, the Martial, Crowned, Verreaux's, African Hawk Eagle, and Ayres Hawk Eagle have all been trained. The most successful is the Martial Eagle, preferably a male, for reasons of weight. One can train a Bateleur, a Hooded Vulture, or a Black-shouldered Kite to come to a lure, but not necessarily to kill anything one wants it to kill.

In selecting a hawk for trial a would-be falconer should study what it naturally kills in the wild state. A bird which habitually kills gamebirds—such as the Martial Eagle, Lanner Falcon, or Bonelli's Eagle—will be more likely to give sport than one like the Bateleur which, although a magnificent flier, in nature kills snakes or eats small dead animals that it picks up on the roads. Though Bateleurs are, I believe, very entertaining birds to keep; I once had one for a time, and it was certainly a strange and intriguing creature.

Among people who are daily in close touch with life in the bush, there may be fables and legends about birds of prey, and there is often a very good understanding of their general behaviour, and of what they eat. This varies from tribe to tribe in Africa, and usually disappears as soon as a smattering of western education is grafted upon native lore. I have met many illiterate African hunters who could put a name to any beast, bird, grass, or tree and, especially if useful, could tell you something about each. But their sons, sent to school, quickly lose most of this knowledge, and gain little useful to them in return.

Fables and legends, not to say superstitious fears, concern nocturnal birds of prey more than the diurnal species. There is hardly a primitive uneducated African who is not faintly alarmed when an owl sits upon his hut and hoots; and in truth the deep hoot of an eagle owl in the dead of night is a forbidding sort of sound. This fear is not, of course, confined to Africans, but is shared by a great many educated Europeans, who ought to know better. Man fears the night for, like a baboon, he is then at a disadvantage; and as a result the creatures of the night tend to be disliked and feared.

I cannot find that there are very detailed accounts of the role of owls in native legend, fable and witchcraft. In some West African tribes wizards are said to embody themselves in owls and on Pemba Island the Russet Scops Owl is said to be viviparous by the local people. It is also said to take a prominent part in native witchcraft (doubtless all effectively stamped out in these enlightened socialist days) but the exact part it plays is not specified. I have seen bits of owls on Juju men's stalls in Nigerian markets; but they would never tell a politely inquiring stranger what these items were for. To acquire this sort of knowledge from the African peoples requires such investigatory zeal and linguistic ability that one has little time for anything else; and I have always devoted most of my time to the living birds and not to fables about them. Some anthropologist should write this up for the convenience of such as myself.

Owls may be generally regarded as birds of ill omen, but in practice I have not found any area, or any African people, who seriously persecute owls on that account. Most owls' nests are none too easy to find, and the adult birds are not easily killed at night with simple weapons; a firearm is needed as well as a torch. I have never met anyone in Africa who persecuted owls as, for instance British gamekeepers used to persecute them, despite the fact that the owls could theoretically have done more harm to roosting poultry than they ever did to British gamebirds. If an eagle owl can take a Lanner Falcon on the roost it can take a fowl too, and I have found the bones of a chicken in the roost ledge of a Mackinder's Eagle Owl. Real or imagined cause for persecution of owls is, however, slight in Africa, and the owls usually live out their natural lives quite happy alongside human beings.

Diurnal birds of prey, being seen about their business by day, are as a rule not the subject of superstitious fears, though there may be curious beliefs attached to them. The Augur Buzzard, for instance, is so called because certain East African tribes use the appearance of the bird as an augury. If it appeared on one side of their line of march the omens were good, if on the other, bad. Such beliefs, akin to the superstitions about the number 13 or walking under a ladder, have not entirely died out. I have been seriously told of them within the last decade, not only in relation to the Augur Buzzard, but also to the Bateleur. Again, such little fables are quite harmless to the birds concerned, and may add to the interest of the daily round.

Dealing with tales about birds of prey I have found that one has to be more careful than I used to think necessary about scoffing at what appear to be thoroughly unlikely statements by Africans. Two instances that I have come across relate to the Bateleur. My Hausa servant, Momo, once told me that when a Bateleur's nest was approached the bird became very angry, shaking itself up and down, and uttering sharp barks. He gave a graphic demonstration of the bird's demeanour, and said that this was the reason for the Hausa name "*Gaggafa, chi yaro*", literally "Gaggafa, eat boy". At the time I discounted the likelihood of any eagle behaving in this way, but I later found that it was true, and that almost all Bateleurs will so behave at the nest. Again, in Mbere, my usually accurate eagle watchers (who put all the world's collectors to shame by pointing out the simple distinction between the male and female Bateleur) told me that Bateleurs in brown immature plumage sometimes incubated eggs. I did not believe it until I actually saw one do it myself. That finally taught me not to be too contemptuous of Africans' travellers' tales.

Another example of the same sort, recently brought to light, concerns the Egyptian Vulture. I would wager that many distinguished naturalists would have automatically discredited the suggestion that the Egyptian Vulture breaks eggs by hurling a stone at them, if they had been told this by, say, a Masai herdsman. But since it has been observed and filmed by eminent scientists and photographers there is no doubt at all about it. Moreover, as long ago as 1877, it was known to some African tribes that Egyptian Vultures did break ostrich eggs. No one however, knew precisely how until a century later, though untold numbers of Egyptian Vultures must have been watched by many eminent naturalists in between.

The raptor I know best is the Crowned Eagle and, perhaps as a result, I have seen some curious things. If anyone had told me, twenty years ago, that Sykes' Monkeys would deliberately bait their potentially deadly enemy I would have been inclined to discount it. But I have now seen it done on at least six occasions, so that if an African hunter gave me a graphic account of a similar happening I should recognise the germ of fact in it. The monkey, in this case, usually baits the eagle on the nest, when the brooding or incubating bird is at a disadvantage; but I have also seen one pluck at the feet of a perched eagle, surely playing with fire, for it is with the feet that the eagle kills. One male monkey living near my house baits the female Crowned Eagle in trees when he can and comes several hundred yards to where she is perched deliberately to annoy her.

In the Gabon this eagle (which is always said to eat many monkeys in true forest environments) is reported to lure monkeys to their doom by uttering a soft whistle. Then, when the monkeys have become curious, it seizes one of them and knocks it to the ground. MacLatchey, who reported this, does not say whether he saw it himself, or whether he is reporting African fables and folklore; I suspect the latter, though that is not necessarily a good reason for discounting it. It is also reported of the Crowned Eagle that it and the leopard may act in concert, the leopard below, and the eagle above, to secure a monkey as prey. Twenty years ago I would have discounted any such tale as pure African imagination; but now I am not so sure. All I will say is that I'd like to see it happen before I made any definite statement on the subject myself.

The bone-dropping habit of the Lammergeier has been doubted by many eminent naturalists, some of whom were very familiar with the Lammergeier. It is now proven to be a common habit, and I have often seen it myself. There is a story that so eminent a zoologist as Sir Julian Huxley was about to go into print to the effect that the Lammergeier never dropped bones when one bombarded him with a bone in the Ngorongoro Crater.

That a shrike should attack a young eagle in the nest seems unlikely; but I have seen it done, and it was first reported to me by my African observers, whom I straightway disbelieved. Nowadays, if I am told an unlikely-seeming tale, I am not so ready to discount it altogether. It is not at all unlikely that the story may be a misinterpretation or even a quite reasonable rendering of behaviour seldom observed and difficult to interpret accurately without binoculars.

I would now even reserve judgement on such thoroughly unlikely tales as that eagles take babies—not that it happens nowadays, but it may have happened once. I would not put it past an eagle to take and kill an infant left out in the open, perhaps uncovered and wriggling, while its mother cultivated a farm. Faced with possible prey too big to carry away at once some eagles such as the Crowned Eagle will kill the animal, dismember it, and cache the limbs in trees until needed. A baby is not as big as a bushbuck calf or a duiker, both of which can be killed by large eagles. And though I will not nowadays believe that a swaddled baby in a pram in Switzerland will be snatched up into the air by a non-existent Lammergeier, I will accept that at some dim and distant time in human memory some such thing may have happened as a factual basis for fable.

Some of these fables continue to result in prejudice against birds of prey. There are still people in Britain who fear that eagles take babies. Far more serious is the effect of the occasional actual crime against mankind. It is useless to deny that eagles will occasionally take lambs or young kids, and that they will often take free-ranging chickens, as will kites, large sparrowhawks, and, for instance, Lanner Falcons. These things do happen, and I have seen them happen. What is wrong is to condemn the bird of prey, either individually or the species as a whole, for an occasional crime probably balanced by many unrecorded good deeds.

In Africa as a whole, especially among relatively uneducated and backward peoples, there is seldom any real or bitter animosity towards birds of prey. If there were there would now be no or few birds of prey. If birds of prey disappear from cultivated and inhabited areas it may well be because other natural conditions have altered rather than because of active persecution. In the areas where I have closely studied birds of prey Africans knew quite well which species were likely to take chickens or goats. They included the Martial Eagle, African Hawk Eagle, Wahlberg's Eagle and Black Kite, all of which did take chickens, young or old, while the Martial Eagle could certainly take a kid wandering from a herd in thick thornbush. Yet no one made any very special effort to destroy the eagles on that account. One found no pole traps dotted about near the eagles' nests, as one would in grouse moors in Britain, and no one lay in wait for them with a powerful weapon. They had no powerful weapons and usually let the birds be, though occasionally a nest tree was cut down when the depredations of a particular eagle so incensed one man that he could muster the energy to do something about it.

Usually, as I have found, the higher the level of education, to a point, the greater the danger of animosity and prejudice towards birds of prey. Some may take an occasional chicken, so every individual of that species, and often anything with a hooked beak and claws, is thereafter suspect. Bush lore has been lost, and its place has been taken by inaccurate statements parroted by rote or thoughtless actions initiated by personal gain. Here again, I have found many European people in Africa far more guilty than Africans. A neighbour of mine, a good naturalist, one day shot a harmless Cuckoo Falcon because it alarmed birds caged in his aviary. Though African schoolboys may climb to and destroy a bird of prey's nest out of sheer wanton destructiveness, they will not often do it because of some such mistaken belief. Probably such prejudices are stronger in South Africa and North-West Africa than anywhere else; but there are still a fair number of birds of prey in these places, and in South Africa there are signs that an enlightened public opinion begins to emerge as the role of birds of prey is better understood, and as education advances to the point where an aesthetic appreciation of the bird itself overcomes existing prejudices.

There may be cases where a recent change in the habits of a particular species may result in a new cause for justified dislike of a raptor which may formerly have been quite blameless. Consider the case of the Cape Vulture, which has—it is said on good authority—taken to killing live and healthy sheep. I have also heard this said in sheep-rearing districts of Kenya in regard to Ruppell's Griffon, and the Lappet-faced Vulture, though a good sheep-farmer friend of mine, who is also a good ornithologist, scouts this suggestion. This may be because the natural supply of carrion has become so scarce that the vultures, driven by hunger, are obliged to kill to eat.

All the same, any such statement should be objectively analysed by properly qualified naturalists—who will not necessarily or probably tell lies to protect birds of prey if they are indeed guilty—before any change in policy towards such normally beneficial species is advocated. If Cape Vultures do in fact kill large numbers of valuable sheep then one can hardly expect sheep farmers to like them. But I would find it hard to believe that in average Karroo rangeland, where the mortality of sheep is certain to be considerable however efficient the rancher may be, vultures would kill many healthy sheep. I would certainly want to be convinced by eyewitness accounts from naturalists first.

A good example of the effect of sheer prejudice on a large raptor species is provided by the Golden Eagle in America. The eagle has been mercilessly persecuted in several south-western states on the ground that it kills large numbers of lambs. It has been shot from aeroplanes (though I am always a little doubtful about how effective this shooting has been), has been trapped on pole traps (outlawed in Britain at the height of the game preserving era because of the abominable cruelty of the practice), and has actually been exterminated as a breeding bird in some areas. Yet an objective study of Golden Eagles on sheep ranges in Montana has shown that Golden Eagles take few or no lambs, and even in Texas, where most of the damage has been claimed, it can be shown that even if Golden Eagles ate nothing but freshly killed lambs the migrant population of wintering eagles could not make serious inroads on the available lamb crop; and they do not eat nothing but lambs, but feed largely on rabbits and hares that are active competitors with sheep.

The parallel case in Africa concerns the Martial and Verreaux's Eagles in South Africa, both of which are accused of taking lambs. Again, an objective assessment of the situation, coupled with a knowledge of what an eagle can and does eat, would show that the accusations are largely based upon prejudice and not upon fact. If this is so in the case of birds that are powerful enough to take an occasional lamb when hungry it is much more likely to be so in the case of many other species which are entirely blameless. What is needed to overcome this prejudice is an accurate knowledge of the facts. Even if these are to a degree disadvantageous to the birds of prey concerned it is better to know what they are before adopting any fixed attitude of animosity or affection towards any bird of prey. So let us make an effort to look at and understand the facts as they affect African species.

(ii) The Facts

The real effect of any species of bird of prey upon man's interests is compounded of the answers to two questions. What does the species prefer to eat, and how much of it? If the answers to these questions are adequately known (as in some cases they are not), then we can assess fairly exactly what possible effect a bird of prey might have on human interests. It will be found that the huge majority of birds of prey are either entirely beneficial or harmlessly neutral as far as man's interests are concerned. If they are harmful at all it will usually be found that a few simple steps would minimise the likelihood of harm done, while a study of the food of a particular species will almost certainly show it does some good.

Food requirements are, as we have seen, a function of body weight. Qualitative and quantitative analysis of prey seen in nests, observed kills in the field, and analysis of castings will tell us what any raptor eats. Knowing its weight we can estimate quite accurately how much prey it needs to keep alive each day. We are then in a position to make an objective assessment of the activities of any bird of prey with reference to our own interests.

For any bird of prey to have a considerable adverse impact upon man's interests it must be, firstly, fairly large, and secondly, fairly common. The Black Kite, which is fairly large and is probably the most numerous bird of prey in tropical Africa, is a good example of the sort. In East Africa birds such as Augur Buzzards or the larger vultures might come into the same category. But a rare species such as Ayres Hawk Eagle, even if it ate nothing but chickens (which as far as we know it never in fact touches) is far too scarce to do any considerable harm.

Such objective examination of the food of any species of bird of prey will show that it is either beneficial to man, in that it eats animals which are themselves harmful to man; neutral in that it eats species that do not harm man's interests, or which do not have much to do with man; or potentially harmful in that, given the chance, it will kill man's domesticated stock or poultry. In Africa, as a rule, one can discount the effect of birds of prey upon game preserving, except perhaps in South Africa; it is the effect upon domestic stock that counts over most of the continent. It is the occasional misdemeanours of the species in the last category that have led to an unjustified level of general animosity towards anything with a hooked beak and claws.

An objective assessment, based upon what we know, and which anyone is at liberty to contest if he can produce better factual evidence than we have, shows how unfair to birds of prey is any general condemnation. Of 89 species of diurnal birds of prey that occur in the continent at one time or another, 37 may be regarded as entirely beneficial to man, 39 as neutral, and only 13 as potentially or actually harmful. As we shall see, even in most of these cases the damage is either so slight as to be negligible, or can be quite easily avoided. Among 31 species of owls 20 are positively beneficial, 8 neutral, and 3 (all fish eaters) possibly harmful. In other words, out of a total of 120 species in Africa only 16, or 13% deserve to be even suspect as possible competitors with man's interests. In this assessment I am of course discounting the possibility that an owl hooting on someone's hut, or a Bateleur crossing from left to right as one sets out to steal someone else's cattle, will lead to disaster directly attributable to the raptor concerned.

Dealing first with the positively beneficial species, these are generally taken to include those that eat rodents that could be harmful to man's grain supplies, or insects that eat either crops or pasture. All vultures I have regarded as essentially beneficial scavengers of refuse and carrion. Among this class too, come such birds as the Black-shouldered Kite, the harriers that frequent grassland, some small sparrowhawks, all buzzards, the eagles that feed upon small mammals, and the small insectivorous falcons such as the Red-footed, Eleanora's, and the kestrels. Out of 31 species of owls the great majority, 20, come in this class. I have included most eagle owls among these until any serious crime is proved against them.

The species that are neutral are those which either seldom or never come in contact with man, such as some rare forest species, or those that occur alongside man but feed mainly on animals that themselves are neutral in respect of man's interests. There is obviously rather more scope for argument over a species that is neutral than there is for one which is definitely beneficial or positively harmful. Among the 39 diurnal species I place in this category I include, for instance, the Bat Hawk, which eats bats and little else. It might be considered more beneficial than neutral, in that few people like having large numbers of bats in their roofs, and it is possible that the Bat Hawk eats a few fruit bats. I include also the Red Kite, which is too uncommon and retiring to do much harm to man, all the Snake Eagles, the Bateleur and the Harrier Hawk, the frog-eating Marsh Harriers, the lizard-eating Chanting Goshawks, some rare forest sparrowhawks too small to take chickens as a normal rule, the bird-eating Booted and Ayres Hawk Eagles, and a number of falcons that have a mixed diet of birds, small mammals, and insects. These have been placed here because they seem less than positively beneficial rather than because they might not be actually harmful.

One could argue individual cases in this list of course, along

Darwinian lines. One could say, for instance, that in fact Snake Eagles are on balance harmful to man, because they eat snakes that are themselves generally beneficial to man, even those venomous species that man tends to dislike and to kill on sight. I have called them neutral here. The Harrier Hawk, on the other hand, is one of the principal predators on weaver bird colonies, and weavers are birds that feed upon man's grain crops and which strip and damage oil palms; but the Harrier Hawk itself occasionally eats oil palm fruit, so that it is perhaps less than positively beneficial. I have known Ayres Hawk Eagle to take domestic pigeons, but most of its prey is forest birds that seldom or never have much to do with man, or doves which may eat a certain amount of grain. Lizards are for the most part insectivorous creatures, and so harmless or beneficial to man. There are several hawks, such as the Shikra and Chanting Goshawks and the Lizard Buzzard which habitually eat lizards and I suppose on that account could be called possibly harmful. But I prefer to regard them as neutral, and if anyone feels like arguing bitterly on the subject he may.

Among owls the eight species I class as neutral are either little-known, or have a mixed diet including some animals that might be beneficial to man. No one knows enough about the diet of the Congo Bay Owl to say whether it is beneficial or not, and Morden's Scops Owl, though entirely insectivorous as far as is known, lives in a forest where it has escaped the attentions of collectors for more than the last half-century, so that it can't be said to affect man's interests either way. The rest of the owls in this category are large or small birds of mixed diet; they are probably on balance beneficial.

The most searching examination of facts needs to be given to those species which I have regarded as potentially or actually harmful to man's interests. In this class I have included the Osprey, the two fish and sea eagles, on the grounds that they *do* eat fish that man might eat. The Black Kite is too common in the haunts of man, and too often takes young chickens to be omitted. The Vulturine Fish Eagle undoubtedly lives mainly on oil palm nuts. The Goshawk, Black Sparrowhawk, and Long-tailed Hawk either do take chickens, or are reputed to do so when they can. The same applies to Wahlberg's, the African Hawk, and Martial Eagles, while the last named is also accused of killing sheep. So are the Golden and Verreaux's Eagles. Finally, I have seen a Lanner take a chicken myself, so although it is generally a neutral bird, feeding on birds that are possibly harmful to man, and on small rodents, I have to include it in this list to avoid being told I am biased.

Among owls I cannot definitely include any but three species that are potentially harmful, and for the same reason as the Osprey, that they eat fish that man could possibly eat. In practice, however, fishing owls are so rare and local that it is inconceivable that their effect is of any economic importance. I have found a chicken bone in a casting of a Mackinder's Owl, and I would suspect that if these large eagle owls could regularly get a roosting chicken they might take one now and again. However, they are generally so overwhelmingly beneficial in the number of rodents they kill that an occasional chicken in recompense would not be too high a price to pay. In any case it is easy to protect chickens from owls by keeping them in a house at night. Owls, therefore, can, as a class, be almost wholly absolved from any harmful effect upon man's interests; all should be protected.

It is when assessing the real adverse effect of a bird of prey upon man's interests that one must depart from the purely qualitative approach, based upon the kind of animal the raptor eats, and attempt the much more difficult quantitative method, which requires thorough and prolonged study to produce any accurate results. The total population of the species concerned, the appetite of its members separately and collectively, and the effect of the gross potential kill of the species on the population of the prey must be accurately assessed. This has never been thoroughly done yet for any species in Africa. But we know enough about it in other parts of the world, and in Africa, too, to be able to say definitely that in all cases the adverse effect upon man's interests is exaggerated, and can usually be regarded as negligible.

Take the case of fish-eating species such as the Osprey and the Fish Eagle, which *could* be accused, and doubtless are accused at times, of taking fish from ponds where they have been reared, and where their activities are consequently definitely detrimental. The Osprey is only a migrant to most of Africa, and there is no doubt that it eats food-fishes to some extent. It also, however, takes fishes that are detrimental to human fishery interests; for instance in Europe it lives largely upon small pike and perch, both of which are carnivorous on more valuable fishes. The same sort of consideration applies to Fish Eagles. They eat fish that man could possibly eat but, at least in African lakes, a high proportion of these fish are carnivorous catfish and lungfish that themselves eat more valuable fishes. And a factual assessment of the amount of fish eaten by the entire Fish Eagle population of Lake Albert proves that in practice they could not, by any stretch of the imagination, substantially affect man's interests in that area.

Fish Eagles also often pick up dead fish, and perhaps take sick fish, which might otherwise spread disease in a population. Their effect could be like that of Great White Pelicans in the Danube Delta, once anathematised and slaughtered by fishermen, but now a national monument because a scientist has proved that they consume a high proportion of diseased fish. Although a Fish Eagle is potentially harmful, in practice the harm it does is completely negligible. This fact is reflected in the complete indifference with which all African fishing tribes of my acquaintance regard this species.

The Palm Nut Vulture or Vulturine Fish Eagle eats oil palm fruits, and sometimes fish, crabs, molluscs and the like. I am afraid that there is nothing really good to be said for it, other than it is a queer and interesting bird. However, although it does subsist largely on oil palms, and although the fruits are potentially valuable food for man, it strikes me as wildly improbable that the Palm Nut Vulture would be sufficiently numerous in any palm-growing area to have any very serious effect on the crop of palm fruit. I know of no record of the food requirements of Vulturine Fish Eagles, but I doubt if they would eat more than a few ounces of fruit per day, in a home range extending over thousands of acres, whereas the yield of palm fruit per acre per annum is measured in hundreds or even thousands of pounds according to the standard of husbandry concerned. In fact, the effect is virtually certain to be negligible.

The adverse effects of the Black Kite, the Goshawk, Black Sparrowhawk, and Long-tailed Hawk (if any) and of the Lanner Falcon are all against poultry. None are sufficiently powerful to attack larger domestic stock. Some small eagles too, notably Wahlberg's and the African Hawk Eagle, are poultry thieves, the latter more serious than the former. Martial Eagles are gamebird killers that sometimes find chickens the easiest of all gamebirds to catch. All of these birds can be frustrated by keeping chickens in a properly constructed wire pen. And if they are not kept in a properly protected manner something else will get them if a Black Kite or a Wahlberg's Eagle does not.

Probably anyone who is really pestered by one of these birds will shoot it or kill it if he can, and this may eliminate an overbold member of the species concerned. So far as the species as a whole is concerned this may not matter much, though it is not to be encouraged. Of those mentioned, the species which attract most animosity, I have found, are the Black Kite, Black Sparrowhawk, and African Hawk Eagle. All of these are a danger to free-range chickens, young or old. Among them at least the Black Kite and African Hawk Eagle can also claim to do some good by scavenging scraps of decaying food or killing insects or mammals that could be harmful.

The most difficult class of avian predators to assess from this point of view are the three large eagles that are accused of taking lambs in rangeland; the Golden, Verreaux's, and Martial Eagles. This also must apply to any large vultures that can be shown to prey on sheep on an important scale. A student of birds of prey cannot hope to convince sheep farmers that such large and spectacular eagles should be left alone entirely on the grounds of their beauty or interest, though there are sheep farmers who enjoy seeing an eagle, like anyone else. Only factual evidence of what the bird of prey eats, and the actual extent of the damage done, based upon a careful and detailed study, will succeed in convincing sheep farmers; sometimes not even then, so ingrown is the prejudice met with. However, provided the evidence is there, and a proportion of sensible people can be convinced, the diehards can then be fairly dealt with according to the law of the land, which often affords protection to large and spectacular eagles.

In this case it is difficult or impossible for the farmer to avoid all danger to his stock from large and powerful birds of prey. He can fence the country with jackal-proof wire, but he can't prevent eagles from flying over it. The range sheep have to be left to find their own living on rough ground. If, as a result of this, they become vulnerable to attack by a predator they must take their chance.

In the case of the three large eagles mentioned any danger is not to the adult sheep, but to the lambs, which are small enough and weak enough to be killed and picked up. Not even the most powerful eagle would attack a healthy adult sheep; it could neither kill it nor carry it away. Large vultures, which although powerful and heavy, have weak feet without strong hooked talons, adapted only for walking and not for gripping, would seem to me even less likely to kill healthy adult sheep. Sheep farmers in this case might well ask themselves whether they have actually *seen* a healthy animal being successfully attacked by a vulture, or whether they have merely been told of the occurrence.

In the matter of eagle versus lamb, a question which crops up in all sheep-rearing countries, all the careful investigation that has been done to date shows that although eagles do take occasional lambs the alleged damage is always greatly exaggerated and usually counterbalanced by the good they do in destroying animals that directly compete with sheep for food. In the case of the Golden Eagle studies in Scotland, Montana, and elsewhere have shown that the eagles either take few or no lambs, and that most of the few that are taken are dead before they are picked up. The main food of the Golden Eagles is medium-sized mammals such as rabbits and hares, which directly compete for food with sheep, or ground squirrels and prairie dogs (marmots) which also burrow in and perhaps damage pastures. They also kill a certain number of carnivorous mammals, such as foxes, and such birds as crows that may be potentially harmful. It is most unlikely that the Golden Eagle does any harm to man where it occurs in the Atlas Mountains and Algeria, as most herds in these parts are in any case accompanied by herdsmen, so that the eagle would be unlikely to attack.

Verreaux's Eagle is the representative of the Golden Eagle group in most of Africa, and although it has been accused of harrying sheep here and there in South Africa it is not so accused elsewhere and is actually almost entirely blameless. Its staple food supply is undoubtedly rock hyrax of various species, but it would hardly be surprising if it took an occasional lamb when sheep run at large in its habitat. In most of its range, it does not normally eat any carrion but occasionally does so in South Africa. I feel quite certain that an objective assessment of the effect of Verreaux's Eagle on a sheep ranch would prove that the eagle was on balance beneficial, in that it is an important predator on hyrax, which directly compete with the sheep for food. If a pair of Verreaux's Eagles and their young were to eat, say, a hundred hyrax in a year, the farmer concerned could accept with equanimity the loss of a few lambs as recompense for this. The hundred hyrax would certainly eat as much as twenty sheep.

The Martial Eagle is somewhat more difficult to assess in this respect, largely because it has been less intensively studied. For choice it appears to be a gamebird killer, but it does undoubtedly eat the young of antelopes, monkeys, and such things as monitor lizards. It is the largest eagle in Africa but not the most powerful. Even so it could, and doubtless does, kill a few lambs if they are to be found free ranging in its territory. The damage that it does to flocks in most parts of Africa is negligible, since in most areas they are accompanied by herd boys and the eagle will not normally attack in these circumstances; it attracts animosity more because it kills chickens than because it takes an occasional kid. However, in open unherded sheep range it would be surprising if the Martial Eagle did not do some small amount of damage. Again, in such country, it probably balances any harm it might do by killing animals such as hares and hyrax, that directly compete with sheep, or predatory mammals such as large mongooses or jackals. It also seems certain that the very large ranges maintained by pairs of Martial Eagles (usually much larger than those of Verreaux's Eagle) would support so many sheep that even if the Martial Eagles fed largely on lamb in the lambing season the aggregate effect would be slight. The Martial Eagle has become very scarce already in South Africa, the only part of the continent where it is actively persecuted, and any harm done by the remaining birds must be negligible. This in fact can be said to be true of any large African eagles; they are relatively so rare, and so small a proportion of their diet is potentially harmful to human interests, that the harm they do in aggregate must be exceedingly small.

Just as one can assess quantitatively the effect of a single pair of a particular species over its home range (see page 221) so one can assess the cumulative effect of a community of diurnal and nocturnal raptors in any given area of country. In any area of country the whole resident and migrant community can be assessed by counts over a period of time. From such counts one can assess the proportion of beneficial, neutral, and possibly harmful species in the population, and can arithmetically estimate the possible effect of each. From this it will be seen that the total theoretically harmful effect to be anticipated from even a large number of miscellaneous birds of prey is very small, and is far more than counterbalanced by effects which can be regarded as beneficial to man's interests.

As an example of what I mean I have taken the diurnal bird of prey community as represented by my own counts on the East African plains, and expressed the result in Table 12 (page 302) and Fig. 18. This is based upon a strip of country a quarter of a mile wide on either side of the line of traverse, in other words half a square mile for every mile covered. It is unlikely that every bird of prey contained in this area has been represented in the table, and in Chapter 19 I have stressed how one is likely to overlook small and skulking species. But the idea is to demonstrate a principle, which can be just as easily applied to any more accurate count that is available. Small, skulking species are by their very nature likely to be harmless or beneficial to man's interests, and the nocturnal owls are all beneficial or neutral, so that the overall effect as expressed here is more detrimental to the birds of prey than it needs to be. I have also tried to include everything that could possibly be harmful, which is barely justifiable. At that, the overall assessment is 85·4% beneficial, 11·2% neutral, and only 3·4% possibly harmful.

"Facts are chiels that winna ding", they say in Scotland. However, in that country as elsewhere there is a reluctance to accept an objective assessment of facts where birds of prey are concerned, and a readiness to be prejudiced against anything with a hooked beak and claws. It has been refreshing to me to find among many unlettered African peoples a far better appreciation of the role of birds of prey in nature than is to be found among much better educated people in Europe, America, and Australia. It is to be hoped that in Africa it may be possible to avoid the acceptance of blind unreasoning prejudice against all birds of prey that has been so characteristic of much of the Western World. By the use of facts I hope to be able to convince reasonable men that birds of prey are more often useful than not, and I would hope that those who may be responsible for lawmaking would be among these. Unreasonable men can then be dealt with by the reasonable, or can at least be ridiculed as ignorant and prejudiced if they will not listen to reason. In such ways one may hope that gradually prejudice and unreason will give way to knowledge and reason, and that men will look at birds of prey not simply as potentially harmful and cruel creatures, but as handsome or spectacular predators that are a necessary part of nature's grand design.

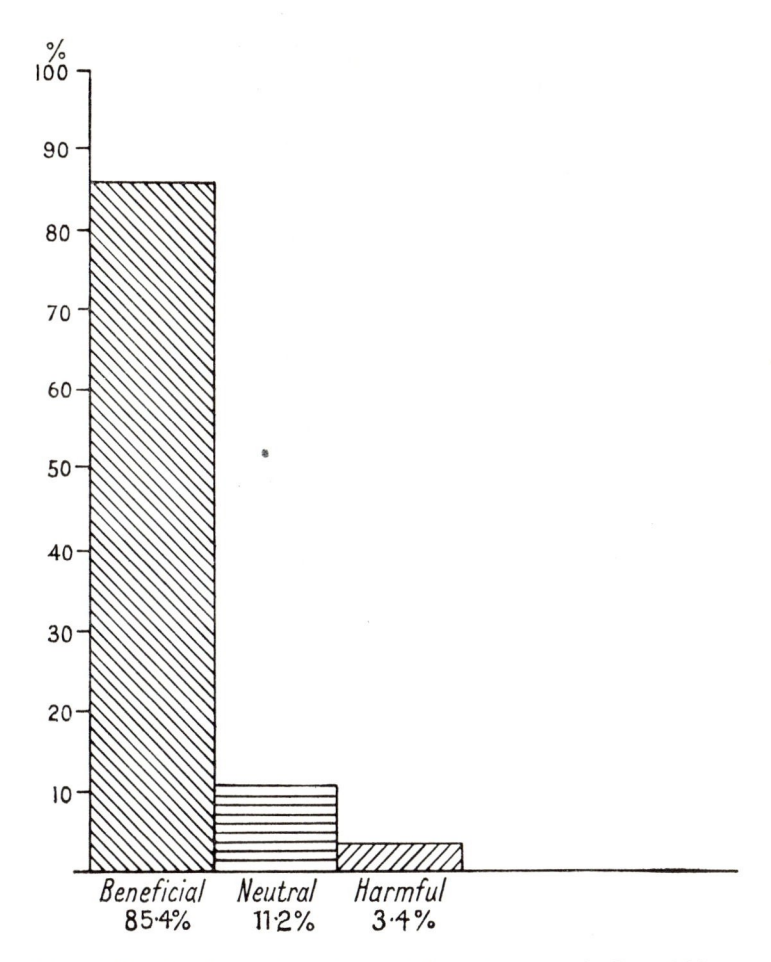

Fig. 18 Beneficial or other effects of diurnal raptors in East African grasslands.

NOTE. The harmful effect is actually overestimated here. Its largest components are the Black Kite and Fish Eagle. The Black Kite in grasslands is virtually harmless, and the Fish Eagle has no significant harmful effects.

Table 1 Raptors counted by G. Rudebeck 1950-51
R=resident   M=migrant   R & M=resident and migrant.

Areas counted and mileage

Species and Status	S and S.W. Cape 12/50– 3/51 1500 m.	S and S.E. Cape 29/1– 16/2/51 1974 m.	W. Karroo 7– 19/11/50 675 m.	Total 4149 m.	Miles/ bird
Osprey ? R or M.	1			1	4149
Black-shouldered Kite R.	20	17		37	112
Black Kite M & R.	20	50	11	81	51
Fish Eagle R.	2			2	2075
Lammergeier R.		2		2	2075
African Marsh Harrier R.	5	1	1●	7	592
Black Harrier R.		2		2	2075
Pale or Montagu's Harrier M.	1		7+ ?3 (10)	11	380
Chanting Goshawk (Pale) R.	2	11		13	320
Unidentified Accipiters R.	2			2	2075
Common Buzzard M.	47	101+ ?1 (102)	1	150	28
Jackal Buzzard R.	6	6	2	14	295
Black Eagle R.	1	1		2	2075
Martial Eagle R.		1		1	4149
Crowned Eagle R.	2			2	2075
Unidentified eagles R.	2		1	3	1383
Secretary Bird R.	6		2	6	690
Lesser Kestrel M.	8000	173		8173	0·51
Lesser or Common Kestrel R or M.	65	43	7	115	36
Red-footed Falcon M.	141	2		143	29
Greater Kestrel R.			10	10	415
Unidentified small falcons	5			5	830
Lanner R.	10	1	9	20	208
Unidentified raptors R.	4	2		6	690
TOTAL	8342	414	68	8824	0·47
Residents	61	44	25	130	31·9
Palearctic migrants	8189	277	11	8477	0·49
Local migrant or doubtful	92	93	32	217	19·1

NOTE: In S. W. Cape and Karroo (cf Table 3) 2175 miles for 105 residents = 21 m/resident species seen.

Table 2   Counts by Rowan and Siegfried 1963-5

R = resident   M = migrant

Species and Status	Areas counted and mileage				
	Rowan S.W. Cape 1960-63 6285 m.	Rowan 1960-63 Central ·Karroo 2850 m.	Siegfried 1963-64 Strandveld 1986 m.	Total 11,121 m.	Miles/ bird
Black-shouldered Kite R.	199		152	351	32
Black Kite M or R.			30	30	371
African Marsh Harrier R.			12	12	927
Black Harrier R.			5	5	2224
Chanting Goshawk R.		49		49	225
Jackal Buzzard R.	28	30		58	191
Buzzards (R & M.)			186 (incl. Jackal Buzzard)	186	63
Secretary Bird R.			2	2	5560
Common Kestrel R.	199	103		302	365
Kestrels (R or M.)			86	86	
Peregrine ? R.			1	1	11121
Other residents	48	64		112	128
Palearctic migrants	97	402		499	22
Unidentified			26	26	425
TOTAL	571	648	500	1719	6·4
Palearctic migrants	97	402	249 (est.)	748	14·9
Definite residents	474	246	251	971	11·4

NOTE: Other residents included e.g. Secretary Bird, Lanner, Greater Kestrel, and Martial Eagle.

Table 3 Counts from Orange Free State, Transvaal & Natal

1955–1965 Rudebeck, Cade and Prozesky
Areas counted and mileage

Species and Status	Transvaal & O.F.S. Rudebeck 12/54, 1 & 2/56 4365 m.	Transvaal & O.F.S. Cade & Prozesky 7–8/65 1709 m.	Pretoria–Pietermaritzburg Rudebeck 1/56 392 m.	Cade & Prozesky 8/65 510 m.	Total 6976 m.	Miles/bird
Osprey M.	2				2	3488
Black-shouldered Kite R.	88	44	5	31	168	41
Black Kite M & ?R.	843	1	2	1	847	8·2
Fish Eagle R.	4				4	1744
Black-breasted Snake Eagle R.	6			2	8	872
Bateleur R.	1				1	6976
African Marsh & Black Harrier R.	40	3			44	168
Pale or Montagu's Harrier M.	22				22	336
Other harriers M.	16				16	436
Harrier Hawk R.	1				1	6976
Gabar Goshawk R.	1	1		1(?)	3	2325
Lizard Buzzard R.		2			2	3488
Common Buzzard M.	108		4		112	62
Jackal Buzzard R.	3	5		3	11	634
Tawny Eagle R.	3				3	2325
Wahlberg's Eagle R.	1			1	2	3488
Verreaux's Eagle R.	1				1	6976
Martial Eagle R.		1			1	6976
Unidentified eagles R.	14	2			16	436

Table 3—*continued*

1955-1965 Rudebeck, Cade and Prozesky
Areas counted and mileage

Species and Status	Transvaal & O.F.S. Rudebeck 12/54, 1 & 4/55, 2/56 4365 m.	Transvaal & O.F.S. Cade & Prozesky 7-8/65 1709 m.	Pretoria– Pietermaritzburg Rudebeck 1/56 392 m.	Cade & Prozesky 8/65 510 m.	Total 6976 m.	Miles/bird
Secretary Bird R.	11	1		1	13	532
Pigmy Falcon		3			3	2325
Lesser Kestrel M.	3184		45		3229	2·15
Common Kestrel R.	19	13		2	34	204
Lesser, Common Kestrel R or M.	87		15		102	68
Red-footed Falcon M.	64				64	108
Greater Kestrel R.	27	8		4	39	178
Lanner R.	12			1	13	532
Peregrine R.	2				2	3488
Unidentified falcons R or M.	81				81	85
TOTAL	4641	84	71	47	4882	1·22

Table 4   Kruger National Park

Species and Status	Prozesky 3 & 12/59, 11/60 734 m.	Cade 8/65 470 m.	Total 1204 m.	Miles/bird
Black-shouldered Kite R.	1		1	1204
Black Kite R.	2		2	602
Fish Eagle R.		8	8	150
Harrier Hawk R.		1	1	1204
Brown Snake Eagle R.	3	3	6	201
Bateleur R.	25	32	57	21
Dark Chanting Goshawk R.	3	1	4	301
Gabar Goshawk R.	4	1	5	241
Little Sparrowhawk R.	6		6	201
Unidentified Accipiters R.		1	1	1204
Lizard Buzzard R.		1	1	1204
Common Buzzard M.	3		3	401
Tawny Eagle R.	9	4	13	93
Wahlberg's Eagle R.	4		4	301
Black Eagle R.		1	1	1204
African Hawk Eagle R.	2		2	602
Martial Eagle R.	3	3	6	201
Unidentified eagles R.		8	8	150
Secretary Bird R.	2		2	602
Dickinson's Kestrel		1	1	1204
TOTAL	67	65	132	9·1
Residents	64	65	129	9·2
Palearctic migrants	3	—	3	401

3. Commonest species (most obvious) Bateleur (57), Tawny Eagle (13), Fish Eagle (8).

Table 5 Kalahari National Park

Species and Status	Prozesky 24–27/4/60	Cade, Prozesky & Willoughby 20/8–1/9/64	MacLean 12/64–3/65	8/64–2/65	Total	Miles/Bird
	350 m.	339 m.	720 m.	2200 m.	3609 m.	
Black-shouldered Kite R.			3		3	1203
Black Kite M.			4	28	32	113
Pale or Montagu's Harrier M.			4	5	9	401
Brown Snake Eagle R.			1		1	3609
Black-breasted Snake Eagle R.			4	28	32	113
Bateleur R.	6	6	64	11	87	41
Pale Chanting Goshawk R.	8	46	56	84	194	18·5
Gabar Goshawk R.	1	10	8	9	28	128
Jackal Buzzard R.	3				3	1203
Tawny Eagle R.	2	8	52	44	106	34
Martial Eagle R.	5	8	3	16	32	113
Secretary Bird R.	7	1	54	79	141	25·5
Pigmy Falcon R.		8	19	152	179	20
Common Kestrel R.	17	4	5	18	44	82
Greater Kestrel R.	2	15	1	11	29	124
Red-necked Falcon R.		6		4	10	361
Lanner R.	1	1	46	4	52	70
TOTAL	52	113	324	493	982	3·64
Residents	52	113	318	464	947	3·8
Migrants	—	—	6	29	35	102

NOTE: It is doubtful if all the species marked resident are regular residents of this particular area. The large fluctuations in their numbers in different counts indicate that the Bateleur, Black-breasted Snake Eagle, and others may concentrate here from time to time.

Table 6 East Africa: Counts in Plains and Thornbush. L. H. Brown. 1965-67

Species and Status	(a) 15 Counts 1613 m. between 1/4 & 30/9	Miles/ Bird	(b) 10 Counts 790 m. 1/10–31/3	Miles/ Bird	Total 2403 m.	No. Counts seen	Miles/ Bird
Black-shouldered Kite R.	19	85	8	99	27	12	89
Swallow-tailed Kite			6	132	6	1	401
Black Kite R. & Local M.	17	94	127	6·2	144	16	16·1
Fish Eagle R.	4	403	9	88	13	6	178
Egyptian Vulture R.	4	403	3	263	7	6	343
Lammergeier R.			2	395	2	1	1202
Hooded Vulture R.	10	161	12	66	22	8	110
White-backed Vulture R.	114	14	62	12·8	176	10	13·8
Ruppell's Griffon R.	9	160	21	37	30	4	80
Lappet-faced Vulture R.	7	230	3	263	10	5	240
White-headed Vulture R.	2	806			2	1	1202
Black-breasted Snake Eagle R.	2	806	1	790	3	3	801
Brown Snake Eagle R.	2	806	1	790	3	3	801
Bateleur R.	33	48	22	36	55	11	44
Harrier Hawk R.	3	524			3	1	801
African Marsh Harrier R.	3	524			3	3	801
Marsh Harrier M.			5	158	5	2	481
Pale or Montagu's Harrier M.			5	158	5	3	481
Pale Chanting Goshawk R.	9	160	2	395	11	4	219
Dark Chanting Goshawk R.			4	198	4	2	601
Gabar Goshawk R.	3	524			3	2	801
Common Buzzard M.			3	263	3	2	801
Augur Buzzard R.	107	15	83	9·5	190	20	12·7
Tawny Eagle R. & M.	36	44·5	61	13	97	18	25

Table 6—*continued*

Verreaux's Eagle R.	2	806			2	1	1202
Long-crested Eagle R.	13	124	5	158	18	11	134
Martial Eagle R.	2	806			2	2	1202
Secretary Bird R.	12	134	11	72	23	11	104
Pigmy Falcon R.	2	806			2	1	1202
Kestrel, Common & Lesser M.			19	41·5	19	7	127
Greater Kestrel R.	2	806			2	2	1202
Lanner Falcon R.	1	1613	4	198	5	3	481
Unidentified	1	1613			1	1	
TOTAL	419		479		898	25	

Summary Table 6.

Total all spp. 898 = average 2·7 m/raptor seen.
Residents including Vultures 826 = 2·9 m./raptor seen.
   without Vultures 577 = 4·1 m./resident raptor seen.
Migrants 72 (Incl. 40 Tawny Eagles) = 33 m./raptor seen.

NOTE: Of the species enumerated the Swallow-tailed Kite is a rare straggler to the area—one might travel 10,000 miles without seeing another.

Frequency of occurrence in 25 Counts.

More than 20 Counts	1 sp.	Augur Buzzard	} Commonest and most widespread.
15–19	2 sp.	Tawny Eagle & Black Kite	
10–14		4 Spp.	Black-shouldered Kite, Bateleur, Long-crested Eagle, Secretary Bird. Widespread but not very common.
5–9		5 Spp.	Fish Eagles, Egyptian, Hooded and White-backed Vultures, Lesser & Common Kestrels. Uncommon except for White-backed Vulture, which is second most numerous.
2–4		15 Spp.	Ruppell's Griffon, Lappet-faced Vulture, Black-breasted Snake Eagle, Brown Snake Eagle, African Marsh Harrier, Marsh Harrier, Pale or Montagu's Harrier, Pale and Dark Chanting Goshawk, Gabar Goshawk, Common Buzzard, Martial Eagle, Greater Kestrel, Lanner Falcon. Uncommon, Local, or rather rare. (Some skulking and difficult to see).
1 only		6 spp.	Swallow-tailed Kite, Lammergeier, White-headed Vulture, Harrier Hawk, Verreaux's Eagle, Pigmy Falcon. Rare, very local, or difficult to see by this method.

Table 7 Raptors occurring in cultivated and inhabited areas.
13 counts 7/66-9/67 625 miles.

Species and Status	Total No.	Miles/ Bird	Recorded in (No. of) Counts	Obsns.
Black-shouldered Kite R.	5	125	4	Uncommon
Black Kite R & M.	211	2·95	9	Numerous widespread
Fish Eagle R.	2	313	1	Rare
Hooded Vulture R.	102	6·0	5	Numerous but local (in towns)
Brown Snake Eagle R.	1	625	1	Rare
Bateleur R.	9	69	1	Locally common
African Marsh Harrier R.	5	125	3	Uncommon
Black Sparrowhawk R.	2	313	2	Uncommon/rare
Common Buzzard R.	3	208	2	Uncommon
Augur Buzzard R.	27	23	9	Common widespread
Tawny Eagle R & M.	2	313	1	Uncommon/rare
Wahlberg's Eagle R. & M.	9	69	2	Quite common
Long-crested Eagle R.	10	63	5	Common: widespread
Crowned Eagle R.	5	125	4	
TOTAL	393	1·59		
Residents	240	2·6		
Migrants	153	4·1		(Migrants include estimated 150 Black Kites)
Residents less vultures	138	4·5		

Of the 211 Black Kites seen 207 were seen in 388 miles between 1/10 & 31/3 = 1·86 miles/bird, and 4 in 237 miles from 1/4–30/9 = 59 miles/bird). A large proportion were migrant individuals in the neighbourhood of towns.

Table 8 National Parks and thinly inhabited country, Uganda

Species and Status	Murchison Falls 219 m. 30/1-2/2	Queen Elizabeth Park 128 m. 3/2-4/2	Ankole 83 m. 5/3	Total 430 m.	Miles/ Bird
Black-shouldered Kite R.	2			2	215
Black Kite R & M.	49	15	23	87	4·9
Fish Eagle R.	14	22		36	12
Vulturine Fish Eagle R.	1			1	430
African Marsh Harrier R.		3		3	143
Marsh Harrier M.	2			2	215
Montagu's or Pale Harrier M.	9	5		14	30·5
Harrier Hawk R.	1			1	430
Hooded Vulture R.	8	5	16	29	15
White-backed Vulture	20	37		57	7·5
Lappet-faced Vulture R.		6		6	72
White-headed Vulture R.	3	4		7	61
Black-breasted Snake Eagle R. & M.	5	4		9	48
Brown Snake Eagle R.	3	3		6	72
Bateleur R.	12	8	5	25	17
Dark Chanting Goshawk R.	1			1	430
Shikra R.	1			1	430
Grasshopper Buzzard L.M.	10			10	43
Common Buzzard M.		4	1	5	86
Tawny Eagle R & M.	12			12	36
African Hawk Eagle R.	2		2	4	107
Long-crested Eagle R.		6	1	7	61
Martial Eagle R.	2			2	215
Unidentified eagles M	2	1		3	143
Secretary Bird R.	4			4	107
Kestrel, Lesser & Common M.	12		4	16	27
Grey Kestrel R.	3	1		4	107
Hobby M.		1		1	430
African Hobby R.		1		1	430
TOTAL	178	126	52	356	1·21
Residents	106	106	32	244	1·72
Migrants	72 (est.)	20	20	112	3·85
Residents less Vultures	75	54	16	145	3·0

Table 9 Relative abundance of raptors other than vultures in unspoiled E. & S. African habitats.

Species and Status	Kruger Park 1204 m.	Kalahari 3609 m.	E.A. Plains 2403 m.	Uganda 430 m.	Total 7646 m.	Miles/ Bird
Black-shouldered Kite R.	1	3	27	2	32	240
Swallow-tailed Kite			6		6	1274
Black Kite R. & M	2	32	144	87	265	29
Fish Eagle R.	8		13	36	57	134
Vulturine Fish Eagle R.				1	1	7646
Black-breasted Snake Eagle R.		32	3	9	44	173
Brown Snake Eagle R.	6	1	3	6	16	476
Bateleur R.	57	87	55	25	224	33
Harrier Hawk R.	1		3	1	5	1529
African Marsh Harrier R.			3	3	6	1274
Marsh Harrier M.			5	2	7	1092
Montagu's or Pale Harrier M.		9	5	14	28	271
Chanting Goshawk R.	4	194	15	1	214	35·6
Gabar Goshawk R.	5	28	3		36	211
Other Accipiters R.	7			1	8	956
Grasshopper Buzzard M.				10	10	765
Lizard Buzzard R.	1				1	7646
Common Buzzard M.	3		3	5	11	695
Augur/Jackal Buzzard R.		3	190		193	39
Tawny Eagle R & M.	13	106	97	12	228	33
Wahlberg's Eagle R.	4				4	1911
Verreaux's Eagle	1		2		3	2549
African Hawk Eagle R.	2			4	6	1274
Long-crested Eagle R.			18	7	25	306
Martial Eagle R.	6	32	2	2	42	181

Table 9—continued

Species and Status	Kruger Park 1204 m.	Kala- hari 3609 m.	E.A. Plains 2403 m.	Uganda 430 m.	Total 7647 m.	Miles/ Bird
Unidentified eagles M.	8			3	11	695
Secretary Bird R.	2	141	23	4	170	45
Pigmy Falcon R.		179	2		181	42
Lesser Kestrel M.						
Common Kestrel R. & M		44	19	16	79	96
Greater Kestrel R.		29	2		31	246
Other Small Falcons R.	1	10		6	17	450
Lanner Falcon		52	5		57	133
TOTAL	132	982	898	356	2368	3·2

Summary Table 9

Total Residents   2146   3·6 miles/resident seen overall
Total Migrants   322   24 miles/migrant seen overall

The figures for a good many species e.g. Lizard Buzzard and small Accipiters are an unsound indication of real numbers.

Mileage for migrants would be lower/bird seen if migration season only were considered, 4140 miles/322 birds = 12·9 m./bird.

Table 10 African raptors and their prey

Diurnal Raptors	Class of Prey	Nocturnal Raptors
As carrion: 11 vultures: *Gyps* (5); *Torgos Aegypius, Trigonoceps, Neophron, Necrosyrtes, Gypaetus.* 4 eagles: *Aquila rapax* and *A. heliaca, Haliaeetus vocifer* and *Terathopius ecaudatus.* 5 buzzards and kites: *Buteo* spp. and *Milvus migrans.* *As live prey:* 2 eagles: *Stephanoaetus coronatus* and *Polemaetus bellicosus* (rarely).	Large mammals more than 10 kg. in weight.	Do not eat carrion and are not powerful enough to kill an animal more than 10 kg. in weight.
As carrion: 19 vultures, buzzards, etc. as above. *As live prey:* 9 Eagles: *Aquila verreauxi, A. rapax, A. heliaca; Hieraaetus fasciatus; Stephanoaetus coronatus, Polemaetus bellicosus,* more rarely *Circaetus gallicus* and *C. cinereus,* and *Terathopius ecaudatus.*	Mammals 0·5–5 kg. in weight; small antelopes, hyrax, hares, mongoose, cane rat, antelope calves, monkeys.	4 eagle owls: *Bubo lacteus, B. poensis, B. shelleyi* (?) and *B. b. ascalaphus.* As live prey only.
As live prey: 9 eagles: *Aquila rapax* and rarely *A. verreauxi; Hieraaetus fasciatus* and *H. dubius; Polemaetus bellicosus, Spizaetus africanus:* less often *Circaetus gallicus* and *C. cinereus,* and *Haliaeetus vocifer.* 3 large falcons: *Falco cherrug, F. biarmicus* and *F. peregrinus.* 4 large goshawks: *Accipiter melanoleucus* and *A. gentilis; Melierax metabates* and *M. canorus.*	Large birds 500–1500 grams; guineafowl, francolins, bustards, duck, crows, etc.	2 eagle owls: *Bubo lacteus* and *B. bubo* rather rarely.
As live prey: 9 eagles: *Aquila rapax, A. clanga,*	Mammals less than 500	*As live prey:* 5 eagle owls: *Bubo lacteus, B.*

A. heliaca, A. wahlbergi; Hieraaetus fasciatus and H. dubius; Lophaetus occipitalis; Terathopius ecaudatus and Spizaetus africanus more rarely. 5 buzzards: Buteo buteo, B. rufinus, B. rufofuscus, B. auguralis, B. oreophilus. 3 kites: Milvus migrans, M. milvus; Elanus caeruleus. 6 Harriers: Circus aeruginosus, C. ranivorus, C. maurus, C. cyaneus, C. pygargus, C. macrourus. Secretary Bird: Sagittarius serpentarius. Goshawks: Melierax spp. (2), Accipiter spp. (2) Harrier Hawk: Polyboroides typus 7 falcons: F. biarmicus, F. cherrug, F. alopex, F. rupicoloides, F. tinnunculus, F. ardosiaceus, F. dickinsoni.	grams: rats, squirrels, shrews etc.	capensis, B. africanus, B. poensis, B. shelleyi, B. bubo. 2 barn owls: Tyto capensis and T. alba. 2 grass owls: Asio flammeus, Asio capensis. Wood Owl: Ciccaba woodfordi. Scops and Little Owls: Otus leucotis and Athene noctua.
About 36 species		About 13 species
Bat Hawk: Machaerhamphus alcinus taking them by day or in dusk, as staple diet. Falco biarmicus, a few.	Bats	Bubo lacteus, B. capensis and B. poensis (a few).
2 eagles: Hieraaetus dubius and Spizaetus africanus. 12 sparrowhawks and goshawks: Melierax gabar, Accipiter melanoleucus, gentilis, ovampensis, nisus, rufiventris, erythropus, minullus, castanilius, tachiro, badius and brevipes.	Small birds 500 grams or less; doves, finches, bulbuls, small waders, small game-birds, e.g. quail.	Bubo lacteus, Bubo africanus, B. poensis. Probably taken when roosting at night and form a substantial proportion of owls' diet.
8 falcons: Falco ardosiaceus, dickinsoni, chicquera, subbuteo, cuvieri, biarmicus, fasciinucha, peregrinus. Buteo spp. (5) Milvus migrans, Elanus, Harriers Circus spp. (6), Harrier Hawk Polyboroides etc. as part of diet		Athene noctua, Glaucidium perlatum—some.

Table 10—continued

Diurnal Raptors	Class of Prey	Nocturnal Raptors
About 36 species, of which 22 feed largely on small birds.		5 species.
Circaetus spp. (4), *Terathopius ecaudatus*; *Melierax* spp. (2), *Kaupifalco monogrammicus*, live or dead, as favourite food items. *Sagittarius serpentarius*.	Snakes and lizards (including large *Varanus* lizards).	*Bubo lacteus* and *B. africanus* rarely. *Glaucidium perlatum* (small reptiles).
Aquila spp. esp. *A. wahlbergi*, *Polemaetus*, *Stephanoaetus*, *Lophaetus*, *Buteo*, *Circus*, *Milvus*, *Falco*, *Accipiter*, *Gypaetus*, as part of diet, usually taken alive.		
At least 30 species sometimes eat reptiles.		Reptiles generally rather rarely taken by owls.
2 eagles: *Aquila pomarina* and *Circaetus cinerascens* 5 *Buteo* spp. rather rarely. 3 *Circus* spp. (*aeruginosus, maurus* and *ranivorus*). *Milvus migrans*.	Frogs	*Bubo lacteus* many; *Scotopelia peli*, *S. ussheri* and *S. bouvieri*.
2 eagles: *Haliaeetus vocifer* and *Gypohierax angolensis*. Osprey: *Pandion haliaetus*.	Fish.	*Scotopelia* spp. (3).
vultures: *Torgos, Trigonoceps, Necrosyrtes, Neophron* but not *Gyps* or *Gypaetus*. eagles: *Aquila rapax, A. clanga, A. pomarina* and *A. wahlbergi*. buzzards: 5 *Buteo* spp. and kites: *Milvus* (2), and *Elanus*.	Large and small insects excluding *Hymenoptera* and termites.	All *Bubo* spp. (6 incl. *Bubo leucosticus*, which is wholly insectivorous). All *Asio* (3), *Otus* (4), *Glaucidium* (4), *Athene* (1) spp.; probably not *Tyto* spp. *Ciccaba woodfordi*. *Jubula lettii*.

Cuckoo Falcon: *Aviceda cuculoides*. sparrowhawks: *Melierax* spp. (3); *Accipiter minullus, erythropus*. Harrier Hawk: *Polyboroides typus*. Secretary Bird: *Sagittarius*. harriers: *Circus* spp. (6). falcons: *F. biarmicus, tinnunculus, vespertinus, naumanni, rupicoloides, subbuteo, cuvieri, eleanorae, concolor*, sometimes others. Pigmy Falcon: *Poliohierax*. At least 43 species include insects in the diet.		At least 20 owls are partly or mainly insectivorous.
Honey Buzzard: *Pernis apivorus* (in winter only). ? Cuckoo Falcon: *Aviceda cuculoides*.	Bees and wasps.	Apparently none.
All vultures except *Gyps* and *Gypaetus* (5). All *Aquila* spp. (5), except *A. chrysaetos, Lophaetus occipitalis*. *Buteo* spp. (5). *Melierax* (3) and some *Accipiter* spp. e.g. *Accipiter minullus*. falcons: *F. biarmicus, tinnunculus, naumanni, subbuteo, vespertinus, cuvieri, rupicoloides*, etc. but probably not *F. peregrinus* or *fasciinucha*. Pigmy Falcon: *Polihierax semitorquatus*. kites: *Milvus migrans*, but not *Elanus*. At least 30-32 species eat termites whenever they can and some spp. such as *Falco vespertinus* and *subbuteo* live largely on them.	Termites (especially flying sexual individuals).	All *Bubo, Asio, Otus, Glaucidium* spp.; probably not *Tyto* spp. ? *Ciccaba* and *Jubula lettii*.

Table 11 Ecological separation of Nocturnal and Diurnal Raptor species

Diurnal Raptors			Prey Class	Nocturnal Raptors		
Arid Steppe and Desert	Savannas and Woodlands	Forest		Forest	Savannas and Woodlands	Arid Steppe and Desert
Vultures, especially Egyptian Vulture and Griffons, sometimes Lappet-faced	*Vultures*: White-backed, Lappet-faced, White-headed also some Griffons. *Eagles*: Tawny Eagle, Bateleur, Fish Eagle	none	Large mammals 10 kg. or more (as carrion)	none	none	none
Golden Eagle (in North-West) Imperial Eagle	Martial Eagle Verreaux's Eagle on hills	Crowned Eagle	Medium mammals 500 gr.–10 kg.	Nduk, Fraser's and Shelley's Eagle Owls	Verreaux's Eagle Owl	Desert Eagle Owl
Tawny Eagle, Lanner Falcon, sometimes also, locally Martial and Bonelli's Eagle and Chanting Goshawk	Martial Eagle Bonelli's (African) Hawk Eagle. Lanner Falcon Peregrine Falcon	Cassin's Hawk Eagle? Ayres Hawk Eagle. Black Sparrowhawk. Goshawk (*A. genitilis*)	Large birds 500–1500 gr.	none	Verreaux's Eagle Owl rarely	Desert Eagle Owl (rarely). Spotted Eagle Owl (occasionally)
Tawny Eagle Long-legged Buzzard; Grasshopper Buzzard (some). (2) Chanting Goshawks; Lanner Falcon	Bonelli's (African) Hawk Eagle; Wahlberg's Eagle; Long-crested Eagle; Bateleur; Augur and Red-necked Buzzards; Black-shouldered Kites	Cassin's Hawk Eagle; Ayres Hawk Eagle; African Eagle; Goshawk; Long-tailed Hawk	Small mammals 0–500 gr.	Nduk, Fraser's, Shelley's Eagle Owls; Barn Owl (Locally). Woodford's Owl; Long-eared Owl	Verreaux's and Spotted Eagle Owls: Cape Grass Owl; Barn Owl; Marsh Owl; Short-eared Owl; White-faced Owl	Desert and Spotted Eagle Owls; White-faced Owl (locally) Little Owl

Lanner Falcon Sooty Falcon Peregrine	Lanner; Peregrine; Red-necked Falcon others sometimes: Shikra; Ovampo; Sparrowhawk; Gabar Goshawk	Ayres Hawk Eagle; Black, Common Sparrowhawks; African Goshawk; Chestnut-bellied and Rufous-breasted Sparrowhawks; Long-tailed Hawk and occasionally others	Birds 0–500 gr. N	Probably none except occasionally Nduk and Fraser's Eagle Owl	Verreaux's and occasionally Spotted Eagle sometimes	Desert Eagle Owl; Little Owl; locally Spotted Eagle Owl
European Snake Eagle; Golden Eagle. Sometimes Lanner Falcon	Brown Snake Eagle; Smaller Banded Snake Eagle. Locally, Black-breasted and Beaudouin's Snake Eagles; Secretary Bird; Wahlberg's Eagle	Congo Serpent Eagle; Southern Banded Snake Eagle	Reptiles, snakes and lizards	probably none	Verreaux's Eagle Owl, sometimes	Desert Eagle Owl, sometimes

Table 12 Analysis of food habits: Diurnal Raptors: East African Grasslands

Species	Classed as	Weight gram	Number	Total Biomass gr.	% Food Cons/Body wt.	Total Food Cons. /day gr.	Total Food Cons. /year kg.	Nature Beneficial	Neutral	Harmful
1 Black-shouldered Kite	B	200 (e)	27	5400	20	1080	392	392		
2 Swallow-tailed Kite	N	120 (e)	6	720	25	180	64		64	
3 Black Kite	⅓ B, N, H	960 (a)	144	138,240	10	13,824	5046	1682	1682	1682
4 Fish Eagle	½ N ½ H	2500 (a)	13	32,500	8	2600	949		475	475
5 Egyptian Vulture	B	1900 (a)	7	13,300	10	1330	485	485		
6 Lammergeier	B	5180 (a)	2	10,360	8	829	303	303		
7 Hooded Vulture	B	1920 (a)	22	42,240	10	4224	1542	1542		
8 White-backed Vulture	B	5690 (a)	176	1,001,140	7	70,080	25,579	25,579		
9 Ruppell's Griffon	B	6380 (a)	30	191,400	7	13,398	4891	4891		
10 Lappet-faced Vulture	B	7500 (e)	10	75,000	7	5250	1916	1916		
11 White-headed Vulture	B	5900 (e)	2	11,800	7	826	301	301		
12 Black-breasted Snake Eagle	N	1700 (a)	3	5100	10	510	186		186	
13 Brown Snake Eagle	N	2000 (e)	3	6000	10	600	219		219	
14 Bateleur	N	1950 (a)	55	107,250	10	10,725	3915		3915	
15 Harrier Hawk	N	1000 (e)	3	3000	10	300	110		110	
16 African Marsh Harrier	N	370 (a)	3	1110	15	167	61		61	
17 Marsh Harrier	N	680 (a)	5	3400	10	340	124		124	
18 Harrier, Mont. or Pale	B	300 (a)	5	1500	20	300	110	110		
19 Pale Chanting Goshawk	N	630 (a)	11	6930	15	1040	380		380	
20 Dark Chanting Goshawk	N	630 (a)	4	2520	15	378	138		138	

21 Gabar Goshawk	N	150 (e)	3	450	25	125	46	46	
22 Common Buzzard	B	950 (a)	3	2850	10	285	104	104	
23 Augur Buzzard	B	1200 (a)	190	228,000	10	22,800	8322	8322	
24 Tawny Eagle	B	2260 (a)	97	219,220	10	21,920	8001	8001	
25 Verreaux's Eagle	$\frac{1}{10}$ H $\frac{9}{10}$ B	3800 (e)	2	7600	8	608	222	200	22
26 Long-crested Eagle	B	1160 (a)	18	20,880	10	2088	762	762	
27 Martial Eagle	$\frac{1}{9}$ B, N, H	4500)e)	2	9000	7	630	230	77	77
28 Secretary Bird	B	4100 (a)	23	94,300	10	9430	3442	3442	
29 Pigmy Falcon	N	60 (a)	2	120	25	30	11	11	
30 Kestrel	B	170 (a)	7	1190	20	238	87	87	
31 Greater Kestrel	B	180 (e)	2	360	20	72	26	26	
32 Lanner	$\frac{1}{4}$ H $\frac{3}{4}$ N	900 (e)	5	4500	15	675	246	184	62
33 Unidentified	B	1000 (e)	1	1000	10	100	37	37	
TOTAL			TOTALS;			68,247	58,259	7672	2318
			%				85·4	11·2	3·4

NOTES: (1) In Weight Column (a) = estimated from actual known weights; (e) = a reasonable approximation.
(2) Annual Consumption/100 square miles = 5687 kg. of which 4855 is Beneficial, 639 Neutral, and 193 Harmful.

Table 13 List of African Raptors with Notes on Status, Habitat, and Prey

NOTE: Habitats (1) Forest; (2) Woodland; (3) Acacia savanna; (4) Steppe and Thornbush; (5) Desert; (6) Aquatic; (7) Towns

(■■ preferred, ■ occurs, ■(m) occurs on passage migration only)

(a) Diurnal raptors (hawks, falcons, eagles, vultures)

	Species	Status	1	2	3	4	5	6	7	Prey Preference
1	*Pandion haliaetus*: Osprey	resident NE/NW migrant to S						■■		fish
2	*Aviceda cuculoides*: Cuckoo Falcon	resident of S Sahara	■■	■■						insects, lizards
3	*Pernis apivorus*: Honey Buzzard	migrant, wintering S of Equator	■	■■	■(m)	■(m)	■(m)			bees, wasps, insects
4	*Machaerhamphus alcinus*: Bat Hawk	resident S of Sahara	■	■					■■	bats, swallows, swifts, insects
5	*Elanus caeruleus*: Black-shouldered Kite	resident S of Sahara		■	■■	■■				rodents, insects
6	*Chelictinia riocourii*: Swallow-tailed Kite	resident S of Sahara intra-continental migrant		■(m)		■■	■			insects, small mammals
7	*Milvus milvus*: Red Kite	resident NW only: some migrants		■■						small mammals, scavenger, insects
8	*Milvus migrans*: Black Kite	resident & migrant	■	■■					■■	omnivorous
9	*Haliaeetus albicilla*: White-tailed Eagle, Sea Eagle	vagrant N & NW				■		■■		fish, birds, mammals
10	*Haliaeetus vocifer*: African Fish Eagle	resident S of Sahara	■■	■				■■		fish, birds, carrion
11	*Gypohierax angolensis*: Vulturine Fish Eagle	resident S of Sahara	■■	■				■■		palm fruit, fish, molluscs, etc.

	Species	Status	1	2	3	4	5	6	7	Prey Preference
12	*Neophron percnopterus*: Egyptian Vulture	resident & migrant			■	■	■		■■	scavenger, carrion, eggs
13	*Gypaetus barbatus*: Lammergeier	resident mountains					■		■	carrion, bones
14	*Necrosyrtes monachus*: Hooded Vulture	resident S of Sahara	■	■■		■■			■■	carrion, scavenger
15	*Gyps africanus*: White-backed Vulture	resident S of Sahara		■		■				carrion
16	*Gyps fulvus*: European Griffon	resident NW in mountains & migrant								
17	*Gyps rueppellii*: Rüppell's Griffon	resident S of Sahara			■	■■■	■■			carrion
18	*Gyps coprotheres*: Cape Vulture	resident, S Africa			■■	■■	■■			carrion
19	*Aegypius monachus*: Black Vulture	President NW; scarce migrant		■						carrion
20	*Trigonoceps occipitalis*: White-headed Vulture	resident S of Sahara		■	■■	■■	■			carrion, young birds
21	*Torgos tracheliotus*: Lappet-faced Vulture	resident S of Sahara		■	■■	■■	■			carrion, young birds, etc.
22	*Circaetus gallicus*: Short-toed Eagle, Serpent Eagle	resident, migrant		■	■	■■				snakes, mammals
23	*Circaetus cinereus*: Brown Snake Eagle	resident S of Sahara		■■	■	■■				snakes, mammals
24	*Circaetus cinerascens*: Smaller Banded Snake Eagle	resident S of Sahara	■	■■	■					snakes, frogs

Table 13—continued

	Species	Status	1	2	3	4	5	6	7	Prey Preference
25	*Circaetus fasciolatus*: Southern Banded Snake Eagle	resident S & E Africa	■	■	■					snakes
26	*Terathopius ecaudatus*: Bateleur	resident S of Sahara		■	■	■				mammals, snakes, birds, carrion
27	*Dryotriorchis spectabilis*: Congo Serpent Eagle	resident equatorial forests	■							snakes, lizards
28	*Polyboroides typus*: Harrier Hawk	resident S of Sahara	■	■	■	■				eggs, small birds, lizards, oil palm fruits
29	*Circus cyaneus*: Hen Harrier	migrant NW				■				small mammals & birds
30	*Circus ranivorus*: African Marsh Harrier	resident S & E Africa		■	■			■		frogs, birds, mammals
31	*Circus aeruginosus*: Marsh Harrier	resident NW, migrant		■(m)	(m)			■		frogs, birds, mammals
32	*Circus maurus*: Black Harrier	resident S. Africa				■		■		frogs, mammals, etc.
33	*Circus macrourus*: Pallid Harrier	migrant		■			■(m)			small mammals, insects
34	*Circus pygargus*: Montagu's Harrier	migrant					■(m)			small mammals, insects
35	*Melierex metabates*: Dark Chanting Goshawk	resident S of Sahara (N & W)		■	■	■	■			lizards, birds, mammals, insects
36	*Melierex canorus*: Pale Chanting Goshawk	resident S of Sahara (E & S)			■	■	■			lizards, birds, mammals, insects
37	*Melierax gabar*: Gabar Goshawk	resident S of Sahara		■	■	■				birds, mammals, insects
38	*Accipiter gentilis*: Goshawk	?resident NW, otherwise vagrant	■	■						birds, some mammals

Species	Status	1	2	3	4	5	6	7	Prey Preference
39 *Accipiter ovampensis*: Ovampo Sparrowhawk	resident S of Sahara		■	■	■				birds
40 *Accipiter melanoleucus*: Black Sparrowhawk	resident S of Sahara	■	■						birds
41 *Accipiter nisus*: Sparrowhawk	resident NW, migrant to N tropics		■ ■	■					birds
42 *Accipiter rufiventris*: Rufous-breasted Sparrowhawk	resident S of Sahara (S & E)	■ ■	■						birds
43 *Accipiter erythropus*: Red-thighed Sparrowhawk	resident equatorial forest								birds, insects
44 *Accipiter minullus*: Little Sparrowhawk	resident S of Sahara		■	■	■				insects, birds
45 *Accipiter castanilius*: Chestnut-bellied Sparrowhawk	resident equatorial forest	■							? birds
46 *Accipiter tachiro*: African Goshawk	resident S of Sahara	■	■						birds, some mammals
47 *Accipiter brevipes*: Levant Sparrowhawk	migrant to N & E		■		■				birds, lizards
48 *Accipiter badius*: Shikra	resident S of Sahara		■ ■	■					lizards, birds
49 *Urotriorchis macrourus*: Long-tailed Hawk	resident equatorial forest	■							? birds
50 *Butastur rufipennis*: Grasshopper Buzzard	resident S of Sahara & intra-continental migrant		■		■ ■				insects, birds, mammals
51 *Kaupifalco monogrammicus*: Lizard Buzzard	resident S of Sahara		■ ■	■	■				lizards, insects, birds

Table 13—continued

	Species	Status	1	2	3	4	5	6	7	Prey Preference
52	*Buteo buteo*: Common Buzzard	resident Atlantic islands and migrant	■	■	■					rodents, insects
53	*Buteo oreophilus*: Mountain Buzzard	resident S & E Africa	■							? mammals, birds
54	*Buteo rufinus*: Long-legged Buzzard	resident NW, migrant		■	■	■				mammals, insects
55	*Buteo auguralis*: Red-necked Buzzard	resident S of Sahara, N & W	■	■	■					mammals, insects
56	*Buteo rufofuscus*: Augur or Jackal Buzzard	resident E & S Africa	■	■	■	■				mammals, birds, insects
57	*Aquila pomarina*: Lesser Spotted Eagle	migrant, wintering in S tropics		■		■(m)				mammals, frogs, insects
58	*Aquila clanga*: Greater Spotted Eagle	migrant, wintering NE tropics			■	■	■(m)			mammals, frogs, insects
59	*Aquila rapax*: Tawny Eagle	resident & migrant		■	■	■	■		■	mammals, birds, carrion
60	*Aquila heliaca*: Imperial Eagle	migrant NE breeding NW?		■	■	■				mammals, insects
61	*Aquila wahlbergi*: Wahlberg's Eagle	resident S of Sahara intra-continental migrant		■	■	■				lizards, mammals, birds
62	*Aquila chrysaetos*: Golden Eagle	resident NW mountains				■	■			mammals, birds, reptiles
63	*Aquila verreauxi*: Verreaux's Eagle	resident S of Sahara E & S mountains		■	■	■	■			mammals

Species	Status	1	2	3	4	5	6	7	Prey Preference
64 *Hieraaetus fasciatus*: Bonelli's or African Hawk Eagle	resident	■	■■	■					mammals, some birds
65 *Hieraaetus dubius*: Ayres Hawk Eagle	resident S of Sahara	■	■■						birds, some mammals
66 *Hieraaetus pennatus*: Booted Eagle	resident NW, migrant	■	■■	■					birds, some mammals
67 *Lophaetus occipitalis*: Long-crested Eagle	resident S of Sahara	■	■						mammals
68 *Spizaetus africanus*: Cassin's Hawk Eagle	resident equatorial forests	■■							? mammals, birds
69 *Stephanoaetus coronatus*: Crowned Eagle	resident S of Sahara	■■	■						large mammals, occasionally reptiles
70 *Polemaetus bellicosus*: Martial Eagle	resident S of Sahara		■■	■■	■				birds, mammals, reptiles
71 *Sagittarius serpentarius*: Secretary Bird	resident S of Sahara		■	■■	■■	■			mammals, reptiles, insects
72 *Polihierax semitorquatus*: Pigmy Falcon	resident S & E Africa			■	■■				insects, birds
73 *Falco naumanni*: Lesser Kestrel	resident NW, migrant				■■	■(m)		■(m)	insects, small mammals
74 *Falco rupicoloides*: Greater or White-eyed Kestrel	resident S & E			■■	■				small mammals, insects
75 *Falco alopex*: Fox Kestrel	resident N & W, local migrant		■	■	■				small mammals, birds
76 *Falco tinnunculus*: Common Kestrel	resident & migrant		■	■■	■■	■		■	small mammals, insects
77 *Falco ardosiaceus*: Grey Kestrel	resident S of Sahara (mainly N & W)		■■	■					birds and small mammals

Table 13—continued

	Species	Status	1	2	3	4	5	6	7	Prey Preference
78	*Falco dickinsoni*: Dickinson's Kestrel	resident S & E Africa		■	■	■				mammals, birds, insects
79	*Falco vespertinus*: Red-footed Falcon	migrant		■	■	■(m)				insects
80	*Falco columbarius*: Merlin	migrant, N only		■		■				birds
81	*Falco chicquera*: Red-headed Falcon	resident S of Sahara		■	■					birds, lizards
82	*Falco subbuteo*: European Hobby	resident NW, migrant	■	■	■(m)					insects, birds
83	*Falco cuvieri*: African Hobby	resident S of Sahara		■	■					birds, insects
84	*Falco eleanorae*: Eleanora's Falcon	migrant: resident NW			■(m)			■(coastal)		birds, insects
85	*Falco concolor*: Sooty Falcon	resident NE, migrant		■(m)	■(m)	■(m)	■	■(coastal)		birds, insects
86	*Falco biarmicus*: Lanner	resident & migrant		■	■	■	■			birds, some mammals
87	*Falco cherrug*: Saker	migrant, mainly NE		■	■	■			■	birds, some mammals, reptiles
88	*Falco fasciinucha*: Teita Falcon	resident S & E Africa			■	■				birds
89	*Falco peregrinus*: Peregrine	resident & migrant		■	■	■	■	■	■	birds

Summary habitat preferences: ■ preferred ■ occurs

		Total
Forest	13 16	29
Woodland	33 30	63
Acacia Savanna	20 43	63
Steppe & Thornbush	20 31	51
Desert	4 20	24
Aquatic	7 3	10
Towns	5 4	9

residents S of Sahara	62
residents only NW	12
residents and migrant	21
migrants only	11

(b) Nocturnal Raptors (owls)

	Species	Status	1	2	3	4	5	6	7	Prey Preference
1	*Tyto alba*: Barn Owl	resident		■					■	rats, mice, insects
2	*Tyto capensis*: Cape Grass Owl	resident S & E			■ ■	■				rats, mice
3	*Phodilus prigoginei*: Congo Bay Owl	resident Congo Highlands ?	■							? probably small mammals, insects, frogs
4	*Asio otus*: Long-eared Owl	resident NW		■						small mammals, insects
5	*Asio abyssinicus*: Abyssinian Long-eared Owl	resident E.A. mountains	■ ?	■ ?						small mammals, insects ? probably small mammals & insects
6	*Asio flammeus*: Short-eared Owl	migrant ? resident NW				■		■		small mammals, birds, reptiles
7	*Asio capensis*: African Marsh Owl	resident S of Sahara		■	■			■		small mammals, insects, ? frogs
8	*Strix aluco*: Tawny Owl	resident NW		■						small mammals, insects
9	*Ciccaba woodfordi*: Woodford's Owl	resident S of Sahara, especially E & S	■	■						insects, small mammals
10	*Otus scops*: Scops Owl	resident & migrant		■		■			■	insects
11	*Otus brucei*: Bruce's Scops Owl	vagrant NE								insects
12	*Otus rutilus*: Russet Scops Owl	resident, Madagascar, Comoros, Pemba Is.	■	■						insects
13	*Otus irenae*: Morden's Scops Owl	resident E	■							? probably insects

Table 13—continued

	Species	Status	1	2	3	4	5	6	7	Prey Preference
14	*Otus icterorhynchus*: Cinnamon Scops Owl	resident W tropical	■							? insects
15	*Otus (Ptilopsis) leucotis*: White-faced Owl	resident S of Sahara		■■	■	■■				insects, small mammals, etc.
16	*Jubula lettii*: Maned Owl	resident W tropics	■							insects
17	*Athene noctua*: Little Owl	resident & migrant N & NW		■		■■				insects, small mammals, birds
18	*Glaucidium perlatum*: Pearl-spotted Owlet	resident S of Sahara		■■	■■	■■				insects, small birds
19	*Glaucidium tephronotum*: Red-chested Owlet	resident Equatorial	■							? probably insects
20	*Glaucidium capense*: Barred Owlet	resident S. Africa		■		■■				insects, etc.
21	*Glaucidium sjostedti*: Sjostedt's Barred Owlet	resident Cameroons	■							? probably insects
22	*Bubo bubo* (including *ascalaphus*) Eagle Owl	resident N & NW		■		■	■			rats, insects etc.
23	*Bubo africanus*: Spotted Eagle Owl	resident S of Sahara		■	■■	■■	■			small mammals, insects, etc.
24	*Bubo lacteus*: Verreaux's Eagle Owl	resident S of Sahara	■	■■	■					mammals, birds, reptiles, insects
25	*Bubo capensis*: Mountain Eagle Owl									
26	*Bubo poensis* (incl. *vosseleri*): Fraser's or Nduk Eagle Owl	resident S of Sahara	■■							mammals, insects
	Bubo shelleyi: Barred Eagle Owl	resident W tropics	■■							? probably mammals, birds, insects

Species	Status	1	2	3	4	5	6	7	Prey Preference
27 *Bubo leucostictus*: Akun Eagle Owl	resident W tropics	■							? mainly insects
28 *Scotopelia peli*: Pel's Fishing Owl	resident S of Sahara						■		fish, frogs
29 *Scotopelia ussheri*: Rufous Fishing Owl	resident W tropical forest						■		fish
30 *Scotopelia bouvieri*: Vermiculated Fishing Owl	resident W tropical forest						■		fish, prawns, birds
	TOTAL	13	15	12	10	2	5	2	
	Preferred	11	6	3	5	—	5	1	
	Occurs	2	9	9	5	2	—	1	
	resident only NW & N	4							
	migrant only	1							
	widespread resident and/migrant	6							

Note: This does not include the as yet unnamed forest owlet from Liberia which would make 31 spp, Forests 14 with 12 preferring this habitat (86%).

313

Index

Figures in bold refer to pages opposite which illustrations appear.

Accipiter, 21, 83-8, 91ff., 118ff., 139, 141, 181, 207, 262, 296ff.
  badius, 200, 298, 307
  brevipes, 298, 307
  canescens, 86
  castanilius, 298, 307
  erythropus, 298f., 307
  gentilis, 83, 296f., 306
  macroscelides, 86
  melanoleucus, 296f., 307
  minullus, 299, 307
  nisus, 83, 217, 297, 307
  ovampensis, 297, 307
  rufiventris, 297, 307
  tachiro, 86, 297, 307
  toussenelii, 86
Aegypius monachus torgos, 296, 305
Agility, 13f., 16, 20-2, 29
Albert, Lake, 75, 230, 278
Algeria, 77, 109, 127, 159, 194, 280
Amadon, Dr. Dean, 37, 120, 133
America, 13, 29f., 49, 109, 131, 150, 152, 165, 220, 258, 265, 272, 282
  North, 133f., 174, 191, 207f., 211
  South, 24, 77, 137f.
Angola, 90
Ankole, 213
Antelopes, 11, 114, 117, 219, 221, 228
Aquila, 92, 105, 181, 298f.
  chrysaetos, 299, 308
  clanga, 296, 297, 308
  heliaca, 296, 308
  h. adalberti, 109
  pomarina, 298, 308
  rapax, 296, 298, 308
  r. nipalensis, 108
  r. rapax, 189
  r. raptor, 189
  verreauxi, 296, 308
  wahlbergi, 297, 298, 308
Arabia, 38, 160
Arabuko—Sokoke Forest, 146
Arussi Mountains, 97, 99
Arvicanthis, 223
Asia, 56f., 72, 77f., 80, 94, 96, 103, 105f., 108, 158, 160, 103-4, 233
Asio, 298f.
  abyssinicus, 311
  capensis, 297, 311
  flammeus, 297, 311
  otus, 311
Astur, 83
  gentilis, 83
Athene, 298
  noctua, 297, 312
Atlas Mountains, 61, 155, 245, 280
Auob, river, 210-11, 212
Australasia, 72, 135
Australia, 77, 94, 134, 174, 208, 211, 282

Aviceda cuculoides, 299f., 304

Bale Mountains, 162
Baringo, 90, 151, 175
Bateleur see Eagle
Bat Hawk see Hawk
Bats, 29, 41, 50-1, 123, 130, 166, 178, 229, 275
Bauchi Plateau, 154
Beak, 12, 14, 37, 49, 119, 139
Beard (of Lammergier), 59
Bees' nests, 48
Benson, C. W., 128
Benue, river, 136, 183
Binocular vision, 17
Birds (as food), 11f., 21f., 25f., 50, 54, 69, 73, 84, 88, 91, 93f., 96, 99, 102ff., 107, 113, 121ff., 129ff., 138, 144, 148, 167, 171f., 202, 221-3, 228, 244, 275, 278, 281
Bones (as food), 26, 58-9, 270
Borassus palms, 124, 254
Bosphorus, 106, 188
Botswana, 106, 188
Bowles, Dr. R., 188
Brachystegia woodlands, 48, 67, 106, 123, 190, 226
Breeding areas, 38, 52, 77ff., 93f., 96f., 99ff., 109, 111ff., 121, 125ff., 129, 131-2, 134f., 143f., 147, 151, 154f., 173ff., 183-7, 191, 195ff., 199-214, 218, 221
Breeding cycles, 50ff., 55, 58, 60, 77, 86ff., 101ff., 114-16, 134-5, 137ff., 147, 149, 153f., 156, 202, 235-7, 245-53, 254-65, 268
Breeding seasons, 70, 91, 93, 135, 147, 152, 154, 160, 168, 174, 186, 196ff., 199-203, 224, 237, 245-53
Broekhuysen, Professor G. J., 168, 255, 258
Brooke, Richard, 49
Bubo, 159, 161, 177, 298f.
  africanus, 177, 297ff., 312
  bubo, 159, 177, 296, 312
  b. ascalaphus, 159, 177, 296, 312
  capensis, 177, 297f., 312
  c. capensis, 177
  c. makinderi, 177
  c. dilloni, 161, 177
  lacteus, 177, 296f., 298, 312
  leucostictus, 177, 298, 313
  poensis, 42, 166, 177, 296f., 312
  p. vosseleri, 177f., 312
  shelleyi, 177, 296, 312

Bulawayo, 111
Bustard, 34, 37, 139, 142
Butastur, 94
  rufipennis, 200, 307
Buteo, 92, 166, 296, 297ff., 308
  auguralis, 95, 200, 297, 308
  buteo, 95, 297, 308
  b. vulpinus, 187
  oreophilus, 95, 187, 297, 308
  rufinus, 95, 297, 308
  rufofuscus, 17, 95, 217, 297, 308
Buzzard, 23, 25, 30, 36, 92-9, 102, 166, 181-3, 217, 226, 230, 275
  Augur, 18, 29, 95-100, 122, 162, 164, 166, 207, 212, 214, 230, 235, 239, 255f., 263f., 268, 274, **113**
  Common, 37, 96f., 180, 187, 190, 192, 230
  European see Common Buzzard
  Grasshopper, 38, 92, 93-4, 181, 191, 200ff., 256
  Honey, 47-9, 180, 182, 186ff., 192, 201, 226
  Jackal, 95-9
  Lizard, 92-3, 239, 256, 276
  Long-legged, 95ff., 180, 256
  Mountain, 37, 95ff., 180, 187, 256
  Red-necked, 95ff., 99, 122, 191, 196, 200ff., 239, 256
  Steppe, 29, 96f., 187, 203, 234

Cade, Professor T. J., 210f., 286-9
Calls, 49, 68f., 85, 91ff., 96, 109, 131, 133, 139, 144-5, 146f., 148-9, 154, 157, 168, 238-41, 259-60
Cameroon, 68, 99, 137, 146, 149, 152-3, 158, 176, 178
Cape Province, 110, 154, 174, 177, 184, 187, 193, 209, 223, 225, 245
Caracaras, 74, 118, 133, 136
Cariama, Crested, 139, 141f.
Cariamas (Cariamidae), 37
Carrion, 13, 30, 40, 54, 56, 58, 61f., 69, 73-4, 107f., 110, 118, 172, 213, 226f., 272, 275, 280
Chad, Lake, 77
Chapin, Dr. J. P., 48, 191
Chelictinia riocourii, 200, 304
Ciccaba woodfordi, 297f., 311
Circaetinae, 65
Circaetus, 65, 69-70, 72, 137
  cinerascens, 298, 305
  cinereus, 217, 296, 305

Index

Circaetus [contd.]
 fasciolatus, 306
 gallicus, 66, 296, 305
 g. beaudouini, 66
 g. gallicus 66
 g. pectoralis 66
Circus, 76, 297ff.
 aeruginosus, 78, 297f., 306
 a. aeruginosus, 78
 a. harterti, 78
 cyaneus, 297, 306
 macrourus, 217, 297, 306
 maurus, 297f., 306
 pygargus, 217, 297, 306
 ranivorus, 297f., 306
Clapham, C. S., 129
Comoro Islands, 145f., 178
Congo, 42, 48, 68, 127, 156, 175, 188, 191, 193
Counts, 80-1, 189, 205-15, 227, 264, 281

Dahlac archipelago, 128-9
Dar-es-Salaam, 51, 141
Darfur, 147, 203
Dedza, 128
Desert, 36, 39, 60f., 64, 67, 71, 78, 90, 95, 110, 112, 129f., 140, 145, 159-60, 172, 200, 202, 227-8
Diatryma, 142
Display, 25, 49, 58, 68, 70, 85, 139f., 154, 162f., 165, 234-5, 239-41, 253, 259
Doum palm, 124
Dryotriorchis, 65
 spectabilis, 306

Eagle, 11-14, 16, 19, 25f., 30, 32-3, 37, 39, 92, 99, 102, 105-17, 139, 171f., 181-3, 187-90, 205-14, 218ff., 226, 229, 262, 266, 270, 275f., 279-81
 Ayres, 88, 112, 115, 188, 234, 242, 248, 257, 262
 Bateleur, 26-8, 32, 65f., 68-72, 73f., 108, 165, 182, 203, 210f., 213-14, 222f., 226, 230, 233f., 244, 257, 265, 267, 269, 275
 Black *see* Verreaux's Eagle
 Bonelli's, 99, 102ff., 257, 267; *see also* Hawk Eagle, African
 Booted, 102f., 180, 188, 256, 275
 Crowned, 20, 22-3, 25, 32ff., 105, 109, 169, 114-17, 175, 178, 182, 203, 209, 213, 217f, 219, 221ff., 228f., 234f., 239f., 242, 249-51, 252-3, 257f., 260-4, 267, 271f.
 Fish, 11, 32, 65, 72-5, 108, 134ff., 167, 213, 220, 222, 230, 233-8, 241, 248, 259, 262f., 265, 276ff., 283; African Fish, 72-5, 229, 257; Vulturine Fish, 23, 65, 72, 133, 135-7, 229, 256, 276, 278, 97
 Golden, 107-11, 116, 166, 231, 243, 257, 259, 262, 272, 276, 279-80

Harpy, 95
Harrier, 65; Brown Harrier, 33
Hawk, 99, 109; African Hawk, 99, 102ff., 222f., 234, 244, 257, 267, 271, 279, 129; Ayres Hawk, 21, 102-3, 222, 255, 267, 274f., 128; Cassin's Hawk, 101, 158, 175, 255; Slender Hawk, 103
Imperial, 109, 180, 188f.
Indian Black, 138
Long-crested, 88, 99-101, 164, 207, 213, 222, 239, 256-7
Martial, 19, 25, 32ff., 103, 105, 108ff., 112-13, 114, 116, 171, 175, 178, 182, 208, 213f., 218, 221ff., 228f., 232ff., 238, 240-1, 244, 257, 263ff., 267, 271, 273, 276, 278f., 281, 144
Sea, 65, 135f., 276; European Sea, 181
Serpent, 66-8, 257; Congo Serpent, 28, 68, 72, 158, 175, 255; European Serpent, 66, 70f., 180
Short-toed *see* Serpent Eagle
Snake, 23, 32, 65-72, 75, 137, 182, 214, 217, 220, 248, 260, 275; Beaudouin's Snake, 66-7; Black-breasted Snake, 23, 66f., 71, 238, 240, 96; Brown Snake, 52, 67f., 71, 222, 239f., 257; Smaller Banded Snake, 67-8, 69-70, 256; Southern Banded Snake, 67-8
Spotted: Greater, 105-7, 109, 180, 188-9; Lesser, 105-7, 180, 186-90, 202, 227
Steppe, 105-8, 110, 188-90, 230
Tawny, 40, 48, 73f., 105-9, 162, 180, 188-90, 192, 203, 210-14, 226, 230, 235-6, 238, 248, 256-7, 129
Verreaux's, 18f., 107, 109, 110-12, 175, 206, 208, 222f., 228f., 231, 234-5, 238, 251, 257, 259, 262, 267, 273, 276, 279f., 144
Vulturine Fish, 23, 65, 72, 133, 135-7, 229, 256, 276, 278
Wahlberg's, 38, 100-1, 103, 109, 164, 188, 191, 203, 210, 213ff., 218, 221-4, 232, 238, 242, 246, 248, 257, 271, 276, 278, 128
Ears, structure, 14, 24, 30-1
East Africa, 36, 61, 67, 78, 80f., 92, 96ff., 107, 118, 121f., 125, 127, 138ff., 145, 147, 152-3, 161, 166, 173f., 177, 184f., 188ff., 192-3, 194f., 200, 202f., 209, 211f., 214, 243, 274, 282

Eggs, electrophoretic analysis of, 139, 142
Elanus, 297ff.
 caeruleus, 297, 304
Elgon, Mount, 97, 99, 131, 176, 187, 239
Elgood, J. H., 183, 191, 201
Elmenteita, Lake, 73
Embu district, 20, 81, 113, 116, 131f., 140f., 160, 183, 185, 199, 205ff., 208, 222, 224, 227, 229, 232, 238, 240, 252, 261
Equatorial Africa, 48, 52, 95, 111, 147, 189, 191-2, 197, 200
Eritrea, 106, 177, 189
Ethiopia, 18, 35, 38, 40, 54, 58f., 63, 78, 81, 90, 97f., 106f., 110f., 125, 143, 150f., 156, 161f., 167, 177, 188f., 193, 265
Eurasia, 56, 226
Europe, 80, 103, 105f., 127, 131, 133f., 143, 152f., 166, 173, 180ff., 201, 207f., 214, 235, 257f., 265, 277, 282
Eye, sight, 13f., 16-20, 66, 113, 241; structure, 16-19, 28, 145, 163

Facial disc, 24, 31, 143, 145, 167
Falco, 112, 120, 298
 alopex, 297, 309
 amurensis, 187
 ardosiaceus, 297, 309
 biarmicus, 296f., 299, 310
 cherrug, 296f., 310
 chicquera, 297, 310
 columbarius, 310
 concolor, 299, 310
 cuvieri, 297, 299, 310
 dickinsoni, 297, 310
 eleanorae, 299, 310
 fasciinucha, 297, 299, 310
 naumanni, 299, 309
 peregrinus, 297f., 299, 310
 p. pelegrinoides, 130, 296
 p. brookei, 130
 rupicoloides, 297, 299, 309
 rupicolus, 173, 297, 299
 subbuteo, 297, 299, 310
 tinnunculus, 261, 297, 299, 309
 t. rufescens (carlo), 173
 vespertinus, 299, 310
Falcon, 11-14, 20f., 23ff., 29f., 39, 49f., 118-32, 133, 171ff., 181-2, 186-7, 222, 226, 229, 232-4, 260, 263, 275
 Barbary, 119, 130-1
 Cuckoo, 28, 47, 49-50, 256, 272
 Eleanora's, 118, 128-30, 180, 186, 257, 275
 Gyr-, 119, 245
 Lanner, 20, 28, 33f., 39, 118f., 125, 130-2, 161, 180, 189, 192, 214, 228, 257, 267f., 271, 276, 278
 Laughing, 118
 Peregrine, 20, 25, 38, 40-1, 102, 118f., 125, 130-2, 174, 180, 207, 214, 234f., 257, 267, 160

Index 317

Pigmy, 11, 118, 120-1, 148, 171, 211, 256
Red-footed, 23, 119, 127-8, 129f., 173f., 180, 182, 186f., 226, 275
Red-headed, 118, 267
Red-necked, 119, 124f., 254, 256
Saker, 119, 180
Sooty, 118, 128-30, 180, 186, 257
Teita, 88, 119, 125-6, 127, 257
Falcones, 120, 133
Falconet, 118, 120
Falconidae, 118, 120, 133
Falconiformes, 12, 37, 133, 139-41, 171, 211
Falconry, 226-7
Feet, structure, 32-4
Fish, 11, 23, 32, 40, 65, 73-5, 134ff., 167f., 220f., 229-30, 275, 276ff.
Flamingo, 57, 61, 73, 107, 226
Flight, 24-8, 65-7, 69, 76, 98, 118-19, 127, 131, 141, 182
Food and migration, 55, 202-3
Food requirements, 64, 75, 112, 216-25, 273f.
Food supply, 53, 100, 123, 161, 171-9, 186, 205, 211, 225-30, 243-4, 245, 247-53, 263
Forest, 28, 35, 39, 42, 48f., 52, 56, 60, 64, 67f., 71, 84ff., 91, 96f., 99ff., 112, 138, 140, 144ff., 149, 155ff., 160, 163, 166f., 172, 175, 177, 182, 188, 198, 201, 208, 213, 227-9, 234, 238f., 267f.
Fort Lamy, 198
Frogs, 11, 23, 32, 70, 96, 165, 167f., 174, 187f., 202, 221, 275

Gabon, 48, 68, 176, 270
Gambia, 184
Gathano, 199
Geranospiza, 137
Gerrhosaurus major, 224
Ghana, 146
Glaucidium, 148
capense, 176, 312
perlatum, 176, 297f., 312
sjostedti, 176, 312
tephronotum, 176, 312
Goshawk *see* Hawk
"Grand Duc", 145, 159
Grasshoppers, 139ff., 174
Grassland, 51f., 60, 77, 95, 122, 139f., 152ff., 174, 184, 188, 190, 212ff., 275, 283
Griffon *see* Vulture
Guinea, 68, 158, 175, 178
Gulf of, 198
Gypaetus, 296, 298f.
barbatus, 305
Gypohierax angolensis, 298, 304
Gyps, 296, 298f.
africanus, 305
coprotheres, 305
fulvus, 305

rueppellii, 305

Habitat, 35-7, 38-43, 77, 81, 90, 108, 122, 171-9, 227-9
Haliaeetus, 72
albicilla, 305
vocifer, 72, 237, 296, 298, 304
Haliaeetinae, 65
Haliastur, 72
Hammerkop, 43, 73, 120, 123f., 151f., 164, 175, 260
Hannington, Lake, 73
Harmattan, 198-9, 201
Harrier, 23ff., 31, 65, 76-82, 91, 121, 135, 137, 153, 174, 181-5, 190, 214, 226, 230, 275
Black, 38, 76f., 78-9, 174, 184, 256
Hen, 76-7, 79, 180, 184
Marsh, 11, 37, 76-8, 81, 180, 184f., 257, 275; African Marsh, 76-7, 78f., 174, 184, 226, 256; European Marsh, 76, 78
Montagu's, 33, 76-7, 78-81, 174, 180, 184f., 230
Pallid, 76-7, 78-81, 174, 184f., 230
Hawk, 11f., 14, 16f., 30, 39, 79, 81, 83f., 90, 94, 96, 138, 171, 216, 226, 267
Bat, 12, 28f., 41, 47, 50-1, 229, 256, 275, **80**
Carrion, 133
Crane, 137-8
Goshawk, 21, 32-3, 49, 83, 88-91, 99, 102, 104, 180-1, 222, 262, 267, 276, 278; African Goshawk, 84-7, 88, 91, 239, 257, 267; Chanting Goshawk, 22, 32, 34, 39, 84, 88-91, 122, 161, 211, 214, 220-1, 228, 239, 267, 275f. (Dark Chanting, 88-91, 220-1, 256, **112**; Pale Chanting, 22, 88-91, 256); European Goshawk, 84; Gabar Goshawk, 84, 88, 91, 216, 256; Little Banded Goshawk, 83f., 256; Pied Goshawk, *see* Black Sparrowhawk;
Harrier, 23, 25, 103, 133, 136-9, 171, 255f., 276, **160**; African Harrier, 76, 136, 276
Long-tailed, 84, 88, 255, 276, 170
Red-winged, 94
Sparrow-, 21-2, 25, 32-3, 49, 83-8, 91ff., 119, 171f., 180-2, 217f., 220, 260ff., 271, 275; Black sparrow-, 33, 83ff., 91, 267, 276, 278, **113**; Chestnut-bellied Sparrow-, 84-5, 87; 255; European Sparrow-, 84, 257; Giant Sparrow-, 83; Levant Sparrow-, 84, 180; Little Sparrow-, 22, 84, 87, 171f., 218, 257, 262; Ovampo Sparrow-, 84,

87-8, 91, 256, 267; Red-thighed Sparrow-, 87; Rufous-breasted Sparrow-, 84, 256
Herbert, Dick, 125
Hieraaetus, 92, 99, 181
dubius, 297f., 309
fasciatus, 297, 309
pennatus, 309
Hobby, 118f., 129, 180, 182, 190, 202, 226
African, 12, 28, 119, 126-8, 130, 257, 267, **145**
European, 119, 126-7, 174, 257
"Home Range", 71-2, 113, 140-1, 214, 218, 222-4, 233-44, 258-9, 281
Honey Badger, 31-2, 47, 91, 161
Hovering, 23-4, 30, 53, 67, 98, 122
Howard, Eliot, 231
Hyrax, 19, 59, 96, 104, 110ff., 162, 175, 224-5, 228f., 238, 252, 280f.

Ibadan, 201
Ilorin, 81, 123, 126, 147, 183, 198, 201, 254
India, 54, 65, 94, 124, 158, 160
Indonesia, 50
Insects, 11f., 23, 28f., 41-2, 49ff., 121ff., 129f., 144, 148, 161, 163, 186ff., 226, 242-3, 275f., 279

Jackson, Sir F. J., 22
Japan, 94
Johannesburg, 151
Jubula lettii, 298f., 312

Kabba province, 183, 201
Kalahari Desert, 31, 90, 106, 121, 124, 139, 160f., 211ff.
National Park, 189, 210
Kampala, 126
Karen forest, 86, 92, 115-17, 138, 234, 239f., 249, 252-3, 261, 264
Karroo, 78-9, 112, 209, 225, 272
Katanga, 127
Kaupifalco monogrammicus, 298, 307
Kavirondo Gulf, 187, 237
Kenya, 20, 42, 48, 50, 66ff., 71, 77ff., 81, 83, 86, 8off., 92f., 96, 98, 100ff., 106ff., 110f., 113f., 120ff., 125ff., 129, 131, 135f., 140, 144, 146ff., 151, 155ff., 161f., 175, 178, 184ff., 193, 196, 198f., 202f., 205, 207, 211-12, 219, 224, 228, 230, 235, 246ff., 258, 261, 263, 265f., 272
Kenya, Mount, 40, 59, 97, 99f., 131, 161, 183, 185, 193, 199, 239
Kestrel, 23, 39, 41, 53, 66, 77, 108, 119, 127f., 1173f., 183-5, 226, **262**, 267, 275
Common, 39, 118, 121ff., 148, 173, 180, 184-5, 214, 257, 261

318 Index

Kestrel [contd.]
Dickinson's, 119, 123-5, 256
European see Common Kestrel
Fox, 119, 122-3, 173, 192, 203, 256
Greater, 119f., 122-3, 173, 185, 230, 256
Grey, 43, 119f., 123-5, 185, 256, 260
Lesser, 118, 121-2, 127f., 130, 173, 180, 184-5, 186f., 209, 214, 233, 241, 256
Rock see Common Kestrel
White-eyed see Greater Kestrel
Khartoum, 197
Kikuyuland, 213
Kite, 20, 23, 25, 47, 49, 51-5, 65, 74, 94, 133, 171, 181-2, 193-203, 213, 229, 232, 234, 238, 271, 80
Black, 35, 40, 51, 53-5, 76, 94, 107f., 180f., 182f., 192, 193-201, 212-14, 234f., 247f., 255, 257ff., 263f., 271, 274, 276, 278f., 283; European Black, 193-7
Black-shouldered, 23, 38, 51, 52-3, 108, 141, 173, 184-5, 207, 230, 242-3, 256, 267, 275
Egyptian, 193-6
Letter-winged, 53
Red, 51, 53-4, 180, 257, 275
Swallow-tailed, 38, 51-2, 191, 200ff., 233, 241-2, 256
Tropical African Yellow-billed, 193-8, 203, 235
Kitui, 131
Kruger Park, 184, 209ff.

Lagos, 147, 201
Lambs, 111-12, 113, 271, 273, 279
Lammergeier, 25f., 28, 34, 40, 56f., 58-60, 61ff., 108, 110, 182, 235, 256, 262, 265, 270
Legends, 268-71
Legs, structure, 32-4, 83, 138
Liberia, 68, 148, 158
Libya, 129
Liversedge, R., 87
Lizards, 23, 70, 90, 92, 100, 110, 138, 148, 171, 222ff., 275f.
Locusts, 189-90
Longonot, Mount, 90
Lophaetus, 92, 298
occipitalis, 297, 299, 309

Machaerhamphus alcinus, 297, 304
Machakos district, 199
MacLatchey, —, 270
Madagascar, 37, 65, 78, 128-30, 133, 137, 145, 178, 186
Magadi, Lake, 57, 61
Malawi, 187
Malaya, 50

Malindi, 41, 51
Malta, 48, 188, 192
Mammals (as food), 11f., 34, 37, 40, 53f., 61, 69, 84, 93, 96, 100, 102ff., 107, 110, 113, 119, 121ff., 131, 138, 148, 150, 163, 165, 178, 190, 221f., 226ff., 230, 275, 279ff.
Manyara, Lake, 81, 136
Marshland, 36, 39-40, 42, 77f., 135, 154, 174
Mastomys, 223
Matopos Hills, 111, 175, 206, 223, 238
Mebs, T., 131
Mediterranean region, 84, 118, 121, 127ff., 134, 143, 184
Meinertzhagen, R., 64
Melierax, 83f., 181, 297ff.
canorus, 89, 296, 306
gabar, 297, 306
metabates, 89, 296, 306
Mendebo Mountains, 162
Merlin, 118f., 124f., 180
Micrastur, 118
Microhierax, 120
Micronisus, 83, 91
Migrants, 37f., 47, 61, 76ff., 81, 87, 97, 105ff., 109-10, 118, 121, 143ff., 173f., 180-90, 191-2, 193-204, 209f., 212f., 221, 226-7, 230, 234f., 246, 255, 277
Migration, 39, 52f., 81, 93, 96, 118, 121, 127ff., 180-90, 191-204, 253
Migration routes, 25, 47-8, 81, 105ff., 127ff., 132, 182-4, 186-90, 190-204
Milvus, 53, 298f.
migrans, 194, 296ff., 299
m. aegyptius, 193ff., 296f.
m. arabicus, 194, 296f.
m. migrans, 193ff., 198f., 304
m. parasitus, 194ff., 296f.
m. tenebrosus, 194, 296f.
milvus, 297, 304
Mombasa, 41, 51, 188
Monkeys, 11, 114, 219, 228, 269f.
Moreau, R. E., 191
Morocco, 54, 77-8, 79, 96, 109, 121, 127, 129ff., 134f., 154ff., 159, 171, 194
Mountains, 41, 58, 63, 77, 95, 99, 106, 109f., 112, 125, 136, 144, 161, 172, 189, 193, 227
Mozambique, 90

Nairobi, 40f., 60, 85, 122, 151f., 173, 183, 188, 230, 242
National Park, 56, 141, 243
Naivasha, Lake, 74, 128, 135, 236-7, 263, 265
Nakuru, Lake, 90, 129
Natal, 147, 157, 177
Natron, Lake, 40
Necrosyrtes, 296, 298
monachus, 305
Neophron, 60, 296, 298
percnopterus, 305

Nests, 37, 50ff., 69, 74, 91, 93ff., 99, 102-4, 108, 112, 118-23, 132, 134-5, 137, 139, 141, 146ff., 151-5, 157, 164-5, 235-7, 254-8, 260; see also Breeding
New World Vultures, 13, 133, 136
Nguka Swamp, 81, 185
Niger, River, 35, 77, 136, 155, 183
Nigeria, 20, 29, 48, 80f., 85, 87f., 93, 99, 118, 121ff., 136f., 145, 147, 154f., 167, 173f., 183, 191, 193, 198, 199ff., 203, 254
Nile, River, 81, 129, 213
North Africa, 38, 47, 56f., 77, 90, 107, 109, 118, 122f., 127f., 139, 143f., 154, 171, 173, 181ff., 214, 245, 266
North Central Africa, 36
North East Africa, 106, 120, 135, 190, 194, 196
North West Africa, 38, 53, 56, 76f., 83f., 96f., 118, 127, 143, 156, 159, 174, 180ff., 195, 272
Nossob, River, 210-11, 212
Nyanza Province, 203
Nyiro, Mount, 98

Oil palm fruit, 23, 72, 135-7, 138, 171, 276f.
Okene, 198-9, 201
Old World Vulture, 56, 65, 133, 136
Omo, River, 167-8
Orange Free State, 210
Osprey, 33, 73, 133-5, 167, 180, 182, 207, 229, 257, 276f.
Otus, 147, 298f.
brucei, 311
icterorynchus, 312
irenae, 311
leucotis, 297
(Ptilopsis) leucotis, 312
rutilus, 311
scops, 181, 311
Owl, 11-15, 28-34, 41-3, 119, 132, 134, 143-68, 171f., 175-9, 180-1 203f., 207, 216, 218, 220, 226, 229, 234, 238, 240, 242, 246, 248, 255-7, 259-62, 267, 275, 276-7, 282
Barn, 30, 33, 42-3, 150-2, 153, 164f., 171, 174-5, 180-1, 204, 258, 260f., 263, **161**
Bay, 255; Congo Bay, 150, 157-8, 276
Eagle, 12, 29f., 32, 42, 145, 150, 159-66, 172, 177, 180-1, 257, 262, 275; Akun Eagle, 159, 166, 177, 255; Barred Eagle, 255; Cape Eagle, 161-3, 172, 177; Desert Eagle, 160; European Eagle, 159, 165; Fraser's Eagle, 159, 166, 177f., 255; Mackinder's Eagle, 161f., 240, 268, 277; Milky Eagle see Verreaux's Eagle

Index

Owl; Mountain Eagle, 161-3, 172, 177; Nduk Eagle, 159, 166, 177f.; Shelley's Eagle, 159, 177f.; Spotted Eagle, 29-30, 32, 34, 159, 160-1, 168, 171, 177, 204, 208, 255, 258, **161**; Verreaux's Eagle, 29, 32f., 163-7, 171f., 177ff., 224, 234, 257, 260, 262f.
Fishing, 11, 32, 42, 150, 166-8, 178, 277; Pel's Fishing, 33, 42, 167-8, 256; Rufous Fishing, 255; Vermiculated Fishing, 167, 256
Grass, 171; Cape Grass, 150, 152-3, 256
Little, 143-4, 181, 258, 261
Long-eared, 150, 155-6, 181, 257; Abyssinian Long-eared, 150, 155-6, 255; European Long-eared, 150, 155
Maned, 33, 150, 158, 255
Marsh, 13, 31, 33, 42, 150, 153, 154-5, 165, 204, 257; Algerian Marsh, 154
Scops, 41-3, 143-7, 148, 171f., 180-1, 204, 240, 257; African Scops, 144-5; Bruce's Scops, 143, 181; Cinnamon Scops, 145-6, 255; European Scops, 144, 146; Morden's Scops, 146, 147; Pemba (or Russet) Scops, 145-6, 255, 268
Short-eared, 42, 150, 153, 154-5, 181, 204, 243; European Short-eared, 31
Tawny, 150, 155-7, 258
White-faced, 42, 143f., **147-8**, 171, 204, 256
Woodford's, 150, 156-7, 171f., 179, 256, **161**
Owlet, 143, 172
Barred, 148-9, 176, 256; Sjostedt's Barred, 148-9, 176, 255
Pearl-spotted, 29, 33, 41, 143, 147, 148-9, 176, 204, 240, 256, **161**
Red-chested, 148-9, 176, 255

Palaearctic region, 38, 36, 79, 84, 110, 135, 156, 159, 174, 183ff., 189f., 209f., 213, 231, 255
Pandion haliaetus, 298, 304
Pandionidae, 133
Pemba Island, 145-6, 178, 268
Perching, 18, 20f., 30, 34, 49, 67, 69, 93f., 98, 108, 122, 127, 207, 239, 259
Peregrine see Falcon
Pernis apivorus, 299, 304
"Petit Duc", 145
Pharaoh's Chicken, 58
Philetairus socius, 211
Phodilus prigoginei, 311
"Piracy", 19, 62, 69, 73-4, 107f., 148

Plumage, 14, 35, 49, 59, 79, 86f., 91, 94, 96, 105-6, 108f., 114, 136, 146, 188
Polemaetus bellicosus, 296, 298, 309
Poliohierax, 299
semitorquatus, 299, 309
Polyboroides typus, 297, 299, 306
Predation, effects of, 75, 216-30, 242-4, 273-82; see also food requirements, food supply
Prey see food supply
Prozesky, O. P., 210, 286-89
Ptilopsis, 147

Rainfall, 38, 57, 64, 126, 147, 154, 168, 186-8, 190, 191-3, 196-203, 228, 243, 245-50
Rand, A. L., 129
Red Sea, 129, 134f.
Reptiles, 221-3, 228
Rhodesia, 48f., 68, 72, 100f., 111, 132, 174f., 183, 187, 193, 197, 203, 206, 223f., 238, 246-7
Rif Hills, 121, 155
Rift Valley, 38, 73, 81, 89f. 121f., 129, 154, 187, 212, 230
Roberts, *Birds of South Africa*, 135
Robin Chat, 92-3
Rodents, 13, 19, 23, 31-2, 43, 53, 70, 72, 77, 96, 99f., 110, 121, 139ff., 151ff., 155, 159-62, 171ff., 189, 202, 208, 222ff., 230, 242-3, 277
Rook, Cape, 120, 122
Roosting, 140, 151, 155, 157; gregarious, 53, 81-2, 128, 187
Rowan, M. K., 209, 285
Rowe, E. G., 111
Ruaha National Park, 129
Rudebeck, G., 184-5, 209-10, 284, 286-7
Rudolf, Lake, 90, 135

Sabaki, River, 129
Sagittariidae, 37
Sagittarius serpentarius, 297f., 309
Sahara, 38, 42, 67, 78, 84f., 103, 109f., 121, 144, 148, 151, 156, 175f., 180, 183, 194, 196, 198, 202, 214
Samburu, 129
Savanna, 34ff., 38-9, 41, 53f., 60, 64, 67, 77, 80, 85, 87ff., 93, 95ff., 100f., 109, 112f., 121f., 126f., 129ff., 136, 146, 148, 155, 158, 160, 163, 166, 173ff., 179, 184, 186, 188, 192, 197f., 200, 202, 205, 213, 226-30, 240, 243
Scavengers, 11f., 26, 40, 43, 51, 54, 56ff., 107, 172, 211, 214, 220, 275, 279
Scotopelia, 298
bouvieri, 298, 313
peli, 298, 313
ussheri, 298, 313
Secretary Bird, 34, 37-8, 76,

90, 120, 133, 139-42, 205, 211, 222, 230, 240, 242-3, 257, 262, **96**
Semien Escarpment, 18, 162
Serengeti National Park, 62, 258
Serle, Dr. W. M., 137
Shikra, 83ff., 87, 191-2, 196, 198ff., 210, 256, 267, 276
Shrike, 11f., 49, 171; White-crowned Bush, 11, 121, 149
Siegfried, W. R., 209, 285
Sierra Leone, 68
Sight, 13f., 16-20, 66, 113, 241
Smith, K. D., 130
Snakes, 26, 28, 32, 37, 65ff., 77, 96, 139f., 165, 171, 220ff., 276
Soaring, 25-6, 48, 63, 65-6, 67ff., 93, 98, 113, 128, 136, 139, 141, 182, 192, 208, 248, 253, 259
Sociable Weaver, 120, 211
Somalia, 96f., 120, 129, 134f., 143-4, 150f., 175, 202
South Africa, 36, 61, 78f., 83ff., 87f., 90, 96f., 108, 111, 116, 120f., 128, 130, 135, 138ff., 152f., 155, 161, 173f., 183ff., 191, 196f., 203, 208-14, 223, 227, 245, 258, 261, 272, 273f., 280
South West Africa, 120, 147, 195
Spain, 54, 80, 102, 109, 121
Spartel, Cape, 48, 80, 188
Species, number of, 37-43; see also counts
Speed, 13f., 16, 20-2, 29, 69, 84
Spilornis, 65, 137
Spizaetus, 101, 109
africanus, 296f., 309
Stephanoaetus coronatus, 217, 296, 298, 309
Steppe, 36, 39, 41f., 52, 61, 67, 77, 80, 88, 96, 108, 121f., 139, 172, 184, 210, 213
Steyn, Peter, 100
Stork, 11f., 103, 108, 187, 191
Strigiformes, 12
Strix aluco, 311
Sudan, 106, 127, 155, 184, 188f., 202f.
Suez, 48, 106f., 188
Sumatra, 51

Talons, 12, 14, 33-4, 83, 134
Tana, River, 131
Tanzania, 40, 61, 90, 93, 111, 125, 129, 147, 175, 177, 184, 187f., 190, 203, 212
Teita, 125, 131
Teratopius, 65
ecaudatus, 297, 298, 306
Termites, 126-8, 130f., 174, 186, 190, 202
Territory, 111, 218, 231-44; see also Home range
Thermal currents, 25, 62-3, 64, 141, 182
Thornbush, 36, 39, 41, 67,

320 Index

Thornbush [contd.]
87f., 90, 92, 100, 109, 120f., 126, 129, 131, 143-4, 146ff., 160, 175, 210, 212f., 238
Torgos, 298
tracheliotus, 305
Towns, 36, 40-1, 42-3, 50f., 54, 99, 145, 150f., 174, 258
Transvaal, 210, 247
Treetops Hotel, 29
Trigonoceps, 296, 298
occipitalis, 305
Tropics, 37, 40, 48, 61ff., 68, 77, 101, 123, 127f., 135, 143, 145, 147, 151f., 154, 163, 166, 181, 186, 188, 192, 196ff., 207, 226, 245, 247, 261, 266
Tsavo National Park, 29, 93f., 148
Tunisia, 155f.
Turkana, 58, 90
Tyto, 298f.
alba, 297, 311
capensis, 297, 311

Uganda, 66, 78, 149, 187, 190, 196
National Park, 185, 213
Urotriorchis, 83, 181
macrourus, 88, 307
Usambara Mountains, 42, 166, 177f.

Van Lawick, —, 57
Van Someren, Dr., 60, 86

Vaughan, R., 128
Vernon, K., 206
Victoria, Lake, 74, 78, 90, 177, 236, 241, 248, 263
Von Heuglin, —, 151
Vulture, 11-14, 19, 25f., 33-4, 37, 39, 56-64, 65, 69f., 108, 133, 171f., 181-2, 211ff., 216, 220, 222, 226f., 233, 242, 257f., 262, 275, 279, 81
Black, 56, 180, 182; European Black, 56, 61, 171, 256
Cape, 56, 60-1, 256, 272, 81
Egyptian, 34, 40, 56, 57-8, 61ff., 136, 180, 182, 225-6, 269
Griffon, 19, 56, 60-3, 233, 242; European Griffon, 56, 60-1, 180, 257; Himalayan Griffon, 171; Ruppell's Griffon, 33, 60-1, 63, 256, 272
Hooded, 56, 60ff., 139, 164, 172, 213, 235, 257, 267
Lappet-faced, 56, 61-4, 171, 211, 256, 262, 272
New World, 13, 133, 136
Nubian, 182
Old World, 13, 56, 65, 133, 136
Palm-nut, 23, 65, 72, 133, 135-7, 229, 256, 276, 278
White-backed, 56, 60-1, 62-3, 211ff., 256

White-headed, 36, 40, 56f., 61-3, 256

Water, 25, 36, 39-40, 42, 73, 99f., 134, 138, 177, 210-11, 213, 230, 277
Weather, effect of, 69, 130, 174, 186-8, 190, 191-203, 208, 216, 220, 224, 243, 244-9, 250-3
Weaver birds, 23, 276
Welty, J. C., *The Life of Birds*, 17, 31
West Africa, 36, 41-67, 80, 85, 90, 93, 96f., 121ff., 127, 130, 136, 138f., 145ff., 151f., 166f., 176f., 184, 188, 191-3, 196, 198, 200, 214, 247, 267f.
Wing loading, 24-5, 62, 76, 138
Wing structure, 25-8, 68-9, 70
Woodland, 35-6, 38-9, 41f., 47ff., 51, 54, 60, 64, 67f., 84f., 87, 91f., 96, 99f., 104, 106, 112, 123, 127, 138, 140, 144f., 155, 163, 171ff., 177, 182, 187, 190, 198, 204, 207f., 212f., 226, 238, 267

Yatta Plateau, 148

Zambezi Gorge, 125-6
Valley, 92
Zambia, 187, 247
Zanzibar, 146
Zululand, 67